# INGLORIOUS, ILLEGAL BASTARDS

*Studies of the Weatherhead East Asian Institute, Columbia University*

The Studies of the Weatherhead East Asian Institute of Columbia University were inaugurated in 1962 to bring to a wider public the results of significant new research on modern and contemporary East Asia.

*elders*

# Contents

*List of Illustrations and Maps*    ix

*Acknowledgments*    xi

Introduction: The Pursuit of Legitimacy
and Military-Society Integration            1

1. The Police Reserve Force and
   the US Army                              25

2. Establishing the National Defense
   Academy and Overcoming the Past         64

3. Becoming a "Beloved Self-Defense
   Force" in Hokkaido and Beyond           111

4. Public Service / Public Relations
   during Anpo, the Olympics, and
   the Mishima Incident                     158

5. The Return of the "Japanese Army"
   to Okinawa                              203

   Epilogue: Whither the SDF and the
   Cold War Defense Identity?             251

*Notes*    *259*

*Bibliography*    *305*

*Index*    *321*

# ILLUSTRATIONS AND MAPS

## Figures

1.1 Police Reserve Force member Irikura Shōzō at
Camp Kurihama, 1950                                              27
1.2 Police Reserve Force members looking for boots, 1950          47
1.3 Prime Minister Yoshida Shigeru and Chief of Staff
Hayashi Keizō inspect National Safety Force troops
in Tokyo, 1952                                                   52
1.4 Residents greet Police Reserve Force personnel arriving
to provide disaster relief in Yamaguchi Prefecture, 1951         60
2.1 The National Defense Academy Obaradai campus
from the air, 1955                                               78
2.2 National Defense Academy President Maki Tomoo
and cadets, 1961                                                 85
2.3 National Defense Academy cadets during a community
open-campus event, undated                                      88
2.4 President Maki and SDF and US military officers
recognizing the US Navy Seabees, 1955                           91
2.5 National Defense Academy dance party, 1961                  101
3.1 The White Snow Castle, constructed by the GSDF
Northern Corps, during the Sapporo Snow Festival, 1958         113
3.2 GSDF Northern Corps personnel providing agricultural
assistance to a local farm woman near Mt. Yōtei, 1967          130
3.3 "Bangai-kun" cartoon, 1969                                  131
3.4 National Safety Force parade in Tokyo, 1953                 135
3.5 GSDF Northern Corps parade in Sapporo, 1964                136
3.6 GSDF Northern Corps training exercise open to the
public on the banks of Toyohira River in Sapporo, 1962         138
3.7 Eleventh Division personnel constructing three snow
statues of figures from Hokkaido's history, 1958               143

3.8 Photograph from the *Akashiya* celebrating
Children's Day, 1964                                                146

3.9 Example of recurring photograph feature in the *Akashiya*
of GSDF Northern Corps personnel interacting with
local women, 1962                                                  152

4.1 Ono Hisako's painting of the 1964 Tokyo Olympic marathon,
GSDF Public Information Center, Asaka Base, Tokyo, 2019   159

4.2 GSDF officials meet with US military officials about plans
for the Tokyo Olympics, undated                                 166

4.3 Tokyo Olympics opening ceremony, 1964                      167

4.4 Tsuburaya Kōkichi and Britain's Basil Heatley competing
in the Olympic marathon, 1964                                    172

4.5 GSDF personnel clearing snow after a series of massive
storms in Hokuriku, 1962–63                                      180

4.6 Mishima Yukio haranguing assembled troops at GSDF
headquarters, 1970                                               197

5.1 Protesters in central Naha marching against the terms
of Okinawa's reversion to Japan, 1972                            206

5.2 GSDF troops celebrating the opening of Naha Base, 1972    214

5.3 Cover of *Kore ga Nihon gun da* (This is the Japanese Army), 1972   217

5.4 Article featuring a local woman in *Shurei*, 1974          240

5.5 *Shurei* coverage of the Okinawa Brigade's march to
Mabuni Hill, 1976                                                246

## Maps

1   Japan, 1950s–1960s                                          26
2   Okinawa Island, 1973                                        204

# ACKNOWLEDGMENTS

It is a humbling task to reflect on the history of this book, which began about twenty years ago. Over the last two decades, my work has benefited from interactions with countless people, who have generously shared their time, expertise, and experiences. I acknowledge their contributions with immense gratitude.

The research that grew into this book began at Columbia University in early 2001, when I was studying the Police Reserve Force (PRF), a forerunner of the Self-Defense Force (SDF). Greg Pflugfelder at Columbia was the ideal mentor, a polymath with an infectious intellectual curiosity who was both encouraging and critical. He, along with Carol Gluck and Henry D. Smith II, formed a trinity of historians who made Columbia a nearly unrivaled setting to study Japan.

Yet, the origins of this book emerged from experiences and education further back in time. This book is dedicated in part to my parents, who stocked our home with books and an interest and concern for people and the wider world. As the youngest of six brothers, followed by three sisters, and without a television in our home (and of course no internet), I spent many hours devouring the written word at the Springville Public Library, a frequent destination on my red Raleigh bike in the small town in Utah where I grew up. Like many of my students today, I was particularly interested in World War II. Thus, a book that examines some of the legacies of that conflict is not surprising. My curiosity about the past in the present was further stimulated by my undergraduate studies of international relations, history, and Japanese at Brigham Young University, interrupted by nearly two years in the Kansai area of Japan as a missionary for the Church of Jesus Christ of Latter-day Saints; by an internship among salaried white-collar office workers in Tokyo one summer; by work as a coordinator of international relations for Gifu Prefecture as part of the Japan Exchange and Teaching Programme; and by a master's degree at Stanford University primarily studying with Peter Duus, who had been Greg's advisor. Some of the questions I began to explore in a paper written for Peter about changing notions of fatherhood in postwar Japan led to this book.

I am thankful that I have had the support to work on this book for many years. In 2002, I received funding to commence research in earnest in the form of a fellowship from the US Department of Education. After several months of archival work, publication opportunities related to a paper I had written during my time at Columbia about human-canine relations led me to change topics, and that research ultimately resulted in *Empire of Dogs: Canines, Japan, and the Making of the Modern Imperial World* (2011), also published by Cornell University Press. All the while, I continued my research on the SDF. I am thankful for a variety of grants I received over the years that helped see this book to fruition: a Fulbright-Hays Doctoral Dissertation Research Abroad Fellowship, a Weatherhead Fellows Program Training Grant, Columbia University; a Twentieth-Century Japan Research Award, Center for Historical Studies and McKeldin Library, University of Maryland; a National Security Education Program David L. Boren Fellowship, Department of Defense; a Research Fellowship, Department of Politics, Graduate School of Law, Hokkaido University; a Fellowship for Foreign Researchers, Japan Society for the Promotion of Science; a Faculty Research Grant, David M. Kennedy Center for International and Area Studies, Brigham Young University; and a Mary Lou Fulton Young Scholar Award, College of Family, Home, and Social Sciences, Brigham Young University.

Funding is vital to research, but the people who help one along the way make it truly enriching. As I began this book, Marianne Scholl, a former Harvard University doctoral student, generously shared many boxes of documents stored in her home in Seattle that she had collected in Japan for a dissertation project that she had not completed. Another early, priceless contact, who shared documents, books, and his personal experiences, was Leonard Humphreys, a US military advisor to and astute observer of the SDF in the 1950s and 1960s. Leonard and his wonderful wife Sally kindly hosted me at their home in Lodi, California, near Stockton where he had recently retired as a historian of Japan at the University of the Pacific. Thanks to his introductions, I also interviewed several other former US military and civilian officials, Raymond Aka, Bob Robens, and Charles Townsend in California and New Jersey, who had interacted with the early SDF as part of the US Military Advisory Assistance Group.

In Japan, I was the beneficiary of more kindness and generosity. My initial year of research funded by the Fulbright was sponsored by Yoshida Yutaka of Hitotsubashi University. I am also indebted to my former employer, Nissho Electronics, which provided me free lodging in its company dorm during my research in Tokyo. I spent the next three years at Hokkaido University in Sapporo, sponsored by Matsuura Masataka and his colleagues in the Faculty of Law. A superb historian, Matsuura-sensei was an invaluable champion of my research, and he and his colleagues asked me to present my work and made key introductions. I am particularly thankful to Yamaguchi Jirō for introducing me to Sakuraba Yasuki, the former mayor of Nayoro, who, like the Humphreys, allowed me to stay in his home and patiently answered my questions. Makabe Jin, another historian in the Faculty of Law, offered tremendous support for my research over the years. I was particularly fortunate to have Satō Morio as a colleague at Hokkaido University. Satō, who had joined the PRF in 1950 and served in the SDF until his retirement in 1992, was conducting graduate research about imperial military intelligence, which he later published as a book. He kindly shared his memories of the postwar force over the course of multiple interviews and many informal conversations. In 2015, over ten years after I first interviewed him, Satō—perhaps wondering if I would ever complete this book—published an account of the PRF, into which he wove his own experiences. One of my greatest regrets in taking so long to finish this book is that he—and doubtless many others—who kindly took time to visit with me have not lived to see its publication. When I last spoke to Satō by phone in the summer of 2019, he expressed his pleasure that I was nearing its completion. A year later, I learned that he had succumbed to cancer at age eighty-eight.

I believe it was Satō who introduced me Irikura Shōzō, another veteran who had also joined the PRF in 1950 and served for many years in the Ground Self-Defense Force (GSDF) Northern Corps public relations office in Sapporo. I could not have asked for a better informant and collaborator. Irikura repeatedly welcomed me to his home, shared his experiences and documents with me, and introduced many other former force personnel, as well as municipal and media officials, who lived throughout the country, including Akikuni Tamehashi, Fujii Shigeru, Furukawa Kumio, Katsu Hidenari, Kuboi Masayuki, Mori Michio, Nishida Hideo, Satō Noboru, Tanaka Kisaburō, and Yanagita Mitsuhara. Irikura's introduction to personnel in the public relations office also gave me the credibility to borrow the office's only copy of the corps's internal newspaper, the *Akashiya*, dating from 1958, which proved to be a source worth copying every single one of its hundreds of pages for over two decades.

Lending what was likely one of the only extant copies of an internal newspaper that had never been used by researchers was just one of the many kindnesses that GSDF officials in Sapporo, Nayoro, Asahikawa, Utsunomiya, Tokyo, Osaka, Kumamoto, and Naha showed to me. They graciously answered my questions, gave me tours, allowed me to make copies of books and newspapers (at no expense), and made invaluable introductions. To provide one key example, officials at Naha Base introduced me to Yamagata Masaaki, a senior officer who had retired in Okinawa and who, along with Ishimine Kunio, another veteran and longtime ally of the force on the islands, met me several times during two research trips to Okinawa.

I am of course indebted to the work and kindness of many researchers. Tony Jenkins of Okinawa Prefectural University of the Arts proved to be an essential contact in Okinawa. His introductions to journalist Kuniyoshi Nagahiro, scholar Yoshida Kensei, and former Okinawa governor Ōta Masahide provided key perspectives on local opposition to the SDF. Thanks to Till Weber for help with lodging in Okinawa. Tony and David Tobaru Obermiller of Gustavus Adolphus College read and provided extensive feedback on an early draft of chapter 5. Sabine Frühstück of the University of California, Santa Barbara provided support from the beginning of this book until its end. Also, Takako Hikotani, a Columbia *senpai* in political science who taught for many years at the National Defense Academy (NDA), made many valuable introductions and kindly read an early draft of chapter 2. Members of the Kyoto University Nichibunken Military Studies group, especially long-time chair Tanaka Masakazu, introduced to me by Frühstück, and Kawano Hitoshi of the NDA, introduced by Hikotani, were extremely helpful. Chapter 2, about the NDA, would not have been possible without Hikotani's introductions to two former academy presidents, Nishihara Masashi and Iokibe Makoto, and the former's introductions to early graduates of the institution: Maekawa Kiyoshi, Shima Atsushi, Shikata Toshiyuki, Tomizawa Hikaru, Ueda Naruhiko, and Yamazaki Makoto, who kindly shared their experiences with me. Ishii Yasuhiro and Umezawa Masako of the NDA's Maki Memorial Hall assisted me in finding some invaluable archival materials and photographs. The guidance of Takahashi Kazuhiro, at the NDA at the time and now at Hosei University, is inestimable. On my first exploratory research trip to Japan in 2002, Hatano Sumio of Tsukuba University kindly took time to meet with me. Seventeen years later, in 2019, on my last research visit to Japan for this book, I met (again) with Takahashi at Hosei and learned that he had been Hatano's student at Tsukuba. My research had truly come full circle and benefitted from the generosity and insights of innumerable people.

Publishing parts of my research helped to move this book forward. Early versions of some of the material in this book appeared as: "Public Service/ Public Relations: The Mobilization of the Self-Defense Force for the Tokyo Olympic Games," in *The East Asian Olympiads, 1934–2008: Building Bodies and Nations in Japan, Korea, and China*, ed. Michael Baskett and William M. Tsutsui

(Leiden, The Netherlands: Global Oriental, 2011), 63–76; "'Ai sareru jieitai' ni naru tame ni—Sengo Nihon shakai he no juyō ni mukete" [To become a "beloved" SDF: Aiming for acceptance from postwar Japanese society], trans. in *Guntai no bunka jinruigaku* [The cultural anthropology of militaries], ed. Tanaka Masakazu (Tokyo: Fūkyōsha, 2015), 213–46; and "Building Snow Statues, Building Communities: The Self-Defense Force and Hokkaido during the Early Cold War Decades," in *Local History and War Memories in Hokkaido*, ed. Philip Seaton (London: Routledge, 2016), 198–214. I am thankful to the editors of these volumes for providing these publication opportunities that helped develop my thinking and moved my research forward.

I have benefitted from the feedback I have received when I presented my research. I did so at the following venues: Graduate Student Conference on East Asia, Columbia University (2002); Annual Conference of the Association for Asian Studies in San Francisco (2006); Department of Politics Research Seminar, Faculty of Law, Hokkaido University (2006); Western Conference of the Association for Asian Studies and Southwest Conference of the Association for Asian Studies at the University of Utah (2007); "Olympian Desires: Building Bodies and Nations in East Asia, Center for East Asian Studies," conference at the University of Kansas (2008); "Revisiting Postwar Japan as History," conference at the Institute of Comparative Culture, Sophia University (2009); Kyoto University Nichibunken Military Study Group symposium held at the National Museum of Japanese History in Sakura (2010); Multidisciplinary Science Forum, Japan Society for the Promotion of Science at the Embassy of Japan, Washington, DC (2014); and Department of Public Policy, National Defense Academy, Yokosuka (2015).

I am also grateful to patient staff at an array of libraries and archives, including the MacArthur Memorial Archives and Library, the US National Archives, the Gordon W. Prange Collection at the University of Maryland, the Library of Congress, the National Diet Library, the National Archives of Japan, the Ōya Sōichi Archive, the Okinawa Prefectural Archives and Prefectural Library, the Hitotsubashi University Library, the Hokkaido University Library, the Hokkaido Prefectural Library, the Ryukyu University Library, the Sapporo City Library, the Hakodate City Library, the Asahikawa City Library, the Nayoro City Library and Nayoro City Museum, the Kumamoto City Library, the Yokosuka City Library, the Kobe City Library, the Kobe University Library, the Carlisle Military History Institute, the University of Hawai'i Library, the George Washington University Library, the US Naval Academy Library, and the Brigham Young University Harold B. Lee Library.

For the last decade and a half, I have been fortunate to teach in the Department of History at Brigham Young University. I am grateful for colleagues in the department writing group who over the years read multiple chapters, and to my fellow East Asianists—Kirk Larsen, Jon Felt, and Diana Duan, as well as Taeju Kim, who joined us as a visiting scholar in 2021—for reading and commenting on the entire book. I also thank administrators, particularly department chairs Shawn Miller and Eric Dursteler, who helped me secure invaluable time and money to move this book closer to completion. I am also thankful to students Reilly Hatch and Michelle Papenfuss for research assistance and interview transcription, respectively, and especially to Devin Sanders for his systematic and detailed work on the notes, bibliography, and index.

I am thankful once again to the Weatherhead East Asian Institute at Columbia University for agreeing to include my book in its monograph series, and to Cornell University Press for publishing it. Ariana King was superb as she solicited a review, shopped my book, and then handed me off for a second time to Cornell. It was a pleasure to again work with Roger Hayden until his retirement and then with Sarah E. M. Grossman, Mary Kate Murphy, Monica Achen, and other members of the fantastic team in Ithaca, NY. I appreciate generous subventions from Columbia University's University Seminars, the Brigham Young University College of Family, Home, and Social Sciences, and the David M. Kennedy Center for International Studies. This book is much better thanks to the anonymous reviews that the Weatherhead Institute and Cornell University Press solicited. Thank you for pushing me in intellectually fertile directions.

Finally, I am thankful for family. Skabelunds and Todate in-laws provided support in many ways over the years. My eldest brother Grant kindly read multiple chapters. My sons Alistor and Mauri grew from boys to men over the life of this book and experienced firsthand the snow-sculpting skills of Northern Corps personnel in Sapporo. Pochi, who joined our family more recently, took me on walks sometimes long enough to nearly read a book chapter. And Seiko, who created the maps, made everything possible behind the scenes.

Asian personal names in this book appear surname (family name) first followed by personal name, except in cases of Asian Americans or Asian scholars based in the West who publish in English. I use diacritical marks for Japanese words and names, except for common words and place names such as bushido and Hokkaido. All translations are mine, unless otherwise noted.

# Introduction
## The Pursuit of Legitimacy and
## Military-Society Integration

"The public called us bastards [*shiseiji*]," recalled veteran Satō Morio, referring to Japan's Self-Defense Force (SDF), the country's post–World War II military organization. Satō joined the Police Reserve Force (PRF), a forerunner of today's SDF, when it was established in 1950, and served in its largest branch, the Ground Self-Defense Force (GSDF) until his retirement in 1992. Over the course of multiple interviews and many informal conversations, he told me that the force and its personnel were regarded as an illegitimate, disreputable half-brother; as the shameful offspring of an illicit relationship with the Americans who became mercenaries serving on behalf of the US military; as "tax thieves" (*zeikin dorobo*) who were a drain on society and worthless in its defense; and as the "dregs" (*ochikobore*) and "outcasts" (*hikagemono*) of society, whom the public preferred to neither acknowledge nor discuss.[1]

Satō was not exaggerating. Commentators regularly used such epithets to characterize the force for several decades after its establishment, and these terms were repeated by foreign journalists and diplomats.[2] The analysis of US academics was not much kinder. Much of society considered the SDF to be a "necessary evil," observed scholar Ivan Morris in 1960.[3] Soldiering, the political scientist (and former US Navy officer) James Auer more tactfully noted over a decade later, was not "a respected profession."[4]

Within Japanese society, such views reflected a widespread and long-standing consensus across a polarized ideological divide. On one end of the political spectrum, progressives saw the force as unconstitutional, a violation of Article 9, the constitution's prohibition against "land, sea, and air forces, as well as other war potential."[5] The left was repelled by the SDF's US patrimony and continuities with the imperial military, which it blamed for leading the country into the disastrous war with the United States. On the other end of the spectrum, those on the right viewed the force as deeply unsatisfying, tainted by its US character and especially by its continuing subordination to the US military. They regarded defense personnel as useless and uninspiring in comparison to the country's storied military figures of the past—samurai and soldiers. Such disregard and disappointment after interacting with GSDF members led the writer Mishima Yukio to create his own paramilitary corps and to commit ritual suicide at its headquarters after deriding the SDF as the "bastard child of the constitution" and "mercenaries for America" in 1970.[6]

It was not just the left and the right that regarded the force in this manner. The view from the middle was not much more favorable. Speaking of society more generally, the journalist Frank Gibney, a longtime observer of the country, declared in 1971: "The Self-Defense Forces in Japan are barely past the status of a public embarrassment. Most Japanese continue to think that a strong economy and a unified society are worth more than numerous divisions. The need for armed forces may be understood by some, but not by many."[7] Indeed, for decades many citizens considered the postwar armed forces to be inglorious, illegal bastards.

The SDF has faced three troublesome relationships: with society, with its predecessor, the imperial military, and with the US military. Wider society—left, right, and center—respectively viewed the force as illegal and unconstitutional, hamstrung by the constitution, and simply suspect. Japanese across the political spectrum also regarded the SDF as inglorious—the successor of and similar to or not enough like the imperial military. And they regarded the SDF as a bastard and were ashamed of the force's US ancestry and its (and Japan's) unending dependence on and subservient status to a foreign military. The US military presence on the islands, in the form of bases and around forty thousand personnel, continues to this day. Japanese citizens found this presence humiliating or at least disconcerting, though many grudgingly supported the status quo because they did not think the country would be safe without U.S military protection.

In these ways, the meaning of military service, not to mention the role of the armed forces, underwent a radical transformation in the wake of World War II. From the late nineteenth century to 1945, with some brief exceptions, most Japanese subjects venerated the imperial military, mourning its setbacks and celebrating its victories. Catastrophic defeat, however, along with the Peace Constitution, which prohibited the existence of the military, education reforms, and strong pacifist and especially antimilitarist sentiment severely eroded public support for military values and for the military as an organization. As a result, the reconstituted armed forces that took shape in the years after their reestablishment in 1950 were isolated and alienated from wider society. Their personnel were less prominent physically, symbolically, politically, and culturally. When the SDF did appear in popular culture, its personnel were transported via science fiction out of their dull peaceful postwar reality by time travel to battle medieval warriors in cultural productions such as *Sengoku Jieitai* (Warring-States SDF), a 1971 novel made into a motion picture in 1979—or remained in the present to combat Godzilla in numerous *Gojira* movies, starting with the original Japanese film made in 1954.[8] This loss of status was not unique to the SDF. In the latter half of the twentieth century, people around the world became disaffected with military principles, ideas, and organizations. Scholars refer to this tension as the "military-civilian divide."[9] Nowhere, though, was this trend as intense and prolonged as in Japan.[10] Indeed, the reconstituted armed forces in Japan were not (and are still not) referred to as a "military" (*guntai*). It was taboo to do so, even though the public understood that the SDF was a military in almost every way but name.

Because of its questionable constitutional status and these political sensitivities, the military nature of the force has been disguised from the start. It was known as the Police Reserve Force (Keisatsu Yobitai) when it was first established in 1950, became the National Safety Force (Hoantai) in 1952, and has been called the Self-Defense Force (Jieitai) since 1954. The coast guard–like Maritime Safety Agency, which conducted mine-sweeping operations during the occupation and maintained considerable continuities with the Imperial Navy, became the Maritime Self-Defense Force (MSDF), also in 1954. That same year, the government created the Air Self-Defense Force (ASDF). These appellations were not mere sophistry. The constitution did indeed constrain the force. Most significantly, Article 9 states that "the Japanese people forever renounce war as a sovereign right of the nation and the threat or use of force as means of settling international disputes" and that "[t]he right of belligerency of the state will not be recognized."[11] These clauses prevented the force from being deployed abroad and from committing to collective defense—coming to the aid of its ally the United States if it were attacked. The government did not deploy the SDF abroad until the 1990s. Even then, it did so only by participating within the auspices of United

Nations peacekeeping operations. From 2004 to 2006, the SDF joined the US-led coalition in Iraq, but it did so under severe restraints and in a limited manner. Only in 2006 did the Defense Agency become the cabinet-level Ministry of Defense, and only in 2015 did legislation allow for the constitution to be reinterpreted to permit collective defense.

From the beginning, the postwar military was also restricted in other ways. Even though the constitution's renunciation of war and prohibition against "land, sea, and air forces, as well as other war potential" came to be interpreted to mean that Japan did *not* forfeit the right to self-defense, legal and political constrictions led the government to maintain a policy of limiting defense spending to less than 1 percent of the country's gross domestic product. Yet, as Japan's economy became the world's second largest by the early 1970s, its defense budgets also became among the world's largest even though they remained below the 1 percent cap. The government has maintained a policy of not acquiring offensive weaponry, including aircraft carriers and, of course, nuclear weapons. But from the time of its establishment, the force has been armed with various kinds of defensive firepower that could be put to offensive use.[12] The SDF has thus long been a de facto military, and I will periodically refer to it as such. More often, however, I will refer to it using the terms that most force members and members of the public have used, because they came to accept it as a defense force rather than as a military.

This book primarily examines the GSDF, one of the three branches, along with the MSDF and ASDF, of the now 250,000-member SDF. Specifically, it focuses on how the GSDF—the land army—even more than the other branches, struggled for societal legitimacy during its iterations as the PRF, the National Safety Force (NSF), and then as the largest, most visible branch of the SDF.[13] In its quest for greater acceptance to overcome postwar Japan's iteration of the military-civilian divide, the GSDF and, to a lesser extent, the other two branches deployed an array of public outreach and public service including off-base and on-base events, civil-engineering projects, agricultural assistance, logistical support for and participation of its athletes in sporting events, and, most prominently, natural disaster–relief operations. The GSDF also sought to mold its future leaders and rank-and-file personnel through education, training, and internal media.

These initiatives achieved some success over the years in garnering greater public support. Yet they did not just change society. They also led the GSDF and the SDF more widely to assume new priorities and traditions. This process contributed to the making of a postwar, or to be more precise, a Cold War defense identity, which was to an extent shared and supported by society. This identity took shape during the decades of geopolitical tension between the United States and its allies (like Japan) and the Soviet Union and its satellite states. It undergirded and was a product of the country's Cold War security posture of "defensive defense" (*senshu bōei*). As a policy doctrine, defensive defense stemmed from the strategies of one of the country's most influential leaders, Yoshida Shigeru, who served as prime minister for most of the first postwar decade and who served simultaneously as foreign minister during much of that time. Yoshida's approach was premised on an (subordinate) alliance with the United States that allowed for "an exceptionally low level of defense spending," a promise to "eschew offensive military missions and capabilities," and the single-minded prioritization of economic growth.[14] A guide for strategy for almost the entire Cold War and beyond, his approach became known as the Yoshida Doctrine and shaped the evolving relationship and identities of the military and society that is the focus of this book.

This process of military and societal change is what I call "military-society integration." This term better captures these dynamics than the term "militarization." Although the concept of militarization may be useful in some circumstances, often it has been used by scholars to suggest a one-way process by which a military organization and military values influence and change society. One well-known theorist of the concept, political scientist Cynthia Enloe, defined militarization as "a step-by-step process by which a person or a thing gradually comes to be controlled by the military *or* militaristic ideas. The more militarization transforms an individual or a society, the more that individual or society comes to imagine military needs and militaristic presumptions to be not only valuable but also normal."[15] Historians, too, have often used the concept of militarization in this manner. Michael Geyer wrote that militarization happens as "civil society organizes itself for the production of violence," and Michael S. Sherry characterized it as "the process by which war and national security became consuming anxieties and provided the memories, models, and metaphors that shaped broad areas of national life."[16] The emphasis of many discussions of militarization, then, is on what happens to society; such discussions tend to neglect the impact of this process on military organizations. This tendency may be in part the result of US (and other) academics since the Vietnam War becoming increasingly suspicious of military organizations and values and concerned about their influence on society, as well as of the decline in military history and other disciplinary studies of militaries and war.

Researchers have used other terms to describe this process, such as "normalization" and "legitimization," but these concepts also sometimes suffer from an attention to just one side of the equation—how the civil-military interaction changes civil society rather than how it transforms both society and the military. In contrast, the word integration indicates the result of the processes by which the developing parts are formed into a functional and structural whole whereby both parts are altered as a result of the integrative and interactive process.[17] Integration more accurately characterizes the development and the outcome of this osmosis-like process, which waxed and waned in an uncertain, unpredictable, and contingent manner. Though the result was not inevitable, the state consistently exercised greater power than society and gradually, incrementally blended itself politically, economically, and culturally into society, though it too was changed by the process. The word "integrate" also is appropriate because it is the equivalent of the Japanese word that GSDF public-relations officials used and indicated was their objective vis-à-vis the public: *shakai ni tokekomu* (to blend into or integrate into society). The word *tokekomu* also means, aptly, "to fit in" and "to adapt to," indicating that the military as well as wider society changed through this interactive process.

Another reason why the term militarization is not appropriate to describe Japan's early postwar decades is that many Japanese who supported rearmament envisioned the reconstituted military to be a self-defense force with no offensive capabilities, rather than a military. Thus, the force and its allies sought to legitimize it and most citizens came to accept it on those terms. Admittedly, some conservatives wanted to revise the constitution and transform the force into a military free from such legal and societal constraints. But many of these same conservatives supported the constitution being interpreted to allow exclusively for self-defense, a status quo that those on the left increasingly came to accept. Therefore, to say that Japanese society as a whole became militarized or militaristic during the Cold War decades is not only an exaggeration but is almost an entirely backward way of looking at what happened.

## Cold War Defense Identity

As the GSDF strived for legitimacy and gained acceptance, its identity, the identity of its personnel, and that of society at large were transformed. Officers and rank-and-file enlisted personnel embraced liberal democratic values, including civilian control of the armed forces, a constitution that constrained their use of arms to military defense, and a strong dose of anticommunism. The *raison d'être* of force personnel became to protect the people, whether from military threats abroad or from nature, and to defend the welfare of the nation through a wide variety of both military and nonmilitary duties. These priorities transformed both the essence of what it meant to serve in the armed forces and the language describing it. Members of the force organization were "personnel" rather than "soldiers," serving the people rather than the emperor. Their leaders urged them to be scientific, rational, and full of spirit, though they redefined the latter term. Personnel were expected to be freedom- and peace-loving, disciplined, and educated gentlemen rather than blindly loyal soldiers. These priorities came to be ingrained in the force, informed its esprit de corps, and become traditions in which personnel took pride and that most citizens came to expect, even as they harbored concerns about the force's constitutionality and its relationship with the imperial and US militaries. The notion that the force was a self-defense force rather than a military, even though that notion increasingly did not match the SDF's capabilities, also became central to its identity during these early postwar decades and beyond. Not only was it called a self-defense force but it came to be accepted as a self-defense force both inside and outside the organization, by the state and society.

During the Cold War, almost all force members were men. Fundamental to the SDF's identity was a reconfigured sense of patriotic manhood. This transformation was imperative because military service, a predominant path to masculinity and mobility for young men before 1945, no longer held that promise for the rest of the twentieth century. Soldiers, veterans, and organizations affiliated with the military permeated many aspects of society in Imperial Japan. But the status of military men plummeted after the war and remained in the doldrums for decades. The organizations they belonged to—the Imperial Army and Navy—were immediately dissolved by US occupation authorities. As millions of soldiers and sailors were demobilized, they—especially army veterans—faced pervasive disdain and discrimination and occasionally even acts of violence as they returned home.[18] Occupation officials placed blame for the war almost entirely on the military. They moved to purge almost all officers from public life and put on trial a group of senior officers for planning and executing a war of aggression. No longer were military men respected, feared, or seen as useful and productive. The government, at the direction of occupation authorities, even stripped veterans of their pensions. These policies were conducted under the two watchwords of the occupation, democratization and demilitarization, goals that first appeared in the Potsdam Declaration in July 1945 and culminated with the promulgation of the US-drafted constitution in 1947 that committed the Japanese people to "forever renounce war as a sovereign right of the nation" and prohibited the very existence of armed forces.[19]

Creating a new patriotic identity was no easy task. Patriotism—especially for the GSDF—had to be divorced from the past and appear to be ideologically neutral, though it was grounded in anticommunism. After the outbreak of the Korean War in June 1950, the reverse course, a shift in the US occupation policies from democratization and demilitarization to economic recovery and support for US Cold War objectives in Asia, which had begun several years earlier, accelerated. To fill the gap created by US forces being rushed from Japan to the Korean peninsula, US occupation authorities working with Japanese government officials established an embryonic military disguised as the PRF. To train a new generation of officers, they founded the National Defense Academy (NDA) three years later. By 1954, the force became the three-branch SDF. Yet Japan and the Japanese had come to identify as and be identified as a pacifist country and people. The constitution renounced war and the existence of a military. "Many Japanese came to define democracy as including peace," as historian Kenneth J. Ruoff observed, "[a] definition of democracy ... arguably specific to postwar Japan." Indeed, the constitution is "commonly referred to as the Peace Constitution not as the Democratic Constitution."[20] Japanese leaders prioritized economic recovery and growth over independent diplomatic policies and reestablishing military power, even as the SDF became a formidable armed force. Culturally, the figure of the salaried white-collar businessmen (*sararīman*), also known as the "corporate warrior" (*kigyō senshi*), came to eclipse the military man and his substitute, defense force members, even as, as the term "corporate warrior" indicates, this figure appropriated the aura of the samurai and soldier as the ideal embodiment of manhood. Some, though, found these developments to be deeply dissatisfying. Mishima's rhetoric and actions were a response to what he and others, especially on the right but also on the left, saw as the emasculation of society and Japanese men, as represented by their defeated and pacified country and the constitutionally constrained SDF with its supposedly weak male members, who were now referred to as "personnel" rather than "soldiers."[21] In the late 1970s, nearly a decade after Mishima's spectacular suicide, the conservative cultural critic Etō Jun, who mourned the lost masculinity of postwar Japanese men in his writings, declared that the authority of fathers could only be restored if Japanese males "face[d] the possibility of doing battle as [did] men elsewhere."[22]

To combat such dim views of the SDF and its personnel, political and defense force leaders worked to craft and nourish a sense of patriotism and masculinity within the force by associating it with the people in both word and deed. Officials from Prime Minister Yoshida and force commander Hayashi Keizō to NDA president Maki Tomoo and individual unit commanders rhetorically dedicated the organization to defend and serve the people, the country, and democratic constitutional principles rather than the emperor and the homeland, as had been the case for the imperial military. More importantly, in an attempt motivated in large part by a desire to win over the hearts and minds of the nation, civilian Defense Agency and uniformed force officials mobilized personnel to work on behalf of and reach out to the people. Such words and actions over time served to shape new aims, attitudes, and practices within the force that went beyond simply providing military security, which, thanks to presence of the US military bases was by default entrusted to the Americans. Senior officials, individual cadets, and rank-and-file members of the force crafted a new identity that included protecting the people against human and natural forces, stoically bearing criticism, dedicating themselves to peace, and being cultured and educated.

As they did this, SDF personnel, who until the late 1980s were all male except for the small, segregated nursing corps, constructed an ethos of military-defense manhood. Bases, training facilities, and schools such as the NDA were almost exclusively masculine spaces. Rather than using women as foils, leaders urged personnel to "be men among men" (*otoko no naka no otoko*), a familiar expression that had been invoked by imperial military officials as well.[23] Leaders often contrasted force personnel with the new archetype of postwar manliness, the *sararīman*, even as the desk jobs that many defense personnel performed transformed them into white-collar workers not so unlike the corporate warriors. Central to these policy and discursive efforts was force leaders encouraging officer cadets and personnel to become gentlemen quietly dedicated to democracy and public service even as they were subjected to abuse and received little praise. Those who crafted this new identity rarely invoked the figure and values of the imperial military man, which the war had thoroughly discredited, as a model for defense force personnel to follow. Sometimes they used samurai and the way of the warrior (*bushido*), a code of martial behavior, as examples for personnel, though this had to be done with care because the misguided and disastrous defeat was blamed on feudal vestiges represented by the samurai. Instead, they had to identify new models. In Hokkaido, where large numbers of GSDF personnel were deployed because of its proximity to the Soviet Union, shapers of this new identity urged Northern Corps officers and rank-and-file personnel to emulate a less threatening martial figure, the farmer-soldier (*tondenhei*) who guarded the northern frontier in the late nineteenth century.

Force proponents and critics on the right and left as well as more neutral observers consistently and repeatedly used another trope, (in)visibility, in discussions of the reestablished military. They often, as Satō mentioned, called force personnel *hikagemono*, literally "someone in the shadows" and more figuratively a "social outcast" or "person who avoids others" and is to be avoided. Government and force officials, media commentators, and even personnel themselves frequently adopted this expression. In 1970, for example, Defense Agency Director Nakasone Yasahiro, who became prime minister in the 1980s, complained, "The Self Defense Forces have been obliged to live in an obscure corner out of the eyesight of the nation."[24] As an organization and as individual members, SDF personnel were regarded as invisible men because, like Ralph Ellison's fictional protagonist, the invisible man, "people refuse[d] to see" them, though for ideological reasons rather than because of the color of their skin.[25] Perhaps because of the term's prevalence, many contemporary media observers and scholars since have written that the force and its personnel were largely invisible within and to wider society.[26] But the force was in fact often quite visible, which is why I prefer to use the parenthetical descriptor "(in)visible men," which suggests both their invisibility and visibility.

Although the SDF may have kept a lower profile than its imperial military predecessor and contemporary foreign military counterparts, civilian political and bureaucratic leaders and force commanders sought for strategic reasons to make it as visible as possible. Moreover, these leaders endeavored to turn its supposed invisibility on its head by casting it as a positive attribute of the force and its personnel. For example, when former prime minister Yoshida spoke to the first graduating class of the NDA in 1957, he declared, "It is possible that many of you may finish your career at the SDF without ever being thanked or welcomed by the people . . . because it is only when our nation is facing crisis and confusion, when we are attacked by foreign forces or when necessity arises for you to embark on disaster-relief missions, that the people will appreciate and praise the SDF."[27] Yoshida concluded by telling the graduates that he wanted them to endure this life in the shadows.[28] Ultimately, to achieve military-society integration, the SDF was at times visible and at other times invisible. As a result, an acceptance of relative invisibility and subordination to other government organizations and the people it served became another defining characteristic of the SDF's Cold War defense identity.

## Overcoming Defeat, Seeking Support

Although this book will focus on the transformation of a national military as it sought to regain societal acceptance, deal with the past, and navigate interactions with an allied military organization, this is not a story unique to

Japan. Many militaries, especially during the Cold War, grappled with such issues, and these processes altered their character and that of wider society. So why does this book focus on Japan?

The history of the SDF invites comparisons with Japan's former Axis allies, especially Germany and Italy. As they did in occupied Japan, the Allies disbanded Germany's military, the Wehrmacht. In West Germany, the military did not reappear until 1955, when Chancellor Konrad Adenauer took the lead in establishing the Bundeswehr. As in Japan, the Korean War along with rising tensions in Europe provided the motivation for US officers to shift their views about West German rearmament.[29] This process began earlier in Italy, with its admission in 1949 to the North Atlantic Treaty Organization (NATO), the US-led multinational regional security apparatus. The war in Korea and ongoing tensions in Europe led the United States to rapidly re-equip the Italian army in 1950 and 1951. As with the creation of the Japanese PRF, US military advisers played a central role in rebuilding the Italian and West German militaries. But whereas secrecy, deceit, and speed pervaded the establishment of the PRF, rearmament in West Germany was regarded as more legitimate because it was marked by gradual negotiations and open political debate and because the Bundeswehr was established within the framework of NATO. This process encouraged West Germans to come to terms with Germany's wartime aggression and required them to reckon more fully with neighboring countries. This did not happen in Japan.[30] Yet similarities exist between the two cases. Many in German society remained suspicious of the Bundeswehr and its personnel, and it too was often over-shadowed by the presence and power of the US military. Like the SDF, the Bundeswehr sought to cultivate public support, and it met with similar reactions. It did so by portraying soldiers as "citizens in uniform (*bürger in uniform*)[31] and, as in Japan, the reconfigured military gained greater backing in the countryside than in urban areas. Likewise, initial concerns about the revival of German militarism gave way to worries that the force might not be as formidable or efficient as its predecessor, the Wehrmacht.[32] And as in Japan, German anxieties about masculinity were rampant in the early post-war years.[33]

Similar trends can be seen elsewhere during the second half of the twentieth century. The French military's relationship with society was strained by three humiliating loses—its "strange defeat," as historian Mark Bloch called its rapid collapse when attacked by the Wehrmacht in 1940, followed by its defeats in the colonies of Vietnam and Algeria. It too faced social isolation and endeavored to regain society's trust.[34] The US military confronted a similar crucible after its defeat in Vietnam. The war and the antiwar movement led not only to distrust of the government but to widespread public suspicion of the military, the use of military force, and military values in 1970s America. Both on a national level and in base towns like Fayetteville, North Carolina, defeat created what historian Catherine Lutz called a "crisis of legitimacy" for the army. Meeting the recruitment goals of a now all-volunteer force became difficult, and recruiters had to "target each and every American high school, cold-calling high school students to sell the military like Pepsi" and create television ads telling their target audience to "Be All You Can Be . . . in the Army." Military recruiters also sought to integrate themselves deeper into society by starting after-school clubs and visiting even middle and elementary schools.[35] Defeat also created a "crisis of masculinity" until popular representations of the war, such as the movie *Rambo*, and a new conflict—the Gulf War in 1990—led to the "remasculinization of America," as scholar Susan Jeffords put it, and a restoration of military legitimacy.[36]

The controversial, lengthy wars in Afghanistan and Iraq have also not been kind to the US military and its relationship with wider society. Though respect for the armed forces as an organization has recovered since Vietnam, especially in comparison to other government institutions, the military—and the army, in particular—continues to struggle to fill its ranks. After the attacks on September 11, 2001, the Pentagon even went so far as to pay professional sports leagues tens of millions of dollars to conduct military tributes in an attempt to boost patriotism and recruitment.[37] Politicians' attempts to politicize the military have also endangered its relationship with society. For example, President Donald Trump's threat to mobilize active-duty military troops to control the wave of demonstrations protesting the police killing of George Floyd and systemic racism in 2020 created concern that such actions would renew divisions between the armed forces and society. The stunning collapse of the US military–trained Afghan government forces and the chaotic withdrawal of US forces from Afghanistan in August 2021, which led to tragic Saigon-like scenes at the Kabul airport, may further strain the military-civilian divide.

Even when not attempting to recover from a defeat or a controversial war, national militaries have worked to maintain good relations with their societies. Since at least the second half of the twentieth century, militaries in both developed and developing countries have participated in public service, such as disaster relief, civil engineering, and agricultural aid, and have engaged in public-relations outreach activities.[38] As historian Mark R. Grandstaff recounted, even the immediate post–World War II US military, which came out of the conflict as the victor with a positive reputation, launched a "national public relations campaign" to persuade the public that it was "an acceptable American institution, both in war and in peace."[39] During the war, citizens were beset by anxieties about whether a powerful military was compatible with democracy. In response, as historian Benjamin L. Alpers argued, "producers of American public culture, from social scientists to Hollywood moviemakers to military officers and politicians . . . attempted to imagine a democratic army."[40] Victory did not entirely resolve these concerns. After the war, to win support for a large peacetime standing military, advertisers working with the military attempted "to create an image of a professional military composed of good, dependable, democratic citizens (the middle class), not the dregs of society (the lower classes)." The military also encouraged "recruiters to become public relations experts, because 'community relations pays off!'" As in Cold War Japan, where the SDF emulated these efforts, they changed both society and the military itself. By the mid-1950s, Grandstaff concluded, such strategies contributed to the military becoming a more democratic American institution.[41]

The SDF's intense engagement in disaster relief and other public service may have made it one of the most economically and socially productive militaries in the postwar era. In some ways, the force became a postmodern military before rather than after the end of the Cold War and long before that notion occurred to sociologists. Although the Cold War–era SDF did not fit all the elements in the sociologist Charles C. Moskos's US-centric typology of a postmodern military, it did include many of them, including a small professional force structure, major missions defined by humanitarian relief, an indifferent public, courtship of the media, and the ideal of the soldier-scholar.[42] Strangely, Moskos's edited volume introducing the concept of the postmodern military in 2000 did not even mention the contemporary SDF, much less the Cold War–era force. Yet the postmodern-military characteristics of the SDF from the 1950s to the 1980s are almost unrivaled by later armed forces, including by the post–Cold War SDF.

This comparative discussion brings us back to the question: Why focus on Japan? Although the SDF's history exhibited similarities to those of the US military, the Bundeswehr, and other armed forces, the suspicion and even antipathy that the SDF and its personnel experienced was unsurpassed in its intensity and length. Therefore, the strategies the force used and the impact their application had on both society and the force itself makes the Japanese postwar military a fascinating and revealing case study.

## Why the GSDF?

Why focus on the GSDF in particular? Because the GSDF's history of relations with society, the imperial military, and the US military described in this book has much in common with that of its fellow branches, I will often speak, as I do in the title, of the SDF in more general terms. Members of the public usually did not (and still do not) distinguish between the three branches and the force, conflating the GSDF with the SDF, for example. They are less likely than Americans to specify which branch of the military they are talking about. This might reflect a lack of familiarity with or interest in the postwar armed forces. Yet, there are compelling reasons to focus mainly on the GSDF. This rationale can be best understood in terms of this branch's relationships with society, the imperial military, and the US Army.

First, the GSDF has always been the largest branch of the SDF and had the most interaction with wider society. In 2016, the GSDF had around 150,000 members, about three-fifths of the entire manpower of the SDF.[43] In the middle of the Cold War in 1964, its manpower ratio was much greater. The GSDF was approximately five time the size of the other two branches combined.[44] It maintained over 160 bases, installations, and training facilities across the country, overseen by five regional headquarters—the Northern Corps in Sapporo (Hokkaido), the Northeastern Corps in Sendai (Tohoku), the Eastern Corps in Tokyo (Kantō), the Middle Corps in Osaka (Kansai, Chugoku, and Shikoku), and the Western Corps in Kumamoto (Kyushu and Okinawa). Its facilities, operations, and personnel are located in close proximity to the general public.[45] Members of the public, therefore, have been much more likely to come into regular contact with the GSDF than with the other branches, which have far fewer bases and whose bases and areas of training and deployment—the sea and air—are farther from the general population. Unlike naval personnel, who are away at sea for extended periods of time, many GSDF personnel commute from private residences to work on base. Their camouflage green vehicles have long been a common sight on public roads, especially on the outskirts of metropolitan areas and in rural areas near bases. Beyond such daily interactions, the GSDF has been much more involved than the two other branches in public service, such as disaster relief and assistance with events like the Sapporo Snow Festival and public-relations efforts such as experiential-enlistment programs.

Second, the GSDF, as the ostensible successor to the Imperial Army, was blamed more for the mistakes of the prewar military than was the MSDF (and of course the ASDF, which was not established until 1954). Such views have endured. As the historian Alessio Patalano described, "the notion of a 'good navy' as opposed to a 'bad army'" began to dominate public memory as soon as the war came to an end and the occupation began. The Tokyo war crimes trials, which conjured up a vision of the war beginning with the army's aggressions in China in 1937, or even in Manchuria in 1931, confirmed the public's dim view of the army especially. The postwar period's most prominent politician, Prime Minister Yoshida, was also more critical of the army than of the navy. Returning veterans, too, contributed to the negative images of the army as they shared their wartime experiences that were filled with stories of internecine cruelty and extreme brutality against enemies.[46] Such deleterious views of the Imperial Army continued for decades during and after the Cold War. Stragglers returning to Japan years later, including two in the early 1970s, reinforced this perspective.[47] And six decades after defeat, in 2006, the *Yomiuri* newspaper published a series of articles, which were compiled into a book, that once again laid blame for the war primarily at the feet of the army.[48] Despite the GSDF having far fewer connections with the Imperial Army than the MSDF had with the Imperial Navy, the ground force was viewed with considerable suspicion as its successor.

In contrast to the GSDF, Patalano observed, the postwar "navy sought to embrace its imperial past."[49] Unlike the army, the navy was never completely demobilized. Instead, in what was arguably a very early violation of Article 9, the US Navy immediately put the remnants of the Imperial Navy to work as part of the Maritime Safety Agency removing mines, first around the archipelago and later in Korean waters after war broke out in Imperial Japan's former colony in June 1950.[50] For this reason, extensive institutional and personnel connections linked the MSDF with the Imperial Navy.[51] Because the public held the Imperial Navy less responsible for the war and because some of its most prominent admirals, such as Yamamoto Isoroku, the architect of the attack on Pearl Harbor, were regarded as cosmopolitan internationalists who were conflicted about the going to war with the United States, it was easier for the MSDF and its allies in the media and literary world to rehabilitate the image of the prewar navy and by extension that of its postwar successor.[52]

As a result, the GSDF became the focus of societal anxieties. Political scientists Robert D. Eldridge and Paul Midford argued that the ground forces "became the primary repository of public and elite fears about a renewed breakdown of civilian control and democracy, and even renewed war."[53] The GSDF's physical proximity to and interaction with society at large, which was greater than that of the MSDF and the ASDF, only served to magnify such concerns.

Finally, the role of the US military in establishing the Police Reserve Force and, even more importantly, its ongoing presence in the country damaged the legitimacy of the GSDF. After being completely demobilized, Japan's ground forces were reestablished by the US military occupation officials in the form of the PRF. As suggested by Satō's comments, US parentage left a stain on the reputation of the GSDF and of the SDF more generally. More significantly, the massive US military bases and presence of US personnel throughout the country continued to undercut the SDF's legitimacy and highlight its and Japan's subordination to the US military and the United States. Such views persisted despite minimal interaction between the SDF and the US forces based in Japan. As the political scientist Sheila Smith explained, this lack of cooperation occurred because the US-Japan alliance, unlike other US Cold War alliances, "did not rest on the assumption of military reciprocity. Japan was not obligated to defend the United States as part of the strategic bargain. Article Nine . . . was interpreted narrowly to preclude the use of force by the SDF on behalf of the United States."[54] Also unlike other alliances, the treaty allowed the US military to intervene in Japan's domestic security until it was revised in 1960. The treaty was also modified "to include an explicit guarantee of U.S. military assistance in case Japan was threatened or attacked. In return, Japan offered the United States [ongoing] access to military bases and facilities on Japanese soil—bases that would support U.S. strategy in the 'Far East.'"[55] The GSDF was nominally tasked with fending off outside threats, but because the United States guaranteed Japan's security from external aggression through the presence of US forces, especially airpower based on Japanese soil, the GSDF in particular seemed to have little reason to exist. Even without the US presence, as Midford and Eldridge observed, "being the land army of an island nation is never an enviable position to be in."[56] The ground force was also ostensibly focused on maintaining internal security, but because political leaders never fully mobilized it for such purposes, it seemed useless in that respect as well.

For these reasons, when leftists and rightists derided the SDF for being American mercenaries and tax thieves and not measuring up to their predecessors, they directed their accusations principally at the GSDF. Not surprisingly, Mishima aimed his scathing critique at ground force personnel, with whom he had interacted the most. He compared them unfavorably with Imperial Army soldiers and regarded them as subordinate to the US military.

## The Lexicon of a Defense Force

All militaries have a specialized vocabulary. But those who established, guided, and otherwise shaped the reconstituted postwar Japanese armed forces created a lexicon beyond the technical organizational and operational jargon that they used and society adopted to characterize the force and its personnel. In turn, as in other organizations, these terms shaped the SDF itself, its personnel, and its identity. Attention to this terminology and its meanings is essential to understand the postwar force and its character. Some of the words were new. Some were influenced by interactions with the US military. Some had been used in the prewar period but were given new meaning during the postwar years. All were influenced by the force's relationship with society. An awareness of this language deepens an understanding of these dynamics and the continuities and ruptures with the past.

The most important vocabulary was the words for the reconstituted organization and its members. As noted earlier, before 1945 the armed forces were known as a military or army (*gun* or *guntai*) in a variety of renderings—the nation's army (*Nihongun* or *kokugun*), the government's army (*kangun*), and the Imperial Army (Teikoku rikugun or *kōgun*).[57] Members of the imperial armed forces, whether part of the army (*rikugun*) or the navy (*kaigun*), were commonly referred to as *hei, heitai, heishi,* or *gunjin* (soldiers). When the SDF was established in 1950, the terms used to refer to the armed forces and their members changed, and though the terminology evolved over time to take on a more military character, it remained different from that of the imperial military in substantive ways. Rather than a military (*gun*), leaders called each postwar organization a "force" (*tai*), as in the Police Reserve Force, National Safety Force, and Self-Defense Force. And its members became "force personnel" or "force members" (*taiin*) rather than "soldiers." Thus, like their samurai predecessors during the Tokugawa period (1600–1868), who were transformed from warriors into administrators during the two and half centuries of peace, soldiers became personnel during the peaceful second half of the twentieth century. Similarly, although some national armies engaged in war after 1945, organizational and technological changes in military service led to warriors to become managers nearly everywhere, as the sociologist Michel L. Martin put it in the French context.[58]

Yet, these changes in military speak were more pronounced in postwar Japan. The PRF, NSF, and SDF used terms for units within the organization and for individual ranks that were analogous to those of a police force, and weapons and vehicles were designated in ways that obfuscated their military character. Tanks (*sensha*), to use the most well-known example, were called "special vehicles" (*tokusha*). The nomenclature for rank and weapons only changed in 1961, when government officials thought that the SDF had secured sufficient societal support to stop using terms that everyone knew were fictions.[59] This vocabulary was the product of subterfuge—US occupation and Japanese government officials hoping to avoid controversy—but it was also to some extent a reflection of the character of the PRF and the constitutional and societal constraints under which it, the NSF, and the SDF operated. Indeed, one might call the PRF a gendarmerie or paramilitary, because US and Japanese officials who created it were primarily concerned with internal security, though it certainly had many military characteristics and many of those same officials expected that it would eventually become a full-fledged military force. That said, the terms used for the force and its units, weapons, vehicles, and employees impacted the identity of the organization and its members over time. As force leaders, personnel, and the public used these terms, it shaped their views about the force's identity and its proper role.

In contrast to the changed lexicon for the organization and its members after 1950, force officials and others continued to use the term *seishin*, which could be rendered in English in many ways, including as spirit, mind, soul, morale, and willpower. A concept fundamental to prewar military and national identity—and to militaries everywhere trained to possess a fighting spirit—the postwar force endowed seishin with new meanings that were both connected to and differed from those of the Imperial Army. According to the political scientist Lewis Austin, seishin is "antithetical to modernization . . . not democratic, not universalistic, not individualistic, not materialistic. It is rather the complex of loyalty, discipline, esprit de corps, and indomitable perseverance that is central to so many of the historical accomplishments of Japanese civilization."[60] This was particularly the case in prewar Japan, when spiritualism came to pervade military education; the military and right-wing leaders used it to inspire the nation during the wartime years of the 1930s and 1940s. The association became so great that *seishin kyōiku* (spiritual education or indoctrination) came to be used to refer to military education in general. Leaders of the reestablished postwar armed force continued to talk of spirit and to conduct spiritual education, but seishin's meaning and purpose evolved. Defeat had discredited the spiritualism and fanaticism of the prewar military, with its emphasis on national mystical essence, the bushido way of the warrior, and seishin trumping science, technology, and rational thinking. Thus, as historian Jennifer M. Miller described, when US occupation and Japanese government officials established the PRF and began to welcome depurged officers into the force, they embraced a hybrid version of seishin, a mix of old and new, as necessary to bolster democracy and fight communism.[61] This redefined spirit was said to be imperative to serve liberal democracy, peace, and the people. It was stoic, moderate, and obedient to the chain of command and civilian control of the military. Likewise, terms similar to seishin, particularly *konjō* (guts, spirit), were used to fashion a positive national and force character. These words were distinguished from—though still linked to and in fact informed by—their prewar connotations, and identified in a positive way with the SDF and its personnel.

Unlike the open discussion about the need for seishin, discussions about gender within the postwar armed forces, though constant, were usually understated. This was true for the prewar military, too. Postwar military leaders rarely used such terms as *otokorashii* (manly) or *otokorashisa* (manliness or masculinity), though PRF chief Hayashi did so in his first official speech to the PRF. Another gendered term that was usually used implicitly was "gentleman." Maki, the first president of the NDA, emphasized the concept of the gentlemen by urging cadets to become gentlemen as well as officers. Maki's notions of a gentleman drew on long-standing ideas about male cultivation and proper form, which were influenced by Confucianism and by interactions with the West from the mid-nineteenth century. The Confucian "gentleman" (*kunshi*), a man of virtue or a sage, had long been a fixture of Chinese civilization. One could also locate the emergence of Japan's gentleman in the way of the warrior that came to define the samurai, who was expected to be proficient in both the literary and military arts. From the second half of the nineteenth century, the *shinshi* emerged as the civilized gentlemen, melding Western Victorian gentility, Confucian civility, and samurai nobility. The *shinshi* as the embodiment of civic virtue, noblesse oblige, and social privilege was to lead the country into the civilized world.[62] Maki's vision of a gentleman, often aptly rendered by cadets using the English loan word *jentoruman*, was also influenced by the cosmopolitan *shinshi* gentleman-officer of the Imperial Navy Academy and by US military academy graduates. Although Maki rarely invoked any specific terms for "gentleman," he constantly encouraged cadets to embody virtue, benevolent leadership, loyalty, stoicism, culture, and service. In turn, when these cadets became officers they conveyed these values to the men they led in the ground force and other branches of the postwar military. In general, SDF masculinity during these decades was (and still is) overwhelmingly heteronormative with indications of homosocial proclivities.

Although few women served in the force and the work that male authorities allowed them to perform was limited during the Cold War decades, they, too, played a role in shaping force identity. Their presence and portrayal—real and imagined—as force personnel, wives, mothers, daughters, and (potential) romantic partners, including the deployment of femininity for recruitment and morale-building, all contributed to the construction of this identity. In this realm too, the SDF's relationship with society, the past, and the US military influenced the actual employment and metaphorical mobilization of women. From 1950 to 1952, service members in uniform were exclusively men. The only women in the organization served as nurses and did so as civilians and not in PRF attire. Because this was identical to the role of women in the imperial military, one of the motivations for creating an Army Nursing Corps in 1952, in which female nurses were integrated into the NSF as service members and wore force uniforms, was, as the sociologist Fumika Satō observed, to "camouflage the continuity with the prewar military . . . to give the impression that this postwar institution represented a break from the Imperial Army."[63] In 1968, influenced by the US military's use of women for clerical work as part of Women's Army Corps, GSDF officials created an analogous organization so that they could "more 'efficiently' use male SDF soldiers in what they deemed to be 'manly' jobs."[64] Soon the ASDF and MSDF also welcomed women in secretarial roles. In subsequent years, historian Sabine Frühstück reported all three branches created "positions considered 'suitable for women,'" a policy change that was prompted in part by the force's, especially the GSDF's, ongoing challenge recruiting a sufficient number of men[65] and in part, as Satō asserted, by officials' hope that the "recruitment of women could play a role in changing public opinion about the SDF."[66] By the same token, from the 1960s onward, SDF recruiters trying to create positive impressions frequently used images of female force members, despite their miniscule ratio in the force. By 1991, the number of women in the SDF had increased to 3.4 percent, doubling from 1.7 percent in 1986, when the national legislature passed a gender equality law that allowed women to assume, theoretically, any role within the SDF. The force opened almost all positions to women as a result, including allowing them admission to the NDA in 1992, which gave women the opportunity to become officers.[67] These changes were motivated not only by pressure from women for more opportunity but also by concerns about the force's image, both domestically and internationally, and recruitment considerations.

## Structure and Contributions

To analyze the (G)SDF's pursuit of legitimacy and the development of a Cold War defense identity that came to be shared to some degree by the public, the following chapters will trace its relationship with society, the imperial military, and the US military during these decades in five chapters organized thematically and chronologically.

The first chapter examines the reestablishment of a military force by US occupation authorities and the Japanese government in the ambiguous form of the PRF from 1950 to 1952. Although US and Japanese officials were often preoccupied with organizational concerns during the force's early years, the challenges they faced and the manner in which rank-and-file personnel responded to them proved to be formative and foundational. Practices and policies strongly influenced by concerns about improving the force's relationship with the public, such as proactively conducting disaster relief, emphasizing its role as the people's force, and resisting being used to suppress domestic disturbances, all began to take shape during these first two years of the military's postwar reestablishment.

Chapter 2 focuses on the establishment of an academy to educate a new officer corps to lead the postwar force. Like the PRF, the NDA was a joint Japanese and US creation. Prime Minister Yoshida and his administration played the central role in its conception, formation, and operation while receiving advice from US military officials, beginning toward the end of the US military occupation and continuing long afterward. As Hayashi did as commander of the PRF, NSF, and GSDF, and then as chairman of the joint staff council of the SDF, academy president Maki, following the charge given to him by Yoshida, sought to create a new identity infused by liberal democratic ideals and masculine *noblesse oblige* that was different from that of the imperial military. Even before academy cadets achieved an outsized influence in the officer ranks as they assumed leadership positions, this defense identity merged with Hayashi's rhetoric to affect the wider force.

As a way of examining the force's search for legitimacy, the dynamics of military-society integration, and the emerging military-defense identity, chapter 3 focuses on the GSDF Northern Corps in Hokkaido, which had great strategic importance and thus hosted a disproportionate number of ground troops and bases during the Cold War years. There, as elsewhere, the force used economic incentives and public service and outreach as part of efforts to become a "beloved Self-Defense Force," as Hayashi encouraged it to do. Drawing on the ideas and actions of Yoshida, Hayashi, and Maki, force leaders sought to mold new traditions and a new identity for the Northern Corps by having its members emulate the figure of late nineteenth-century farmer-soldiers, the tondenhei. A focus on this regional army acts as a case study for similar developments throughout the country during the 1950s and 1960s.

Chapter 4 returns the focus to Tokyo during the 1960s, a tumultuous decade for the force and for the country. An existential policy question for political and force leaders was whether or not to mobilize the SDF to deal with massive and sometimes violent protests that shook Japan's political foundations during these years. During the huge demonstrations against the US-Japan Security Treaty in 1960 and in the face of the violent radical left-wing protests in the final years of the decade, the authorities decided not to deploy the force, in large part out of concern about how doing so might irreparably damage its relationship with society. But for the same reason, officials mobilized the SDF to provide logistical support for and participate as athletes in the Tokyo Olympics in 1964. The chapter uses the Olympics, which along with disaster-relief work did much to increase public acceptance of the SDF, to frame the chapter. It also examines Mishima's suicide at GSDF headquarters. Mishima's actions were shaped by the anti–security treaty protests, the Olympics, and GSDF experiential-enlistment programs conducted in hopes of boosting military-societal integration, all of which led to his rejection of the Cold War defense identity.

The final chapter turns its attention to Okinawa. In 1972, after twenty-seven years of US occupation and the establishment of huge military bases, the United States returned the islands to Japan. As it did so, all three branches of the SDF established bases on Okinawa to assume responsibility for its defense. Many Okinawans, who were once enthusiastic supporters of reversion, were angered by its terms, especially the unchanged status of US bases but also the arrival of another military, the existence of which they saw as a violation of Article 9. Even worse, they saw the SDF as the successor of the imperial military, which had sacrificed and even deliberately killed islanders during the horrific Battle of Okinawa in 1945. Such associations created a relationship with Okinawan society that was fraught with hostility and distrust and even more challenging than the situation that the reconstituted force had faced on the mainland in the 1950s. The chapter analyzes the opposition to and response of the SDF and especially the GSDF as it drew on familiar yet recalibrated tactics in its search for greater legitimacy. Though the force achieved a degree of often grudging acceptance in Okinawa, the chapter concludes that the particularly difficult challenge of integrating with society made it harder to create a strong sense of defense identity within and beyond the organization in Okinawa.

Although these dynamics continued beyond the 1980s, this book concludes with that decade for the following reasons. In a geopolitical context, the end of the decade marked the close of the Cold War. In terms of relations with society, by the 1970s and arguably by the 1960s on the mainland and the 1980s on Okinawa, the SDF had achieved a level of support that would largely remain stable until more recent post–Cold War interrelated international and domestic developments led to greater acceptance and backing. In addition, the 1980s marked a watershed moment as former imperial military officers retired; as a new generation of graduates from the NDA, who embraced and helped create the new military identity, began to advance to senior leadership positions; and as women began to be accepted as regular enlisted personnel in the GSDF from 1986 (they were accepted as cadets at the NDA from 1992). Finally, by the 1980s the SDF and the US military had begun to act more like allied armed forces, conducting their first joint training exercises, which was a step toward a more equitable intermilitary relationship.

In addition to advancing the concepts of military-society integration and Cold War defense identity, this book makes several other contributions to our understanding of the postwar era more broadly and of postwar Japanese history specifically. First, it sheds light on the contested nature of identity, particularly military identity in a peacetime democracy. For good reason, historians have focused on the development of pacifist and leftist movements as well as right-wing nationalist movements in the early Cold War decades. They have also highlighted the transwar continuities of prominent conservatives such as Yoshida. Studying other conservative and liberal democratic developments adds greater texture and complexity to the dueling political and social perspectives of the time. It also acts as a point of comparison for the complicated status of militaries in other democracies, such as the United States and Western European countries, during the Cold War.

Second, that greater texture and complexity is made possible in part by expanding the focus on elites beyond Yoshida to other leaders such as Hayashi and Maki. Scholars have written almost nothing about these two in either English or, for that matter, in Japanese. The leadership that each took in organizationally and ideologically laying a foundation for the postwar military-defense establishment is a reminder that individuals matter in shaping the contours of history.

So do nonelites. A third contribution of this book is its recognition of the roles and voices of rank-and-file personnel and cadets, some of whom rose to top leadership positions, but many of whom did not. It draws on oral history interviews—many of which I conducted—and a variety of eclectic sources, including internal force newspapers secured through relationships built with veterans and active-duty personnel. These sources do not simply enrich the narrative. They demonstrate that these rank-and-file force members played a proactive part in the creation of the force and its identity.

A third contribution is this book's discussion of how the organization and personnel of the SDF generally and GSDF specifically helped establish the peace and democracy that have characterized Japan since the end of World War II. They did this despite or perhaps because of their questionable constitutional legitimacy, suspicious foreign origins, the delegitimizing unending US presence, imperial military legacies, and alienation from society. Like other peaceful, liberal democratic regimes, Japan's has not been without its flaws, contradictions, and dark undersides, and it is now increasingly threatened and in need of reform. Yet, we should not be blind to its success and should recognize that the SDF's leaders and personnel often contributed to its stability. Though not apolitical and certainly anticommunist, they did not get actively involved in politics and did not attempt to subvert civilian control. They acted as a defensive rather than offensive force and never committed any acts of aggression. They acted on behalf of the nation—contributing economically and socially in myriad ways to the welfare of the people they pledged to serve. All in all, the organization and its leaders acted as a moderating force, and though they never became as beloved as they hoped during the Cold War decades, they gained a measure of respect that, in the end, is deserved.

# Chapter 1

## The Police Reserve Force and the US Army

On September 18, 1950, the day after eighteen-year-old Irikura Shōzō joined the PRF, he entered Camp Kurihama in Kanagawa Prefecture, about a one-hour train ride from Tokyo. The PRF recruitment drive had begun in August, a month after the creation of the force in early July, which was triggered by the outbreak of war on the Korean peninsula in late June. Until Japan's surrender in September 1945, Kurihama had hosted a navy communications school. In anticipation of an US invasion of the mainland, it became a center where military personnel and civilians, including women and children, prepared to defend the capital. That anticipated invasion would not have been the first time that an intimidating US force had arrived in Kurihama. In 1853, Commodore Matthew C. Perry landed his three warships there to commence negotiations that forced the Tokugawa regime to open the country to US trade. After the war, the communications school sat empty, rusting away for five years until the PRF was established. When Irikura and his fellow recruits arrived, their first task, under the direction of US soldiers, who oversaw PRF camps across the country, was to make the facilities livable.[1]

In late October, enlistees began weapons training. Irikura recalled feeling distinctly "troubled" when he was given his first rifle—an US-made M-1 carbine—and realized that guns like the one he held in his hands had been used against his fellow countrymen only five years earlier.[2] A photo that he sent to me in 2020 shows him sitting on the edge of a US Army jeep at Camp

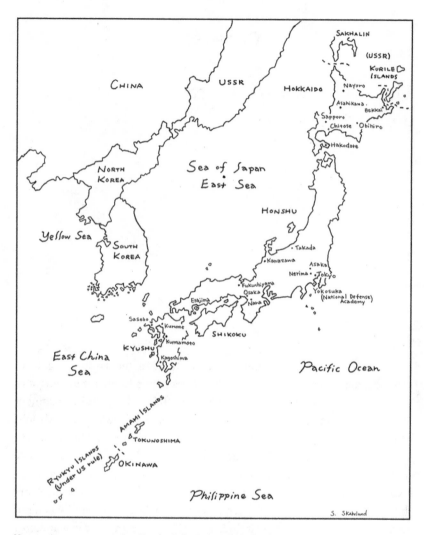

**MAP 1.** Japan, 1950s–1960s. Map by Seiko Todate Skabelund.

Kurihama (figure 1.1). Irikura was thirteen when the conflict came to an end in August 1945 and he had been taught that the Americans were a demonic enemy during the war. Yet his ambivalence must have paled in comparison to that of over half of PRF recruits, who had served in the imperial military.

Like most of those who enlisted, Irikura was primarily motivated by economic concerns. He wanted to help feed his family. But like many men, although he was not sure whether the reserve was a police or military force, he thought that Japan should at least be able to defend itself. He thought the new constitution, announced three years earlier, did not or

**FIGURE 1.1.**    Irikura Shōzō, a newly inducted member of the PRF, posing as he half sits in a US Army jeep at Camp Kurihama in late 1950. Used courtesy of Irikura Shōzō. Author's collection.

at least should not prevent it from doing so, whether the threat was a war across the strait or internal conflict. If the force was to be an army, he, like most recruits, had no interest in it emulating the imperial military, whose reckless actions had brought utter defeat and occupation. Despite this commitment to defend the country, Irikura remembered that he and other personnel were the target of verbal abuse off base. The men even rented a room just outside the base's gate so they could change out of their uniform and into civilian clothes when leaves began and then change back into their uniform when they ended.[3] This practice continues to this day, though now the motivation to be less visually prominent is to blend into society rather than to avoid jeers.

Irikura's experiences are emblematic of the first two years of the country's reconstituted military, a formative period in which its relationships with society, the imperial military, and especially the US armed forces left a strong imprint on the character of the force and its personnel. As Gen. Douglas MacArthur, the Supreme Commander for the Allied Powers (SCAP) in Japan, rushed US troops from Japan to Korea, he ordered Prime Minister Yoshida Shigeru to "establish a national police reserve of 75,000 men and expand the existing authorized strength of the personnel serving under the Maritime Safety Board by an additional 8000," to fill the gap.[4] His immediate concern was internal security and order, but he recognized that the police reserve would be the kernel of a resurrected military force. (The Maritime Safety Board had been formed in 1948 as a coast guard.) Yet his vision, and Yoshida's, of the development of the police reserve was more restrained than that of other Americans and Japanese who hoped for rapid rearmament and a force not unlike the Imperial Army.[5] Regardless, recognition that the organization violated the constitutional ban against the maintenance of war potential led occupation authorities to call it a police reserve and to minimize any public discussion of the force's true nature through reinvigorated censorship.

Despite the censorship, the force's questionable constitutionality, its foreign pedigree, and the ongoing US presence contributed to the image of it as an illegitimate subordinate of the US military. As suggested by Camp Kurihama's US commanders, US Army soldiers took a leading role in the formation of the force. This was not surprising given its establishment during the occupation and the urgency of the situation. Former Home Ministry police officials, whom the government appointed to many of the most powerful civilian and uniformed positions with the approval of occupation authorities, also shaped its character. SCAP occupation authorities and Japanese government officials prevented almost any former Imperial Army officers from joining the force until late 1951. After the occupation ended in 1952, they came to compose about 15 percent of the PRF's officer corps.[6] Some former police officials and some former army officers begrudged and distrusted US power and resented being subject to it. When Japan regained its sovereignty as the occupation came to a close, its reconstituted armed forces also secured greater autonomy. But both the government and the military, though independent, remained subservient to the United States and its military. The United States maintained bases across the archipelago and Japan remained dependent on the United States for its security. This bilateral security relationship was mirrored on a military organizational, personnel, and personal level. Because of the US military presence and the US-Japan Security Alliance, the two countries were partners in an unequal relationship. Because the narrow interpretation of Article 9 prevented collective self-defense, the two militaries conducted almost no joint training exercises for three decades.[7] While American Forces–Japan projected US power throughout Asia, the SDF, constrained constitutionally and by public opinion, assumed the character it would retain for decades: concerned with internal threats but wary about exercising its power against them, nominally providing defense against foreign invasion but protected by the overshadowing US military presence and nuclear umbrella and struggling to gain legitimacy in the eyes of society. These dynamics involving the US military, societal interactions, and the legacies of the imperial military all served to mold the priorities and identity of the postwar armed forces and its personnel during and after the occupation.

This chapter focuses on the establishment of the PRF, a seminal period for the reconstituted military, on the experiences of its recruits, both enlisted men and former Imperial Army officers, and on their relationships with US soldiers, society, and the prewar military. Scholars have focused more on the PRF era than on any other period of the postwar military, with an emphasis on the political and diplomatic story.[8] This chapter is more of a social history. It argues that although early postwar civilian and uniformed leaders were consumed by the organizational challenges of reestablishing a new military defense force, and although—or perhaps because—the process was characterized by competing interests, uncertainty, and contingency, the two years of the PRF were foundational in the development of a new military identity. Part of that identity was the tension between invisibility and visibility—maintaining a low, noncontroversial profile versus attempting to justify the PRF's existence. The chapter also tells the experiences of rank-and-file recruits and emphasizes the force's relationship with society, whose stability and order was the impetus for its creation. It begins with MacArthur's directive and the array of conflicting motivations that the establishment of the PRF unleashed, which provide political and diplomatic context.

## A Police Force or an Army?

Less than two weeks after Kim Il-sung sent North Korean troops across the 38th parallel on June 25, 1950, MacArthur sent his memo ordering the creation of the force to Yoshida on July 8. Communist forces had advanced rapidly, capturing Seoul within three days of crossing the border, and they continued to move south, sweeping beleaguered Republic of Korea troops before them. MacArthur's only viable option was to rush to South Korea four Eighth Army divisions, some eighty thousand men, who were stationed in occupied Japan. Their departure created a domestic security vacuum, which led MacArthur to order the establishment of a Japanese security force. His memo was only the beginning of the formation of the PRF (called the National Police Reserve, or NPR, in English). Despite this urgent beginning, a variety of disparate, sometimes competing and sometimes cooperating political actors shaped the creation of the PRF.[9]

Remarkably, in his memo to Yoshida, MacArthur did not mention the Korean War but instead couched the decision as a response to the government's request for an "augmentation" to its police forces.[10] His primary concern, though, was filling the hole left by the departing US divisions. Even if he did not think in these terms when he drafted the letter, MacArthur appears to have come to think of the force as an "embryonic army," because within a week of issuing the letter, his top lieutenant, Maj. Gen. Courtney Whitney, met with Chief Cabinet Secretary Okazaki Katsuo to confirm the meaning of the memo.[11] It would not be a normal police force, Whitney explained, but would respond to internal disturbances and attacks by foreign enemies. The force was to be armed with carbines, and equipped with artillery and tanks in the future.[12] Five days later, SCAP occupation officials informed the government that "the new force would be placed under direct Cabinet control by Potsdam decree, not Diet legislation, and organised separately from the regular police."[13] Calling it a "police reserve" from the beginning allowed occupation authorities to avoid what was politically unacceptable: violating the constitution that occupation officials themselves had crafted just four years earlier. That said, MacArthur appears to have imagined the PRF becoming a small military capable of dealing with civil disorder and helping to defend against a foreign invasion.[14] Although MacArthur had relinquished his presidential ambitions by that time, for several years he had been concerned that rearmament would undermine his legacy of having bestowed the peace constitution on the country, threaten SCAP's credibility, and endanger Japanese democracy.[15]

Like MacArthur, other SCAP officials were conflicted about what the PRF should be. Most recognized that, given the conflict in Korea, Japan needed an armed force that went beyond a police organization. But they, too, were restrained by MacArthur and by public opinion. Occupation authorities were also far from unified in how they viewed the nature and the leadership of the PRF. Some officials wanted to ensure that the force was not led by former Imperial Army officers, most of whom were still subject to the Allied purge of militarists that been implemented soon after the war. They wanted to draw mainly from the former Home Ministry and from the police for top leadership. But some officials, such as the fiercely anticommunist Maj.

Gen. Charles A. Willoughby, had other ideas. He hoped that the PRF would resemble the Imperial Army and be led by its former officers. He and others worked with former officers to achieve this objective. By August, his attempt to have appointed as commander Hattori Takushirō, a former imperial general staff officer and military secretary to Gen. Tōjō Hideki, was rejected by MacArthur, much to the relief of Yoshida.[16]

Prime Minister Yoshida, though initially confused about the nature of the PRF, soon figured out how to manipulate the situation to his advantage, as he often did. Indeed, Yoshida, a master negotiator, believed that "a defeated nation, by exploiting the shifting relations among world powers, could contain the damage incurred in defeat and instead win the peace."[17] Over the next several years, he repeatedly achieved this objective, though his emphasis on economic recovery over geopolitical independence, which became known as the Yoshida Doctrine, came at a cost to the national psyche. On receiving McArthur's directive and even after Whitney clarified the intent of the letter for Okazaki, Yoshida told the British ambassador on July 13 that he was "naturally most grateful" for the order and that he would like "to model this new force upon the London Metropolitan Police."[18] Two days later he told the Diet that MacArthur had authorized strengthening the police to a level like that of other democratic states.[19] Even after he clearly understood the US intent to transform the gendarmerie-like PRF into an army, Yoshida continued to maintain that it was and would remain a police force. One of the earliest examples of this strategy, which was suggested by SCAP, was his use of a cabinet order to bypass the Diet and legislative debate to order the creation of the PRF in early August. To minimize political discussion and deflect opposition, Yoshida continued to insist that the reserve was merely a police force and that Japan was not rearming, and when that position became obviously false, his government maintained that it was just an "army without war potential" (*senryoku naki guntai*).[20] This was not a naive view but rather a politically calculated expression on the part of Yoshida. Although he supported the strengthening of internal security capacities, he was concerned, as historian Jennifer Miller noted, about "the return of militarist power, ideologies, and personnel" within the PRF.[21]

The newly appointed civilian and uniformed leaders of the force, most of whom had previously served as police officials in the pre-1945 Home Ministry, had their own set of motivations. The interactions of officials such as Utsumi Hitoshi and Gotōda Masaharu with SCAP authorities made them realize that they were not overseeing a normal police force but something more like a gendarmerie that was going to become an army. Utsumi, Gotōda, and others were opposed to this but realized that it was pointless to contest the power of SCAP. They hoped to maintain some control over the force, though these former Home Ministry officials, too, came to recognize that a military needed experienced army officers, so long as they did not displace them. They did not, however, want the force to be created in the image of the imperial military, but wanted it to be "an organization appropriate for Japan under its new constitution."[22] Officials like Utsumi felt humiliated by the occupation, burned with a desire to rebuild their country, and were frustrated by the "ambiguity" (*aimai na mono*) of occupation policies.[23] They doubted whether US officials truly had Japan's interests at heart and whether the United States would be willing to defend their country. Some of them even went so far as to ask, when the occupation ended, that US military advisers leave Japan.[24]

Many senior officials in Washington, the most prominent of whom was Secretary of State John Foster Dulles, wanted Japan to rearm and contribute to the Cold War. Even before the outbreak of the Korean War, Dulles argued for rearmament. As he negotiated with Yoshida in late 1950 to bring the occupation to end, Dulles pushed Yoshida to rearm more rapidly. But Yoshida cleverly used public opposition and the economic costs of more rapid rearming to fend off Dulles's demands.[25]

Although a greater public outcry would have certainly greeted more rapid rearmament, Yoshida exaggerated the opposition. In midst of the Red Purge, the removal of thousands of leftist leaders from public and private positions that had begun before and continued after the outbreak of the war in Korea, the leftists were on the defensive. Public opinion was also mixed. With the travails of war still a fresh, raw memory, many citizens supported Article 9, were suspicious of rearmament, and did not believe Yoshida's denials that Japan was rearming. But war next door led to increased support for the idea that the country should at least be able to defend itself. Still, the lack of debate stemming from the Red Purge, increased censorship, and government machinations led to confusion on the part of the public.[26]

Finally, actual and potential enlistees shaped the character of the force. Like Irikura, the majority of men who applied to and joined the PRF did so for economic reasons. Some of them resigned as soon as they realized that the force was more military than police-like in character. Others left at the end of their two-year contracts, when they became eligible for generous severance pay. Given the economic difficulties of the era, the PRF did not have trouble recruiting a sufficient number of men, but retention remained a concern. Recruits continued to be motivated more by financial concerns than by ideology. This dynamic influenced the rhetoric of force leaders and the PRF's policies and practices.

Former imperial military officers whom the government eventually turned to fill the leadership vacuum also helped shape the force. These ex-officers were not a monolithic group. Almost none were aligned with Hattori. Many of the more than fifty-three thousand army officers who had been purged—"every military officer above the rank of captain, approximately one-half of the captains, and all graduates of Japan's military schooling system, including wartime officer candidate schools"—wanted to join the force.[27] Like most rank-and-file recruits, many were motivated by economic concerns, because the purge had made life difficult for them and their families. Nationalism was likely stronger among such recruits than among enlisted men, but many were supportive of the occupation's democratic reforms. They were also motivated by personal pride and a sense of professionalism. Many did not want to join the force unless they were sure they would be able to use their military expertise and leadership skills.[28]

These diverse stakeholders represented the range of interests that animated the establishment and development of the early force. The mix of constitutional constraints, geopolitical imperatives, and competing parties and personalities led to subterfuge, sophistry, and uncertainty. The contradictions of this process were apparent in the messaging of the recruitment campaign and by the experiences of the young men who answered its call.

## "Peaceful Japan Wants You"

The ambiguous nature of the PRF was underscored by its recruitment drive, which began on August 9, 1950. The campaign's messaging and its organizational structure served to create more confusion than clarity. It represented the force as a constabulary policing body, and because the National Rural Police largely conducted it, both at their own stations and at local police stations, it further gave the appearance the PRF was merely an extension of these policing agencies. But some elements of the campaign suggested to discerning potential recruits that it was the foundation of a robust military force.

One of the most distinctive characteristics of the recruitment campaign was its rushed nature, which was motived by the need to form a strong security body to take the place of departing US troops. The government announced the campaign just a month after MacArthur issued his memo. Four days later, on August 13, the government began to accept applications. The deadline to apply was just two days later. Testing began on August 17, and successful applicants began training a week after that. Occupation authorities directed the Japanese government to have a force ready to be mobilized by October 12.

Posters, newspaper reports, advertisements in train stations and trains, radio announcements, news broadcasts, announcements at sporting events, appeals from PRF officials, movies, slides, and leaflets were all utilized to spread the recruitment campaign.[29] The government implemented a "carefully planned series of informational programs on regular newsbroadcasts [sic] and spot announcements three times daily" and on a dozen radio programs, such as *Women's Hour*, *School Newspapers*, and *Recess for Farmers*. Recruiters also distributed more than eight hundred thousand leaflets throughout the country.[30] Interested men were told to apply at their local police station, suggesting the supposed police nature of the force. The name of the organization, of course, did so as well. On July 27, the force was officially designated the Keisatsu Yobitai, a translation of the phrase that MacArthur had used in his memo, "national police reserve."[31] The name could be understood as "reserve personnel of the national police." Even when government officials announced that the PRF would be a separate force and have "army-like strength," as they did in early August, its name still gave the impression that it was no more than a constabulary—or at the most a paramilitary—policing organization.[32]

Recruitment materials sought to subtly assuage fears that the force violated the constitution and country's new peace identity. Over a hundred thousand copies of one recruitment poster, with a "striking design of red, gold, blue, and white," declaring in large characters and letters "Peaceful Japan Wants You" (*Heiwa Nihon ha anata o motomete iru*), were displayed across the country. The designer, who is unknown, placed a large white dove, its wings spread, superimposed over a red rising sun surrounded by golden rays emanating from it. The design, particularly the golden rays, suggested either police or military insignia, and the PRF's subsequently issued shoulder patch and cap insignia would resemble it. Below the dove were the words "Police Reserve Personnel Recruitment" in large letters, and below that was a detailed description of the qualifications, benefits, length of service, examinations, and period of recruitment. In "faint lettering" spread over this description were the words "75,000 Men."[33] The poster's first word, "peaceful," and its centering of the dove, a symbol of peace, seemed designed to lessen any concerns that the force contravened Article 9. At the same time, placing the dove in front of a rising sun allowed the poster to appeal to patriotic sentiments by associating peace with the nation.

Recruiters realized, though, that for most young men practical concerns were a greater priority than ideology. The deciding factor for most of those considering applying was probably the detailed description at the bottom of the poster. That explanation indicated that monthly pay would be 5,000 yen, with a severance payment of 60,000 yen at the end of two years of service. This made the PRF highly attractive employment. A monthly salary of 3,000 yen was considered high for government work at the time.[34] Plus, during one's service all clothing, food, and housing would be provided for free. Those interested were instructed to pick up an application form at any police station, substation, or police box, or at city, town, and village offices.[35]

The organizational structure and uniforms of the PRF also gave the impression that the force was just another police organization. Some newspaper reporters, though, suspected that this was not the case. In mid-July, after the government had announced that the force would be composed of thirteen ranks, each with a name typical of a police organization, the left-leaning daily newspaper *Asahi* provided a listing of the ranks with their equivalent Imperial Army rank. A police chief (*keisatsu shichō*), for example, was equal to company officer (*ikan*).[36] In the same story, the reporter introduced the design of the PRF uniforms and featured an illustration of a uniform-clad figure, who looked more like a policeman than a soldier. The authorities could have presented several different uniform styles. Significantly, they chose to introduce a formal outfit, which was most like what policemen would normally wear. Regardless, the masculine strength and idealized order that the newspaper image expresses is unambiguous. The man is tall, broad shouldered, with a muscled physique perceptible under his long-sleeved, double-pocketed shirt. He stands upright and at attention. In midst of turmoil at home and not far away across the sea in Korea, people may have found such as figure reassuring. He was associated with the police, an organization that combated the specter of violence and anarchy.

The uniform's designer further linked the PRF to the police. The same newspaper article reported that the designer was Ebine Shundō, who had drawn the likeness of Hirozawa Sadamichi, the defendant in the Teigin (short for Teikoku Ginkō, Imperial Bank) Incident in January 1948. Hirozawa had allegedly entered a branch of the bank in the capital and, posing as a public health official, announced to those in the bank that dysentery had broken out in the neighborhood and convinced them to drink a supposed antidote. The mixture, which contained cyanide, killed twelve people. The suspect then stole 160,000 yen and fled. The police arrested Hirozawa seven months later. A sketch rendered by the police artist Ebine was instrumental in Hirozawa's apprehension, and he was applauded for his artistic talent that helped solve the crime. In early August 1950, the incident was very much on the minds of the public because just weeks before a court had convicted Hirozawa and sentenced him to death.[37] Though his selection as the designer of the PRF uniforms, which the government touted, may have not been intended to give the impression that the PRF was a police entity, it probably further contributed to that notion.

In response to the recruitment campaign, a huge number of men applied for the PRF. When the application period began on August 13, interested candidates swarmed local recruiting offices and many local police stations quickly exhausted their allotment of the four hundred thousand enlistment forms.[38] According to the daily *Mainichi* newspaper, many "enthusiastic" applicants in Tokyo, hoping to be first in line, arrived "before dawn waking up dozing policemen" at the recruitment centers. "Both in cities and the countryside," the paper reported, "many applicants were former Imperial Army noncommissioned officers. In the cities, unemployed applicants were fewer than expected. Applicants came from various occupations such as cooks, officials, industrial / construction laborers, and shop workers. Among the most unusual applicants was a student studying oil painting at a college of the arts and a temple priest from the Zen Buddhist Eihei Temple [in Fukui Prefecture]. In the countryside, many second and third sons from such backgrounds as textiles and farming applied."[39] Government data confirms that these observations were generally accurate. Over a third of applicants worked in agriculture and forestry, and 13 percent were unemployed. Besides an "other" category, the "unemployed" category was the second most numerous, followed closely by industrial and construction laborers. Applicants with some high school education numbered about one-third. Over 40 percent of the applicants were between the ages of twenty and twenty-two. Despite the recruitment guidelines stipulating that applicants must be between twenty and thirty-five years old, twenty-five thousand eighteen and nineteen-year-old men applied, and over a quarter of these were accepted. Eighty percent of all applicants were single men.[40] Among these applicants, over half had served in the Imperial Army. Of these, 27 percent were rank-and-file soldiers, 18 percent were noncommissioned officers (NCOs), and 4 percent were low-ranking officers. Among those accepted, the percentage from each group was roughly equal to its percentage of applicants, though a slightly higher percentage of former NCOs and officers were accepted.[41]

In the end, a huge number of men—over two hundred thousand—applied for the seventy-five thousand openings. Given the ongoing postwar upheaval, including a severe recession and the austerity measures that the government, following the advice of SCAP financial adviser Joseph Dodge, had begun to implement in 1949, it is no surprise that most applicants were motivated by economic concerns. Satō Morio, the veteran who in this book's introduction recalled the derogatory names the force and its personnel were called, was in many ways a typical applicant. Eighteen years old and a Kyoto high school graduate, Satō was ill from working long hours as a machinist in a Mitsubishi factory in Nagoya when he saw a recruitment poster in the company employee room. He had no interest in national security. Rather, as the only son and oldest child of a family of eight whose father, an employee of Mitsubishi Petroleum, had perished during the war when the ship he was on, bound for the Dutch East Indies, was sunk by a US submarine, Satō was motivated by a desire to earn more money to send to his mother and younger sisters.[42] Although no data exists to show that economic concerns were the primary motivation for applicants, ample anecdotal evidence from contemporary newspaper coverage, memoirs, and oral history interviews indicate this was likely the case.

That said, a desire to protect their country may have been a motivation for some applicants, or perhaps a way to ennoble a decision chiefly motivated by economics. The southern island of Kyushu—known for its distinctive martial masculinity—produced nearly one-third of applicants, although its inhabitants made up only 10 percent of Japan's population. This may, however, have reflected its widespread poverty rather than ingrained military values. For decades, young men from poor lower-class families in the farming villages and small towns of Kyushu especially, as well as to a lesser extent Hokkaido and the northeastern Tohoku region and Yamaguchi Prefecture on the main island of Honshu, would be significantly overrepresented among the enlisted members of the force.[43] A similar dynamic occurs in the US South, which has historically supplied a significantly higher percentage of recruits to the US military than its share of the country's population.[44] Compared to other regions, Kyushu's high population density and lack of arable land led to a prevalence of small family farms and more difficult economic conditions. It may have been more socially acceptable for applicants, as the historian Tomoyuki Sasaki argued, for Kyushu's young men to rationalize their decision to apply for the force with cultural rather than economic reasons. "Ideology," Sasaki observed, often is mobilized in this way "to disguise material conditions."[45]

Although many men were unsure if the PRF was to be a police or a military force, some—particularly those with previous military experience or schooling—suspected from the recruiting messages that it would likely be or become a military organization. This was the case for Mori Shigehiro, who had just completed accelerated coursework at the Army Academy when the war ended and whose father had been an army engineering officer. In 1949, Mori became a police officer. But the following year, when he saw

PRF recruiting announcements, he explained to his commander that he had trained for the military and so belonged in the PRF rather than in the police.[46]

But the character of the PRF was not clear to many other enlistees. That ambiguity, the strong US influence on the force, and other factors led to many resignations and to ambivalence among some who remained. An examination of the immense US influence on the establishment of the PRF and how enlisted personnel responded to that dynamic and other aspects of training and camp life reveals much about the foundations of the Cold War defense identity.

## "As Though . . . Made in the United States"

After applicants successfully passed a series of physical examinations and a background check, they were sworn into the PRF at five National Rural Police regional schools that served as induction centers. Following four days of paperwork, medical tests, and orientation, recruits traveled to one of twenty-eight newly opened camps to begin training.[47] These camps were either former imperial military installations, like Kurihama, property of other government agencies, or US bases that had just been vacated by the Eighth Army. The Americans allowed the PRF to temporarily use the latter before those troops returned from Korea and/or replacement troops arrived from the United States.[48]

Wherever newly enlisted personnel were sent, one element was consistent: they found US military officers in charge. Enlistees recalled arriving at the camps to the greeting of a US major: "I'm the camp commander."[49] Although the emergence of Japanese leadership within the PRF reduced the role of US military personnel over time, US soldiers played a central role not only in organizing the force but also in fashioning its identity. Indeed, "American policymakers and military leaders did not conceive of security simply in terms of expanded military capabilities. . . . They also hoped that the [force] would produce the responsible and committed citizens and leaders believed necessary to create a physically, ideologically, and psychologically 'sound' democracy. . . . They increasingly hoped that Japanese defensive forces, built under American supervision, could infuse Japan with the military, political, and psychological strength to oppose communism."[50]

Because of a dearth of Japanese leadership, US servicemen played a leading role at all levels, whether at PRF headquarters or at the training camps. On the day MacArthur issued his letter to Yoshida, SCAP began preparations to establish the force. Within days, the Civil Affairs Section created a Civil Affairs Section Annex (CASA), led by Maj. Gen. Whitfield P. Shepard, to oversee the staggering task of recruiting, equipping, billeting, and training the force.[51] Shepard selected Col. Frank Kowalski as his top assistant. A graduate of West Point in 1930, Kowalski served in Europe in 1944 and then, after several years in the United States, was assigned to serve in the occupation of Japan in 1948. In the spring of 1950, he was transferred to work under Shepard. After war broke out in Korea, Kowalski hoped to be assigned to command a combat regiment on the peninsula. Instead Shepard promoted him to his chief of staff and shared with him, as Kowalski recalled in his memoir, secret plans to create "the beginning of the Japanese army."[52]

For the next two years, Kowalski and other CASA officers, working with Japanese civilian and uniformed officials, played a central role in directing the new security force. Kowalski took charge of developing and implementing a basic plan for the force, overseeing policy and logistical matters and working closely with the top Japanese officers selected by Yoshida and approved by him and other SCAP officials. He was supported by a staff of over 400 the first year. By April 1952, CASA had expanded to its largest size, 975 personnel made up of 322 officers, 599 enlisted men, and 54 civilians.[53] Calling the PRF a "little American Army," as Kowalski did, may have been an exaggeration, but it was not much of one.[54]

The influence that US officers like Kowalski had on the new force's leadership in shaping a more democratic force is illustrated by an experience Kowalski had with Hayashi Keizō, the uniformed chief. After a visit to Korea during which Kowalski witnessed a South Korean major brutally slap a recruit, which a US adviser there claimed was something Koreans had "picked . . . up from the Japanese army when it occupied Korea," Kowalski vowed that this sort of behavior would not be tolerated in the new Japanese Army. Soon after his return to Japan, he read about a PRF captain who had slapped and kicked a civilian on a streetcar for failing to offer him his seat. Shocked, he asked Hayashi to come to his office. In response to Kowalski's questions, Hayashi said the PRF would conduct an investigation. A week later, he reported that the inquiry had confirmed the newspaper account and that the captain would be fined two weeks' pay. Kowalski was indignant. "Is the Japanese Army," he demanded, "going to become a viable military of a democratic people, or are you going to permit the officers of the new force to slap, kick, and push your citizens and soldiers around?" Hayashi protested that the captain came from an influential family, to which Kowalski countered, "Is his family, and is he, more important than the [PRF]? Is he more important than the dignity of the individual citizen? This captain doesn't look to me like an officer and a gentleman." Three days later, Hayashi returned to report that the captain had been dismissed from the force.[55] This incident highlights the influence that occupation officials like Kowalski exerted on Hayashi and other senior PRF officials and how they sought to redefine the identity of the organization, especially in terms of its relationship with society and the legacies of the imperial military.

US Army personnel also exerted a strong influence as commanders at PRF camps across the country. Given that almost all prewar military academy graduates had been purged and were not allowed to join the force, SCAP officials had no one to turn to other than US soldiers to provide leadership and training to incoming recruits. These men supervised the force as part of the US Army Advisory and Control Group. But officers were hard to secure because of the urgent need for leadership in Korea.

Because of this leadership deficit, Kowalski and his colleagues decided to assign at least one officer, usually a major but, failing that, a noncommissioned officer, usually a sergeant, to each one thousand inductees—and no more than two NCOs per camp. Finding available NCOs for the task, especially as the first groups of recruits left the induction centers for the training camps, was not easy. A day before the first group of a thousand recruits was to arrive at one camp, a desperate Kowalski considered sending his deputy, a lieutenant colonel. Then a major appeared in his office. Like Kowalski a couple of months earlier, the soldier was looking forward to being sent to Korea. Instead Kowalski assigned him to oversee a PRF camp. "You are going to take over one of the most challenging and exciting jobs you have ever had in the Army," Kowalski told him, "You are going to be daddy to a new Japanese military force. You will organize, house, administer, equip, and train a Japanese infantry battalion, the first in the new Japanese army. And you're going to do that without letting a single Japanese know that they are anything but part of a police force." None of the enlistees, Kowalski continued, would be officers or NCOs, though some of the inductees may have served as NCOs in the Imperial Army. Kowalski's instructions to the major indicate the degree to which Americans exercised control over the PRF both at the central headquarters and at the training camps.[56]

Given this situation, Kowalski's comment elsewhere that "Americans managed these troops like a private army" seems like no exaggeration.[57] His language, particularly his use of "daddy" to refer to the major's impending role overseeing Japanese recruits, also suggests a sense of superiority that resonates with the criticisms of the reconstituted defense forces as the bastard child of the Americans and dovetails with MacArthur's infamous denigration of Japanese civilization as being as developed as "a boy of twelve."[58] Although Kowalski wrote his memoirs years later and these reconstructed passages are certainly not the exact words that were used, they do capture underlying attitudes of the time. A Japanese civilian translator for the PRF, who kept Kowalski apprised of political and societal developments while he oversaw the force and after he returned to the United States, used similar language, referring to Kowalski as the "Foster Father" of the PRF.[59] Although archives unfortunately appear to contain next to nothing of the perspective of US camp commanders, accounts by Japanese recruits in these camps confirm that US commanders exercised considerable sway over the enlistees with whom they interacted and likely exhibited such attitudes.[60]

Additional evidence confirms the profound influence of the US Army on the PRF. A SCAP political adviser, William Sebald, recalled that the "new Japanese army . . . looked as though it had been made in the United States. On a visit to one of the training camps," he remembered, "I thought at first I had stumbled into an American base, for everything from guns to fatigues was G.I."[61] A reliance on US military clothing, equipment, and weaponry was the rule. US influences did not end there. Photographs of camps show signs labeled both in Japanese and in English: "kitchen," "mess hall," and "work room," as well as "no smoking within 50 feet" on a building presumably housing explosive material.[62] US camp commanders spoke little to no Japanese, so all orders were issued and training was conducted in English, often translated into Japanese by US soldiers of Japanese descent. CASA rushed translated parts of the US basic training curriculum to the camps. Sometimes individual recruits were tasked with translating other training materials.[63] Specialized training was based on the US Army's basic field manual. As SCAP's Civil Affairs Section scrambled to translate, print, and distribute the manuals, the process was slowed by an attempt to hide the military character of the organization. US officers sought to "omit objectionable terms such as enemy, combat, attack, artillery, helmets, infantry, soldier, tanks et cetera" and substitute "'police' terminology,'" which "was a must."[64] The GSDF did not begin revising the basic field manual it had adopted wholesale from the US Army until 1956, after years of using "extra cushions on the seat and extensions on the pedals" for the "drivers of tanks and armored cars and other vehicles turned over" to them by the Americans.[65]

When training got underway, lasting, in typical US military boot-camp fashion, for thirteen weeks or 624 hours, Japanese leadership began to emerge. US camp commanders, or the recruits themselves through voting, selected men for leadership positions. The process, the historian Ayako Kusunoki noted, was "generally haphazard, with a tendency for those with some [NCO] experience or English fluency to be chosen." Gaps in leadership, though, remained a problem at headquarters and within divisions. Recognizing this, US occupation and Japanese government authorities agreed to fill two hundred high-level PRF positions by selecting officials from other government agencies and to fill some eight hundred mid-level positions through recruitment, this time allowing purged imperial military officers younger than forty-five years old who had been carefully screened to join the force.[66]

As former military officers entered the PFR, US anticommunism led to a reevaluation of concerns about a revival of Japanese militarism and military spirit. During 1951, US occupation authorities and Japanese officials such as Hayashi began to reconsider their views of imperial military officers' "'devotion' to militarism." Instead, concerned about the force's "tactical and spiritual deficiencies," they "recast" what was once seen as fanaticism as "patriotism," found common ground in anticommunism, and lauded former officers for their vigor and spirit (seishin).[67] The Cold War anticommunist context also became a "powerful integrative force" as the West German government, assisted by the Americans, reestablished a military in the 1950s.[68] In Japan, Kowalski, who had earlier opposed admitting imperial military officers into the PRF, came to praise them, as he later recalled, for what "they could give the new force: military competence, strength of character, devotion to country, and hopefully a deep understanding of past mistakes."[69] He came to welcome their "military spirit." "Spirit, heart, guts, or *seishin kyōiku*, whatever one calls it," he claimed, "is the essence of a fighting force. Without it, no soldier is worth his salt and no army worth its budget."[70] Kowalski's reassessment of spirit aptly illustrates how this core martial character trait, which was so closely associated with the imperial military, was reinterpreted and repackaged and gained wider acceptance in the context of the Cold War.

When Japanese leadership emerged in 1951, US military officers who had been acting as commanders gradually became advisers, though the process was gradual and halting. At the beginning of 1951, CASA issued orders telling personnel that "their function [was] advisory in nature."[71] Yet US advisers continued to exercise an influence beyond their newly prescribed role. The mixed messages that senior officials issued probably did not help. On the one hand, a memo from the Fourth Region Kyushu Headquarters of the PRF in June 1951 informed Japanese camp commanders and division and section chiefs that "success of NPR operation depend[ed] upon the extent of cooperation and liaison with advisors' groups" and encouraged them to, as necessary, "hold a daily conference" with them.[72] On the other hand, in October CASA issued a memorandum reminding regional officials across the country, "U.S. Army Advisory personnel are not in command of elements of the NPR."[73] Despite or perhaps because of this sort of messaging,

Furukawa Kumio, a former imperial military officer who joined the force in November 1951, remembers advisers still having an inordinate amount of influence after he joined.[74] Even in early 1952, just months before the end of the occupation, advisers continuing to play an outsized role remained a concern for Japanese officials and one recognized by the Americans. A SCAP memo reported the tactful comments of the cabinet minister who oversaw the PRF: "At the present time, there are over 600 US Army officers with the [force], and they have been very kind to the Japanese leaders, but at the same time, the Japanese feel very much subjected to their authority." Although expressing these concerns, the minister communicated the government's hope that advisers would continue to work "closely with the Japanese military organizations" after the occupation came to an end.[75]

## An Incomplete Restoration: PRF Camp Life

Joining the PRF was an ambiguous experience. Several factors contributed to the ambiguity. Once recruits left the induction center and arrived at the training camps, many recruits who thought they had joined a police force soon realized from its organizational structure and training they were receiving that it was more akin to a military. True to the stated mission of the PRF, commanders instructed members in riot control, but they moved to field exercises that resembled combat more than policing and utilized weaponry more powerful than "pistols and other small arms."[76]

For roughly half of the enlistees, the PRF was their first taste of highly regimented, military-like life. For those with imperial military experience, what they were experiencing was more familiar, but the US inflection made it equally if not more disconcerting. For one thing, their camp commanders had been the enemy just five years earlier. Now the close but wholly unequal relationship between Japan and the United States that characterized the occupation was personal. They were now experiencing it firsthand every day. Being trained by a US NCO, holding US guns, and wearing US-style uniforms made some of them, like Irikura, the young recruit introduced at the beginning of the chapter, uncomfortable. Even the first official history of the SDF admitted that "during this period, American camp commanders were the ones actually in charge of some personnel matters and of giving orders for most management and operational matters. From time to time, some camps experienced a lack of mutual understanding, leading to ambivalence."[77]

Recruits also found that much of society viewed them with suspicion or at least did not revere them like they imagined it once had imperial soldiers before 1945. Some members found these contradictions related to wider society and the US and imperial militaries difficult to stomach.[78] Yet some, including those who had served in the Imperial Army, may have felt a restoration of confidence in returning to uniform. Handling weaponry again probably satisfied some masculine egos. Some recruits may have felt a sense of liberation at taking back the buildings and barracks previously occupied by the US troops. However, vivid reminders of their country's occupied status and their force's subordinate position vis-à-vis the US military may have tempered such feelings of redemption.

Whether the camp they moved into had been previously occupied by US troops or was an old imperial military facility that had largely sat empty since the end of the war, enlistees often experienced culture shock. Harsh conditions awaited recruits who entered the latter camps. Onetime imperial military facilities were often in disrepair and cold in the fall and winter weather. Recruits spent the first weeks fixing up barracks and other buildings to simply make them inhabitable. A six-page illustrated account by an enlistee named Satō Yukio depicts various aspects of his group's first weeks at Camp Takada in Niigata Prefecture. It shows their arrival by train, their march from the station through the streets of Takada to the camp (which was on the grounds of a centuries-old castle), their work to put the barracks and grounds in order, including putting together their bunkbeds, and their riot suppression training.[79] Some camp accommodations were even more primitive. Fujii Shigeru, who grew up in Bibai in Hokkaido and worked in a coal mine there before joining the PRF in September, slept in a horse stable for about a year while based in Hakodate.[80]

Enlistees who were assigned to camps where US troops had been stationed before being sent to Korea enjoyed more comfortable conditions, but this situation did not make them immune to ambivalence. Unlike their fellow members who went to facilities like Kurihama, they did not need to repair the buildings. But for weeks they had little to do because none of the camps except for the Etajima training school near Hiroshima had any equipment or weapons with which to train.[81] Satō, the young man who quit his machinist job at Mitsubishi to join the PRF, remembered marching around the camp during the mornings and playing baseball or softball most afternoons. He found the field with its green grass outfield and groomed infield so beautiful that he imagined he was in the United States, and he enjoyed the sense of comradery and teamwork fostered by the games.[82] Such an effect may have been just what US camp commanders were after. Occupation authorities, the historian Sayuri Guthrie-Shimizu argued, "championed baseball as a tool for democratizing the former enemy."[83] Or, it may have just been a great way for the new recruits to kill time until the materials needed to conduct military training arrived. Regardless, recruits experienced many things for the first time in the PRF. Irikura recalled that he had never drunk coffee and Coca-Cola until he joined the force.[84] Many recruits had never used a Western-style toilet before. Some remembered the bodily and emotional discomfort of using toilets and urinals that were too high for their short legs and of using showers instead of baths—and even worse, showers located in the same room as the toilets without any walls between them.[85] Fujii remembered having no idea how to use the toilet he encountered at the training camp in Chiba near Tokyo, so the first time he stood on seat and squatted.[86] He and others laughed when recalling these incidents many decades later, but at the time they found them embarrassing, even humiliating. Several force veterans recalled the odd sensation of sleeping in raised beds or cots and the difficulty it took to become comfortable sitting in a chair.[87] Adjusting to US ways required PRF recruits to adapt bodily.

These cultural shocks were not simply the result of differences between Japanese and US daily living practices, but also of differences between civilian and military life. Conscripts in the prewar imperial military, many of whom came from rural areas, also had difficulty adjusting to military practices that were heavily influenced by the Army's and Navy's adaptations of Western conventions.[88] This did not necessarily mean that adapting to the living quarters on onetime US bases was easier for imperial military veterans. For many of whom came from the countryside and from lower-class backgrounds, some of the practices may have been familiar, yet they were not the same as to those they had once experienced.

Some of the clothing worn by recruits may also have dimmed any sense that the force represented a restoration of national sovereignty. Because domestic apparel and footwear manufacturers were unable to meet the PRF's huge, sudden orders, many recruits were initially outfitted in an eclectic mix of US uniforms, service caps, and boots, and sometimes in old Imperial Army khaki summer uniforms and cheap white tennis shoes. Wearing the clothes and boots of the former enemy appears to have made a strong impression on many recruits, though some veterans remember wearing Japanese-made uniforms and only US-made boots.[89] Yūmoto Yūzo, who had served briefly as a sailor in the Imperial Navy before the war ended, recalled that until proper uniforms and caps came he wore the "smallest US Army jumpsuit that barely fit the bodies of Japanese. The shoes" he remembered, "were, of course, US Army boots—the lace-up kind of boots that females wear.

At first, really big ones came, and we found that they were loose when we put them on. Everyone complained continuously that they were useless, but evidently smaller ones arrived soon thereafter, and we were able to exchange them."[90] A photograph shows new recruits looking through a pile of boots for sizes that fit them (figure 1.2). Yūmoto's description of the boots as being like the "kind . . . that females wear" is telling. It is not clear if the boots were indeed the kind that women wear, but his comment suggests that recruits felt emasculated because they had to wear such boots and because the male sizes were too large for them.[91] Yūmoto was not alone in his reaction. Satō Yukio's illustrated account of PRF troops moving into Camp Takada also highlights the surprise of recruits encountering the massive US boots. One scene shows a puzzled-looking soldier holding a boot, which is bigger than his upper body and so large that a bird has perched on its toe. Both gaze at the boot, their bewilderment given expression by a question mark placed above them.[92] Putting on the smallest of the US uniforms and boots must have made recruits physically aware of the corporeal disparity between US and Japanese soldiers. This difference was not just imagined. On average, US soldiers were "about a foot taller and fifty pounds heavier than [their] Japanese counterpart[s]" in the early 1950s.[93]

Recruits also took notice of differences in language and military practices. Yūmoto remembered that commands were often the direct translations of US army commands. For many, these commands were unlike the familiar phrases of the Imperial Army and sounded odd. The US command to turn one's head about forty-five degrees to the right during a military drill is "eyes right." This order was translated directly into the archaic sounding "manako migi" (eyes right) instead of using the traditional Japanese command "kashira migi" (heads right).[94] This strange rendering caused some trainees to shift their eyes rightward on command without moving their heads. Not only were the words different but training drills, too, were all conducted US-style.[95]

While the subordinate status of the PRF warped military terminology, the efforts to make a military appear like a police force led to ludicrous names for the increasingly powerful weaponry employed by the fledging force. Initially, beginning in October 1950, the PRF trained with carbines like the one issued to the eighteen-year-old Irikura. By the following year, the PRF was training with 105-millimeter and 155-millimeter artillery, incendiary projectiles, and tanks. In part because SCAP directives outlawed Japanese industry from researching or producing any weaponry, the PRF was completely dependent on the US military to supply it with arms. Such weaponry, however, could not be called by its common names. SCAP officials instructed

**FIGURE 1.2.** New members of the PRF look for boots in sizes that fit them. August 1950. Used with permission of the Asagumo Newspaper Company.

the PRF to call artillery "special instruments," tanks "special vehicles" (*toku-sha*), and so on. This sort of doublespeak continued for decades, although by the early 1960s some of the "camouflage used to hide the military flavor in vocabulary" began to be replaced.[96]

Recruits seem to have generally liked their US camp commanders, though some found the idea that they were subject to US military officers to be demeaning. Because one or two commanders were assigned to train as many as a thousand recruits and because commanders spoke little to no Japanese, most force personnel did not form close personal relationships with them. Fujii, the former coal miner from Hokkaido, recalled feeling angry about being trained by an American but figuring that because Japan had lost the war, nothing could be done about it. As he used his M-1 carbine during target practice and found he could fire off eight shots in a single round, compared to three shots with the Japanese guns that he used as an Imperial Army soldier, he realized why his side had lost.[97] Other former recruits had a less complicated view of the camp commanders and other military advisers. Satō, the former Mitsubishi machinist, had more contact with his camp commander than many personnel because he was involved in translating training materials. He remembered him as a "gentleman" and the epitome of military professionalism.[98] Interactions with or observations of the advisers also led to moments of cultural shock. Irikura recalled seeing something he thought was unimaginable: the morning routine of a military wife dropping off her adviser husband at the base each day in a Buick.[99]

Interaction with interpreters, almost all of whom were Americans of Japanese ancestry, was more complicated. Irikura remembered Nisei (Japanese American) linguists having more influence than camp commanders on training and camp life because of their intermediary status and language ability. He thought they had a favorable view of the PRF as an organization, but that some seemed to hold a grudge against Japanese and to bully them on purpose.[100] Likewise, a former Japanese civilian driver for a US adviser remembered that interpreters looked down on the PRF. He recalled an incident involving a Nisei "Sergeant K" who took a knife without permission from a PRF kitchen and when asked by a Japanese private to return it, got angry. He belittled the PRF by saying all their equipment including the knife came from the US military, and then he hit the private.[101] These memories dovetail with the analysis of the historian Eiichiro Azuma, who argued that "the position of Nisei linguists resembled that of colonial middleman" in occupied Japan and that they behaved in contradictory ways, sometimes moving from "oppressed to oppressor[s]" and engaging in "overcompensation" or "hyper-disidentification" by "despis[ing] the vanquished Japanese more intensely than other Americans because they shared the same ancestry."[102] As the former driver noted, the fact that some of them had been sent to Japan from the frontlines of the Korean War may have intensified such tendencies because of post-traumatic stress disorder.[103]

Beyond the training camps and bases, PRF recruits were often taken aback by the chilly reception they received from wider society. On the streets, personnel faced jeers of "tax thief" and "there is 60,000 yen walking along," references to their large salaries. Critics accused them of only enlisting for the pay and staying in the force so that they could collect the generous severance payment.[104] Critics on both the left and the right thought the force was a waste of public money. The media was also critical of the PRF, though the censorship that intensified after the outbreak of the Korean War tempered some criticism.[105] SCAP censors appear to have been most concerned about media descriptions of the force as "the new Japanese Army" and they objected to reports that included mention of "machine guns" and the use of "expressions and terms which suggest[ed] the reappearance of the former Army." They also objected to references to and photographs of "dilapidated buildings and poor equipment" and "U.S. personnel . . . with [force] personnel (including U.S. military installations and equipment therein)."[106] The historian Masuda Hajimu observed that what media discussion did occur "remained principally a conversation about domestic order" because most "politicians and officials" were concerned about a "'red-menace' at home" rather than a "direct military attack."[107] The lack of an open and robust political debate about the PRF contributed to the force's lack of legitimacy in the short and long run.

Not surprisingly, these contradictions, ambiguities, and uncertainties, along with personal and financial concerns such as late pay and being stationed far from home, led to feelings of discontent and retention challenges. Nearly ten thousand men (almost one in seven enlistees) left the force during its first year of existence. Eighty percent of the loses were resignations. "Dismissals, death, medical discharges, and the elimination of Communists," records showed, "accounted for the other 20 per cent." SCAP concluded that many of the dismissals and most of the resignations could be "traced to the fact that the [PRF] was posing as a police rather than a military organization." As successful applicants discovered this was the case, they often resigned even before they had been inducted into the reserve, and recruits continued to do so after training began and "especially after cold weather set in." In the spring of 1951, the reserve tried to "stem the tide of resignations" by transferring nearly thirty thousand members to camps near their homes, and this appears to have helped decrease the number of resignations.[108]

Communists tried to sow discontent and increase resignations by criticizing the PRF's many ambiguities. They argued that it was a violation of the constitution. They asserted it was a military and that its men were being treated as poorly as Imperial Army soldiers once had been, but without getting any of the respect that the emperor's soldiers had received. Their leaflets highlighted the prominent role of US advisers and called PRF soldiers slaves and mercenaries. It is impossible to know the degree to which Communist efforts influenced enlisted personnel to quit, but there is no denying that the reserve's incongruities likely made many men susceptible to such messages. Rumors that the PRF would be sent to Korea also alarmed members of the force.[109] Such rumors were not entirely unfounded. Although any military involvement in the conflict by Japanese would have been a violation of the Potsdam Declaration and there is no indication that US or Japanese authorities ever considered sending PRF personnel to Korea, some politicians in both countries called for Japanese volunteers to be allowed to fight there. Also, as mentioned, the US military had the Maritime Safety Force conduct minesweeping operations off the Korean coast, and it had Japanese crews of landing vessels put US and South Korean soldiers ashore at Incheon in September 1950.[110] This mobilization of sailors, most of whom were former Imperial Navy personnel and went on to serve in the MSDF, contributed to the continuities between the wartime and postwar naval forces, whereas discontinuity and incongruity characterized the PRF and the GSDF.

Even recruits who remained in the PRF and GSDF for their entire careers were bothered by these inconsistencies years later. Remember Satō's comments, mentioned in the introduction. He did not simply say that people called the force the "bastard child of the Americans." He himself adopted the acerbic language of the force's critics. Irikura did not go so far, but the former longtime SDF public-relations specialist expressed discomfort about the subordinate status of the PRF and the GSDF.[111] Yūmoto, who was interviewed in 1980, repeatedly used the adjective *chūto-hanpa*, a word meaning something like "half-baked, half-way, incomplete, deficient, or unsatisfying" to describe his PRF experience. He described his own checkered career path before joining the force as *chūto-hanpa*, and then applied the word to the PRF. "It wasn't quite a police force, nor was it quite an army. It was the incomplete quality that made me sick."[112] Later he again described its half-military / half-police nature in the same way: "It was all sort of half-baked. For us who had served in the imperial military, we did not really care which it was. If it was going to be a police force, then it should be one. If it was going to be an army, then it should be one. We just wanted it to be one or the other. Company chiefs on up claimed, 'This is no army, it's a police force.' But all the while, our everyday life was actually that of an army. One only had to look at the fact that we were attached to a U.S. Army sergeant and had to follow all his instructions. It really did not make any sense."[113]

Ambiguity also characterized the experience of the former Imperial Army officers who were allowed to join the force. The change in policy took place in April 1951 when Gen. Matthew Ridgeway replaced MacArthur, who had steadfastly refused to admit former officers. The force had not been able to fill that leadership gap that made it rely on Americans for training. Many former officers received a PRF recruitment letter along with the notification that they had been depurged, as if to insinuate that joining the force was a condition for lifting their banishment. In June 1951, the force welcomed some three hundred former second lieutenants. They were followed by four hundred former lieutenant colonels in October.[114] For these men, many of whom had retired to the countryside—embittered, discredited, impoverished, and purged—a return to a military position of authority must have held the promise of a restoration of honor and dignity. But like the men they commanded, the former Imperial Army officers who joined the force found that it offered only partial redemption. It was, at least initially, regarded by most former officers as "a body of mercenaries established mainly for the benefit of a foreign power, and as anything but a source of national pride and power."[115] That dismissive view dissipated, but ambivalence about the force lingered as it and its men remained alienated from society and it and Japan remained woefully subservient to the United States. Kuboi Masayuki, who graduated from the army officer academy in 1945 and joined the PRF as one of those three hundred former second lieutenants in June 1951, expressed as much. Fiercely proud of both his service in the Imperial Army and in the GSDF, Kuboi remembered thinking that if he joined the PRF and worked hard, then the Americans could and would go home. But, he bitterly recalled, the politicians and the people did not allow that to happen.[116]

## Defining the Force's Identity and Mission

In midst of these contradictions and ambiguities, government and force officials sought to formulate an identity for the force even as there was confusion about what the PRF was supposed to be and become. Needless to say, its relationship with the US military, with the imperial military, and with society influenced these formulations. The most important figure in this process was Hayashi, the reserve's top uniformed officer, who can be seen in a 1952 photograph standing next to Prime Minister Yoshida reviewing NSF troops (figure 1.3).

When Yoshida appointed Hayashi to lead the PRF, it was not clear that he would become such an invaluable leader, though he had considerable

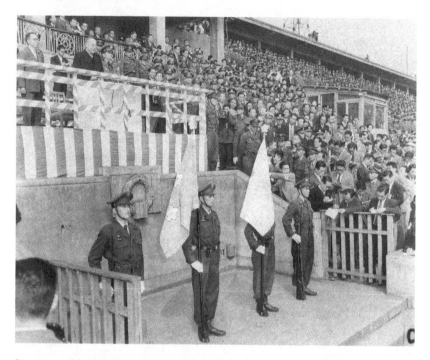

**FIGURE 1.3.** Prime Minister Yoshida Shigeru, at the front of the stand in the black suit, and Chief of Staff Hayashi Keizō, in uniform to his immediate left, review troops at a ceremony celebrating the creation of the NSF, the successor to the PRF, in Tokyo on October 15, 1952. The civilian director general of the force, Masuhara Keikichi, stands to Yoshida's right. Used with permission of the Asahi Newspaper Company.

promise. Like many other civilian and uniformed officials in the PRF, Hayashi had a Home Ministry background. He had no military experience and, for that matter, little police experience. An official in SCAP's G-2 Intelligence Section, led by Willoughby, who hoped to have Hattori and other former Imperial Army officers lead the new force, accused Hayashi of being an arrogant "misfit."[117] Not surprisingly, G-2 opposed his appointment. Hayashi did, however, have considerable credentials. The son of an Imperial Army general, Hayashi Yasakichi, he had been appointed a prefectural governor after the war at the age of just thirty-nine and was serving as the vice minister of the Imperial Household Agency when Yoshida asked him to serve as the force's top uniformed officer. He also apparently had an "irreproachable character," despite what G-2 officials claimed.[118] He continued to lead the NSF, the GSDF, and then the entire SDF until 1964—a leadership tenure five times as long as that of any of his successors. His formidable ideological legacy matches his unrivaled time at the top. As a leader of the reconstituted military defense force, Hayashi sought to tie the organization and its personnel as closely as possible to the people and to maintain some distance from the imperial military as well as from the US military.

Gaining the trust and respect of society was a consistent priority for Hayashi. In his first speech delivered immediately after his appointment in October 1950, Hayashi declared the force must become the "people's Reserve Force" (kokumin no Yobitai).[119] In 1954, he adjusted the phrase to a "Self-Defense Force for the people" (kokumin no tame no Jieitai) or "the people's Self-Defense Force" (kokumin no Jieitai). He used the phrase both to appeal to wider society to alter its view of the force and to encourage force members to strive to be worthy of public support. In his opening speech, which was disseminated to force members in a weekly internal publication, Hayashi reminded personnel of their pledge "to maintain the peace and order and protect the welfare of all citizens." He continued, "You must cultivate a love of our country and our people." "This means a spirit [seishin] of love for our fellow countrymen, for our parents, brothers, sisters, wives, and children to live in peace. . . . We must never forget that the PRF belongs to the people."[120] Hayashi encouraged personnel to always be on their best behavior, whether on or off base, in or out of uniform.[121]

Hayashi also invoked the language of masculinity. Conduct to gain trust and respect, he concluded, were nothing less than "manly behavior" (otokorashii kōdō).[122] This demeanor, as he explained, included mastering proper etiquette, such as table manners and how to write a letter. Service members, no matter how humble their economic and educational background, were expected to not only develop the arts of (defensive) war but also to be gentlemen and be cultured.[123] Hayashi repeated this message over the early years of the reconstituted military and it had a lasting legacy on the force.[124]

Although the content of Hayashi's message was clear, how it was communicated to the force is less so. How it was received is even more uncertain, especially during this formative period when officials were consumed with everyday organizational concerns as the PRF, the NSF, and then the GSDF took shape. During the two years of the PRF's existence, effectively disseminating Hayashi's ideas would have been a herculean task, and the organization certainly did not seem to have the resources to carry it out. When the organization became the NSF, all service members were required to carry a handbook that contained Hayashi's speeches and the objectives for moral improvement, and the GSDF used similar methods to try to inculcate these ideas and practices. Like other militaries and other organizations more broadly, it sought to instill them in its new members through an initial training regime and ongoing education. Irikura, who became responsible in 1958 for communicating guidance from senior officers such as Hayashi to rank-and-file personnel in the Northern Corps in Hokkaido, did not think that the GSDF was able to devote serious resources to instilling a new identity in recruits until the late 1950s. In his estimation, Hayashi's ideas began to yield the desired effect when that began to happen, though he admitted that reception is difficult to ascertain.[125]

Though his message certainly took time to spread, Hayashi attempted to redefine military identity and the meaning of patriotism during his fifteen-year tenure at the helm of the force. He endeavored to implement Yoshida's idea of a force that would be "divorced both structurally and in personnel from the former Japanese military and that, with American assistance, would become a 'democratic military force.'"[126] He hoped the people and the state, as represented by elected officials, would take the place of the emperor as the object of loyalty for the reconstituted military.[127] Unlike imperial military leaders, he did not hold up soldiers or samurai who had performed acts of bravery and had been motivated by devotion to the emperor as paragons for personnel to emulate. Rather, postwar military identity was to be rooted in a spirit of love for the Japanese homeland and for its people.

## Domestic Security and Disaster Relief

Although MacArthur's main motivation for establishing the PRF was the maintenance of internal order, officials proved reluctant to use it for that purpose, primarily because of public distrust of the force and a concern that its tenuous relationship with society would be irreparably harmed if they did so. Instead, motivated once again by concerns about public opinion, government leaders, starting with Yoshida, deployed the PRF to deal with a different sort of internal disturbance—natural disasters—that was not part of its stated mission. In this way, concern about society and people's welfare, as well as a desire to distinguish the new force from the imperial military, contributed to the formation of new duties and traditions and a new identity. Deployment for disaster relief also increased the force's visibility, as it was intended to.

As previously noted, during the creation of the PRF, the principal decision-makers agreed that one of its primary purposes was to maintain internal order. Regardless of their stance on whether the force should be a gendarmerie or full-fledged military, top officials—US and Japanese—were united about the need for a force that would, as MacArthur put it in his memo, "strengthen the police" in the face of domestic threats.[128] Conservatives had long been concerned that the 1947 police law, which created a decentralized policing system, was inadequate to contain communist activity. In early 1950, the Communist Party fanned those fears when, in the face of US pressure on the Japanese labor movement and criticism from Moscow, it abandoned working peacefully for change within the political system and began a campaign of demonstrations, strikes, and industrial sabotage. SCAP responded by purging alleged members of the Communist Party from public and private sector jobs in June 1950, just weeks before the outbreak of the Korean War. In turn, this purge led to more radical measures and violence by labor activists.[129] Even before these incidents, SCAP had deployed occupation troops to restore public order, and US officials were concerned that they might need to be mobilized again. With the departure of US troops for the Korean peninsula, both US and Japanese leaders worried about whether the police had sufficient power to deal with such internal threats.[130]

PRF commanders emphasized the force's mission to maintain public order via training, indoctrination, and where they stationed troops. Such exercises, as the historian Thomas French pointed out, composed the largest part of the PRF's first two thirteen-week training courses. During the first session, "when combined with guard duty, another internal security task, these elements took up more than one third of the total programme."[131] Maintaining internal order was also part of the rhetoric of the force. Every morning, the men recited the PRF Pledge vowing to "maintain . . . peace and order in our country and preserve the public welfare."[132] They also sang songs like the PRF's official anthem, "Protecting the Public Order" (*Chian o mamori*), that emphasized that role.[133] Another song, "Fighters for Public Peace and Security," is equally telling. A SCAP translation rendered it in the following manner:

> The bells toll, the sun rises, the drum of liberty,
> Gallant, stern, straight and mighty,
> Stand we up for peace and security,
> Ah! This inspiration, this mission,
> Stir up for action, we are the Fighters for Peace and Security.
>
> Mills and streams of the old home, parents, and children,
> Ye comrades too: Mark, the battle-cries, cries of righteousness,
> With truncheons at wickedness to strike, train we day and night;
> Ah! The hearts with vigor brimming,
> Stir up for action, we are the Fighters for Peace and Security.

Tempest, come! Rioters, come! What can they do?
Here we stand, firm and resolute, death defying;
With our blood hot and intense, shall we the paradise build, the land
    of our ideals,
Ah! Forward we look, to that day to come;
Stir up for action, we are the Fighters of Peace and Security.[134]

Although the language is vague and threats to "public peace and security" can be interpreted as either external or internal, the song suggests that dangers to "home, parents, and children" are primarily internal ones—"rioters"—and must be confronted by men who are sons and fathers armed with "truncheons . . . firm and resolute." Finally, the fact that officials concentrated the bulk of the PRF near industrial cities, where support for the Communist Party was the strongest, confirms that domestic threats were the main concern, at least initially, of SCAP and the government.[135] Surprisingly, in spite of the uptick in the Communist campaign in 1951 and 1952, there were no major incidents serious enough for authorities to call out the PRF during the rest of the occupation period.

Regardless of this training, rhetoric, and placement, officials were reluctant to deploy the PRF to maintain internal order. This disinclination seems to have primarily stemmed from concerns about the force's relationship with society rather than from a desire to differentiate it from the prewar military or worries about repeating the mistakes of the past. The imperial military had been mobilized for internal public security operations five times, most prominently in response to the nationwide Rice Riots of 1918—widespread popular protests against inflationary food prices—and to the Great Kantō Earthquake in the Tokyo-Yokohama region of 1923.[136] The former deployment was "one more factor alienating the army from the people" during the early 1920s,[137] but it is unlikely that this precedent over three decades earlier added to the hesitancy of the postwar military leaders to use the force for internal security.

As soon as the occupation ended and the Japanese government became responsible for dealing with internal security challenges, a violent incident occurred that led authorities to mobilize the PRF, though only grudgingly and in a limited manner. The signing of the US-Japan Peace Treaty in the fall of 1951 and the Japanese Communist Party's call for an armed struggle caused tensions to rise as the occupation ended and the peace treaty went into effect on May 1, 1952. On that day, May Day—commemorated as International Workers' Day by socialists and communists since the late nineteenth century—an estimated four hundred thousand leftists gathered at the Meiji

Shrine Park (Meiji Jingu Gaien). They were part of more than a million people who took part in some 330 rallies nationwide. The demonstrators called for workers' economic rights and protested rearmament, remilitarization, war, US military bases, and the continuing occupation of Okinawa, as well as "April 28—the Day of National Disgrace" (the date the occupation had come to an end) because it had not resolved these issues. As the rally came to an end, an estimated ten thousand protesters marched to a plaza in front of the Imperial Palace, three miles away, which the government had forbidden organizers from entering. There violence erupted when, without warning, police attacked with teargas and pistols. As protesters fled into the surrounding streets, mayhem spread as demonstrators overturned and burned cars and threw three US soldiers, who happened to be in the area, into the moat before they were rescued by other Japanese. When the melee ended, two demonstrators were dead and over two thousand police officers and protesters were injured.[138] Alarmed by the incident, Yoshida ordered the PRF to mobilize for the Commemoration of the Effectuation of the Peace Treaty and Fifth Anniversary of the Enforcement of the Constitution, scheduled for May 3.[139]

Because Yoshida's order did not go through the formal legal procedures and was vague, how to implement it was left to others. Both civilian and uniformed leaders, including Hayashi, were conflicted about carrying it out. Ultimately, officials decided to have five hundred men from the First Infantry Regiment attend the ceremony. The troops stood in the background, behind a considerable police presence. Officials had the men carry unloaded carbines and rifles. They ordered another unit, ready with light machine guns loaded with ammunition—though with mostly less deadly tracer bullets—to wait near the Meiji Shrine in case of an emergency. Fortunately, the ceremony ended without incident, but the hesitation to mobilize the PRF and the partial way it was done highlight the "strong psychological resistance" to deploying the PRF for internal security.[140] That opposition, fueled by concerns about the force's relationship with society, continued and led officials to resist mobilizing the NSF and then the SDF, including—as discussed in chapter 4—in response to the massive demonstrations against the renewal of the US-Japan Security Treaty in 1960.

Concerns about the force's relationship with society also prompted Yoshida to mobilize the PRF for disaster relief. Yoshida readily admitted as much in his memoirs:

> I was apprehensive that such a cold reception from both the political Left and Right, so to speak, might have adverse effects upon the young men in the force, and searched for some means whereby to encourage

people to look upon the new uniformed men with affection and respect. To this end, I issued instructions to the authorities concerned to turn out the force to undertake rescue work whenever floods, typhoons or major fires occurred—calamities to which we Japanese are only too frequently subject—in order to foster a closer relationship between the men of the force and the inhabitants of the districts where they were stationed. . . . . I cannot say to what extent these and other measures actually influenced public sentiment, but it appears that in the provinces, at least, the Self-Defense Force has come to be regarded with a more friendly feeling than formerly.[141]

It is, indeed, unclear how much influence the force's natural disaster–relief activities had on public opinion, but even as early as 1960, when Yoshida was writing his memoirs, their positive impact on society was evident.

The military's deployment of personnel and equipment to respond to disasters was not without precedent. The Imperial Army, the historian Yoshida Ritsuto argued, came to regard disaster-relief operations as an important part of maintaining internal security after the Russo-Japanese War of 1905–06.[142] The imperial military responded to natural disasters large and small, including the eruption of Mt. Sakarajima in Kyushu in 1914 and the Great Kantō Earthquake in 1923. The quake's severity and a civilian leadership vacuum—the prime minister had died just days before and the new government had been formed the day before the quake hit—led the military to immediately mobilize its considerable resources. Within a week, thirty-five thousand troops were deployed not only to restore order but also to conduct rescue work and infrastructure repair. This number would grow to fifty-two thousand—nearly a fifth of the standing army. Army engineers relit streetlights, cleared roads, and repaired or reconstructed forty-five bridges.[143] They remained in the capital for weeks. They were motivated by altruistic concern to aid stricken inhabitants, but also harbored ulterior motives. Because the army had become the object of widespread and open disrespect after its deployment to restore order during the Rice Riots of 1918, it "consciously labored to recoup its position of esteem." Its efforts were rewarded as "popular treatment of the army took a dramatic turn for the better, not only in the capital but throughout the country."[144] The army responded to smaller emergencies, too. Local commanders, who oversaw men conscripted from surrounding regions, sometimes allowed soldiers to return home for several days to help when their communities faced a crisis, especially an agricultural one. However, army leaders regarded disaster relief as not core to the force's mission and only justifiable because it contributed to internal security. In part, they took this position because they could usually afford to. Highly organized army reservist and youth-association organizations mobilized their members for disaster relief, and hence there was limited need for the active-duty military.[145] But there was also a difference in attitude. The imperial military was not designed to serve the people, but rather to serve the state and the emperor; it often looked down on the people. Except for several years in late 1910s and early 1920s, strong public support for the military gave its leaders little to worry about. The hostility toward military values, the military, and military men was far greater in the 1950s, and so the postwar military followed Yoshida's directive to proactively provide disaster relief.

During its two years of existence, the PRF mobilized six times for natural disasters. Its first deployment came in 1951 in response to flooding in Fukuchiyama, a city in northwest Kyoto Prefecture. A rural agrarian community that had hosted an Imperial Army base since the late nineteenth century, Fukuchiyama was one of the first cities to invite the PRF to establish a base in its community. Perhaps because of that history, the mayor did not hesitate to request aid and the local regimental commander did not hesitate to deploy his troops, doing so without asking for approval from his superiors and, ultimately, the prime minister, which was a violation of civilian control of the military. Residents were thankful for the aid, like those elsewhere (as seen in figure 1.4). Nevertheless, PRF headquarters reprimanded the commander. This incident led force officers to become more careful about following civilian control in response to subsequent requests for assistance, but the favorable public praise for the relief led disaster operations to become one of the four main duties of the postwar military, "ranked as equivalent with 'Defense Operations' . . . and 'Public Security Operations'" in the SDF Law of 1954.[146] It also became a proud tradition of the SDF and particularly of the GSDF in a way that it had not been for the imperial military. Yoshida probably did not anticipate this outcome when he directed the force to conduct disaster relief, in part to improve its relationship with the public.

On August 9, 1952, Lt. Joel J. Dilworth, a US Army adviser to the force, delivered a short address during a visit to a PRF camp near Maebashi, a city north of Tokyo. Dilworth's visit came several months after the occupation had ended and two months before the PRF became the NSF and took another step toward greater rearmament. It also occurred around the time of the second anniversary of the PRF's establishment, two years to the day from when the organization began its recruitment campaign in 1950. For that reason,

**FIGURE 1.4.**    Local residents greet a PRF unit arriving in Yamaguchi Prefecture to provide disaster relief in response to a typhoon in October 1951. Used with permission of the Asagumo Newspaper Company.

Dilworth decided to wish the PRF a happy birthday. He read from a prepared text written in simple romanized Japanese, indicating that he may have had some Japanese speaking ability but was not proficient in reading Japanese characters. He may have had help preparing the address, but it likely reflected his thoughts. Like many Americans and some Japanese at the time (and since), Dilworth opted to use the condescending trope of describing the postwar force, and by extension Japanese more generally, as a child. The force, he began, was "growing incredibly quickly" because it was young and full of energy and because "it received good things from its parents," who went unnamed but may have represented the Japanese government and US officials. The child, Dilworth continued, "would benefit its entire family," who would soon be "proud of" and "respect" the child as "he provided protection for the house." No doubt, this statement alluded to the force's complicated relationship with the public and its efforts to win the latter's affection and support. Finally, as an adviser to the force, Dilworth concluded by saying, "[I] tried to help but you deserve the credit. I wish you a happy birthday as your friend."[147]

The creation of the military defense force in the form of the PRF and the formulation of its emerging identity was the product of a complex configuration of factors. The communist invasion of South Korea created a security vacuum in occupied Japan as MacArthur rushed US troops to the peninsula. The urgency of the situation, plus the absence of Japanese military leadership because of the purge, led US Army personnel to oversee the establishment and training of the new force, from its headquarters to its hastily opened camps across the country. But Americans did not call all the shots. Prime Minister Yoshida, newly appointed civilian and uniformed personnel, and average enlistees and depurged imperial military officers who were eventually allowed to join the force all helped forge a new organization and identity. Given these numerous collaborating and contending stakeholders, the estrangement of society in general from military values, the disparity in power between Japan and the United States, and legacies of the imperial military, it should be no surprise that these foundational years of the postwar armed forces were riven by contradictions, both for the organization as a whole and for its individual personnel.

As the PRF became the NSF and then the GSDF, these contradictions persisted and continued to be embedded in its complicated relationships with society, the imperial military, and the US military. The first two dynamics, in particular, remained unchanged, but as the occupation came to an end, the force's interaction with the US military became much more limited. The two countries may have been allies, but their militaries conducted little to no joint training exercises and hardly coordinated. The relationship was asymmetrical and unequal. The end of the occupation brought about subordinate independence on a geopolitical level and in the two country's macrolevel and microlevel military relations.

One indication of that asymmetry was the continued presence of US military advisers. By the time Dilworth visited the Maebashi base, senior US officers like Kowalski and US camp commanders had stepped away from leadership roles within the PRF, and many had left Japan. The CASA was disbanded as the occupation came to an end in April 1952. But hundreds of US military advisers and support staff remained in Japan for nearly another two decades. They were part of a network of advisers providing guidance to US Cold War allies across the globe. As the occupation ended, some government and PRF officials concluded that US advisers were unnecessary. US authorities, though, were concerned about the force backsliding and becoming like the old Imperial Army. Hayashi wanted them to remain to balance the power of former Imperial Army officers at each camp, but other officers were concerned that having advisers stationed at every camp would undermine the appearance of Japanese independence.[148] As a part of an agreement for Japan to receive US Mutual Security Assistance aid in 1954, which Prime Minister

Yoshida adeptly used to boost the economy while deflecting US pressure for Japan to drastically expand its military forces, the U.S advisory organization changed again. The Safety Advisory Group—Japan, which had succeeded the CASA advisory group that had overseen the PRF, became the Military Assistance Advisory Group (MAAG) and continued to provide assistance and advice to "organize, equip, train, and maintain" the force. For most of the 1950s and 1960s, MAAG's triservice—army, navy, and air force—personnel strength of officers, enlisted men, US civilians and local nationals numbered in the hundreds, though its US personnel numbers dropped from 650 in 1954 to 131 in 1964.[149] MAAG advisers provided coordination for the schooling and training of force personnel, filed reports, and attended military and diplomatic social and ceremonial events until MAAG was greatly reduced in size ("from an 82-man office to a 16-man office") and became the Mutual Defense Assistance Office in 1969.[150] By 1961, approximately 100,000 force personnel had completed US military schooling and 30,000 had undergone training within US units based in Japan.[151]

Another little known, long-running form of assistance was the instructions that tens of thousands of SDF personnel received in the United States. From 1950 to 1968, over 15,000 personnel did so.[152] By 1971, the Defense Agency estimated that over 70 percent of current SDF officers had completed training or education courses at US military facilities or at schools in the United States.[153]

More visibly, tens of thousands of US military personnel continued to be stationed on bases across Japan, despite the end to the occupation. They are still there to this day, though, except on Okinawa, to a lesser extent. Sometimes US personnel were stationed adjacent to Japanese forces, but interactions between the two militaries were minimal, even at the highest levels. Most notably, the two militaries did not conduct any joint exercises for over three decades. Officials engaged in some coordination, but maintained a strict division of labor, with the US military using the archipelago and Okinawa as a base to project US power beyond Japan and fight wars in Korea and Vietnam and the SDF nominally responsible for Japan's defense. The GSDF had particularly little interaction with the US military, as the political scientist Sado Akihiro noted. Because its primary mission was defined as dealing with "indirect invasions . . . and internal security, the possibility of joint operations with the U.S. military [was] extremely small," so even coordination was rare.[154] In 1978, the relationship between the two militaries became closer and more collaborative when formal consultations began. In the 1980s, bilateral exercises began, though they "stopped well short of an integrated contingency plan" regarding how to respond to war.[155] Only after the end of the Cold War did the two militaries begin to work together much more closely.

During these early formative years, US military advisers, including Dilworth, also contributed to the creation of the force's officer training academy. Like the PRF, it was influenced by the US military, grappled with legacies of the imperial military, and navigated a fraught relationship with society. The academy is the subject of the next chapter. The education of a new officer corps, combined with Hayashi's emphasis on the reconstituted military being a "force for the people," also redefined its identity during these early Cold War years.

# CHAPTER 2

# Establishing the National Defense
# Academy and Overcoming the Past

Just six months after the opening of the rees-
tablished military officer college, known at the time as the National Safety
Academy (and later as the National Defense Academy, or NDA), its administrators and faculty of academic professors and military science instructors
gathered for an emergency meeting in September 1953. It is unclear if the
US military advisers who sometimes participated in faculty meetings were
present or not. An entire platoon of thirty cadets was on the verge of being
kicked out of the school. Apparently, just before summer break began in July,
one student revealed to his cohort that he might not return to the academy
after the vacation period. His classmates decided to send him off with an
informal farewell party, arranged for some bottles of saké to be smuggled
onto campus, and gathered late one night in their dormitory. When the
cadets returned from the break, they learned that another student on night-
watch duty had noticed them drinking and reported them. Expecting expulsion, Shima Atsushi and his fellow platoon members began to pack their
belongings as the faculty debated about how to respond to the violation.
Instructors who had served in the Imperial Navy called for their dismissal.
Alcohol was not allowed on naval ships because of a history of accidents
caused by drunkenness; unauthorized drinking was a blatant breach of conduct. Former Imperial Army instructors called for leniency; the army had
been far less strict about consuming alcohol in its barracks. Moreover, they

said, when confronted about the incident and told to close their eyes and raise their hands if they had participated, every member of the platoon did so. This showed, the instructors argued, that they did not understand the seriousness of their transgression and were honest, and that their motives were pure. The superintendent of the academy, Maki Tomoo, a civilian who had studied at Oxford University and then taught at one of the country's most prestigious private institutions, Keiō University, for three decades, listened to both sides. Finally, he opted to forgive the cadets.[1] Perhaps this was because those arguing for forgiveness were in the majority and Maki touted the importance of democracy. Perhaps it was because he valued the spirit over the letter of the law.

This incident illustrates several themes of this chapter, which focuses on the reestablishment of military officer education after the war. Most importantly, the story highlights the philosophy that guided Maki, acting on directions that Prime Minister Yoshida gave him, as he sought to educate a new generation of officers. That philosophy was grounded in lofty standards and strict discipline balanced with liberal democratic ideas and gentlemanly humaneness. The last two elements were a departure, though not a complete one, from the ethos of the imperial military. Two other factors influenced this incident and other developments at the academy: interactions with the US military and relations with society. As was the case for the wider force, the interplay of these dynamics—with the imperial military, with the US military, and with society—shaped the academy's policies and practices, and ultimately came to define a Cold War military-defense identity that the academy and its graduates helped to mold.

For the academy, the vestiges of the imperial military formed the most important dynamic. Yoshida stressed that he wanted an academy that educated a new generation of officers who would be different than those produced by the prewar Imperial Army and Naval academies. Accordingly, Maki expected cadets to become gentlemen as well as officers, to value democracy, and be endowed with humanity. He ensured that the academy's curriculum emphasized science rather than irrational spirit—associated with the imperial military—and prioritized a broad general and liberal education.[2]

Yoshida wanted the school, unlike the prewar academies, to be egalitarian by accepting young men from all socioeconomic backgrounds. Students at the academy received their education, training, room, board, and food, as well as a small allowance at no cost, yet they were not bound to enter the military on graduation.[3] Although obedience, discipline, rank, and hierarchy were unavoidable aspects of military culture, Maki sought to infuse the school with democratic ideas and practices. Shima and his fellow cadets had committed a serious breach of a rule, but Maki would not countenance severe verbal, much less corporal, punishment, which would likely have been meted out even for minor offenses at the imperial military academies and in the prewar armed forces more generally.[4] That said, continuities with the past endured. Former imperial military officers joined the faculty and administration, and some prewar practices and traditions lingered. But the dominant characteristic of the postwar academy was rupture. The impetus for much of that change came from Yoshida and Maki, whom the prime minister entrusted to guide the academy. Maki did so for its first twelve years until his retirement in 1965, a tenure almost as lengthy as Hayashi's at the helm of the ground forces and entire SDF. Like Hayashi, Maki left a lasting institutional and ideological imprint on the NDA and the force more widely that continues to this day.

Although the US military did not have as much influence on the establishment of the academy as it did on the founding of the Police Reserve Force, it played a key supporting role. Occupation officials contributed to planning for the academy, and Yoshida and Maki saw the US military academies, especially West Point, as models to emulate as they sought to create a different kind of academy than the prewar army and navy academies.[5] US influence on the academy continued long after the end of the occupation. US military advisers, who numbered among the hundreds of US officers who provided guidance and technical assistance to the wider force, remained posted at the academy until 1963 and had regular interaction with Maki, other administrators, instructors, and cadets.[6]

The academy's relationship with society, like that of the wider force, was no less complicated. Situated in the port city of Yokosuka, which had long hosted Imperial Navy facilities and after the war became one of the largest overseas US Navy bases, the academy was generally welcomed by the community, though interaction between cadets and residents was (and continues to be) minimal.[7] In terms of its relationship with society more widely, the academy—as part of a vast and sprawling military organization that came to be composed of a quarter million personnel stationed at bases across the country—was and remains the SDF's most recognizable and visible component. Like the force as a whole, the school was criticized as illegitimate by the left and the right for reasons that sometimes overlapped. Pacifists saw its creation as further evidence of rearmament and a return to a recent militaristic past, and as violation of Article 9. Rightists saw it—with its civilian superintendent, liberal arts–heavy curriculum, emphasis on education over training, and cadets' extracurricular activities—as not measuring up to the prewar academies. Both sides looked askance at the US military influence on the academy, even though the US advisers kept a low profile.[8] The academy's proximity to the capital, its reputation as an elite yet contested educational institution—attracting some of the nation's brightest young men, who could have gained admission to many other top universities—and the fact the NDA was the only university graduation ceremony that the prime minister attended every year certainly heightened its visibility. Unlike the force's rank-and-file personnel, cadets represented the SDF's future leaders. As a result, the academy and its cadets were the focus of considerable scrutiny and high expectations, both externally and internally.

These relationships—with the imperial military, the US military, and society—combined to shape a reconfigured democratic, masculine military identity that its graduates as officers spread to the SDF during the Cold War. Critics, particularly some conservatives outside the NDA (and a few inside), contested and challenged this identity. But the traditions that Maki created, his influence, and the embrace of his ideas by many cadets formed an ideological bulwark that has shielded the academy to some degree from such attacks. Always having a civilian as president of the academy (which is not mandated) and emphasizing a humanistic, liberal arts education have been particularly important buffers. Both these practices were products of plans for the academy that began with Yoshida, were informed by a reaction to the war as well as by US influences, and were solidified by Maki's long, influential tenure.

## Planning for an Academy

Preparation to create a new academy began less than a year after the government created the PRF. Although the impetus this time began on the Japanese side, the process of planning for the school was collaborative, involving both Japanese government and US military occupation officials. Japanese authorities certainly had a freer hand than they did with the PRF. This was in large part because the process began a year later and during what turned out to be the last year of the occupation and continued on for a year after it ended. It was also because Yoshida again played off US desires for Japanese rearmament. In the case of the PRF, he and the Japanese government were forced to scramble and then took advantage of MacArthur's order to establish a police reserve after the outbreak of the Korean War. In the case of reestablishing a military officer academy, Yoshida took the initiative. Yet US influences, in the role of SCAP officials advising the Japanese government and in the form of US military academies as models, loomed large. They also at times produced unexpected outcomes. Although one would think that the

US influence would contribute to discontinuity from the imperial military academies, sometimes the US advisers argued against innovation.

The initiative to establish an academy seems to have begun at the very top, with Yoshida. As the challenge of providing the PRF with competent leadership led Yoshida to approve depurging former captains, majors, and lieutenant colonels and recruiting them at the staff level from mid-1951, he came to the realization that, although a revived military officer academy would not resolve the problem of leadership in the short term, it was imperative that it do so in the long run. Yoshida also hoped that the creation of an officer academy would help satisfy the demands of US Secretary of State Dulles, who was demanding that Japan rearm more quickly.[9] The first record of a conversation about establishing an academy comes from Masuhara Keikichi, the civilian director general of the PRF. He recalled that on May 17, 1951, he spent "a little more than an hour" at the funeral of Dowager Empress Teimei (Kujo Sadako) with Yoshida, who "used that whole time to explain his concept for the Academy."[10] Clearly Yoshida had given some thought to the subject.

One of Yoshida's primary concerns was differentiating the new academy from its predecessors—the Imperial Army and Navy academies. As the historian John Dower noted, "Yoshida's prewar career imbued him with no particular love for the military establishment as a whole."[11] Though not an opponent of the country's drive to establish an empire, Yoshida objected to how military leaders had gone about doing so. From his perspective, they, especially army leaders, had needlessly confronted Britain and the United States, which he thought Japanese leaders could have accommodated to achieve the country's strategic geopolitical objectives. Yoshida's distrust of the military was also personal. His part in a plot to bring the war to an early end had led to his arrest and imprisonment for ten weeks by the Kenpeitai military police in 1945.[12] Yoshida believed that to avoid repeating its prewar mistakes Japan needed to train a new generation of military leadership. "The problem that we now faced," he wrote in his memoirs, "was to remedy the shortcomings of the former method of imparting military education as practiced in the pre-war institutions and to ensure that the men, as members of a defense force forming part of a democratic system of government, have a sound knowledge not only of the technical aspects of their work, but also of the world at large: to turn out, in other words, officers who would be sensible citizens as well."[13] Educating officers to work within a democracy, to have a broader perspective, and to act rationally—these were the criteria that Yoshida believed were essential.

Yoshida turned to his advisers, including a few former military officers, to flesh out his ideas. Tatsumi Eiichi, a former officer who was an army attaché in London while Yoshida was the ambassador to Britain and who advised Yoshida as prime minister on defense matters, along with a few other ex-officers who had joined the PRF, began working on a plan. They discussed it briefly with SCAP officials led by Gen William P. Ennis in the summer of 1951. The proposal emphasized "instruction of the doctrine of a true democratic force and also that of . . . military science principally based on the United States Army equipment."[14] This document, discovered by the historian Takahashi Kazuhiro, shows that substantive discussions about the academy began more quickly than historians have thought and that US officials were involved sooner and more extensively than has been supposed.[15]

In September 1951, the signing of the peace treaty and security pact created a sense of urgency and spurred discussions within the Japanese government and SCAP circles about establishing an academy. These conversations continued over the fall and winter months. Around this time, Utsumi Hiroshi and Gotōda Masaharu, two ex-police PRF officials who were among those troubled by the half-baked nature of the new force mentioned in chapter 1, were tasked with coming up with a more detailed proposal. Utsumi recalled that they drafted the following criteria. First, the academy must not represent a return to the prewar schools. Second, it must educate officers in "scientific knowledge and thinking, and the rejection of a reliance on the gods or spirit [seishin]." Third, graduates must be free to choose a different career path and to not serve in the force.[16] These conditions represented a reaction against the imperial military, which had infamously valued spiritualism over both technical and military science and had prevented graduates from pursuing other careers because its leaders had regarded any other occupation as inferior to military service.[17] After formulating this list, Utsumi and Gotōda asked occupation officials for their feedback. Utsumi remembers that two unnamed US lieutenant colonels, one whom was probably George B. Pickett, Jr., who had recently been transferred to SCAP from Korea, listened to their presentation with interest but skepticism.[18]

During these and other discussions in late 1951 and early 1952, different US officials appear to have given their Japanese counterparts mixed messages about the proposals under consideration. One contested issue was the status of the academy's president. In February, Tatsumi met twice with Assistant Secretary to the Army Earl D. Johnson. At the first meeting, Tatsumi left with him an English copy of "A Plan for the Training of the Cadre of the Defence Corps of Japan," which had been drafted the previous summer.[19] Tatsumi emphasized that the school would be led by a civilian rather than a military officer. In response, Johnson noted that although West Point was led by an officer, its board of trustees were all civilians. His response seems to have conveyed his approval of a civilian being appointed as superintendent. Around the same time, however, the head of the US Safety Advisory Group, Brig. Gen. LeRoy Watson, suggested that the academy should be led by a uniformed officer.[20] Some Japanese officials, especially former imperial military officers, shared this view.[21] This joint opposition by Japanese conservative figures and some US military officials to some of the progressive plans for the academy was similar to the shared attacks on Yoshida's cautious pace of rearmament.

Another issue that led to disagreements between Japanese officials and some of their US counterparts was whether a single academy should serve both branches of the military or whether separate academies were necessary. As in the United States, the Imperial Army and Navy had operated distinct officer-training schools before 1945. For Yoshida, educating cadets who would become officers of the ground and sea forces in the same academy was of the utmost importance. Pickett remembered the prime minister remarking that during the war "our Army and Navy spent almost as much time arguing among themselves as they did fighting their enemies."[22] Ultimately, planners decided that the academy would accept 400 applicants per year (which was increased to 530 when the Air SDF was added in 1955). Only after their first year do cadets choose which branch of the force they will enter, and for the entire four years they live, study, and often train together regardless of their chosen branch. After cadets graduate from the academy, they attend their branch's officer candidate school and only then are commissioned as officers. In meetings with senior government officials, General Johnson appeared to support the idea of a single academy. A memorandum of the meeting noted, "[He] pointed out, that if we in America did not have a history of separate Service academies, we might well have a single academy for general courses with separate schools for the advanced ones."[23] Other US military officers, however, did not agree. Utsumi remembered that other US advisers "mocked [the] idea" and saying it would be like a "circus": "They said they were aware of only one such program, and that was in India."[24] Citing impoverished, newly independent India as a precedent was obviously not meant to be a compliment. These advisers were probably not aware that in 1943 and 1944 the US Joint Chiefs of Staff had considered consolidating West Point and Annapolis into a single institution to stop graduates, as they put it, from forever "playing the Army-Navy [football] game" that "obstructed full and effective interservice cooperation."[25] Although some US officers objected to a joint army-navy academy, some former imperial military officers were not opposed to the idea. Miyano Masatoshi, a former major general who had served as an administrator in the Imperial Army Academy and whom

Maki later sought out for advice, was a strong supporter of an integrated academy.[26] Perhaps he knew from personal experience the pitfalls of branch rivalries.

After many months of discussions, formal preparations to establish an academy began in earnest when a planning office was created within PRF headquarters in March 1952. Pickett, joined by Lt. Col. Dilworth (who gave the speech at a PRF base mentioned in chapter 1) and a naval officer as well as several PRF officials, began to examine the curriculum of the US academies, Japanese universities, and the imperial military academies. West Point, specifically, was regarded as a worthy template by Yoshida.[27] The group debated the nature of the curriculum, specialized subjects, and what sort of instructors should be recruited. In the end, they decided to structure the academy's curriculum, which emphasized science and engineering, on that of the Tokyo Institute of Technology. In a 1964 report, US military advisers called the NDA "more of a technical school than a military one," noting the limited courses and hours devoted to warfare and military training.[28] Although the academy would not have a social science track until 1974, the curriculum stressed general knowledge, the humanities, and a liberal arts education over specialized military subjects. Interestingly, these elements were similar to recommendations considered by the Joint Chiefs of Staff for the US academies during the war, which were ultimately adopted.[29]

One of Yoshida's greatest concerns was who to select as the academy's first president. His first choice was Koizumi Shinzō, an anti-Marxist prewar liberal who had served as president of Keiō University from 1933 to 1947. Koizumi declined because he was overseeing the education of Crown Prince Akihito for the Imperial Household Agency.[30] The fact that his face had been severely scarred by a US bombing raid on Tokyo during the war may have also been a factor. In his stead, Koizumi recommended that Yoshida appoint Maki, a graduate of Keiō University and Oxford University who taught political science at Keiō until Koizumi appointed him to serve as a director (*riji*)— a role similar to that of a provost at US universities—when Koizumi became president of the university in 1933. Like Koizumi, Maki was an anti-Marxist liberal. This background and his studies in Britain made him acceptable to Yoshida, who was a well-known Anglophile, in part of because of his Foreign Ministry postings to Britain in the 1920s and 1930s, including as ambassador from 1936 to 1938. In response to a reporter's question, Yoshida declared that the reason he had chosen Maki was that his "English education" would help him produce soldiers unlike those of the prewar years.[31] After his appointment in August 1952, Maki immediately took charge of preparations to open the academy.

One of Maki's most pressing tasks was selecting faculty. Pickett recalled that there "were many applicants for the . . . professorships who were technically qualified," but "large numbers of professors whose communist sympathies and radicalism were sources of real concern." Most former military and naval officers, unless they held radical views (usually on the other end of the political spectrum), were deemed acceptable as military science instructors.[32] Maki selected Matsutani Sei and then Takayama Shinobu, both whom were former Imperial Army colonels, as his assistant superintendents. Their presence as senior administrators at the academy gave some comfort to former imperial military officers who were suspicious of the academy and its civilian superintendent.

Finally, there was the question of the location of the school. Yoshida felt strongly about this issue, too. He wanted the academy to be located near Tokyo to help with recruitment of professors and to expose students to the "trends of the present day world at home and abroad."[33] This concern about the geographic placement of the academy was also a response to a prewar precedent that Yoshida did not want to repeat. The Imperial Navy Academy had been in Kure, near Hiroshima in southern Honshu. The Imperial Army Academy was relocated in 1937 from the Ichigaya area of Tokyo to the small town of Zama, about forty kilometers to the southwest in Kanagawa Prefecture, in part to create greater physical separation from society.[34] Maki was unable to secure a permanent location by the time the new academy opened in April 1953, so it was housed at Camp Kurihama, the former naval communications school that became a PRF base in Yokosuka and was the facility that Irikura Shōzō entered in September 1950, as mentioned in chapter 1. One former cadet remembered that when he entered the school in 1953, its wooden warehouse buildings were still rickety and decrepit.[35] Like other preparations to open the academy, readying its physical infrastructure was rushed. During the opening ceremonies, a US adviser remembered, workers were still replacing a roof on one barracks but "it was all ready by bedtime."[36]

## Maki-ism: Redefining Military Service

When incoming students arrived at Kurihama for the academy's first year of classes, they were greeted by Maki, whose impact on the school is hard to exaggerate. Maki's ideas redefined military leadership, character, and values, and came to hold such sway that they became known as "Maki-ism" (Maki-shugi), if not during his life then soon after. In his dozen years as superintendent, over five thousand young men graduated from the academy and went on to exercise influence on the SDF officer corps disproportionate to their numbers. Maki alone does not deserve credit for fashioning this new identity. Yoshida, Koizumi, and Hayashi also contributed to its formulation. But Maki was the most important. Yoshida empowered him, as the prime minister put it, to make cadets "sensible citizens . . . inculcated by liberal education," who were not "cast in the mould of the officers Japan had before" and would not "meddle . . . in fields beyond their ken."[37] To do this, Maki applied his worldview, shaped by his upbringing and experiences at Keiō and Oxford, to create a generation of officers who spread his views to the wider force.

Maki's educational and career experiences made him an ideal superintendent. Born in Sendai as the oldest son in a family with warrior ancestry on both his father's and mother's sides, Maki received an education at home and school that was both traditional and modern, Eastern and Western, and liberal and nationalist, and that emphasized freedom and discipline. Maki graduated from Keiō University, which had been founded by the country's great nineteenth-century intellectual Fukuzawa Yukichi, with a degree in economics in 1914.[38] Fukuzawa had made the idea of "independence and self-respect" (dokuritsu jison) the "founding principle" of Keiō. This idea, historian Justin Aukema explained, "envisioned a symbiotic relationship between individual and national liberty: on the one hand the state guaranteed and protected individual liberty while, on the other hand, the individual defended the liberty of the state." Based on these principles, instructors at Keiō during the early twentieth century "encouraged students, as dutiful national citizens, to render their services to state and military institutions—the guarantors of individual liberty."[39]

After graduating from Keiō, Maki enrolled at Oxford University in 1916 during World War I. Maki immersed himself in the university's communal dormitory lifestyle, its intense sporting traditions, and its intimate intellectualism. They likely seemed familiar to him. Fukuzawa had "conceived of Keiō as both a functional counterpart to the British public schools and a preserver of at least some of the genteel pedagogical traditions associated with . . . Shōheikō," a neo-Confucian school dedicated to the education of samurai men of talent.[40] Maki was also exposed to the mobilization of Oxford students for war. During the conflict, the proportion of males in Oxford's undergraduate population was significantly reduced—from 66 to 88 percent from 1915 to 1918—as a result of a massive surge of patriotic enlistment. Because the university was a center for the treatment of disabled and wounded soldiers, he surely witnessed the effects of the war's carnage and later the disillusionment to which it contributed.[41] Yet, Maki's intellectual influences at Oxford were consistent with those at Keiō. He studied with the political scientist Ernest Barker, a late Victorian liberal-conservative who embraced both classical liberal values such as constitutionalism, tolerance, and civil and political freedom and the "value of nationalism . . . and the existence of 'national character.'"[42] Barker, who served as Maki's don, provided him with individual study guidance.[43] These influences made an imprint on Maki's political philosophy and his administrative policies.

After graduating from Oxford in 1920 and returning to Keiō in 1921, Maki began to apply these ideas as a teacher, writer, and administrator. He taught classes on political thought and the history of the British constitution and published *Seiyō seiji seido shi* (History of Western political systems) in 1931. In the lecture hall, he often praised and embodied in dress and deportment the customs and manners of British academic culture. In 1927, he established Keiō's Yamanaka cottage in the mountains of Yamagata Prefecture, a place for student group study retreats that was inspired by his experiences at Oxford and the belief that education was not just acquired in the classroom.[44]

Maki gained valuable administrative experience after Koizumi appointed him as academic director of Keiō in 1933. Over the next dozen years, he oversaw the construction of Keiō's Hiyoshi campus in Yokohama and the establishment of several new departments.[45] During his tenure, he once again witnessed the impact of total war, and this time may have actively supported it. Keiō's students began to be conscripted in 1943 when the government removed the draft exemption for college students and lowered the age of conscription. And in 1945, US bombs began to fall on Keiō's campuses, including the Hiyoshi campus, which by then had become the Imperial Navy's headquarters as it prepared for an anticipated invasion of the archipelago. As Keiō's president, Koizumi invoked Fukuzawa's belief that "individuals [should] defend . . . the liberty of the state" to voice support for the war and encourage students to serve in the military.[46] It is unclear if Maki encouraged students in this manner. It appears that, unlike Koizumi, he did not make any such statements in Keiō's student newspaper, *Mita shinbun*, or elsewhere.[47] Yet, given the liberal-conservative influences on Maki, his closeness to Koizumi, and what we know about his ideology before and after the war, it is logical that Maki had views like Koizumi's during the war. At any rate, in 1947 when Koizumi retired as president, Maki also left Keiō. Three years later, Koizumi recommended that Yoshida appoint him as president of the academy.[48]

The historian Tanaka Hiromi argued that as academy president, Maki did not create new ideas or reach into the past to revive old ideas but distilled the ideology of the time and made that the basis for officer education.[49] No idea was as important in the early postwar years as democracy. Maki apparently liked to repeat the charge he received from Yoshida: "Now is the age of democracy. Do it well."[50] Democracy was one of two objectives of the US occupation. It was embraced by the public and retained overwhelming support even as SCAP reversed course and prioritized the country's economic recovery over democratic reforms as the Cold War began, and even as Japan regained its independence and the government reversed some of the reforms. The other objective of the occupation was demilitarization. That, of course, was also reversed with the creation of the PRF and the "creeping rearmament" of the NSF and the SDF.[51] Yet pacifism, as enshrined in Article 9, enjoyed widespread public backing even as it came to be paired with the contradictory idea that Japan should, at a minimum, be able defend itself. While Yoshida resisted US pressure to rearm quickly, Maki sought to instill in a future officer corps guiding principles that would prevent the military from repeating the excesses of the wartime years. In a newspaper interview a month before he welcomed the first group of students, Maki declared: "We do not intend to train war technicians. We intend to create first-class human beings who can present themselves anywhere in society. With as much freedom as possible, we will train the highest caliber men and give them the highest caliber technical education."[52] Even as Maki presided over the establishment of the academy, which could be seen as another step toward rearmament and militarism, he adhered to the principles of democracy, including civilian control of the armed forces. He himself was an emblem of civilian control—a civilian overseeing a military academy. He championed democracy and challenged cadets to come to understand it so they could defend it. While avoiding the question of whether the force was recognized by the constitution or not, Maki argued that it was only natural for citizens to protect their nation's peace and independence. Patriotism, he asserted, was caring about one's nation's heart—both seen and unseen—and being willing to defend it.[53]

This new form of patriotism was liberal and democratic but conservative, like the thought that Maki had encountered at Keiō and Oxford. As evidenced by these lines from the first matriculation ceremony, Maki, like Yoshida, was a proud patriot who was optimistic about his country's prospects: "As a people, we are endowed with a boundless attachment and pride for our country. Our ancestors lived here, worked hard, and bestowed upon us a priceless heritage. The value of those traditions, culture, diligence, and a persistent spirit [tamashii] is beyond estimation. For a long time, we have experienced many vicissitudes. But there is always a reason for rises and causes for declines. Lately, we as a people have faced a disastrous series of hardships. But we should not give up hope, throw away our pride. We must set our hearts anew, discover what will lead us to prosperity, and single-mindedly pursue that path."[54] This statement illustrates Maki's liberal, conservative, nationalist, and realist impulses as he and other like-minded social scientists of this era sought to recreate a cohesive national community based on native and international intellectual influences.[55]

Even as Maki promoted patriotism and democracy, he reminded cadets that freedom must be restrained by discipline, especially as military officers. His repeated emphasis on discipline and obedience was a reaction against both the Imperial Army's extreme emphasis on "absolute obedience" and, paradoxically, its "culture of military insubordination" of the 1930s.[56] "Order has been described as the habit of reasoned compliance," he repeatedly declared. "Your compliance to orders must move as soon as possible from simple passive compliance to cooperation and ultimately to confidence. You have freedom of opinion. But once something has been decided by the Japanese people, you must conform to that decision. This is the spirit of democracy and it is the first step in the trust that the Japanese people have placed in you."[57] Obedience and discipline, Maki insisted, do not contradict democracy and freedom, but are tempered by these values and are what make them possible.

Maki's reworking of military identity incorporated notions of manliness with a variety of influences from home and abroad and from the past and the present. His formative educational experiences reinforced his upbringing in a family with a samurai heritage. Learning at both Keiō and Oxford emphasized character, cultivation, courtesy, civic virtue, and noblesse oblige. Likewise, practices from West Point and Annapolis shared by US military advisers and observed by Maki during his visit in 1956 played a role. On his return, Maki praised the "manliness" (otokorashisa), "manly virtue" (otoko no tokusei), and "public spirit" (kōkyō no seishin) he witnessed at the US academies.[58] Domestic prewar masculine ideals that valued self-cultivation (kyōyō) achieved through the acquisition of a broad liberal education, which prevailed at elite prewar universities such as Keiō, were also important.[59] Fukuzawa himself was "steadfastly committed to the conservative social idea of leadership by men of broad learning and cultivated élan."[60] Similar views also pervaded the Imperial Navy. After his appointment as president and in preparation for the opening of the academy, Maki visited Inoue Shigeyoshi, an admiral who had become isolated within the navy because of his moderate views, including his opposition to the Tripartite Pact with Nazi Germany and fascist Italy, and was eventually transferred from command duties to oversee the navy academy from 1942 until the end of the war. Inoue urged Maki to produce officers unlike those that came to dominate the army as well as the navy during the war. At the navy academy, Inoue said he tried to "educate cadets to be gentleman [*jentoruman*]."[61] Inoue represented a powerful, longstanding tradition of well-educated, self-cultivated cosmopolitan internationalism among naval officers. Such martial masculine identity, which Maki later touted, contrasted with and represented a critique of a strand of military manliness that emerged among officers, especially army officers, in the wake of victories in the Sino-Japanese and Russo-Japanese Wars, and culminated in the assassinations and attempted coups of the late 1920s and the 1930s. This unfortunate streak led some young officers to devalue education and self-cultivation, read only books about military tactics, substitute spirit for rational and scientific thinking, be uncouth and unruly in their manners as well as disobedient, violent, and rebellious.[62] These attitudes drew on earlier Tokugawa-era primitive and unrestrained strains of masculinity that fed a late Meiji-era nativist backlash against the figure of the Westernized gentleman in the late nineteenth century.[63] Like Inoue, Maki rejected such prewar notions that valued men primarily as warriors and soldiers. Instead, he preached that cadets were to become gentlemen first at the NDA, and then military officers in officer candidate school.

This did not mean that physical strength did not matter. Here, too, Keiō, Oxford, and influences from overseas military academies likely left an impression on Maki. At both Keiō and Oxford, gentility and public spirit were to be paired with ample though constrained masculine courage and valor. Maki embraced the Victorian and late Meiji ideas of a muscular masculinity that valued athletics and saw sporting competition as an essential element of personnel development, group loyalty, and military training. Such influences were prevalent at both universities, where students romanticized a past of knights and samurai. As the historian Donald Roden showed, an intense participation in sport was the mark of manliness at elite Japanese national high schools and universities such as Keiō.[64] Likewise, "prowess in and a conversational knowledge of sport," as Paul R. Deslandes observed in his study of contemporary Oxford and Cambridge, "signaled the attainment of a level of education, culture, and status that was deemed essential."[65] Maki relished his memories of playing rugby and drew lessons from them that he applied at the academy. These inclinations were surely reinforced by the US advisers and his trip to foreign military academies in 1956. According to the itinerary, for example, Maki took time during his busy day-and-a-half-long visit to the US Naval Academy to "observe informal athletic practices."[66] In his speeches, he touted sport as invaluable for national defense, character

FIGURE 2.1.   The National Defense Academy Obaradai campus from the air in 1955. The main access road from central Yokosuka that winds up to the top of the bluff and enters the newly constructed campus to the right of the photograph can be seen in the foreground. The Pacific Ocean is visible in the distance. Photograph by Kubota Hiroyuki, National Defense Academy Archives. Used with permission of Maki Katsura and the National Defense Academy.

building, physical training, and mental strengthening.[67] He praised the value that the British and Americans placed on the concept of fair play. The emphasis that the postwar academy placed on sport was in sharp contrast to the prewar military academies. In general, neither the Imperial Army Academy nor the Imperial Navy Academy had cadets participate in sports, other than some martial arts training and calisthenics.[68] This was not the case at the postwar academy, where the administration required cadet participation in athletics and encouraged team sports in particular.[69]

Another legacy bequeathed by Maki was the Obaradai campus that the school moved to in 1954, and where it is still located. Like Kurihama, Obaradai is in Yokosuka, but its location is much more striking, as can be seen from an aerial photograph (figure 2.1). It stands on a bluff situated 80 meters above the surrounding area with views overlooking Tokyo Bay in one direction. On clear days, Mt. Fuji is visible in the distance in the other direction. In that respect, the academy followed the imperial military academy custom of being situated at a higher elevation than the surrounding terrain, thus the suffix *dai* (heights).[70] Despite meager funds and limited public support, Maki acquired the property. He had been interested in locating the academy on beachfront land occupied by the US Army base at Camp McGill, located in

Hayama on the opposite side of the Miura Peninsula from Yokosuka. When US Army officials indicated they were not ready to return the base to the Japanese government, Maki turned his attention to Obaradai. The property owner was planning on using it to build a golf course, hotel, theater, and clubhouse that would primarily serve US Navy personnel stationed at the nearby port of Yokosuka, which had become the home of the Seventh Fleet in 1952.[71] But with the assistance of city officials, Maki was able to persuade the owner to sell the land to the government. The US advisers at the academy arranged for a US Navy Seabee civil engineering team to level 160 acres of land for training and athletic fields for the new campus, work that was still underway when the third class of students arrived in April 1955.[72] One student in the first graduating class remembered being told to pray for Obaradai and wondered if perhaps the US Navy was the answer to those prayers.[73] The academy's departure from the dilapidated imperial military buildings at Kurihama, Maki's central role in acquiring the Obaradai property, and the assistance of the US military all aptly symbolize some of the principal aspects of the early postwar academy.

Not every aspect of the new academy represented a departure from the past. Like the imperial military academies, the postwar academy remained a masculine space, except for a few women who worked in the health clinic, cafeteria, and post exchange (PX) and who were much older than the cadets. (The academy did not begin accepting women until 1992.) As has been noted, Maki's view that officers should be educated, cosmopolitan gentlemen had a long history, especially in the Imperial Navy. Likewise, his liberal-democratic beliefs that the state should protect the individual and that individuals should serve and be willing to fight and die in defense of the nation-state represented a continuity with progressive forms of prewar ideology. Personnel—the academy's administrators and instructors—linked the new academy to its prewar predecessors, too. Maki had little choice but to hire former military officers to teach the academy's military science classes. He also selected some former officers as senior administrators. Needless to say, some of these instructors and officials may not have been entirely in agreement with Maki's philosophy and policies. Indeed, the journalist Maeda Tetsuo argued that "not a few . . . conservative tenets [of the imperial military] survived attempts to sever all links" with the past. Specifically, he cited the example of Maki's assistant superintendent, Matsutani, a former colonel in the imperial military who had served as Tōjō Hideki's secretary. Maeda contended that Matsutani "was no believer in the new philosophy of military education."[74] In contrast, some early NDA graduates, such as Sakuma Makoto, a member of the first graduating class, claimed that Matsutani and other prewar officers came to embrace Maki's vision and methods.[75] Matsutani himself, writing in the early 1980s, praised Maki and stated that Maki, unlike himself, understood the postwar generation.[76] Perhaps Maeda's judgment was too harsh, but it is unlikely that all the former Imperial military officers in the administration and serving as a military science instructors supported Maki's ideas about officer education. As discussed below, tension between cadets and instructors in the classroom and disagreements between some instructors and Maki over extracurricular activities indicate that was the case.

## "To Be Men among Men": The Cadet Experience

The academy was shaped not just by Yoshida, Maki, other administrators, US advisers, professors, and instructors but also by the cadets themselves. It was they who adopted the identity of gentlemen officers and embraced the task of building a new democratic defense force dedicated to protecting the peace and welfare of the people. These ideas were not only inculcated via Maki's speeches and classroom instruction but also through a new academy culture that was more open, liberal, and democratic, nourished and shared by upperclassmen and underclassmen. After graduation, the contribution of cadets to this new esprit de corps continued as graduates spread the ethos across the wider force and some returned to the academy to teach as instructors of military science, over time replacing all the prewar officers.[77] Within a few years of their graduation, cadets began to serve as unit commanders in the three branches of the SDF and by the 1980s began to ascend to the most senior positions in the force. Though academy alumni formed a relatively small percentage of the SDF officer corps, their promotion and thus their clout were vastly disproportionate to their numbers. As we shall see, many of these early cadets have been the most vocal defenders of Maki's ideas and legacy while in the service and in retirement.

The young men who entered the academy came from a variety of backgrounds. This was by design. Yoshida wanted the new school to avoid the elitism of the prewar academies.[78] Because of a lack of data, it is difficult to ascertain how successful it was in achieving this goal, but by all indications the postwar academy drew from a much wider segment of society than did its predecessors. The only available information about the background of early cadets comes from anecdotal evidence mentioned in oral history interviews, from contemporary media coverage, and from limited statistics reported in the academy's student newspaper, the *Obaradai*. Entrance into the academy was highly competitive; only one out of thirty-two applicants, for example, was accepted in 1953. Not surprisingly, those admitted were academically gifted. That year, they also came from a variety of backgrounds. The media reported that 28 percent came from white-collar households, 26 percent were the sons of government officials, 17 percent were from farming families, and 15 percent were the sons of small-business owners.[79] Several early students mentioned that many cadets came from military families, which likely means that their fathers were officers and/or enlisted soldiers who died while serving in the military and thus became identified primarily with that role. One member of the first graduating class estimated that as many as one-third of his peers fit this category.[80] Unfortunately, no data exists to support these observations. Likewise, early students mentioned that many of their classmates came from families who were repatriated returnees from the empire.[81] Both these groups—sons of military families and repatriates—may have had an ideological inclination to join a newly established military. But this may not have been the case. Difficult economic circumstances may have led them and their families to take advantage of the academy's free tuition and room and board, which put a university education within the realm of financial possibility.

The average age of incoming students in 1953 was twenty-one years old. That was higher than in following years, when those accepted were, increasingly, recent high school graduates or *rōnin*, students who were a year or two out of high school attempting to pass the college entrance exams on the second or third try. These *rōnin* were, like their namesake—premodern masterless samurai—no longer affiliated with a group, or a school in this case. In 1953, some incoming students were as old as twenty-four. Some were students at other universities. Several were personnel who were serving in the NSF and who had been recruited to provide leadership for the first class of students.[82] Some of these NSF members had only graduated from junior high school. They apparently struggled academically at the academy and it appears that most or all of them returned to the force within a year.[83] And of course, other incoming students had just graduated from high school or were *rōnin*.

As was the case for rank-and-file recruits, a disproportionate number of students during the 1950s and beyond came from the cities, farming villages, and small towns of Kyushu. In the first five classes, about one-third of all students who were admitted (four hundred each the first two years and over five hundred each year for the rest of the decade, when the number of students admitted increased after the ASDF was formed) were from the seven prefectures in Kyushu.[84] Interestingly, this percentage was about the same as the percentage (29.7) of successful rank-and-file recruits from Kyushu in the PRF, NSF, and SDF from the 1950s to the late 1970s.[85] Remarkably, despite only having about 14 percent of the country's population, Kyushu accounted for nearly one-third of academy cadets and force personnel.[86] The Kantō region (Tokyo and surrounding prefectures), which had a higher ratio of young men because of its universities and schools for *rōnin* preparing to retake the college entrance exams, and Shikoku, the smallest of the four main islands, were the only other regions with application rates higher than their percentage of the population. In both cases the application rate was only slightly higher, whereas in Kyushu the application rate was more than twice as high. As mentioned in chapter 1, the historian Tomoyuki Sasaki explained the disproportionate number of applicants from Kyushu to the wider force in the 1950s as resulting from economic rather than cultural factors—the latter being the region's high esteem for samurai and soldiers, its similar overrepresentation in the Imperial Army and Navy, and its celebration of the hyper-masculine "Kyushu man" (*Kyūshū danji*) archetype. For Sasaki, uneven development between cities and the countryside, the agrarian nature of much of Kyushu, and the high number of farmers applying to join the wider force was the "key to understanding the geographical variance among applicants" between Kyushu and the rest of the country.[87] Certainly the academy was an attractive option for bright young men whose families had little means to send them to college.

But culture seems to have been a factor, too. Indeed, in addition to economic motivations, a sense of national pride appears to have contributed to the decision of young men to apply to the academy. For some, going to college would have not been an option if tuition and living expenses had not been covered by the government. The family circumstances of Nishimoto Tetsuya, a member of the third graduating class, who grew up in Kagoshima in southeastern Kyushu, were so bleak that the academy was the first place where he got enough to eat.[88] Although Nishimoto himself was from neither a military nor a repatriated family, Kyushu's poverty may in part explain the island's disproportionate share of soldiers in the imperial military, and hence its high number of sons of purged or deceased military men and repatriated families. It may also help explain the many applicants from Kyushu, though if that were the only factor one would expect more applicants from other economically depressed areas, such as Tohoku and Hokkaido. Economic criteria alone, therefore, are not a sufficient explanation. Culture, at various levels, matters.

Identity, family background, and personal experiences were certainly factors that led some young men to apply, whether they were from Kyushu or elsewhere. Shikata Toshiyuki, a student in the second graduating class whose military officer father died while imprisoned in a Soviet camp several years after the war, was already thinking of applying for economic reasons when his mother showed him his father's final letter, which expressed his hope that his son would join the military if it was reestablished. This experience doubtless strengthened his resolve.[89] A student in the first graduating class from Tokyo, Ueda Naruhiko, decided that he wanted to help protect the nation after seeing the clash, mentioned in chapter 1, between the police and protesters in front of the Imperial Palace on May Day in 1952. Unlike Ueda and Shikata, some members of the first graduating class did not understand that the university was a military academy. The former remembers five or six students quitting once weapons training began and they realized what they had gotten themselves into.[90] Others, like Shima, the cadet who thought he would be kicked out with his platoon, clearly did. He was impressed by the uniforms of the NSF troops he encountered in Kagoshima. The son of a government official, Shima had few financial concerns. He claimed that he was motivated by love of country and Satsuma samurai values.[91]

Applicants to the academy encountered both support and opposition from family members, teachers, and friends. Fathers, it appears, were generally more supportive than mothers. High school teachers, who were often members of the Japan Teacher's Union (Nikkyōso) whose slogan was "Never send our students to the battlefield again,"[92] sometimes voiced their opposition. Teachers sometimes—though not always—showed support after students had been accepted. When Suzuki Akio, who entered the first academy class, asked a teacher at Nishi High School in Sapporo for some necessary paperwork to apply to the academy, the teacher asked him if he was "intent on destroying the country again with militarism like that of the prewar army."[93] One of the favorite teachers of Nishimoto, the impoverished high school student from Kagoshima, was more subtle in her disapproval. She suggested that he apply elsewhere.[94] In the politically divisive environment of the 1950s, applying to the NDA was not for the faint of heart, even when on a personal level many people avoided confrontation.

Once successful applicants arrived at the academy, daily life at the school was similar to that at other universities, but far more regimented. Like at the prewar academies, Oxford, and some other Japanese universities, students were required to live in on-campus dormitories. At Kurihama, for a time around a hundred cadets slept in a single room.[95] After moving to Obaradai students generally slept on bunkbeds eight to a room, with two students from each class (from 1956, when all classes were on campus for the first time), and were not separated by their chosen branch. Mornings began at 0600 with the sound of a recorded bugle blast playing over loud-speakers. Cadets rushed to make their beds, put on tactical pants, boots, and a cap, and assembled outside for roll call, their upper bodies naked. They then returned to clean common areas. Breakfast began an hour later. "The food," recalled former student Tomizawa Hikaru, "was nutritious but never delicious." After being dismissed from breakfast, students briefly returned to their rooms and then reassembled for a morning ceremony, sometimes as an entire student body and sometimes in smaller groups, during which the colors were presented and the national anthem sung. Most of the day was spent in class, like at other universities. Compared to prewar and US military academies, NDA cadets spent less time on training, and less of their studies was devoted to military science. Cadets usually spent the evening studying, taking a bath, and visiting the PX. At 2200, it was lights out.[96] This was the daily routine Monday through Friday, as well as Satur-day morning. Saturday afternoons were largely dedicated to club activities. Students were permitted to leave campus on Sundays. From their second year, students were permitted to leave from Saturday evening to Sunday evening.[97]

According to many early students, Maki-sensei had an immense influ-ence on them. This is said to be especially true for the first graduating class, but later graduates expressed similar sentiments. Shima's experience of Maki interceding on his platoon's behalf may have been atypical, but his feelings of reverence for Maki were not. He brought to his interview with me the record of reprimand he received from Maki nearly seventy years earlier, which he still treasured as a sort of good luck charm (o-mamori). He credited Maki with laying the foundation for his service in the SDF.[98] Another former stu-dent, Yoshikawa Keisuke, took notes of Maki's speech at his matriculation ceremony, which he still cherished. At his interview with Japanese research-ers, he shared two quotes from the speech, based on those notes, that challenged cadets to become upstanding citizens of the nation and highly educated members of society, and to gain a proper understanding of democ-racy and nourish a seishin that valued order and obedience.[99] In addition to Maki's speeches, which students heard two or three times a year and which later students sometimes read in their classes, Maki's dress and deportment, like at Keiō, made a strong impression on students. Former cadet Sakuma, who became the navy chief of staff in 1989, remembered Maki as a "gentle-man" who was dressed impeccably no matter the occasion.[100]

Early academy graduates also remember the words of Yoshida, who visited the academy regularly as prime minister and even more often after he left office, as well as those of Koizumi and Hayashi.[101] Their messages confirmed what cadets were hearing from Maki. He was an erudite, sophisticated, strict, but warm fatherly figure, and his vision of democracy, patriotism, and manliness found a receptive audience among cadets at a formative time in their lives. One can get some sense of that relationship from the body language and facial expressions of the cadets pictured in a photograph, surrounding President Maki at a school reception (figure 2.2).

Many early cadets formed a strong impression that it was up to them to create a new kind of military and committed to doing so. Although Maki did not directly criticize the imperial military, students came to contrast his vision of gentlemen officers with the defeated officers of the past. Former cadet Ishizu Sadamasa remembered Maki instilling in students a "concept of a soldier that was completely different" from that of prewar officers.[102] Cadets were sometimes openly dismissive of the imperial military, including their own military science instructors. Shima remembered an incident when such tensions broke into the open. During a training exercise at the GSDF base in Kurume in northwest Kyushu, an instructor derided the cadets, the

**FIGURE 2.2.** National Defense Academy President Maki Tomoo surrounded by cadets at a teacher thank-you party held in conjunction with the graduation of the fifth class in March 1961. The only cadet I have been able to positively identify is Kimura Yoshihiro, who became a major general in the GSDF. He is looking toward Maki on the right side of the photo. Photograph by Kubota Hiroyuki, National Defense Academy Archives. Used with permission of Maki Katsura and the National Defense Academy.

academy, and Maki. The students did not mind being the object of criticism themselves, but they were so angered by the belittling of Maki that they went on strike and insisted that the instructor apologize for insulting Maki.[103]

The attitudes of cadets, though, were not a complete departure from the past. Although the wartime suffering and postwar education that early students experienced as youngsters may have made them critical of the imperial military, cadets looked further back in history to the figure and ethos of the samurai for inspiration in reviving a new officer corps. They also invoked the country's natural wonders as inspiration. These conflicted views are aptly illustrated by the lyrics of "Song of the Academy Cadet Corps," which were composed by Maekawa Kiyoshi, a member of the first class, and sung at his graduation ceremony in 1957:

> Majestic Fuji soaring skyward
>> In the light of dawn.
> Waking from a nightmarish dream
>> The waves of the Black Current are rough and cruel.
> Yet they strive to rebuild the homeland.
>> On the rocky cliffs of the Eastern Sea
> We men of talent are being nurtured.
>
> O'er the verdant mountains the white clouds soar,
>> The road ahead is long.
> Though our mission be strenuous,
>> We stake our lives in sweat and tears,
> With the surge of the tides in our breast,
>> We look forward to lofty aspiration.
>
> Cloud formations over Obaradai,
>> O'erlooking the sea and distant peaks.
> Soaring skyward our school at Obaradai,
>> Is a sentry to keep vigilance
> Over the mountains and rivers of our homeland.
>> By steeling our bodies and whetting our minds,
> Warriors here surge over onward.
>
> As the chilly wind blows on a wintry night,
>> Sprinkling stars meet the eye.
> Our thoughts are ever high.
>> Prayers in Peace, Heaven, and Earth are ever pure.
> Though the warrior spirit is latent within us,
>> Ah! Who is to know of our sorrows.[104]

Within the conflicted emotions of pride in one's homeland and regret about the "nightmarish" war, an identity as "men of talent" is evident. In the song, the cadets claim that they are like warriors of old learning the arts of war and culture—"steeling our bodies and whetting our minds"—to "rebuild" and defend their country.

As suggested by these lyrics, an element of this new identity was a reconceptualized notion of military manliness. Cadets accepted Maki's charge to become cultured gentleman first and foremost. They embraced Maki's challenge to devote themselves to personal development by gaining a broad liberal arts education; to dedicate themselves to a career of unglamorous, unselfish public service; and to adopt a gradual, long-term approach to changing the SDF as they advanced in rank. They contrasted this worldview with the "simple-minded" nature of prewar officers, which some of their instructors suggested they emulate. Instead, they sought to follow Maki's counsel to not seek fame because achieving it would be a disaster for their country. It would mean they had become involved in politics, which they were legally prohibited from meddling in; that their country was again at war, which they aimed to avoid; or that it had been struck by a natural disaster, to which the SDF was entrusted to respond.[105] One former cadet repeated Koizumi's Confucian-inspired counsel that the "duty is heavy and the journey long" to steady his commitment.[106] Several graduates echoed Maki's advice that they did not need to be immediately useful to the SDF. Unlike the prewar officers, they were not being trained to quickly lead units into combat. Rather, they were being trained for a future when they would eventually be ready to command a force to defend the country. As Shikata recalled, cadets "had to be men among men," "the finest gentleman among gentleman," and, of course, as he and other graduates repeatedly declared, "gentlemen and officers."[107]

This redefined military masculinity was a fusion of ideas of various national, temporal, and international origins. Perhaps most importantly, the cadets had vivid memories of the war and occupation. They were also the recipient of Maki's experiences at Keiō and Oxford and of his visits to the Western academies. Several graduates mentioned the influence of another Keiō professor, Ikeda Kiyoshi, who described his eight years studying at the Leys public school and Cambridge University during the 1920s in *Jiyū to kiritsu: Igirisu no gakkō seikatsu* (Freedom and discipline: English school life), a best-selling book published in 1949. Ikeda's account confirmed the importance of democratic freedom combined with civic duty and order. Professors, former cadets said, recommended they read the book to help them better understand Maki's philosophy.[108] Like Maki, Ikeda had much praise

**FIGURE 2.3.**   National Defense Academy cadets engage in a contest of *bōtaoshi* (topple the pole) during a community open-campus event. The structure in the background is a stage used for dancing and other performances. Date unknown. Original photograph is in color. Photograph by Kubota Hiroyuki, National Defense Academy Archives. Used with permission of Maki Katsura and the National Defense Academy.

for English sport and sportsmanship, which he touted as an excellent method for students to come to understand the relationship between freedom and discipline.[109]

Indeed, cadets' enthusiasm for athletics was another way that they adopted Maki's vision and used it to shape new academy traditions. Students devoted themselves to sport to a degree that would have impressed Oxbridge men and did impress US advisers who were West Point and Annapolis graduates. In response, the advisers provided support for academy athletics. In addition to arranging for academy fields to be graded in 1955, one adviser worked with Willy N. Sugihara, an officer stationed at nearby US Army Camp Zama, to secure equipment for the academy American football team that was established that year.[110] The support provided by US advisers and the US military at the academy, as well as at PRF camps, as noted in chapter 1, was likely a continuation of occupation-era policies that sought to nourish democracy in Japan through the promotion of team sports.[111] Thanks to such assistance and cadet passion for football and other team sports, the academy became a collegiate contender, including in a native Japanese sport that emphasizes teamwork, *bōtaoshi* (topple the pole), which can be seen in a photograph probably dating from the early 1960s (figure 2.3). That status continues to this day.[112]

## Advising the Academy

The US military's continuing influence on the academy went far beyond football. For over a decade after the academy was established, US military officers served as advisers to Maki. They were among hundreds of advisers in the Safety Advisor Group (until 1954) and in MAAG who supplied guidance to the wider force for nearly two decades after the end of the occupation. The nearby location of the advisers' offices at both Kurihama and Obaradai symbolized the ready and regular access to Maki and other officials that they enjoyed. Such routine interaction and the work that the advisers performed extended the influence that the US military had on the academy well beyond its establishment.[113]

Because all the officers assigned to the academy were graduates of West Point or the Naval Academy, they could speak from personal experience about the US military officer training system. Most were lieutenant colonels or majors, and each served at the academy from one to three years. When the school opened in 1953, the eight officers—seven army officers and one navy officer—serving as advisers were reduced to two. For the next decade, one or two advisers were posted at the academy and were assisted by a staff of enlisted and civilian personnel that included a supply sergeant, an administrative sergeant, and interpreters.[114]

The advisers performed a variety of duties. They acted as liaisons to the US military by arranging for administrators, faculty members, and cadets to visit US military facilities in Japan and sometimes in the United States, and vice versa. For example, one of the first advisers after the academy was established, Lt. Col. Dilworth, coordinated a visit by Gen. John E. Hull, head of the US Army Far East Command, to the school in 1954. A presentation Dilworth prepared ahead of that visit is revealing. In an addendum, he reminded Hull, "It is considered inadvisable . . . to make any specific remark linking the Safety Academy to a future Army, Navy, or Air Force. It is presently considered to be serving the National Safety Force and the Coastal Safety Force, and no more."[115] This caution illustrates that even as late as 1954 and even within military circles, both sides continued to maintain the fiction that the force was not and would not become a military. Maki also asked the advisers to reach out to the former imperial military officers now serving as military science instructors. Specifically, Dilworth remembered Maki "actively" seeking his "assistance in developing an understanding of the concept [of civilian control] among the military men of the Defense Academy staff."[116]

The next senior military adviser assigned to the school, by then called the NDA, played a key role in helping to arrange Maki's nearly two-month-long tour of officer-training facilities in the United States, Britain, and France in early 1956. "Major [Archibald D.] Fisken," wrote Maki, "was actively involved with the development of the NDA and regularly provided me with advice and suggestions. He was a graduate of West Point and was a strong believer in its education system and never got tired of speaking about the wonderful aspects of the academy. We learned a lot from him."[117] On his trip, Maki seems have been most impressed by West Point. In addition to the US army and naval academies, Maki visited the Army Language School in Monterey; the California Institute of Technology in Pasadena; the Air Force Academy at its temporary location at Lowry Air Force Base in Denver and its new location in Colorado Springs, which was under construction; Purdue University; the Pentagon; and Harvard University. Next, Maki returned to Britain for the first time in over thirty years and visited the Royal Naval College at Dartmouth, the Royal Air Force College in Carnwell, the Royal Military College at Sandhurst, and of course Oxford. In France, he toured three military academies and École Polytechnique.[118] In the years after this trip, stories of what he learned filled his speeches on campus and writing that appeared in the *Obaradai* student newspaper.[119]

The next adviser, Lt. Col. Francis E. Kramer, by his own account, took an active role in tweaking the academy's education and training and in the school's extracurricular activities. Specifically, Kramer provided advice about matters from the "proper performance of arms to the value of ballroom dancing," an activity that, as discussed below, caused considerable controversy. Kramer also recalled being asked "in staff and faculty meetings . . . about

American military doctrine, customs and courtesies of [the] military services, cadet education and training methods at [the] service academies, and character development, particularly the Honor Code at West Point." In addition, he met with cadets to help them practice their English conversation. He also responded to several members of the fourth graduating class who came to his office "with a rather large and unexpected appeal." Despite the earlier civil engineering work performed by the US Navy, the academy still lacked "suitable athletic fields" that were not on "rough and uneven ground." Thanks to Kramer, once again a Seabees crew arrived with bulldozers, graders, and dump trucks to level the fields (figure 2.4).[120]

Another intervention by Kramer dovetailed with Maki's efforts to instill patriotism in the SDF's future officer corps. On his arrival in Japan with his family, he declined housing on a US base and requested to live where he could more easily host academy civilian professors, military instructors, and especially cadets. Students, whom he regularly hosted in his home

**FIGURE 2.4.** President Maki, in the black hat, recognizing the work of the US Navy Seabees for their "construction of a training field at the new academy" (quote on the back of the photograph). Among the Japanese SDF and US military officers observing is Major A. D. Fisken, Jr., senior advisor to MAAG, who can be seen in the rear row, second from the left. September 26, 1955. Official US Navy Photograph, National Defense Academy Archives. Used with permission of the National Defense Academy.

in nearby Kamakura, shared with him their concerns about entering an "unpopular military profession" at a time of pervasive "anti-military sentiment." Kramer tried to "reassure them" by pointing out "the justness of a man's right to defend his family and hence his nation when attacked," that "in such situations profession of arms [was] considered an honorable one," and that "by their devotion to duty . . . the people would eventually respect them as their protectors." In this context, he explained the West Point motto of "Duty, Honor, Country."[121] These conversations may have influenced the formulation of the NDA Cadet Code. Created in 1965, it, like the West Point motto, had three keywords: "Honor, Courage, Propriety." Earlier samurai ethics probably influenced the code's formulation, too. Ōta Fumio, who attended the academy after the code was announced, claimed that it was inspired by Yamaoka Tesshu, a warrior who became famous during the Meiji Restoration and who emphasized "Propriety, Valor, and Honor."[122] Kramer also influenced other practices at the academy. He noticed that cadets did not present the (de facto) national flag, the Hinomaru, during the school's regular parades. "It seemed to me that carrying the National flag," Kramer recalled, "the symbol of the Nation, in parades would lessen the cadets' concern over their choice of career by reassuring them of their essential role in Japanese life and thus raise their self-esteem." Kramer suggested to Maki, "When he thought the time was right, the cadet Color Guard [should] be authorized to carry both flags [the Hinomaru flag and the NDA flag] in parades. . . . He must have been thinking along the same line, too, for not long after, I saw the two flags flying proudly as the Color Guard passed in review."[123]

US military advisers continued to be assigned to the academy for four more years, until MAAG decided the position was no longer needed in 1963. The last adviser, Lt. Col. William J. Brake, remembered, "[My] position became more like that of an ambassador, promoting . . . a spirit of international cooperation through exchange programs with cadets from other countries. My wife and children contributed to the Cadets' extracurricular activities by participating in social events and conducting informal English speaking sessions. We enjoyed entertaining cadets (and their girl friends) in our quarters on weekends." In 1963, Brake was transferred to MAAG headquarters in the Tokyo embassy.[124]

During the decade that US advisers served at the academy, their presence and work heightened the influence of the US academies, especially West Point. Thanks to close relationships with Maki, other administrators, and faculty members, as well as interaction with cadets, the advisers bolstered the ties between the SDF and the US military. Some former cadets remember having little contact with the advisers and only seeing them at official events. One, the strong-willed Shikata, recalls thinking the advisers should not even be at the academy, if Japan, politically and militarily, was truly independent and not subordinate to the United States.[125] Their presence and their privileged status, as Shikata recognized, were another sign of the uneven and unequal relationship between the two countries and their militaries, which continued well after their disappearance from Obaradai. Like the school's relationship with the surrounding community of Yokosuka and society more broadly, its interactions with the US military shaped the academy and the wider force.

## Yokosuka and the NDA

Largely because of its long history as a "military town" (*gunto*), Yokosuka's relationship with the new military academy was a generally positive, if limited, one. Since the late nineteenth century, Yokosuka had hosted the Imperial Navy, and by 1953 it hosted the US Navy's Seventh Fleet and the Maritime Safety Force in its massive port. The addition of the academy did not significantly change society-military relations in a port city that was already awash in military-related facilities and personnel, both domestic and foreign. Local political leaders welcomed the academy's opening at Kurihama and supported Maki's effort to have the government acquire the Obaradai bluff, the last large undeveloped tract of land in the city. Because cadets only left campus on weekends—often to go into town to watch a movie—city residents did not have much contact with them, and relations seem to have been cordial.

Yokosuka had long been a navy town. Its strategic location on the Miura Peninsula at the mouth of Edo (now Tokyo) Bay made it a natural site for maritime defense installations. During the Tokugawa period, the shogunate maintained control over the peninsula to fortify the security of Edo. Authorities required all incoming ships to stop for inspection at the Uraga commissioner's office and later installed artillery batteries along the coast. Despite these measures, US Commodore Perry came ashore near Kurihama in 1853, an event that helped trigger dramatic political, economic, and social changes over the next several decades. In 1866, the shogunate established a foundry and shipyard at Yokosuka as it struggled to maintain its grip on power. After the regime fell two years later, the new Meiji government took control of the facilities and established the Yokosuka Naval Station, which oversaw maritime operations for the entirety of eastern Japan.[126] By the early twentieth century, the Imperial Navy had transformed Yokosuka into one of the largest arsenals in the country. Remarkably, US planes rarely hit the city with bombs, other than carrying out a few tactical raids during the final months of World War II. After the conflict ended, the US Navy took over the port and made Yokosuka the headquarters of the Seventh Fleet in 1952, which it still is today. Perhaps because the military presence gave the city security against economic troubles and natural disasters—allowing it, for example, to recover quickly from the Great Kantō Earthquake of 1923[127]—and because the city suffered little during the war, its residents generally maintained a favorable view of the extensive military presence in the city, including the academy.[128]

Graduates experienced few negative interactions in the city, except for an occasional shout of "tax thief" or "you're not going to ever find a wife," or other theater goers moving to a seat farther away when cadets sat down to watch a movie.[129] Because of the brief lengths of their leaves, cadets could not venture far from campus, though they often found Yokohama to be a more interesting destination than Yokosuka. Like members of the wider force, some cadets would jointly rent an apartment off-campus just so they could have a place to change out of and back into their uniforms at the beginning and end of their leaves. Though the economic and societal impact of cadets was relatively small, local businesses welcomed their spending and some residents attended the academy's annual student festival.[130]

The administration took care to remind cadets that they should be on their best behavior when they left the academy's gates and descended the hill into Yokosuka. Maki's messages about being gentlemen of course spoke indirectly to this issue. Another reminder appeared in the *Obaradai* in 1957. The article summarized the results of a survey that gauged Yokosuka residents' knowledge and impressions of the academy and its cadets. It concluded that although "city residents regarded the academy dispassionately, cadets generally had a good reputation." The author of the article did not simply convey the results of the survey but used them to "reflect on the many ways cadets should improve." It enumerated reasons why some city residents regarded cadets negatively: "Bad language, poor conduct when drinking, not removing their cap and smoking while in a movie house, not dressing appropriately." Then it suggested what cadets could do to improve their image: "Don't do things that would embarrass the academy." Specifically, the suggestions included "behaving appropriately on buses and trains, maintaining proper relations with females, not overdrinking, and making room for others on the sidewalk." In response to the survey, some residents also suggested that more dance lessons be provided to cadets, who had recently begun a social dance club and were practicing in Yokosuka each

Sunday.[131] This very issue—students dancing—would soon be debated on the floor of the national legislature. That debate provides one example of the academy's relationship with society and the media as seen through the lens of critiques from the left and right.

## "What the Hell Are You Teaching These Cadets?"

Probably no other institution within the SDF received as much media attention as the academy. The press covered its establishment and early years extensively. Newspapers dispatched literary luminaries and public intellectuals to write commentaries about it and its cadets. As in the media's coverage of the wider force, many stories were critical of the academy, particularly if they came from either end of the political spectrum, and it was difficult to be neutral in the 1950s about an issue so divisive as rearmament.

Some of the prominent public intellectuals who visited the early academy used their experience to comment more generally on young men who had come of age during the early postwar years. Within months of the opening of the academy in April 1953, the Asahi Newspaper Company sent Mishima Yukio, already a famous novelist thanks to the success of the semiautobiographical *Confessions of a Mask* (1949), to write about the academy. Mishima was not yet the right-wing ideologue he would become after the protests against the renewal of the US-Japan security treaty of 1960 (which will be discussed in chapter 4). At a mere twenty-eight years old, he was not much older than some of the cadets. Former cadet Maekawa Kiyoshi remembered fulfilling an assignment to guide the writer around the Kurihama campus.[132] Mishima met with Maki, whom he described as a "well-built, cheerful, elderly gentleman, . . . who is well-suited to be the principal of a university being subjected to so much public scrutiny." When Mishima expressed some misgivings about US influence at the academy, Maki replied that the US military officers were merely advisers whom he was glad to have at the school. Elsewhere in the article, Mishima poked fun at the name of the Safety Academy, joking that if its Chinese kanji characters were rendered equivalent to how they were translated into English, as "safety" rather than as "security" academy, there would be fewer objections to the academy's existence from the left. Always fashion conscious, Mishima made light of cadet uniforms, which he thought were a "ridiculous" mix of Imperial Navy and US military styles. But principally Mishima, as his title, "Gendai shōnen no mujun o han'ei" (Reflections on the contradictions of modern youth), suggests, used the article to contemplate the situation of young men more generally, who he argued were navigating young adulthood "buffeted by moral and economic pressures" in a world without firm political bearings.[133] The cadets, he concluded, were not all that different from other university students.

Two other well-known intellectuals came to a similar conclusion when they visited the school later that academic year. Ōya Sōichi, a nonfiction writer, and Miyagi Otoya, a Tokyo University psychologist and social commentator, published a transcript of their conversation with a group of unnamed cadets followed by shorts essays by each of them.[134] Ōya expressed surprise that the cadets read translations of existentialist works by Jean-Paul Sartre and Simone de Beauvoir, and especially that the best-selling magazine at the academy PX was *Sekai* (World), a decidedly left-leaning publication. For him, these reading habits underscored that the cadets were like students at other universities, critical of the political system and US influence but not doing anything to apply those views.[135] By the same token, Miyagi expressed surprise that almost none of the students were obsessed with "defending the homeland" and the emperor, and found that they believed gradual but minimal rearmament was imperative to achieve true independence.[136] Both authors noted that the academy's affordability provided intelligent, ambitious young men who came from poor families an opportunity to obtain a higher education. Like Mishima, they repeatedly compared the cadets to other young men their age, often doing so in positive terms.[137] Mishima's, Ōya's, and Miyagi's skeptical approach, and perhaps their pleasantly surprised reaction, to the academy seems to have been typical of media coverage of the institution in the early 1950s.

Those further to the right or left often had harsher views of the academy. In 1958, two individuals from opposite sides of the country's deep ideological divide separately criticized the academy but did so in ways that were similar. Both critiques highlight how the legitimacy of the NDA, like that of the wider SDF, was questioned, often in terms of its relationship with the imperial and the US militaries. As demonstrated in varying degrees by these two incidents, critics cast doubt on the masculinity of cadets and personnel, often, as in these cases, by using women as a foil to try to make their point. How Maki and individual cadets responded to this criticism also illustrates the application of the attributes that Maki sought to instill in students.

The challenge from the right, not surprisingly, came from a former military man. Tsuji Masanobu was one of the most fascinating and fanatical figures of the twentieth century. Although only a colonel, he played a key role in the planning of the Imperial Army's lightning-fast invasion of Southeast Asia in the opening weeks of the Pacific War. He also likely had a hand in atrocities, especially the Sook Ching killing of Chinese in Malaya and Singapore and the Bataan Death March in the Philippines that followed Japanese victories.[138] When the war came to an end, Tsuji went underground to avoid prosecution as a war criminal, moving from Thailand through Burma to Nationalist China. In 1948, he snuck back into Japan, where, because of his intelligence expertise and anticommunist credentials, he was protected by MacArthur's intelligence chief, Major Willoughby, and by Japanese former officers working in SCAP's Repatriation Bureau, until his criminal status was lifted in 1950.[139] Unlike former officers like Hattori (mentioned in chapter 1), Tsuji did not try to enter the PRF but instead turned to politics and built a following in the countryside, fueled and funded by fame and profits from the sales of a several books detailing his wartime exploits.[140] Elected to the Diet in 1952, Tsuji became a fierce critic of communism, the security alliance with the United States, and the government, which he regarded as having sold out to the Americans. He founded the Self-Defense League (Jiei dōmei), which promoted rearmament and neutrality and was designed to provide support for armed forces that were a worthy successor to the imperial military.[141] He obviously did not believe the SDF was such a force. His attack on the NDA in 1958 was just one example of that view and of his adversarial relationship with other conservatives, such as Prime Minister Kishi Nobusuke. Like other unrepentant imperial military officers, Tsuji derided the reconfigured military's leadership and its more moderate conservative political allies.[142] He found it particularly abominable that a civilian led the resurrected academy and thought its curriculum would not produce officers capable of defending the country. But in the end, cadets engaging in social dancing led him to launch what was probably his most public denunciation of the force.

It is not surprising that social dancing upset a rightest like Tsuji. As in other societies, Western-style dancing had repeatedly become a flashpoint in Japan since the late 1800s.[143] Government critics, for example, derided a fancy costume ball held by top Meiji leaders at the Rokumeikan, a garish Western-style building, in 1887. They criticized the event, which had been attended by Prime Minister Itō Hirobumi and his "Dancing Cabinet," as a "demeaning attempt to win the approval of foreigners no matter the cost to Japan's national dignity."[144] Likewise, during the 1920s—another period of rapid cultural change—Western social dancing became the focus of critique, as illustrated by its fraught status in Tanizaki Junichirō's novel *Chijin no ai* (A fool's love, 1924; translated as *Naomi*).[145] Despite such disapproval and growing anti-Western conservatism, social dancing remained popular deep into the war years of the 1930s. Finally, the government could countenance it no longer and shut down all dance halls and jazz performances on November 1, 1940.[146] In all these historical moments of sudden social and cultural change—the 1880s, the 1920s and 1930s, and the 1950s—the debate was about much more than dancing.

Former military officers, both those outside the academy and some military science instructors within it, were not happy that cadets were dancing, which they saw as symptomatic of more serious flaws in the officer education paradigm. In the West, being able to elegantly guide a woman around a dance floor was the mark of a gentleman and an officer. Prewar Japanese military officers, by contrast, would have never participated in dancing, except perhaps as military attachés posted abroad. Not surprisingly, young people, including university students, embraced Western-style dancing. They associated social dancing with democracy and formed dance clubs at their universities. At the academy too, cadets wanted to form a club.[147] After Maki returned from his trip to visit Western military academies in 1956, students used his report's praise of West Point cadets participating in dances to ask for the administration's blessing to form a club. Maki, naturally, granted their request. Like Fukuzawa, who encouraged the development of "associational skills" in male students with refined young women at Keiō, Maki believed in the value of "etiquette [in] proper escort, dress, and conversation."[148] At Oxford, he likely participated in the "balls, dinners, wine parties, picnics, and teas" with the "gentler sex" that were an "important component" of the "education [of] gentlemen" at the university.[149]

Cadets named the social dancing group the Akashiya Club, after acacia (black locust) trees that had recently been planted on the Obaradai campus, and Maki volunteered to become its honorary president. Because the nearest dance hall in Yokohama had an unseemly reputation, the club arranged for two instructors to come to teach lessons in Yokosuka each Sunday at a civic hall. Late that year, the club held its first dance at a hotel in the nearby coastal resort town of Zushi, and then organized two more that academic year. Soon student participants increased to around a hundred. In March 1957, the *Obaradai* reported that "because of the particularities of our university and because of how society views dancing," administrators and club leadership, concerned about attracting public criticism, were extremely strict and "nervous to a ridiculous degree." Before the dances began, the newspaper reported, Maki talked about maintaining the correct "frame of mind" and administrators distributed guidelines for proper behavior to all attendees. The school's concerns were not unwarranted. Over time, reports emerged of an "unsavory atmosphere" and of "amorous" young women coming and going as they pleased from dances. These reports led to steps to reassert tighter control over dances while keeping the club "open to all with a bright atmosphere."[150]

For reactionaries like Tsuji though, any dancing was intolerable. In December 1957, Tsuji ambushed the year-end dance held at a hall in the Station Hotel near Tokyo Station. Apparently tipped off about its whereabouts by an unknowing cadet who invited Tsuji's daughter (of all the young women he could have invited) to the dance, he crashed the party and confronted assistant superintendent Takeshita Masahiko because Maki had not yet arrived with his wife. Takeshita himself was a former Imperial Army lieutenant colonel who helped plan but ultimately did not participate in a military coup d'état to stop the government from surrendering at the end of the war. But Takeshita's credentials did not give Tsuji pause.[151] "What the hell are you teaching these cadets who will become military officers in the future?" he demanded.[152] He then reportedly accused participants of being "feeble womanizers."[153] Although Maki was apparently not present, former student Ishizu remembered him being there and not being the least bit intimidated. Tsuji threatened him with "I will be questioning you at the Diet" as he left.[154]

A few months later, on March 7, Tsuji got his chance to grill Maki on the floor of the Diet. After a series of questions to Defense Agency Director Tsushima Juichi about geopolitical matters, Tsuji turned to issues related to the NDA. After asking about the cost and purpose of building and maintaining the academy, he pivoted to the subject of dancing. According to the official Diet transcript, this is how the exchange began:

> TSUJI: University President Maki-sensei, please come forward. I'd like to ask you some questions. Is it not true that the Defense Academy has a club called the Akashiya that is dedicated to dancing? I'd like to know if this club was created because you think that dancing is indispensable in educating SDF officers to become full-fledged members of society?
>
> MAKI: I can answer that question. At the Defense Academy, not that many students are participating in this group, but we do think that learning how to properly interact with women is an important part of the education of cadets and we support this club.[155]

Tsuji continued his questioning by claiming that he had "stumbled" on the cadets going to the party near the station, followed them into a "dimly lit" dance hall, and found an estimated two hundred of them dancing with young women whose bodies were "exposed from their hands to their shoulders."

In a comment that elicited laughter from fellow legislators, Tsuji claimed that the cadets were not just dancing, but also that they were in fact excellent dancers. That ability, he alleged, was in stark contrast to their marching in formation for review, which he claimed was inferior to the close-order maneuvers of average GSDF personnel. He then claimed, disingenuously it seems, that he was not taking issue with the dancing *per se* but was concerned that such privileges were unfair to students at other universities, whose education and living expenses, unlike those of academy cadets, were paid by their hard-working parents and their own part-time jobs. Was sponsoring such a dance, Tsuji demanded, not a misuse of taxpayer money? Were not the cadets also "tax thieves," he seemed to imply?[156]

Maki refused to back down. He contended it was important for future officers to learn how to choose a good female partner, both for dances and for life. For the purposes of the dance party, the club worked with local women's groups and the friends and sisters of cadets living in the Tokyo area to find dates for cadets. When Maki had visited West Point, he learned that the US military academy worked with nearby colleges such as Vassar, which only accepted women at the time, to arrange dates for cadets.[157] He insisted that social dancing was not a bad influence on cadets and that it was in fact good preparation to become an officer.[158]

Tsuji's attacks became more heated and personal. He launched a barrage of criticisms: denigrating the quality of education and training cadets were receiving at the academy; faulting it for not measuring up to military academies elsewhere; questioning whether the cadets were receiving the spiritual (*kokorogamae*) training necessary for officers; accusing it of aping US military academies; and dismissing Maki as a "mere professor at some private university who thinks he can be the president of a military academy." Defense Agency Director Tsushima responded to these criticisms using a combination of concessions—perhaps the dance party in Tokyo was excessive—and justifications—there was nothing bad about dancing. Only after Prime Minister Kishi rose to endorse the academy's education and training did Tsuji move on to other topics.[159] In what was surely a rarity, a Japan Socialist Party (JSP) politician, perhaps tiring of Tsuji's histrionics, came to the defense of the academy during the lengthy exchange. He reportedly yelled out, "Hey, just let them dance, we don't care."[160] And that the cadets did, though in more discreet locations than near Tokyo Station (figure 2.5).[161]

Although Tsuji's criticism may have been idiosyncratic, it sheds light on the right's dissatisfaction with the NDA specifically and with the SDF more generally. Hard-core rightists, including many former military officers, despised the civilian control of the academy and larger force. They thought

**FIGURE 2.5.** A dance party sponsored by the National Defense Academy in December 1961. Photograph by Kubota Hiroyuki, National Defense Academy Archives. Used with permission of Maki Katsura and the National Defense Academy.

both were soft, inadequately trained, and a poor shadow of their predecessors. They dismissed both as the illegitimate offspring of and beholden to the US military, and they longed for the spiritualism of the imperial military.[162]

A few months after Tsuji attacked the NDA and its cadets in the Diet, a critic from the other side of the political spectrum launched an assault that was emblematic of the left's objections to the academy. The critic was Ōe Kenzaburō, a twenty-three-year-old Tokyo University student whose publication of short stories earlier that year had rocketed him to literary fame and who would be awarded the Akutagawa Prize, one of the country's most prestigious literary awards, just a month later. (In 1994, Ōe was awarded the Nobel Prize for Literature.) On June 25, Ōe published a short column in the *Mainichi* newspaper entitled "Joyū to Bōei daisei" (The actress and Defense Academy students). As he mentioned, Ōe was responding to a photograph that appeared in a brief newspaper blurb introducing a radio program in which the actress Arima Ineko visited the NDA and interviewed cadets and Maki.[163] Ōe's column read:

In a newspaper a few days ago, I noticed a brief article that included a photograph of Arima Ineko surrounded by a group of Defense Academy students. The article reported that she said she felt much affection for the cadets and that she had been led to reconsider her negative views of them.

If she is in favor of rearmament, there is nothing I can say. But after meeting her and asking her about this article, she said she absolutely did not say anything about having affection for the cadets.

If this article and photo, for example, exerts some influence on young men in some farm village to join the SDF, then this is a problem of the newspaper reporter misusing the commercial power of the media. The reporter who wrote that article is responsible for committing a political act while using someone else's name without their permission. We must be more careful in the words we use and in what we report, in order to resist the "quiet rearmament" that is attempting to slowly infiltrate everyday Japan and the lives of all Japanese. Even the seemingly most insignificant acts have political dimensions to them and potentially threaten to expand infinitely.

What I say next I say with a clear understanding of my political perspective. I think Defense Academy students are a defect and a disgrace to my generation of young Japanese. I think we need to work toward eliminating the possibility of anyone applying to study at the NDA.[164]

Ōe's final paragraph, particularly the phrase "Defense Academy students are a defect and a disgrace to my generation," grabbed the public's attention.

In response to Ōe's criticism, the *Mainichi* received many letters from readers. The newspaper published several of them, including one from Yamaguchi Susumu, a cadet from the fourth graduating class who criticized Ōe's call for disarmament and the SDF's elimination as unrealistic.[165] A couple of weeks later, the paper published a long article entitled "'Our Pride' and 'Disgrace?'" ("'Hokori' to 'chijoku'"), that analyzed the letters it had received, solicited commentary from several public intellectuals, and gave Ōe the opportunity to respond to the letters and commentary. The reporter noted the editor's surprise that about 70 percent of the letters did not agree with Ōe. Many of the letters came from young people, the generation who were supposedly disgraced by academy cadets, and most were signed letters. Almost all the commentators interviewed for the article criticized Ōe's letter. One of the commentators was the writer Ōya who had visited the academy five years before. As in his earlier observations, Ōya argued that most young men enrolled at the academy for practical, economic reasons rather than ideological ones and that Ōe was an elitist who, as he put it, was like "someone living in a lovely apartment who criticized the janitor who kept it clean." Ōe in turn criticized Yamaguchi's logic and arguments like Ōya's and asserted that even if young men like Yamaguchi attended the academy for economic reasons, they bore responsibility for the choice that they had made. He predicted that their choice would not make them, their families, or the country happy.[166]

Although most people on the left would not have expressed their feelings so directly, harshly, and personally—calling an entire group of people a "disgrace"—Ōe's views were probably representative of how many on the left felt about the SDF and the NDA. Leftists feared rearmament, which had begun with the formation of a disguised but embryonic military organization, the PRF. After a couple of name changes and personnel increases, and the acquisition of US heavy weaponry, the organization had unquestionably become a military. Likewise, a military academy that some thought was masquerading as a university was competing for some of the country's brightest students to provide future leadership for what leftists saw as an unconstitutional entity. Maki may have been a liberal and a civilian, but he was complicit in the country's rearmament and remilitarization. Like rightists, leftists such as Ōe found the NDA and its cadets to be like but not quite like the imperial military. Unlike rightists, they feared that it would become more so. Leftists, like rightists, resented the influence of the United States on the NDA and the SDF, though Ōe did not mentioned this in his critique.[167]

Even more so than Tsuji's criticism, Ōe's was personal, slighting not just the academy and its aims but also its students.

Though on polar ends of the political spectrum, both Tsuji's and Ōe's critiques struck at cadets' manhood by using women and cadets' association with them. The conservative Tsuji found cadets dancing with young women scandalous, with the nakedness of women's arms in the dark adding to their supposed disrepute. Ōe found the thought that an acclaimed and attractive actress like Arima, the star of several recent films by the director Ōzu Yasujirō, might feel any affection toward cadets so reprehensible and unbelievable that he felt compelled to seek her out and confirm that this was not the case. He could neither imagine female romantic interest toward a cadet trumping ideology nor his ideological enemies being worthy of such affections. Despite being diametrically opposed ideologically, Tsuji and Ōe regarded any hint of female affection directed at cadets, the representatives of an illegitimate organization, as politically threatening.

Cadets, in turn, metaphorically mobilized women in response to Ōe's challenge to their masculinity. One student, Konagaya Satoshi, wrote the lyrics for what became the official "cheer squad [oendan] song" of the academy.[168] He recalled being inspired to do so because of the incident. He also remembered that cadets wanted a song of their own that they could sing on marches, because all the others originated from the imperial military era. Like many of those songs and other cheer songs, which are shouted out by male squads with heightened masculinity, Konagaya's alluded to nature, in this case blossoms, Mt. Fuji, and the sea. It expressed hope for peace. And in conclusion, it alluded to Andromeda, a mythic Greek goddess "dancing in the eastern sky." The song's message, Konagaya said, was to inspire cadets to be like Perseus, the warrior who saved the beautiful goddess from the sea monster Cetus.[169]

In other ways, the response of Maki and individual cadets to these insults reveals how they applied Maki's ideas. Ishizu's observation that Maki kept his composure when confronted by Tsuji is telling (even though Maki had yet to arrive at the dance party and was not the school official who interacted with Tsuji). Other former cadets remarked on the contrast, evident to them at the Diet hearing, between a calm, rational gentleman who was their superintendent and the unhinged former officer who represented discredited prewar military masculinity. Cadets seemed to take this as a cue for how they, too, ought to behave. But criticism from Ōe, one of their peers and a popular writer, appeared to be much harder to stomach for many cadets. It may have stung all the more because it echoed insults thrown at the cadets by their female peers in recent memory. As Shima recalled, female students from schools such as the venerable Ochanomizu University in Tokyo traveled to Yokosuka during May Day protests and held up placards outside the gates of the academy declaring that they would never marry a cadet.[170] Yamaguchi acted by writing the letter to the *Mainichi*, but the administration reprimanded him for doing so. Most cadets kept their poise, gritted their teeth, and did not respond. Tomizawa, whose father, Uio, had been awarded the Akutagawa Prize in 1936, remembers another student drafting a response to Ōe's column, only for a professor to discourage him from sending it. In this instance and others, Tomizawa believed that cadets were "saved" by remembering the counsel of Maki as well as of Hayashi, who had quoted the words "great souls endure in silence" (*doch grosse Seelen dulden still*), from the German writer Friedrich Schiller's 1787 play *Don Carlos*, at a speech at the academy.[171] This was the kind of manliness that Maki was seeking to foster in cadets. Though Ōe's attack has become part of the collective memory of academy graduates, it and Tsuji's went unmentioned in the pages of the *Obaradai* at the time.[172] As Shikata put it, the attitude of cadets was "it's okay if we are called an embarrassment."[173] As cadets graduated and became unit commanders of rank-and-file personnel, they sought to instill this same attitude of quiet determination in their men.

## Maki's Influence on the Wider SDF

The impact on the SDF of Maki's decade-long tenure at the NDA is evident in the force's core values and leadership. In the realm of ideas, Maki's as well as Hayashi's pronouncements both came to be encoded and even enshrined as the ethos of the force. A new code of duty was formulated in response to the imperial military past and to incidents blamed on former officers who joined the force and acted in abusive ways associated with that past. In terms of personnel, the impact of academy graduates was slower, as it took time for them to advance in rank and move to top positions within the force. But as they did so, they reshaped the force and further helped to spread Maki's ideas throughout the officer corps and to rank-and-file personnel.

The influence of Maki and Hayashi is perhaps most obvious in a code of ethics for SDF members that was adopted in 1961. Known as the "Jieikan no kokorogamae" ("Ethical Principles for Personnel of the Self Defense Force"), the code, which remains the core text of personnel indoctrination to this day, was clearly informed by the redefinition of the character and mission of the SDF. Although the Imperial Precepts to Soldiers and Sailors (1882) and Imperial Rescript of Education (1890) were never used as official texts to be studied and followed in the SDF, the media depicted "Ethical Principles" as a de facto replacement of them.[174] Unlike the two prewar foundational texts, which commanded imperial subjects and soldiers to serve the emperor and were infused with bushido, "Ethical Principles" does not include any reference to the emperor or the way of the warrior. Instead, patriotism and national defense were based on a love of country, "freedom and peace . . . stand[ing] on the principles of democracy." The spiritual foundation of SDF personnel became the "elevation of oneself as an individual, love for one's fellow countrymen, and concern for one's people and country." The central values of the new guidelines—loyalty, responsibility, discipline, and solidarity—are analogous to traits esteemed in the Imperial Precepts and Rescript, but they were tied to protecting the people and defending democracy rather than to serving the emperor and the land of the gods. The "obligations" of "personnel as members of a family, society, and country," the principles directed, must derive from an individual's conscience and be balanced by a "strict observance of . . . the law . . . and . . . orders." Personnel, it continues, must avoid ignorance and fanaticism and must not participate in "political activities." SDF leaders clearly wanted to avoid the mistakes and excesses of the imperial military. Finally, the document lists five "fundamental principles" that personnel must follow: "Awareness of mission, self-improvement, fulfillment of responsibility, strict observance of discipline, and strengthening of solidarity."[175] The language of the entire document echoes themes that Maki had imparted to cadets at the academy and that Hayashi had been promoting in the force. Although it appears that Maki was not directly involved in crafting the code, his influence and that of Hayashi, who was part of the committee that formulated the statement of principles, is obvious.[176]

In contrast to these values, those associated with the prewar military were viewed with suspicion both within the force and by the public at large. Several incidents demonstrated this tendency, but the most well-known came to be called the "Hiroshima Death March," though it paled in comparison to the Bataan Death March. In early 1957, GSDF commanders conducted a training exercise that required troops to march for twenty-four hours, during which platoon leaders "encouraged" them to keep walking by beating them with bamboo sticks. Although the division commander who ordered the exercise was an ex–Home Ministry bureaucrat, former imperial military officers dispensed the abuse during the march, and as a result the civilian-dominated Defense Agency censured them most severely for the incident.[177] In this and other cases, prewar values and officers were often blamed and were contrasted with new postwar ideals and leadership.

Academy graduates, who represented the new ideals and leadership, further extended the influence of Maki's ideas. "In 1961 former members of the Imperial Army and Navy occupied most [force] officer posts" in all three branches "above the rank of captain, naval lieutenant and flight lieutenant. By 1968 former Imperial officers occupied no more than about 15 per cent of such posts. By 1982, only 127 former Imperial Army and Naval personnel remained in an officer corps numbering more than 42,000" in all three branches.[178] As the number of former imperial military officers declined, the number of NDA graduates increased. By 1967, after ten classes had graduated and an estimated 2,000 cadets had been commissioned, NDA graduates composed about 10 percent of the 20,000 officers in the GSDF.[179] A similar rise also occurred in the MSDF and the ASDF. By the 1960s, many of these graduates were already commanding units and conveying Maki-ist ideas to their men. Shikata, who claimed to not care about being called an embarrassment, remembered overseeing a civil engineering unit leveling grounds for a high school and being confronted by leftist teachers who used the school intercom to warn students that the personnel were "killers" and not to get close to them. It was times like that, Shikata said, that he was glad he had shared with his enlisted subordinates Maki's ideas of keeping one's composure and being a gentleman.[180] In the late 1960s, about 80 percent of the GSDF officer corps came from sources other than the NDA: the direct commission of former police officers in the early 1950s, former rank-and-file soldiers who had come up through the force ranks, and college graduates who had chosen to enter the GSDF's Officer Candidate School in Kurume. (The MSDF's school is located at Etajima near Hiroshima and the ASDF's is in Nara.) In the late 1960s, the proportion of NDA graduates in the ground force was about the same as the proportion of West Point graduates in the US Army.[181] But their influence was probably much greater than that of their US counterparts, and came to be even more so by the late 1980s and the 1990s, as academy graduates came to dominate the highest positions of the GSDF, the MSDF, and the ASDF. By the 1980s over 70 percent of the upper echelon of officers in the three branches were former cadets who had studied at the NDA during Maki's tenure.[182] In the 1990s, this influence became even more pronounced. After Shima, the student who nearly got kicked out of the academy, became the first NDA graduate to ascend to chief of staff of the Ground Staff Office (Rikujō Bakuryō Kanbu) in 1990, every person who has held the position since has been an NDA graduate.[183] As evidenced

by graduates' recollections and their defense of Maki's legacy, their disproportionate domination of top posts has extended the ideological clout of
Maki-ism to this day.

The formative early years of the NDA shed light on a key reconfigured postwar military institution and how its interactions with the imperial armed
forces, the US military, and society contributed to the development of a
reconstituted military identity. Most of Yoshida's conceptual ideas about
how to restructure the academy were in reaction to the excesses of the prewar military. Maki implemented these reforms to create an institution that
sought to educate cadets who understood and were committed to democracy and were endowed with a broad perspective, rational scientific thinking, and humanism. They were to be gentlemen as well as officers. Cadets
who experienced the war as children and were teenagers during the occupation years also contributed to the creation of an academy culture by embracing
and spreading Maki's ideas to underclassmen and to the wider SDF. Before
and after the establishment of the school, US military advisers who were
graduates of West Point and Annapolis helped Maki make the US academies
even more of an officer-training model for Obaradai. The residents of Yokosuka welcomed another military facility to their city, but cadets' interactions
with the local community were limited and the academy's relationship with
broader society was even more complicated. The media and critics on the
left and right focused much attention on the NDA, reflecting and contributing to its visibility in the debate over security issues. Because Maki's legacy
lives on both at the academy and within the SDF, it makes sense in closing to
analyze developments over the course of the more than half-century since
his retirement.

After Maki stepped down as president in 1965, his influence ebbed and
flowed. In the final years of his presidency, his allies began efforts to secure
his legacy. In 1965, the NDA published many of Maki's speeches in *Bōei no
tsutome* (Duty of defense), which helped spread his ideas to a new generation
of students and the wider public. Until then, few of Maki's speeches or writings had been published, even in the *Obaradai*. Member of the ninth graduating class Yamazaki Makoto remembered buying the book just before his
graduation in 1965 and it helping him come to a much better understanding
of Maki's ideas.[184] The book was reprinted in 1968 and 1971, but not again for
over forty years. In 1970, two years after Maki passed away, alumni dedicated
a bust of Maki that stands in the middle of campus. Although humanities
and social science classes had always been central to the curriculum, the
administration established new degrees in the humanities in 1974 during the

tenure of the third president, Inoki Masamichi, who, like Maki was an academic and political scientist dedicated to liberalism and social democracy.[185]
Perhaps tellingly, in response to Mishima's failed coup attempt and suicide
at GSDF headquarters in 1970, Defense Agency Director Nakasone Yasahiro, who served as prime minister in the 1980s, turned to Inoki to draft an
official response. Inoki reaffirmed the SDF's core values found in "Ethical
Principles" and its commitment to defend the nation.[186] After Inoki retired in
1978, Maki's influence seemed to fade. The next two presidents came from
bureaucratic backgrounds. Although little curricular change occurred at the
NDA, Maki-ism seemed to have less of a presence at Obaradai as the Cold
War came to an end and debates about the SDF waned after the Socialist
Party recognized the constitutionality of the force in the mid-1990s.[187]

In the first decade of the twentieth-first century, as political debate intensified over security issues, the future of the SDF, and war memory, new
NDA presidents and alumni who had studied under Maki and were by then
retired from the SDF began to invoke Maki's liberal democratic ideas to
defend the academy and the force from the rise of a revisionist, nationalist
right. In particular, Iokibe Makoto, who was appointed president in August
2006 by Prime Minister Koizumi Jun'ichirō, repeatedly cited Maki to combat these challenges. A Kobe University professor of international relations,
Iokibe was no stranger to controversy. Less than a month after his appointment by Koizumi, Iokibe criticized the prime minister for supporting the
Iraq War and US President George Bush's call for US allies to put boots on
the ground by dispatching the SDF to help with relief and reconstruction
efforts. Iokibe also objected to Koizumi's visits to Yasukuni Shrine, which
honors the country's war dead, including fourteen military and civilian officials who were convicted at the Tokyo war crimes trial.[188] (Unperturbed,
Koizumi asked Iokibe for permission to include the essay, which otherwise
positively evaluated the prime minister's foreign policy performance, in
his electronic newsletter.[189]) Two years later, in the same column, Iokibe
expressed his support for the government's dismissal of Tamogami Toshio,
a 1971 NDA graduate and the ASDF chief of staff, who had published an
essay in a far-right magazine that justified Japan going to war against the
United States, claimed that Japanese imperialism brought prosperity to
its colonies, and criticized the Tokyo tribunal. Elsewhere, Tamogami had
repeatedly called for the SDF to draw on the traditions of the imperial military, including bushido, and for Article 9 to be revised so that the SDF would
be less constrained.[190] Iokibe argued that Tamogami's essay was a serious
threat to civilian control and reminded readers of Maki's efforts to educate officers who, unlike their prewar predecessors, would follow orders.[191]

Iokibe's comments fueled the controversy and angered those on the far right, who denounced him as anti-Japanese and called for his resignation. Extremists in black sound trucks blaring vitriol from loudspeakers appeared outside of the academy's gates, and some alumni and others sympathetic to Tamogami successfully pressured a veteran's group to cancel a speech that Iokibe was to give in Osaka.[192] Most alumni, though, rallied to his defense, and they, too, deployed Maki's memory to defend the NDA and the SDF. Shikata, for example, believed that Tamogami's statements were diametrically opposed to those of Maki and he would not have been so susceptible to such extremist views if Maki or Inoki had been president when he studied at the NDA.[193]

Iokibe's memory-making went beyond using Maki to combat rightists. In his essay about Tamogami, he mentioned that the academy had "coincidently" just opened a permanent exhibit about Maki in a new campus museum.[194] The timing may have been coincidental, but it was motivated by the desire of Iokibe and his predecessor Nishihara Masashi, also an academic, to instill Maki's democratic ideas in a new generation of cadets at a time when those ideas were being increasingly challenged by the right.[195] Indeed, Iokibe declared in the official published introduction to the exhibit that as "the SDF faced a variety of missions both at home and abroad at the beginning of the twenty-first century, . . . now, more than ever, it must stand on the spiritual foundation established by its leader" Maki.[196] The next year, in 2009, Iokibe arranged for *Bōei no tsutome* to be republished for the first time since 1971. The new edition, which tellingly bore a new subtitle, *Jieitai no seishinteki kyoten* (The spiritual basis of the SDF), included new essays by Maki that had not appeared in the previous editions and an introduction by Iokibe. Thanks to these efforts, Maki's writings are now being read more often by cadets and the general public. In addition, on the sixtieth anniversary of the establishment of the NDA in 2012, the academy's then president, Kokubun Ryōsei, who like Maki had taught politics at Keiō, unveiled *Monument to the Establishment of the Academy*. In the center stands another bust of Maki, with the words *noblesse oblige* engraved on the base of its pedestal, flanked by two granite markers on which are inscribed the Cadet Code—"Honor, Courage, Propriety"—and the Cadets' Anthem, which was composed by a graduate of the first class. Alumni who studied at the academy during Maki's tenure provided the funding for the monument, which celebrates the values and identity that he and they as cadets forged in those formative years of the 1950s and early 1960s.[197]

# CHAPTER 3

# Becoming a "Beloved Self-Defense Force" in Hokkaido and Beyond

Sapporo, the prefectural capital of the northern island of Hokkaido, is famous for its snow festival. Visitors, now numbering over two million annually, have flocked to the event since the early 1950s. Almost from the beginning, the GSDF's Northern Corps played a vital role in its success. In 1953, the corps's brass band performed at the festival, which began in downtown Ōdori Park. Two years later, the corps went beyond merely making music to fulfill the most important role at the festival—constructing its celebrated massive snow sculptures, like the castle built in 1958 (figure 3.1).[1] When it started in 1950, junior high and high school students built the statues, but within a few years organizers asked corps commanders for assistance because parents were concerned that students were neglecting their studies, and reportedly also because some people were anxious that teenagers were being exposed to nudity through some the shapely figures that the youngsters were sculpting.[2] Since then, GSDF personnel have provided much of the labor in Ōdori Park. In 1963, the corps went even further; it began constructing sculptures at its base in Makomanai in the southern part of the city. Two years later the base became an official festival site. By the second half of the 1960s, base personnel were annually donating over ten thousand aggregate days of work to haul several thousand truckloads of snow and to build over a dozen large statues and several dozen small and medium statues at Ōdori and Makomanai.[3] As Martin Heflin, a US consular official in Sapporo, reported in 1971:

> Early in January each year columns of SDF trucks piled high with fresh snow gathered in the high Hokkaido mountains begin to roll into Sapporo. They dump their loads in the city's broad, mile long central park, and then they return again and again to the mountains for fresh loads. In the park, large working parties of SDF men shovel and bull-doze the new snow higher and higher, while others mold it into shapes. By the end of January the park will be graced with a dozen mammoth snow statues, and several dozen smaller ones. In addition, the grounds of the Eleventh Division within the Sapporo city limits, will boast dozens more. For four days, throngs of tourists will visit this famous Sapporo annual Snow Festival, which was featured in the December, 1968 issue of *National Geographic*.
>
> Last January a total of 18,000 SDF men worked on the snow statues. SDF trucks hauled 5,500 loads of snow into the city, and SDF honor guards and bands added to the festivities. Without the assistance of the SDF, this biggest community event of the year in Sapporo could not be held. The city, with a population in excess of one million, simply could not muster the workers and the vehicles needed to build the statues. Even if it could, it would lack funds to pay for them. So the SDF does the essential work, but the civic leaders get most of the credit and merchants reap most of the rewards.[4]

That was the scene in Ōdori Park every year, as well as at Makomanai until 2005, when security concerns prompted by the September 11, 2001, attacks and the SDF's subsequent deployment to Iraq led organizers to move the event off base. Although Northern Corps personnel collectively work thousands of hours each year, its accountants have only charged festival organizers for the expense of gasoline required to haul the snow. The Sapporo Snow Festival is just one of an array of services—of which the best known are disaster-relief operations—that the ground force has rendered in Hokkaido and across the country since its establishment as the Police Reserve Force.[5]

The Northern Corps's support for the snow festival is illustrative of the story of military-society integration and part of the defense force's long-standing, concerted courtship of society in the pursuit of acceptance. As described by several researchers, these public service and public-relations efforts have continued into the twenty-first century with considerable sophistication.[6] The SDF justified the organization's outreach activities by labeling them public service and training exercises, but, as force leaders

**FIGURE 3.1.** GSDF personnel standing in front of the White Snow Castle, which the 101 Communications Unit of the Northern Corps constructed for the Sapporo Snow Festival in Ōdori Park in 1958. The number and shape of the gables make it appear as if this castle was modeled on Osaka Castle, but given its name and the numerous castles being reconstructed across the country in the late 1950s, it is probably channeling that trend in a more generic way. The sign to the left of the group being photographed reads "Protecting the North," a reference to the Northern Corps. Used with the permission of the Northern Corps.

readily admitted, these activities were also motivated by a desire to increase public understanding, as well as to bolster the morale of force personnel. As Hayashi and other force leaders declared throughout the 1950s and 1960s, they hoped that the organization would become the "beloved Self-Defense Force" (*ai sareta Jieitai*).[7]

This chapter focuses on these public service and public-relations efforts during the first few Cold War decades by using Hokkaido as a case study of developments in the GSDF's relationship with society throughout the country. I have not chosen to focus on Hokkaido because it is necessarily representative. In fact, the prefecture may be peculiar for several reasons. First, Hokkaido was regarded as having special strategic value because of its proximity to the Soviet Union, Japan's primary Cold War rival. Second, because of that strategic value, the island was home to more GSDF bases and personnel than any other region. After MacArthur rushed US troops to Korea, occupation officials dispatched around sixty thousand newly commissioned

PRF members to Hokkaido. By the mid-1950s, over 30 percent of GSDF troops were stationed in three infantry divisions (the Second, Fifth, and Eleventh) and one armored division (the Seventh) on dozens of bases across the island, which accounted for 40 percent of all SDF land.[8] The heavy GSDF presence in Hokkaido continued throughout the Cold War and only decreased slightly after it came to an end. Third, from the time of the establishment of the PRF and especially by 1954, few US troops were stationed in Hokkaido. Almost all army personnel left the island as part of MacArthur's deployment of troops to Korea.[9] A small Air Force unit remained in the southern city of Chitose until 1971.[10] The absence of US troops, unlike in many other regions of the country, provided the GSDF with much greater visibility in Hokkaido. Thus, in this chapter, the relative absence rather than the presence of the US military and what that meant for the force's relationship with society is an underlying theme. Finally, compared to other regions, Hokkaido was a stronghold of the left during these early postwar decades. And leftists, as represented by the Japan Socialist Party (JSP), the primary opposition party, as well as by the much smaller Japan Communist Party (JCP), regarded the SDF as unconstitutional. Except in a few "military base cities" (*gunto*) that had hosted an Imperial Army base, creating a comparative affinity for the military within society, resentment of the military, its personnel, and its values persisted in much of Hokkaido. This was true both in Sapporo and, to a greater degree than in other parts of the country, in rural areas. If the GSDF could integrate itself into local communities in Hokkaido, it likely could do so elsewhere. Although Hokkaido may be distinctive in some ways, interactions in this strategically important, base-heavy, and left-leaning region shed light on wider military-societal relations, if only in that the island is but one instance of how militaries everywhere seek to integrate themselves and their members into society, and how elements within local communities encourage and facilitate the process of overcoming the military-civilian divide.

The Northern Corps's efforts influenced society's view of the force. The public in Hokkaido came to accept the SDF to a remarkable degree during the 1950s and 1960s. Part of this acceptance grew out of economic dependence, but some of it can be attributed to affinities nourished by the Northern Corps's public service and outreach, as well as to interactions with personnel and their families as neighbors and fellow community members. These developments mirrored similar trends elsewhere in the country. Already by 1961, the US consul in Sapporo reported, "Local communities in Hokkaido readily accept SDF men. This results from their cooperativeness, the assistance they provide during natural disasters, and the aid they furnish in such matters as installation of telephones and landscaping of school grounds, together with the fact that the SDF men participate in local recreation programs."[11]

Simultaneously, these efforts changed the force and its personnel. The service they provided and the standards they were encouraged to adhere to shaped new military traditions, specializations, and even a distinctive Northern Corps masculine identity, which was one manifestation of a wider Cold War defense personnel image. As the SDF justified building snow statues and rescuing civilians from the vagaries of nature as training for a core mission of the force—the defense of Japan—units and personnel took pride in this service and the skills they developed. Even as and probably because the SDF leveraged its service to try to improve its image by, for example, arranging for personnel who built snow statues to share their experiences in national and internal force newspapers, those personnel and their fellow soldiers in the wider force found fulfillment in the benefits they brought society and the expertise they had gained in the process.[12] Likewise, SDF personnel over time became intertwined with local communities through marriage, friendships, and experiences in ways that seemed to justify the training and encouragement they received. In Hokkaido and elsewhere, these ties bound the organization to society and have made it difficult for the SDF to, for example, close bases or scale back or end its participation in events like the Sapporo Snow Festival as strategic priorities have changed.

Wooing society was not easy anywhere during the early postwar years. In former Imperial Army base cities, the GSDF was able to take advantage of some of the networks that its predecessor had created with society that still survived. But the force could not permeate society or exercise the same kind of political or economic power as the prewar military. Defeat and occupation reforms, as well as public opinion, severely undermined and legally restricted or outlawed these possibilities. Spending on defense, which the Diet consistently capped at less than 1 percent, for example, prevented the creation of anything like Imperial Japan's or the United States' Cold War military-industrial complex. Perhaps more significantly, because a military cabal was blamed for a reckless war and defeat, the GSDF could not assume the place and practices of the Imperial Army without being hampered by the latter's lingering negative associations. Moreover, most Imperial Army bases, many of which had been located inside cities, including many on castle grounds in city centers, disappeared after the war, becoming schools, parks, and sometimes US military bases. Therefore, the postwar armed force often found itself physically separated from society on newly opened bases on the outskirts of populated areas. Thus, the GSDF had to come up with new ways to build grassroots support and make positive visible impressions. As an examination of Hokkaido during these decades shows, this is precisely what the force did through contributing to the economies of local communities, engaging in public service and outreach, and shaping personnel who could be beloved.

## An Anatomy of Dependence: GSDF Base Communities

In commemoration of the tenth anniversary of the establishment of the PRF, in November 1960, Kishimoto Shigekazu, a Northern Corps commander, boasted that the GSDF was the "trailblazer of Hokkaido's development." As evidence of this pioneering role, he called attention to an increase in the island's population that had been aided by the influx of force personnel. Consequently, industry, transportation systems, and culture, he contended, were prospering as never before.[13] Although Kishimoto's claims may sound self-congratulatory, the GSDF had indeed made significant contributions to regional socioeconomic development. Yet as in military base communities elsewhere, SDF contributions to Hokkaido's development had a downside; they enhanced dependence on the central government and foreclosed other opportunities.

Hokkaido's position as a frontier periphery of defense and development has a long and complex history. Greed for the island's untapped natural resources and fear of Russian intrusion led the Tokugawa shogunate and then the Meiji regime to transform the island—called Ezo until it was renamed Hokkaido in 1869—into an internal colony. As early as the eighteenth century, the Tokugawa regime began to transform what Japanese regarded as a foreign place into a "northern administrative district."[14] Meiji officials continued this process by seeking to exploit the island's resources by setting up the Colonization Agency (Kaitakushi) in 1869. Five years later, the Kaitakushi began to recruit former samurai, principally defeated Tokugawa warriors from the three southern main islands, to settle in Hokkaido as farmer-soldiers (*tondenhei*). The government expected them to keep one hand on a plow while holding a gun in the other as they reclaimed new land for cultivation and defended the imperial frontier against Russia. Over the next several years, over seven thousand tondenhei helped to establish about forty settlements on the island.[15] In 1886, Meiji leaders founded the Hokkaido Agency (Hokkaidō chō), which allowed them to govern the island more directly than other regions in the country. In fact, Hokkaido only became a prefecture in 1947, with the implementation of the Local Autonomy Law during the US occupation. Greater regional autonomy did not last long.

In 1950, over the initial objections of occupation authorities, Japanese leaders again used the pretext of defense—the threat of the Soviet Union—and development—the imperatives of postwar economic recovery—to reestablish central government control in the form of the Hokkaido Development Agency (Hokkaidō Kaihatsu chō). The agency undermined local autonomy by overseeing major infrastructure projects and answering to bureaucrats in Tokyo rather than prefectural officials in Sapporo. To exploit the island's resources, strengthen its defenses, and relieve population pressures on the main islands (*naichi*) of Honshu, Shikoku, and Kyushu, the agency continued the colonizing development policies of Imperial Japan.[16]

When the PRF moved into Hokkaido in late 1950, the reconfigured armed forces became an agent of defense and development. Throughout the country, PRF troops settled in bases vacated by departing US troops, but these sites were far from sufficient. Immediately after the war, people displaced by US air raids and returning from overseas used imperial military barracks for temporary housing, and the population, trying to fend off starvation, used army training grounds to grow food. As occupation education reforms were implemented, the government converted many of these facilities into university campuses. They turned others, especially bases that occupied castle grounds, into public parks. After the Korean War erupted and the PRF was established, local political and business elites who were eager for economic stimulation began to lobby government officials in Tokyo to establish bases in their cities and towns. These efforts, which occurred across the country, replicated Meiji-era initiatives by local areas to attract imperial military bases. In Kanazawa, a city on the Sea of Japan in central Honshu, for example, officials were so anxious to host the PRF on the grounds of a former Imperial Army base—in an area that after the war had been renamed Peace Neighborhood (Heiwa chō)—that they took back land that had only recently been given to nearby Kanazawa University and pushed aside opposition to their recruitment efforts. As the historian Matsushita Takaaki observed, despite Japan apparently taking a "180 degree turn from a militaristic country to a peace country based on the principle of eliminating war," the only thing that seemed to have changed between the prewar and the postwar eras was the emergence of some local opposition to such efforts.[17]

The immediate and ongoing economic benefits of newly established bases made it difficult for local critics of rearmament to raise objections, even though they were often opposed to the very existence of a reestablished military. How could they align their political beliefs with local needs? In the north-central Hokkaido town of Nayoro, the dilemma became apparent instantly. In 1951, after city officials learned that the government was interested in finding new locations to station the PRF, local chamber of commerce executives urged the city, which had never hosted an imperial military base, to invite the force to Nayoro and contributed two million yen to the effort. In his memoirs, then mayor Ikeda Kōtarō recalled that the night before he departed for Tokyo to meet with top PRF officials, he encountered Sasaki Tetsuo, a Socialist city council member, putting up protest handbills downtown. In response to Ikeda's question about where he stood on inviting the force to town, Sasaki reportedly replied, "I'm a citizen of Nayoro, too. How can I be against something that will lead to this town's prosperity? Look at what is written on this flyer. It doesn't say we're opposed to inviting the PRF; it says we're opposed to rearmament."[18] Given such pressures, perhaps it is not surprising that when Nayoro voters elected the city's first Socialist mayor, Sakuraba Yasuki, decades later in 1986, they did so only after he broke with the party's official stance and recognized the PRF. After his election, Sakuraba went even further. In a clever move to deflect criticism from local conservative rivals, he asked the Defense Agency every year to increase the number of troops in Nayoro rather than simply maintaining the status quo, a request he knew would go unfulfilled as the Cold War came to an end and Hokkaido's strategic value decreased.[19]

Despite the obvious economic benefits of hosting a base, many local residents did not welcome the reconstituted military with open arms. Even in the military base city of Asahikawa, which as the host of the Imperial Army's Seventh Division was known for its strong prewar ties to the military, citizens greeted arriving National Safety Force troops with decidedly mixed emotions in 1953.[20] Many people viewed rearmament, bases, and soldiers as necessary evils. Thanks to its existing base infrastructure, Asahikawa's campaign to host an PRF base proceeded smoothly, though the force did not arrive until it had been renamed the NSF. It was one of a handful of cities in which a former Imperial Army base had not become school grounds or a park and was still available. Almost a decade later, in 1962, the city became the headquarters of the corps's Second Division. Likewise, despite an immediate PRF economic boom, base officials and their allies in Nayoro sensed that many residents only grudgingly accepted the base, which was located a few miles outside of the city. Some citizens openly expressed their resentment. Initially, young people were among the most vocal. In 1952, over half of the town's high school students signed a petition calling on the PRF to not construct a building near the high school grounds and to prevent the establishment of an entertainment district catering to soldiers.[21] Another way that such ambivalence manifested itself was for citizens to welcome the reconstituted military but to express their desire that it (and Japan) not be allied with the US military but remain unaligned in the Cold War standoff between the United States and the Soviet Union. This sentiment was evident in a large banner that greeted in the force personnel in the town of Shibetsu, near Nayoro, as they conducted winter drills in 1954. The sign read, "Welcome Japan's Neutral Army."[22]

Gradually, such ambivalence faded and complaints subsided. Leftists, such as the future Nayoro mayor Sakuraba when he appeared on the political scene in the 1960s as a young public-employee union leader, continued to oppose the SDF in principle and the introduction of new weaponry such as Hawk air-defense missiles to the local base during the early 1970s. But it was virtually impossible for those on the left to directly criticize the base or its troops, who by then had ingrained themselves into the socioeconomic fabric of Nayoro and other base communities. Such criticism might appear to disparage their neighbors, active and retired personnel whose families increasingly made up a sizable portion the town's or city neighborhood's population. The fact that SDF personnel were hybrids—both soldiers and residents—obviated opposition to the organization they belonged to and the ideology they seemed to embody, especially in small, tight-knit communities like Nayoro and in neighborhoods adjacent to bases like Makomanai in the south part of Sapporo.[23] Such developments animated military-society integration in its micro form.

Like classic colonial relationships, interactions with base communities required a degree of give and take, but power was primarily in the hands of the state. The armed forces had to rely on the cooperation of municipalities to supply them with land to locate bases, airfields, and ports. Yet local governments, like Nayoro's, were often so eager to have the economic benefits of a base that they acquired the land from private owners, made basic infrastructure improvements, and then handed it over to the military for free. To make requests and curry favor, local officials repeatedly made "tributary" visits, as Sakuraba called them, to Tokyo.[24] Senior bureaucrats in the Defense Agency granted requests not only to further strategic interests but also, in consultation with Hokkaido Development Agency bureaucrats, to support efforts to further populate and develop the island. After the initial opening of bases in the early 1950s, their placement became more heavily colored by such considerations. The starkest example of such discretion was the establishment in 1988 of a base in Bibai, a city in central Hokkaido, about halfway between Sapporo and Asahikawa. Bibai had absolutely no strategic value but had been economically traumatized by the decline of the coal industry since the 1970s.[25]

Defense and Hokkaido Development Agency bureaucrats joined with local political elites to incentivize GSDF personnel, most of who came from outside of Hokkaido, to become active agents of internal postwar colonization. For instance, top Northern Corps officials encouraged their male subordinates to literally court Hokkaido's female citizens. That is, bureaucrats sought to facilitate marriages between active soldiers and local women. Official worries about servicemen having difficulty finding women willing to marry them was not without precedent. In the early 1920s, imperial military officers were concerned about soldiers' marital prospects when the organization struggled with fleeting unpopularity.[26] Government officials had also collaborated with private matchmakers to find brides for disabled veterans during the war.[27] But the military working with the regional and local government and other groups to address such concerns for military personnel in general was unprecedented. It spoke to the severe and protracted unpopularity of military values and personnel in the early postwar decades.

Marriage mediation on the behalf of force personnel began in earnest in Hokkaido after Liberal Democratic Party (LDP) politician Machimura Kingo was elected governor in 1959, bringing an end (until 1983) to Socialist control of the governorship, which had begun in 1947. SDF, prefectural, and local marriage consultation centers worked jointly to bring soldiers and women together through introductions and a variety of less formal gatherings. The GSDF usually assigned soldiers from the southern islands to Hokkaido for two to three years. For several decades, roughly a third of service members in Hokkaido hailed from Kyushu. The lowest ranking members of the GSDF—privates—could renew their contracts once or twice and remain in the force if they were promoted to the rank of noncommissioned officer. Intermarriage with local women allowed commanders to extend a soldier's stay in Hokkaido for good and helped boost the permanent population of the island. Equally important for the Northern Corps, its leaders believed that matrimony and kinship between force members and local women and their families would bind communities to the organization and dampen local criticism of the force.[28] Such interventions into the affairs of personnel also were designed to boost morale and individual members' sense of manhood. Facilitating marriages was no easy task, and ideological opposition to the very existence of soldiers made the effort even more challenging.[29] Such marriages represented military-society integration at its most personal level.

The GSDF's support for the development of Hokkaido included attention to personnel leaving the force, as well. During the mid-1950s, the Defense Agency teamed with the Hokkaido Development Agency to send discharged soldiers and their families to establish two new farming communities in northeastern Hokkaido. The plan was ambitious, even audacious. It aimed to recruit three hundred personnel leaving the service in 1956 to become the first group of settlers.[30] In a revival of the early Meiji-era practices of the Colonization Agency, the government, once again concerned about overpopulation, promoted migration to Hokkaido and land reclamation policies. Government bureaucrats hoped that former service members would emulate nineteenth-century tondenhei and carve out a livelihood despite the region's long winters and short growing season. They provided financial support and agricultural training and had local GSDF engineering units build roads to the settlements. The program, though, was not a success. It failed to meet its initial recruiting goals; only a few discharged members, including several who had married local women, joined the program.[31] Within a few years, the hamlets disappeared when the farms proved to be a financial failure.[32]

The Defense and Hokkaido Development Agencies also sought to place personnel leaving the force with local companies and settle them in Hokkaido. In 1963, Governor Machimura partnered with over four hundred public and private employers to establish the Hokkaido Employment Council for Discharged SDF Personnel (Hokkaidō Jieitai jotaisha koyō kyōgi kai), a branch of a national organization that had been founded a year before.[33] Each party was able to serve its self-interest through the partnership. The SDF secured employment for some of its departing personnel; the prefecture and Development Agency boosted skilled employment and the population; and employers, in exchange for agreeing not to try to hire force personnel before their service was complete, got introductions to those whose contracts were up. Further the SDF gained increased support within society as former members filled the latter's ranks. Such programs became common throughout the country in the 1960s.[34]

Another effort to enhance support for the force within society took the form of groups established in collaboration with SDF political and business allies from the mid-1950s. Two of the first organizations the Defense Agency and its allies created were the Jieitai kyōryoku kai (SDF Cooperation Association) and the Bōei kyōkai (Defense Association). Specifically, they sought to increase support for national defense and recruitment. The 1954 SDF Law required all municipalities to cooperate with the force in the area of recruitment. In practice, the law obliged local governments to publicize openings and refer any interested parties to the SDF. In addition, some local governments chose to provide these associations with administrative assistance. By 1968, SDF supporters had founded nearly a thousand chapters with nearly a half-million total members in cities, towns, and villages across the country.[35] These booster societies included subsidiary groups for women and groups for youngsters. In 1964, supporters of the SDF founded the country's first force-booster youth group in Sapporo, which was dedicated to bolstering "patriotism and love of nation."[36] Seven years earlier, in 1957, allies of the force had established the Fukei-kai (Fathers and Brothers Association), a support group "concerned with the welfare of force personnel. Local chapters help[ed] to arrange marriages, arrange[d] for relatives to make visits to distant camps, ma[de] tape recordings by enlisted men to be broadcast over their home radio stations, help[ed] former personnel find suitable jobs after discharge, and assist[ed] SDF families in their personal affairs." A US embassy official in 1960 reported that the organization "provide[d] a significant link between the civilian population and the SDF."[37]

Defense Agency and SDF officials also helped to organize groups for veterans of the organization, which in turn provided further societal support for the force. The first such groups for discharged PRF and NSF personnel appeared as early as 1953. Eventually organizers consolidated these groups into the Taiyū-kai (Force Friends Association) in 1959. Irikura Shōzō, mentioned in chapter 1 as a conflicted enlisted member of the PRF, was transferred to Sapporo in 1958 and began serving in the Northern Corps's public-relations office. He remembered the Defense Agency making the establishment of such groups in Hokkaido a priority by sending Sasaki Masanobu, a Tokyo University graduate, to the Provincial Cooperation Office.[38] Irikura remembered that Sasaki spent most of his time interacting with local business, political, and community leaders and most days smelled strongly of sakè from nights of drinking with such officials.[39] Such efforts of course took place across the country to varying degrees, depending on military-community relations. A US Army attaché wrote that the Force Friends Association "represent[ed] another potentially significant means of creating a closer feeling between the SDF and the various civilian communities."[40]

The SDF also received support from another group of veterans—those of the imperial military, who sought to educate the public about the "necessity of defense." These veterans, in groups such as the Gōyū Renmei (Native Friend League), were at times critical of the SDF for what they considered its supposed amateur leadership and dismissive of its volunteer force. Such criticisms, and the desire of postwar force veterans to maintain some distance from their predecessors and their values, hampered efforts to forge a closer relationship between veterans of the prewar and postwar militaries. This tension was still palpable when I interviewed top Gōyū Renmei officials in 2002. They made much of the fact that unlike the Force Friends Association, their organization and officer veteran groups, specifically the Kaiko-sha and Suiko-sha (representing the Imperial Army and Navy, respectively), had never received financial assistance from the government, which allowed them to be involved in politics.[41] In 1960, the Japanologist Ivan Morris published an in-depth study of contemporary right-wing politics and observed that the Force Friends Association was "very much less backward-looking than that of the associations of pre-Surrender ex-servicemen."[42] His observation aptly captures the orientation of these prewar and postwar veteran groups.

Indeed, the nature and influence of SDF-related groups was different than that of their prewar predecessors, though the inspiration and some of the practices of these groups were similar. In Imperial Japan, such groups formed a "total mobilization system" or a "social basis for prewar Japanese militarism," as the sociologist Hitoshi Kawano and the historian Richard Smethurst have respectively argued.[43] Transwar continuities existed, but the times, if not all the people and values, had changed. The core membership of the SDF support groups tended to be made up of local LDP politicians and neighborhood association representatives, as well as businesspeople and sporting association leaders, who relied on the force for contracts, assistance, and access to facilities. Though their impact, as US embassy officials observed, was significant, they did not have the clout of their forerunners. Postwar SDF support groups, the political scientist Peter J. Katzenstein noted, generated well-organized but limited backing for the force.[44]

In the 1970s, government officials took further steps to bolster military-society relations. After a decade of high economic growth lessened the dependence of many communities on military installations, the Defense Agency added direct financial payments to further strengthen the bonds between local base communities and the SDF. In 1974, the agency allocated the distribution of mandatory and discretionary compensation for localities that hosted SDF as well as US forces. The pretext for the payments was noise and other harmful side effects of military operations. The agency also wanted to shore up local support. Localities in Hokkaido that host ASDF airfields and GSDF live-fire maneuvers, such as Chitose and Bekkai, respectively, collect considerable redress mainly through improvements to public facilities. Because the base in Nayoro houses only a small-arms firing range, the nuisance allowances the city has received have totaled approximately 1 percent of the city's annual budget during the last few decades of the twentieth century. But the indirect economic impact of the base reaped by Nayoro through consumption and subsidies from the central government, which are based on population figures, has been close to 20 percent. Yet these programs were motivated by the Defense Agency's desire to discourage antimilitary sentiments from emerging and to maintain support in communities that were the most closely connected to bases.[45] These financial payments secured the ongoing support of key local political and economic elites who benefited from local public works projects and other inputs. The importance of these payments has been so great that Katzenstein and Nobuo Okawara argued they form "a local welfare state which generates its own distinctive type of politics."[46] They also continued the economic dependence of communities. Some segments of society benefited more than others in the process of military-society integration, and the military-defense identity that became embedded in society was embraced by those groups. Money talks, of course, and it was bolstered during these early Cold War decades by other, softer strategies that reach out to other segments of society.

## "Strengthening the Foundations of Defense": SDF Outreach

"Public relations," according to an SDF handbook from the 1960s, "is one method of combat for the SDF and requires the application of the theories and techniques of psychological warfare."[47] This declaration suggests how seriously force officials viewed the task of endearing the organization to the public. GSDF commanders, in particular, believed that the ground force would have to rely on the assistance and cooperation of average citizens if the country ever became involved in another conflict, and they were not satisfied with their narrow margin and fragile foundation of support. The repeated inability of recruiters to meet the organization's enlistment goals, especially after the economy took off in the 1960s, was another cause for concern. Moreover, leftists repeatedly contested the constitutionality of the SDF in court. Many of these cases stemmed from disputes by a few citizens who were unhappy to have the force as a neighbor and bore an ideological grudge against the existence of the military. The cases generated press that reminded people of the questionable legitimacy of the force. More worrisome was, as US officials observed, a public that accepted the fact that the SDF was "here to stay" but showed "no active enthusiasm" for its existence.[48] To combat these domestic adversities, the SDF, under the direction of the Defense Agency, strategically deployed several outreach programs whose objective was "strengthening the foundations of defense" (bōei kiban no ikusei), which contributed to military-society integration.

The Defense Agency's embrace of public relations in the late 1950s was inspired by and adapted from public information programs that the US military had established after World War II. In his pathbreaking study on US civil-military relations, *The Professional Soldier* (1960), the sociologist Morris Janowitz described what he called the "new public relations" that had emerged within the US military. "Public information ha[d] become a specialized military career," he wrote, with each branch employing several hundred "public information officers" who were focused both on "internal informational programs" and outside "public relations activities." "The new public relations requires converting all personnel of the military establishment into informal spokesmen," Janowitz observed, "for military managers are aware that the behavior and manners of military personnel lies at the root of public images of the services." He also noted the military opening its bases to the public to win support and that "even wives [were] mobilized" in the effort to foster "cordial relations" with society.[49] As discussed below, the SDF emulated many of these strategies beginning in the late 1950s.[50]

Because the SDF and its personnel were proscribed by law from engaging in politics, other than voting, the organization had to resort to means other than political arguments to build understanding and elicit the interest of the public. Leonard A. Humphreys, who acted as an adviser to the GSDF as an officer in the US Army in the 1950s and became a historian of the Imperial Army after leaving the service, observed in 1975, "[Since its establishment] the SDF [has attempted] to maintain as low a profile as it can, passively accepting its innocuous and completely apolitical role in the government bureaucracy, despite its numerical strength and relatively large budget."[51] Humphrey's observation is both true and untrue. To a degree, force personnel could make arguments based on strategic concerns, but because the line between politics and security was so thin, especially in the early postwar decades, this was fraught territory for soldiers. It was best to leave politics to civilian allies, especially LDP politicians. As an alternative, SDF officials resorted to finding as many ways as possible to generate positive visual images and directly interact with the public. Although cautiously, they sought to increase the force's profile. They did so in ways that can be divided into two broad categories. First, the organization undertook ventures that were almost or entirely unrelated to national security to instill in the public a sense that the organization was indispensable to society, even outside of the traditional realm of military security. Second, SDF leaders emphasized the defensive role of the force and that it could be trusted with that role. Both strategies sought to increase the visibility and profile of the force, which supporters and critics alike routinely called a force hidden in the shadows.

Without question, the most prominent nonmilitary activity that the SDF engaged in was disaster relief. As evidenced by Prime Minister Yoshida's order for the PRF to proactively engage in disaster-relief operations to garner "respect and affection," mentioned in chapter 1, the reconstituted military commenced relief operations in part to gain greater public acceptance, though it was not proper for the organization itself to boast too loudly about its work for publicity purposes. Fortunately for the SDF, its actions spoke loudly and calamities were decidedly newsworthy. As noted earlier, the PRF as well as the NSF conducted several operations to aid citizens caught in the wrath of typhoons and floods.

As the PRF was transformed into the NSF in 1952 and the GSDF in 1954, disaster relief became an established duty of the force. The SDF Law of 1954 required the organization to respond to calls for assistance from prefectural governors "if they deem[ed] it necessary for the protection of lives and/or properties because of natural calamities and/or other disasters,"[52] but allowed the organization to dispatch troops without waiting for a request if the situation demanded it.[53] Initially, the GSDF was proactive, and prefectural governors routinely sought out its help. Commanders interpreted the law as liberally as possible and made soldiers available not only to battle major natural disasters but also for a variety of situations in which threats to life and property were loosely defined. Sometimes leftists criticized the force for dispatching troops too quickly, and these rebukes contributed to a hesitancy on the part of commanders to act until all the procedural steps had been taken.[54]

Even so, motivated in part by a desire to be beloved, the force defined disaster relief in broad terms. The GSDF performed tasks, such as search-and-rescue operations for lost hikers and emergency flights from remote localities to hospitals, which in many other countries come under the purview of the police or other government agencies. From 1951 to 1960, the SDF was mobilized to deal with 476 fire-related emergencies, 229 water-related disasters, and 353 other problems. Among these, Hokkaido accounted for 208 mobilizations, almost four times as many as the second-ranking prefecture.[55] In 1955, GSDF troops stationed outside Nayoro rescued the town's citizens from floodwaters even as their base itself was being inundated. In June 1960, they flew children stricken by polio to hospitals in Asahikawa by helicopter, while units based elsewhere spread DDT (dichlorodiphenyltrichloroethane) in the coal-mining town of Yūbari to halt the outbreak.[56] The GSDF particularly played a valuable role in rural areas. It regularly dispatched doctors to remote villages with limited access to health care to provide check-ups and other medical services. In 1966, for example, force physicians treated 2,300 people in twenty-six villages in Hokkaido.[57]

As a result, rendering disaster relief became a core element in the SDF's sense of public responsibility. Its dedication to such work even surprised veteran observers. James H. Buck, who served in Japan during the occupation and for several years after, became a "language and area student and was the first US Army officer to serve in a Japanese military unit (GSDF 12th Infantry

Regiment) since 1940." He was shocked by the "diversion of military man-power . . . for nearly three months to assist during the typhoon season in western Japan" in 1965. "To me," he wrote, "this was an inordinate diversion of these forces from their primary mission of training. But to the Japanese the activity was appropriate and without doubt contributed handsomely to the development of a favorable image of the SDF in that particular area." Buck concluded, "In terms of ideological orientation ... [the SDF] differs fundamentally from its predecessor. This is true with regard to stated mission and legal status. All indications are that the SDF reflects the core values of postwar Japanese society and simultaneously reinforces them."[58] What Buck described was the development of the GSDF's Cold War defense identity that resulted from the process of military-society integration.

The degree to which disaster-relief service transformed the SDF during its first decade of existence and differentiated its role from that of the imperial military is illustrated by an exchange in midst of its response to a massive typhoon that struck Ise Bay in central Honshu in September 1959. At the request of a prefectural governor, a local brigade responded to the emergency immediately. Once it became clear that reinforcements were needed, Defense Agency Director Akagi Munemori issued an order for another ten thousand personnel to be deployed. In response, an officer in the GSDF Staff Office who had also been an officer in the Imperial Army objected, saying, "Disaster relief operations are not part of the main duties of the [GSDF]." To this, the vice chief of staff, Ōmori Kan, an officer who had joined the PRF in 1950 by way of the police replied, "The SDF does not simply protect the nation and its citizens against direct and indirect invasions. It is an important duty for the force to protect the lives of the people during times of disaster as well."[59] A decade of disaster-relief operations had clearly shaped how some senior officers defined the force's mission. That sense of purpose and the expertise personnel gained by conducting such operations made the force ready to respond to such emergencies, which in turn strengthened the sense that disaster relief was part of its identity. As it turned out, the typhoon proved to be the largest mobilization to date for the force. For the first time ever, air and maritime forces joined the GSDF in responding to a disaster, as did the US military.[60]

As dependence on the GSDF to deal with disasters grew, opinion polls revealed, somewhat to its leaders' displeasure, that the public valued the force's disaster relief more than its military capabilities. Many people assumed that the US nuclear umbrella was largely guaranteeing their country's security. As time passed few residents of Hokkaido, for example, took the threat of a Soviet invasion of the island seriously. Thus, they wondered, was the GSDF necessary for defense? Still, commanders welcomed opportunities to use their expertise and mechanical power to be of assistance and enjoyed the resulting praise. But sometimes they resented the demands. In February 1964, for example, the Fifth Division, headquartered in Obihiro in south-central Hokkaido, issued a statement that it would start to turn down requests for help unless they were exceptional. Apparently local hospitals had repeatedly asked the division to send over soldiers to donate blood after traffic accidents. Asking for the GSDF's help had become "as easy as picking up the phone and ordering ramen," one official complained, and it was time for the city to establish a blood bank.[61]

The GSDF's civil engineering projects were also in high demand. Unlike for natural-disaster operations, there was almost no Imperial Army precedent for such activities. The Imperial Army, of course, had engineering units, but these focused on constructing infrastructure, such as buildings, roads, and water systems, which may have benefited the public as a byproduct, but were focused on military-specific outcomes.[62] This was not the case for the postwar organization. Many of its engineering projects had nothing to do with improving the physical infrastructure for the force. It does not appear that GSDF leaders regarded the US Army Corps of Engineers and its massive public-works projects as a model. Rather, force officers responded to smaller, more immediate needs and were motivated by the desire to sow positive relations with local communities. From 1953 to 1959, NSF and SDF personnel were responsible for 1,193 projects nationwide.[63] These projects, which included building and repairing roads and bridges, leveling land, clearing snow, and stringing communication lines, made regional equipment battalions (chiku shisetsu tai), which the GSDF formally established in 1958, a favorite of local governments and the public. The Defense Agency estimated "that the SDF contributed almost eight-million man-days of labor" to 1,200 such project from 1953 to 1959.[64] As in the case of the Sapporo Snow Festival, bookkeepers did not charge a single yen for labor and billed materials and fuel at their actual costs.[65]

The Northern Corps often coordinated these projects with the Hokkaido Development Agency, as well as with prefectural and local governments. The corps's engineering battalions were responsible for thirty-four of seventy-four major road-building projects during the 1957 fiscal year.[66] Hokkaido relied heavily on the corps to complete public works, and these projects on the island constituted a significant proportion of all the force's projects nationwide.[67] While the Hokkaido Development Agency's projects linked major cities, Northern Corps projects—both large and small—benefited specific municipalities and local residents.[68] The force's service did not go unrecognized, especially in local municipalities. Hokkaido's citizenry especially appreciated the mechanization that the GSDF brought to snow plowing. When the NSF acquired its first bulldozer in 1953, Nayoro city officials and many residents celebrated.[69] For the next three decades, the GSDF and the Hokkaido Development Agency split the work of plowing roads around Nayoro. The former chief of the Eleventh Division's equipment battalion, Kuboi Masayuki, a native of Kyushu who spent much of his career and his retirement in Hokkaido (and is briefly discussed in chapter 1), recalled being overwhelmed by requests and scrambling from one job to the next.[70] Because the GSDF during the 1950s and 1960s was one of a few organizations, private or public, that owned heavy equipment such as bulldozers, graders, and cranes, its provision of construction services rarely competed with privately owned firms. This was particularly true in peripheral regions such as Hokkaido. The corps stopped accepting jobs that had previously been of no interest to private construction companies in Sapporo in the early 1970s but continued to accept them in rural areas like Nayoro even in the early twenty-first century.[71]

The GSDF also engaged in agricultural assistance. When the booming economy led to a shortage of workers on farms, especially in Hokkaido and northern Honshu, the force dispatched thousands of soldiers to plant and harvest rice, beets, and other crops. As mentioned, local Imperial Army commanders periodically dispatched troops to help local farmers during planting and harvesting season, but its activities paled in comparison to those of the GSDF in the 1960s. Initially, commanders dispatched only personnel—over fifty thousand in 1965—who volunteered or were strongly encouraged to perform such work. A proliferation of requests the next year, however, forced them to send entire units, regardless of individual wishes.[72] Personnel, many of whom were second and third sons from the countryside, could sympathize with the plight of rural areas and were apparently supportive of these efforts. They were, in effect, replacing young men who had left for jobs in urban areas, including perhaps themselves. Commanders rationalized agricultural relief as "'disaster relief' to defend the land" that was also good for recruitment and community support.[73]

The free assistance may have won the hearts of shorthanded farmers, as well as of some of their daughters, including a number who married soldiers laboring in their villages. This byproduct surely pleased SDF commanders and their local allies. The Northern Corps's internal newspaper, the *Akashiya* (which happens to be the same name as that of the NDA social dance group mentioned in chapter 2), featured photographs of soldiers and local women working side by side in the fields and fraternizing during breaks (figure 3.2).

**FIGURE 3.2.** A photograph of GSDF Northern Corps personnel planting rice near Mount Yōtei in southwestern Hokkaido as a local farm woman gazes at the camera, June 2, 1967. This photo appeared on the front page of the *Akashiya* on June 25 and was one of a number of such photos that were featured in the paper showing personnel providing agriculture assistance and interacting with women in rural communities during the 1960s. Used with the permission of the Northern Corps.

Irikura, who had joined the force in 1950 and was transferred to Hokkaido, where he joined the public relations office and became an *Akashiya* writer and editor from 1958 to 1977, admitted that he and other staff members aimed to take and feature such photographs to encourage romantic relationships and participation in the work, as well as to boost personnel morale. Similar scenes appeared in two Northern Corps newspaper cartoons that were published on the same day in different internal newspapers in 1969.[74] The first reflected the reality of the hard work of planting rice seedlings in wet fields. It appeared in *Kawashidai*, the paper of a regiment based in Obihiro in south-central Hokkaido. On the first day of the work, a soldier comments that the work is "interesting," to the surprise of a shapely farm girl bending over in the paddy near him. By the third day, his back aches from continuously being bent over and he cannot wait for five o'clock, when the work will come to an end. And on the final day, his back has gotten strong and he has become used to what is back-breaking work.[75] The second cartoon, which appeared in the *Akashiya*, shows the outcome that corps commanders, and probably some personnel, hoped for and in some cases achieved; a force member and village woman are mutually smitten and pair off away from the

**FIGURE 3.3.** This "Bangai-kun" cartoon strip appeared in the *Akashiya* on June 1, 1969. After the commander issues "10 rules" to follow when engaged in "agricultural assistance" in the first scene, the troops greet the villagers in the second scene. For Bangai-kun and a village woman it appears it is love at first sight in scene three. The fourth and final scene shows that the two have paired off and separated from the others in the midst of planting rice. Used with the permission of the Northern Corps.

rest of the group as they plant rice seedlings (figure 3.3).[76] The cartoon aptly represents the military-society integration that the SDF sought and to some extent achieved as the postwar military and society, once apart, came closer together in a process that changed both.

More glamorous than—though not as potentially romantic as—farm work was GSDF support of sporting events. In Hokkaido, personnel regularly prepared ski slopes and other facilities for regional and national competitions, and units across the country provided aid for sporting events from the 1950s onward. Like civil-engineering projects, logistical support for sporting and other events was unprecedented. As discussed in chapter 4, the Imperial Army showed limited interest in having its soldiers engage in sports, much less in supporting sporting events. This was not the case for the GSDF. Such work prepared it for the task of providing assistance for the Tokyo Summer Olympics in 1964, which is also discussed in the following chapter. The size of the 1972 Winter Olympics in Sapporo was much smaller, but the GSDF played a major role in ensuring its success as well.[77] Decades of involvement won the organization powerful friends among sporting-association executives and those involved in such activities.[78]

Through these public-service activities the GSDF and its allies sought to instill the idea that society, or at least certain segments of society, could not do without the military. This strategy was aptly illustrated by the experience of the future Nayoro mayor, Sakuraba. As in Sapporo and elsewhere in Hokkaido, the corps played a central role in Nayoro's snow festival. In fact, Nayoro Northern Corps units founded the festival as an open-base event in 1959. Five years later the event moved into town and personnel continued to construct its snow sculptures. In 1970, organizers decided to cancel the event because many base soldiers were scheduled to be away for training maneuvers. In response, union organizer Sakuraba and others rallied around the slogan "snow statues created by the hands of citizens" and obtained the aid of six local groups to organize what they dubbed the Mini Snow Statue Festival. Instead of constructing large statues like the corps, the upstarts put their efforts into creating attractions such as slides and mazes that would appeal to children. Around fifteen thousand people attended, which made the event a resounding success. Soon afterward, a chamber of commerce leader summoned Sakuraba to his office and scolded him for spoiling the possibility of residents realizing how boring winter in Nayoro would be without the Northern Corps.[79] Somewhat ironically, Sakuraba's efforts may have inspired the force to make the event more appealing to children, as slides and mazes subsequently became regular fare.[80]

The service rendered by the GSDF certainly won it backing, but it also opened it up to criticism. People of a variety of political stripes, including on the right, accused the force of stealing or wasting taxpayer money or wondered out loud if it engaged in outreach because the GSDF had nothing else to do. Labor leaders sometimes accused it of stealing jobs from workers; more than one leftist suggested that the force was so proficient at these nonmilitary tasks that the organization should turn its swords into plowshares and become dedicated to protecting people and property, aiding agriculture, and conducting civil engineering projects. In 1959, the Socialist Party recognized the SDF, but not as a legitimate defense force. Rather it proposed that it become the "Peace National Construction Force."[81] Praise for the organization's public service by its supporters sometimes unintentionally strengthened the arguments of the SDF's critics. Yoshida, who as prime minister a decade earlier had encouraged the force to proactively engage in disaster relief to bolster public support, now expressed concerns that such praise was leading people to forget the SDF's main purpose: "Disaster relief operations are part of the duties of the SDF, but they are not the reason for the existence of the SDF. I fear the public has a tendency to forget this fact."[82] To fend off suggestions that it become a force dedicated to disaster relief and civil engineering and remind people that its true value and primary mission was national defense, GSDF leaders insisted that all of these activities were indispensable training for defense. They justified, for example, farm work as a way for personnel to learn how to grow food in case they might need to wage an insurgency against an invading force and asserted that sculpting snow statues provided personnel from warmer climates with invaluable winter training.[83] Such statements were a bit ironic, because at the same time the GSDF was still using euphemistic words, such as "special vehicle" instead of "tank," to disguise its military nature.

## To Become a Trusted Self-Defense Force

Paradoxically, SDF commanders' second strategy to win public support during these early years—trying to increase trust in the force as essential for the defense of the country—highlighted the fact that it was indeed a military or at least a reliable, well-armed defense force. The historian Tomoyuki Sasaki observed that criticism from opponents of rearmament "made it impossible for the SDF to identify combat against foreign enemies as its reason for existence, as most national armies do."[84] But in fact, the message that the force often sent was one of realism; strong defensive capabilities were the best guarantee of peace. Commanders believed that a more prominent profile and greater interaction with the force would convince the public that its members were not the militarists of yesteryear that had brought the country misery and humiliation. The SDF was not just battling the legacy of the imperial military but also the deceptive way in which US occupation authorities and Japanese government leaders had created a military while calling it a police reserve force, a safety force, and finally a defense force. It also had to contend with the presence of the US military, which led many people to doubt even the defensive military value of the SDF. Many citizens did not believe the country faced a direct or immediate security threat because the United States was treaty-bound to protect Japan. If an attack did come, many people—on both the left and the right—did not think that the SDF was capable of adequately defending the country or even "contributing greatly" to its defense. This led them to regard the SDF and especially the GSDF as a waste of money that created the risk of the reemergence of militarism or, even worse, led Japan to become entangled in war because of the alliance with the United States and its bases on the islands.[85] This complicated calculus led to the public's lukewarm view of the SDF and was a constant dilemma faced by the organization and its personnel.

Perhaps the most subtle but effective means of attracting the gaze and thus the support of the public was to first catch their attention through music. The PRF organized bands almost immediately for internal ceremonies, but as evidenced by the participation of the NSF band in the 1953 Sapporo Snow Festival, the reorganized military also deployed music as an outreach tool. In the 1950s, few bands existed, and fewer still had the skill and time to practice like these official ensembles. Parading bands were less controversial and confrontational than other elements of the force. Band members wore uniforms, mainly performed popular numbers, and usually performed a familiar (prewar) and a new military march or two in conclusion. Their concerts were always free. And these bands visited remote towns and villages throughout the countryside where concerts were a rarity. The Defense Agency estimated that in 1959 alone, over 3.2 million people heard the GSDF Central Band play.[86] Performances by regional bands surely multiplied that number several times; the Northern Corps Band performed a remarkable 203 times at public events that year.[87] SDF bands continue their live free performances to this day.

The GSDF also used parades or processions to increase its exposure. Parades were held near regional headquarters at least once a year during the 1950s and 1960s. They began at the behest of Prime Minister Yoshida during the PRF years as an effort to win greater public support. Yoshida wrote in his memoirs that, in addition to proactively participating in disaster-relief operations, he had the force "parade in formation through the streets of large cities, such as Tokyo, so that the people might have the opportunity of being stirred by the sight."[88] On its first anniversary, on August 10, 1951, the

**FIGURE 3.4.** Troops based at Camp Nerima march through Hibiya in central Tokyo as part of a parade celebrating the one-year anniversary of the Police Reserve Force becoming the National Safety Force, October 15, 1953. Used with permission of the Asagumo Newspaper Company.

PRF held parades across the country, and then did so each fall to celebrate the establishment of the NSF and then the GSDF (figure 3.4). The following year (1952) when the NSF was established, its armored vehicles rolled through Ginza, Tokyo's central shopping district, on October 15. A photograph shows "NPRJ" (National Police Reserve Japan) still painted on one of the vehicles' front bumpers.[89]

After the SDF was established in 1954, it held anniversary parades every year on November 1 throughout the country. In Tokyo, Defense Academy cadets, servicemen (and some women), and weaponry paraded down the streets around Meiji Park in the morning for inspection by the prime minister, top officers, foreign dignitaries, and members of the public. The spectacle, however, extended far beyond central Tokyo, as hundreds of trucks, artillery pieces, and tanks departed after the morning review and wound through the capital on four long parade routes in all directions to return to bases at Asaka, Nerima, and, the centrally located GSDF headquarters, Ichigaya.[90] Depending on the location and event, processions did not necessarily restrict private traffic on entire streets or attract that many spectators. Many parades, though, seem to have concluded with a tank unit lumbering down the street.

Regional armies also held parades across the archipelago on the same day. In Sapporo, the preferred route was along Ōdori Park, which ran for twelve blocks through the center of the city (figure 3.5). The GSDF did not have any qualms about showing off its weaponry as though to demonstrate to society just what arms it did and did not have. It didn't neglect rural areas, either. On the way to exercises at training grounds such as Bekkai, in eastern Hokkaido, top brass ordered the convoys to go out of their way to roll through rural towns to get as much exposure as possible.[91] Such parades continued until the early 1970s, when opposition from progressive governors and mayors led the GSDF to begin holding them, or modified versions of them—more reviews than parades—on rather than off base.[92] By then, holding parades or processions was less necessary for the SDF because it had gained visibility with and greater support from the public, and the political downsides of trying to continue to hold them off base had become too high.

Well before that, the SDF sought to bring the public onto its bases rather than to just engage with people off base. These events usually were of three varieties. First, during the late 1950s and early 1960s, the SDF organized or participated in expositions throughout the country, some of which were held on base. Private companies often served as sponsors, organizing them

**FIGURE 3.5.** A GSDF Northern Corps fourteenth-anniversary parade featuring M4 tanks along Ōdori Park in central Sapporo, November 1, 1964. The GSDF held such parades across the country throughout the 1950s and 1960s, including just six months after the Anpo anti–security treaty protests. Used with the permission of the Northern Corps.

and partnering with the Defense Agency. The goal of such expos, declared agency chief Akagi, at the opening of the Defense for Peace and Modern Science Exposition held in Sendai in September 1959, was to "heighten defense consciousness" to ensure the "cooperation of the people" with the SDF.[93]

Expos used a variety of methods to bolster support for defense and strengthen public cooperation. These tactics were evident at a month-long exhibition held in Sapporo in the summer of 1958. As a part of the multisite Hokkaido Industrial and Science Exposition, the Northern Corps's Makomanai Base served as an exhibit space. Corps officials made every effort to attract as many people as possible. They understood the power of spectacle. As an *Akashiya* reporter reminded readers, "A picture is worth a thousand words, and this event is a golden opportunity to showcase the SDF's current situation."[94] Fortunately for the SDF, as a military it possessed plenty of hardware to create a feast for the eyes that could get the attention of young and old alike. Personnel prepared panels about the force, exhibited jets, helicopters, tanks, and artillery, made parachute jumps onto the spacious base, and arranged for leggy female dancers to perform. Like the expo in Sendai, the Sapporo exhibition highlighted science and space exploration, which were of intense interest to the public at the time because of the international space race and were used to make military weaponry seem less threatening.[95]

The names of the exhibitions themselves were telling. The Defense for Peace Exposition held in Nara Prefecture in 1958, and symbolic gestures, like the release of doves of peace at the start of the expos, underscored the SDF's goal of convincing citizens that a strong defensive posture would keep Japan peaceful and secure.

Some events specifically targeted families and children. Visitors could stay overnight in a tent for free to experience the outdoor life of a soldier, and on Children's Day youngsters could enjoy jeep rides. A photograph of one of the activities on Makomanai Base of the 1958 Hokkaido exhibition shows several children, watched over by two soldiers, standing on top of an M24 tank, which the caption of course calls a "special car" (*tokusha*). One child, wearing a helmet with goggles, aims what appears to be a 12-mm heavy machine gun, while other children wait for their turn.[96] Exposition organizers estimated that some 190,000 people visited the base during the event.[97]

Open-base events, live-fire demonstrations, and air shows were a second and more frequent way of creating opportunities to interact with the public. Sometimes these events mixed a bit military spectacle into more lighthearted entertainment. For example, the Eleventh Division organized a base event in the southwestern port city of Hakodate in 1963 in commemoration of its twelfth anniversary. On Saturday, its band performed a "citizen appreciation evening." Local SDF support associations organized dancing on Sunday morning and then in the afternoon held a sports day (*undōkai*), which featured drills demonstrated by specially trained rangers.[98] Other events were more serious. In 1962, the division staged a training exercise open to the public along the Toyohira River in Sapporo (figure 3.6). An estimated sixty thousand spectators, who gathered along the river's levees and bridges, watched a flyover by twenty-five ASDF jets, displays of artillery and tanks, and live-fire infantry maneuvers.[99] Such events were designed to increase the visibility of the SDF as an organization that could be trusted with the nation's defense. Leaders noted with pride that an estimated four million people participated in such events in 1959. They made special note that the number of women and children attending was increasing; nearly half of the participants were females between the ages from ten to forty years old. This demographic was of special interest to the SDF because many of the fiercest proponents of pacifism were women, and officials believed that they needed the support of mothers and sisters to successfully persuade young men to join the force.[100]

**FIGURE 3.6.** The GSDF Northern Corps's Eleventh Division conducting a public training exercise along the Toyohira River in Sapporo in the summer of 1962. The event, which included a parade of tanks and a flyover by twenty-five ASDF jets, attracted sixty thousand spectators, some of whom can be seen on the far side of the river. Based on the location of Mount Moiwa, to the left, it appears that this event took place just outside of Makomanai Base, which borders the river. Used with the permission of the Northern Corps.

The Northern Corps's initiative to start a snow festival at Makoma-nai in 1963 that ran simultaneous to the Sapporo Snow Festival was part of this strategy that sought to bring the public onto its bases. This event went beyond its personnel hauling snow and constructing snow sculptures, which was done behind the scenes and before the festival began. Welcoming visitors to their base gave community members the opportunity to inter-act with personnel and become more comfortable with the force. The first year, the base partnered with local junior high schools to build twenty-seven statues. Attendance, however, was not good. The site did not have a media sponsor, and transportation to the base on the outskirts of the city proved to be a challenge. The corps addressed the former issue by persuading the Mainichi Newspaper Company to become the base event's sponsor. It also persuaded festival organizers to recognize Makomanai as an official festival site in 1965.[101] Like in Nayoro, the corps created snow slides and live enter-tainment that appealed to families and children. Eventually, the transporta-tion challenge was addressed when a subway line including the Jieitai-mae (literally, "in front of the SDF") Station was constructed in preparation for the 1972 Winter Olympics. But already during the second half of the 1960s, organizers estimated that an extraordinary number of people—over a million—visited the base during the festival, among the three million who attended any of the festival's three sites.[102]

The GSDF's prominent and public role in the snow festival did not go unnoticed. In the mid-1960s, leftist critics of the force complained that such involvement was a "waste of tax monies" and argued that "even if the snow sculptures were small, they should be built by city residents" rather than an illegitimate military. The criticism so worried Satsu Kazuo, the festival's chairman and chief of the Sapporo Tourist Association, that he visited the Defense Agency to ask Director Matsuno Raizō for the SDF's continued sup-port. Matsuno readily agreed, apparently calling the division commander immediately, and then led a delegation of LDP Diet members to visit the festival the following February as part of a trip to observe Northern Corps winter training exercises. Satsu recalled later that in the end the SDF's desire to be "beloved" and "contribute to local society" ensured its continued sup-port.[103] This interpretation was confirmed by the division's public affairs chief. In a roundtable discussion marking the fiftieth anniversary of the festi-val in 2000, he repeatedly mentioned that individual personnel and the orga-nization as a whole thoroughly enjoyed some "two million people admiring their work" each year.[104]

"Join the force for a day" (nyūtai taiken) programs represented the third type of on-base event. In the late 1950s, SDF bases began offering the public, especially young men and boys, the opportunity to experience the life of personnel for a day, or at least a few hours. These events were often administered in collaboration with organizations like the Boy Scouts to try to minimize criticism from leftists, who feared the militarization of youth that had been a routine part of the prewar era.[105] As discussed further in chapter 4, despite such criticism, these programs grew dramatically in popularity and scope in the 1960s.

The SDF also used the mass media to reach an even wider audience. The organization produced programs that were shown in theaters or aired on television with the cooperation of national and local media companies.[106] To nourish relationships with media companies, the SDF provided movie studios with assistance to make commercial motion pictures and provided free aerial and marine transportation to assist reporters. In Hokkaido, the Northern Corps attempted to partner with the island's left-leaning, widely read, and, after 1998, only prefecture-wide daily newspaper, the *Hokkaidō shinbun*. The newspaper served as the principal sponsor for the snow festival, though never for the Makomanai venue specifically. The force got more positive coverage from a rival conservative newspaper, the *Hokkai taimusu*, which sometimes featured headlines and content so laudatory they seemed to have been produced by the SDF's public-relations office. Headlines marking the SDF anniversary in 1966, for example, read, "With the People of Hokkaido for 16 Years," "The First Time the SDF Saved the People of Hokkaido" (referring to a disaster-relief operation), and "The Continually Deepening Relationship between the Northern Corps and the People of Hokkaido."[107] Regardless of these efforts, media coverage of the SDF during the 1950s and 1960s largely matched the views of society at the time—acceptance of the force's existence paired with little enthusiasm and mild suspicion.

The imperial military had engaged in public outreach too, though less directly than the SDF. Instead it relied on a host of affiliated organizations to "mold . . . an obedient rural following."[108] Its bands and troops also performed and marched through the streets on special days, such as Army Anniversary Day (Rikugun Ki'nenbi), held throughout the country each March 10 from 1906 to celebrate the 1905 victory against the Russians at Mukden.[109] Local bases annually hosted open-base "military flag festivals" (*gunkisai*) on the anniversary of the date they had received their regimental flag from the emperor. Compared to postwar open-base days, military flag festivals emphasized martial ceremonial spectacle, such as precision drill marching and rifle salutes. But they also included plenty of eating and entertainment— such as sumo wrestling, theatrical and equestrian performances, and bicycle races—during which the public could interact more casually with the emperor's soldiers.[110] The annual autumn grand maneuvers, during which two competing units simulated battle, also offered a visual and audible spectacle for the public, and it required thousands of locals to provide lodging in their homes for visiting troops.[111] Many villagers enjoyed the band concerts the army put on during fall maneuvers.[112]

Yet, these events were merely the most prominent ingredients in a constant diet of militarization, and especially for base communities, daily social and economic interaction with the imperial military, which was heightened by the physical proximity of prewar bases. The steady fare of militarist ultranationalism and close contact led locals to strongly identify with the military and its soldiers, most of whom were conscripted from the region where they were stationed. In the city of Sakura in Chiba Prefecture, for example, residents referred to the regiment headquarters, located in the heart of the city, as Sakura-jō (Sakura Castle), which demonstrated its strong association with the community.[113] That said, the relationship between the imperial military and society was starkly unequal. Whereas postwar leaders and force supporters worried about SDF personnel having an inferiority complex, before 1945 the public often regarded military officers as arrogant and pitied conscripted men. Organizational and personal interactions shaped such views. For example, whereas GSDF maneuvers were held on vast government-owned grounds in remote areas like eastern Hokkaido, imperial military exercises were often held on private lands and left property damaged, to be repaired at the expense and with the labor of farmers.[114] The imperial military served the emperor rather than the people, and the people were expected to be at the service of the emperor's army.

Unlike its predecessor, the GSDF did operate from a position of strength. It had to deal with the Imperial Army's checkered legacy and the presence of foreign troops on Japanese soil. In the face of these challenges, the GSDF sought to be useful in a variety of decidedly nonmilitary functions and to prove that it could be trusted with the defense of the country. Both these strategies necessitated trying to make the organization as visible as possible. They also involved trying to influence the force's personnel in specific ways.

## "Shōwa Era's Farmer-Soldiers": Constructing the Northern Corps Man

As the SDF pursued strategies to justify its existence to society, officials attempted to shape personnel to represent the force in a positive manner. Through training, standards for appearance, and media produced by public-relations specialists, the force's leadership tried to mold, as well as represent, force members as thoroughly democratic and patriotic soldiers who were physically and ideologically prepared to protect the nation. These efforts were primarily aimed at male soldiers, who composed almost the entirety of the force, and were thus gendered in that way. The force's education and training regime sought to boost morale and internal unity and to inculcate in personnel a prescriptive form of patriotism redefined for a democratic defensive force. The indoctrination of the Northern Corps soldier illustrates one variety of this regimen. As elsewhere, senior officers wanted to foster a military-defense masculine identity. This identity took a unique form in Hokkaido, where over 70 percent of the troops stationed on the island came from elsewhere in the country.[115]

In Cold War Japan, one of the principal ways that top officers communicated with enlisted personnel was via internal newspapers, which each regional headquarters began to publish monthly in the 1950s. The oldest of these regional newspapers was the Northern Corps's *Akashiya*, which began publication in 1954.[116] It was initially published monthly, and then bi-weekly. According to the *Akashiya* staff member Irikura Shōzō, the paper had two main goals: fostering internal unity and disseminating information to individual members from senior officers, who exercised editorial control. Articles in the *Akashiya* took many forms, including greetings from commanders; announcements of force-wide and regional events and public service; reports about training; articles celebrating special moments in the lives of members, such as marriages and births; poetry and other literary compositions; and letters written by average soldiers that allowed them and others to "blow off steam."[117] Although it is difficult to ascertain what personnel thought of what they read, they did read the paper, as shown by two polls the paper conducted in the early and mid-1960s.[118] Commanders hoped not just that personnel would read the newspaper but also that it would influence their thinking and actions.[119] For this reason, they used the *Akashiya* to encourage, chide, and guide their underlings.

Through the *Akashiya* and other indoctrination, Northern Corps leaders sought to encourage troops to identify with Hokkaido in several ways. One of the most prominent methods of doing so connected personnel to the tondenhei, the farmer-soldiers the Meiji government sent to colonize Hokkaido beginning in the 1870s. The tondenhei were probably appealing to senior Northern Corps officers because they were former samurai who were associated with the spirit of the way of the warrior, and because they were not imperial military soldiers, associated with the darker excesses and mistakes of a more recent martial past. In contrast to the attention given the tondenhei, the *Akashiya* and other Northern Corps materials from the

Cold War decades rarely mentioned the samurai and bushido directly. This was not the case on the pages of *Chinzei*, the GSDF Western Corps's internal newspaper in Kyushu, a bastion of military tradition. Nevertheless, during these decades the force in general seems to have been reluctant to encourage its personnel to emulate the figures of the imperial soldier, and, to a lesser extent, the samurai.[120]

As commanders sent thousands of soldiers into the countryside in the mid-1960s to engage in agricultural assistance, the *Akashiya* channeled the figure of the tondenhei, one hand on a plow carving civilization out of the wilderness of Hokkaido and the other holding a rifle ready to defend family and community against a possible Russian (now Soviet) attack. A massive snow sculpture of a farmer-soldier that corps personnel constructed for the 1958 Sapporo Snow Festival may have deepened the corps's connection with the tondenhei (figure 3.7). This statue was not the only use of this memory. On the pages of the *Akashiya* and in training sessions, leaders repeatedly reminded personnel that they were the current "Shōwa era's farmer-soldiers"

**FIGURE 3.7.** Eleventh Division personnel at work constructing "three grand figures" (*eikō sannin zō*) from Hokkaido's early history, including a farmer-soldier (tondenhei) and an indigenous Ainu, at the ninth annual Sapporo Snow Festival in 1958. The third figure, in the rear, depicts a Kaitakushi (Colonization Agency) official. The full name of the statues was "three grand figures of the Hokkaido Exposition," referring to the Hokkaido Industrial and Science Exposition that was held that summer in venues across Sapporo, including on the Northern Corps's Makomanai Base. Used with the permission of the Northern Corps.

(*Shōwa-jidai no tondenhei*). Newly arrived soldiers from Kyushu and other regions, as well as local recruits, learned of the valiant sacrifices of these supposed kindred soldiers in lectures and tours of local museums that were an established part of training. Not surprisingly, Northern Corps versions of the tondenhei story match those identified by cultural studies specialist Michelle Mason in her analysis of dominant narratives about colonial-era Hokkaido. Like those told in other circles, narratives shared by GSDF trainers emphasized the role of male tondenhei, their connection to the central government, their national mission, their defense of the island (and thus Japan) vis-à-vis Russia, and their supposed patriotic and pioneering spirit.[121] From the time *Akashiya* commenced publication, its editors frequently printed articles that highlighted such themes. A five-part series of articles about the tondenhei, for example, ran for the express purpose of nourishing in personnel "a sense of affinity" for the corps's supposed farmer-soldier predecessors.[122]

In 1968, the same year that Japan celebrated the hundredth anniversary of the settlement of Hokkaido, in which the tondenhei played a central role, the Eleventh Division opened a history museum on Makomanai Base that was used both for internal training purposes and to educate the public. Museum exhibits narrated the defense of Hokkaido "from the tondenhei to the SDF," as the title of a pamphlet produced for its opening put it. Although exhibits did mention "the pride of Hokkaido," the Imperial Army's Seventh Division, it received far less attention as a predecessor to the Northern Corps than did the tondenhei, who did not produce the same kind of complicated memories as the Imperial Army.[123] Near the museum, personnel and visitors could also see a silo that dated from when the area was a ranch during the Meiji colonial years and a small building built by the US Army in the shape of the Pentagon after they converted the ranch into Camp Crawford at the beginning of the occupation. Unfortunately, neither one is still standing.

Another tactic to strengthen an affinity with Hokkaido was to encourage an attachment for the beauty of Hokkaido—both natural and feminine. The very name of the primary medium of instilling such identity, the *Akashiya*, quietly symbolized this goal. *Akashiya* means acacia, the yellow and white flower-bearing black locust tree that had come to be identified with the island. The tree was in fact an invasive "botanical colonizer."[124] Endemic to North America, the acacia proliferated throughout the world, spread by human colonizers. By 1873, it found its way to Japan, embraced because it was both useful and aesthetically pleasing. Meiji foresters recognized that its extensive root system was ideal for denuded landscapes such as industrial mines. It's beautiful, fragrant white flowers also made it immediately popular in newly constructed parks and along streets. Thanks to lyrics of a popular children's song, "Kono michi" (That street), that referred to "acacia flowers" in the trees around the Sapporo train station and the Sapporo Clock Tower, by the late 1920s the tree became associated with the city and with Hokkaido more widely. It was not surprising then that Northern Corps leaders chose it as the name of the paper and featured its blossoms along with an outline of the island for the newspaper's masthead.[125] Other ways that the corps highlighted its ties to Hokkaido were also subtle—or not so subtle. In 1963, the corps published a coffee-table book of photographs edited by Irikura, entitled *Hokkaidō to Jieitai* (Hokkaido and the SDF), which included many photos that depicted the Northern Corps's activities in the island's natural scenery. One photograph shows fighter planes flying over the snow-capped Daisetsuzan National Park, whose peaks rise in the middle of the island. Other images show a uniformed male soldier with a woman in civilian clothing strolling below the famous promenade of poplar trees on the campus of Hokkaido University in central Sapporo, scenes of flora and fauna, and attractive women posing in pastoral scenes.[126]

Commanders pushed their subordinates to emulate their tondenhei forefathers by putting down roots on the island. In the *Akashiya* and through programs such as marriage consultation centers, leaders encouraged personnel from outside the prefecture to marry local women and settle permanently on the island. In this way, corps personnel were told to "go native" (*dochakusei*), as it was called.[127] After extolling the scenic wonders of the northern island, introductory copy in the aforementioned book of photographs reminds readers that they "must not forget that the SDF staunchly defends the innumerable tourist treasures of Hokkaido."[128] As if to demonstrate that, the book is divided into sections showing Northern Corps personnel training in military maneuvers and living on base, exhibiting military hardware at expos, providing disaster relief, agricultural assistance, engineering work, and medical assistance to villages without doctors, and of course building sculptures at the Sapporo Snow Festival. Actual training, and images of all these activities, not only sought to prepare the troops for their defensive mission but also helped personnel embrace the identity of the Northern Corps and physically identify with the region they were tasked to protect. In this way, Northern Corps leaders sought to nourish in their personnel a pride in protecting Hokkaido and by extension all of Japan, and to instill in them and a wider audience a sense that the security and well-being of the northern frontier—both natural and human—was dependent on the SDF.

Northern Corps publications often portrayed personnel as men who could be entrusted with the protection and care of women and children.

The *Akashiya* featured many photographs of soldiers, almost always tall and handsome, posing with a woman or children. One photograph, taken by Irikura and published in the paper in May 1964, aptly captures this message (figure 3.8). A corps member stands with a young boy sitting on his shoulders. The boy has the soldier's cap on his head and seems to be trying to salute. The soldier has his arm around a slightly younger-looking girl who stands at his side. Both children are presumably his.[129] In the background are three carp-shaped windsocks, which are flown to celebrate the national holiday Children's Day on May 5, streaming in the wind from a pole above a rooftop. The carp, known for its vigor and power in swimming upstream, is associated with Boy's Day, which became Children's Day in 1948. The photo caption reads, "Happiness is the carp protecting the sky in May," and the image and text allude to the lyrics of the famous song "Koinobori": "Carp streamers are higher than the roof / The biggest carp is the father / The small carp are children / Enjoying swimming in the sky." These elements seem to suggest that the man, as a father and as a member of the defense force, protects all the country's children and provides for their happiness. The sociologist Satō Fumika found that SDF recruitment posters from the 1960s to the 1990s sent a similar message by portraying personnel, almost always depicted as male, as guardians of women and children.[130]

**FIGURE 3.8.** A photograph featured in the May 25, 1964, edition of the *Akashiya*, noting the celebration of Children's Day earlier that month. Used with the permission of the Northern Corps.

Such images served to create for the public a softer vision of the force and to distinguish it from the highly militarized masculine aura of the imperial military.[131]

Another way that the Northern Corps, the GSDF, and the entire SDF sought to build internal solidarity was to create a sense of group pride. A favored technique to bolster unity was the identification of "others," groups that allegedly represented something different. This principally took two forms, one political and one social. In the Cold War, Japan's geopolitical enemy was the Soviet Union, so the SDF's enemies were communists and socialists, represented domestically by the JCP and JSP. Because of the prohibition against involvement in politics, official publications like the *Akashiya* had to avoid being explicit about this view. Occasionally, Northern Corps leaders openly criticized these political parties, especially the JSP, the largest opposition party, but doing so publicly was risky. A broadside against the JSP in the *Akashiya* in February 1966, for example, caused an uproar in the Diet, and resulted in the dismissal of a top officer who was the editor of the PR section. As a result of this controversy, a private company rather than the GSDF became the publisher of the *Akashiya* in April 1967, even though all the writing and editing were still being done by the Northern Corps. The number of unsigned articles also increased, to provide protection for the organization. (The move to publish the paper privately also allowed the paper to begin publishing advertisements.)[132]

*Akashiya* editors used other techniques to criticize the organization's political foes. A relatively safe one was to include an insert in the *Akashiya* published by one of the force's nongovernmental support groups that advanced explicitly political arguments. For example, *Ezo sakura* (Ezo cherry), a special insert published by the Fathers and Brothers Association in April 1967, argued that a strong military defense was the best way to ensure peace. Another subtler but often used method employed by Irikura and his fellow *Akashiya* newspaper staff was having "average" citizens speak for them. This way the force could not be held responsible and could just claim to be quoting what people wrote or said. In 1961, the year after the anti–security treaty protests, the *Akashiya* added a regular feature "Shimin no koe" (Voice of citizens) for this purpose. In one, an unidentified citizen from Asahikawa urged SDF personnel to keep their chins up: "Hey SDF, don't blow your horn weakly. You are not the communist party, and citizens want the beloved SDF to be a more courageous organization."[133] In November 1966, after communists used a loudspeaker to protest the SDF's sixteenth-anniversary parade, Irikura turned again to sympathetic citizens to censure those who criticized the force. An unidentified "Student K" (K-sei) of Sapporo, in an ostensibly unsolicited letter to the paper, expressed his disgust at "obnoxious" communists and pleaded for the corps to "tell its young members of the unlimited love and support that many citizens feel for the SDF."[134] In these ways, the paper sought to boost the morale and unity of personnel by giving voice to others criticizing the force's political opponents.

SDF personnel also exhibited anxieties vis-à-vis another "other"—salaried white-collared workers (sararīman), the prototype of postwar masculinity who for many Japanese represented the "bright new life" in the 1950s and 1960s.[135] During these postwar decades and beyond, the figure of the salaryman symbolized manhood and social mobility, thoroughly eclipsing the military man, who had been completely discredited by defeat and occupation. By that same token, people regarded the reconstituted military and defense personnel as illegitimate and half-baked. It was the salaryman, as the sociologist Ezra Vogel found, whom the "young Japanese girl hope[d] to marry" rather than "independent shopkeepers, craftsman, and farmers," or in particular, I would add, SDF personnel, who "complain[ed] that they [could not] compete with salary men in attracting desirable brides."[136] Because it would have been inappropriate to denigrate members of the public that the force was defending, *Akashiya* editors once again allowed guest writers to express resentments directed at these men who were celebrated in the media as "company warriors." For example, Miyata Yoshifumi, a Waseda University student who served as a Spanish translator at the Olympic Village during the 1964 Tokyo games, asserted that force personnel were much more disciplined and responsible than salarymen.[137] Another letter from an unnamed but photographed second-year Sapporo high school student published that same year was more pointed. He urged SDF personnel to cast aside the "salaryman spirit" (*sararīman konjō*) and stop relying on US weaponry, so the public could respect them.[138] The SDF using salarymen, as well as US military men, as foils continued after the Cold War. In her anthropological fieldwork observing ground force personnel in the late 1990s and early 2000s, Sabine Frühstück found,

> [Force members] measure their masculinity primarily against that of other men, not women. Hence, the sense of community and comradeship of men in the Self-Defense Forces is not rooted in the marginalization of women. Rather, the Self-Defense Forces' organizational identity and the militarized masculinity of their service members are informed by past and present militarisms and have been molded by the until recently near-hegemonic position of the "salaryman," or white-collar worker, as the ideal representative of Japanese masculinity, the

legacy of the Imperial Army, and the tens of thousands of American troops stationed on Japanese territory.[139]

As Frühstück's analysis suggests, the construction of a defense force identity based on comparisons with the salaryman has been a constant for the SDF.

Unlike the post–Cold War SDF, the *Akashiya* and other corps publications rarely mentioned the Imperial Army and the US Army. As previously discussed, the *Akashiya* invoked the figure of the tondenhei farmer-soldier and largely ignored the imperial military soldier. It did include articles with war tales (*senki*) from the Asia-Pacific War, but these were less personal than those about tondenhei and did not seek to connect the soldiers involved with Northern Corps personnel. Likewise, the *Akashiya* almost never mentioned the US military and its soldiers. This silence was made easier by the fact that from the end of the occupation until the 1980s, although the US military was a partner in the defense of Japan, only top officials coordinated. In contrast, almost all personnel had almost no interaction with the US military unless they were among the relatively few who had contact with the military advisers, received training at US bases in Japan, or were dispatched to the United States for training. This was even more true for the Northern Corps because of the departure of almost all US personnel from Hokkaido by the mid-1950s.[140] The challenge that the US nuclear umbrella created for SDF efforts to forge a closer relationship with society, though, did not go unnoticed. In 1960, the US Army Attaché Col. Horace K. Whalen noted in an assessment of the public image of the force that the "tenuous concepts of 'state' and 'democracy,'" compared to the "pre-war images of Emperor and national destiny," "have failed to re-establish the identification of the people with their military forces." One of the primary reasons for this lack of affinity, he posited, was that Japan's "comparative military insufficiency and its dependence upon the United States" prevented it from "creat[ing] a popular image of strength and potency." For that reason, the force, "particularly the GSDF," was "acutely aware of its dubious status," and sought to win public support through outreach and public service.[141] It is therefore not a surprise that the GSDF as a whole, like the Northern Corps, brought as little attention as possible to its "dependence upon the United States," and its military.

From the founding of the PRF, politicians beginning with Prime Minister Yoshida, Defense Agency officials, and senior uniformed officers expressed considerable concern about SDF morale and, by extension, manliness. The *Akashiya* only rarely mentioned such fretting and it usually only appeared in pronouncements by top politicians and Defense Agency officials. In 1962, Director Shiga Kenjirō publicly voiced worry about the sense of "servility" and "inferiority" from which "SDF men" suffered. In an interview with the conservative daily newspaper *Tōkyō shinbun*, he declared it a priority to "infuse new spirit [seishin] into each individual SDF man as quickly as possible and make the SDF an SDF of the people in the true sense of the term." "As a long-term policy," he continued, "I started advocating the 'building of men' as soon as I took office." Concretely, Shiga emphasized education and job-training, specifically helping SDF personnel earn high school degrees at night schools and acquire technical skills while in the service, which would help those discharged be more employable and boost recruiting efforts.[142] But as Shiga's comments indicate, he was also concerned with intangibles, such as spirit, manliness, and morale.

Another way that civilian and uninformed leaders sought to boost force morale was through rules about physical appearance. Like other militaries, the SDF maintained a strict dress and grooming code. Communicating these rules and enforcing them internally was straightforward. At least as early as 1960, the appearance of personnel as they commuted to and from work became a sensitive issue. In metropolitan areas, some soldiers were reluctant to wear uniforms because of taunts and because it was unseemly for a uniformed soldier to "fight" for a train seat when commuting.[143] In 1960, Defense Agency Director Esaki Masumi publicly deplored the practice of members wearing civilian clothes, which made them look like salarymen, as they commuted to the office or barracks, and then changing into their uniforms while on duty.[144] In 1966, another director went further and ordered soldiers in Tokyo to don their uniforms while commuting to and from the agency's headquarters. In Sapporo, the *Akashiya* staff employed a familiar but cleverer persuasion technique: They let attractive young single women on the pages of the newspaper do the talking. In a 1965 article, a twenty-two-year-old Asahikawa college student, Keimatsu Rumiko, asserted that SDF soldiers "looked good in uniforms" and that she was impressed by their "disciplined manliness and spirit."[145] In another article, Kabeno Yōko, a young Sapporo bus attendant, was blunter. "There are force members who wear civilian clothes when they go out," she claimed, "but because they are Mr. Force Member [Taiin-san] it would be best if they wore a uniform. Maybe it would help them remember to be responsible for their actions." Kabeno, who of course was photographed in her bus uniform, added, "Girlfriends and fiancées will not feel any resistance about being seen with a soldier in uniform."[146]

Kabeno's latter message—that uniformed SDF personnel were desirable—was one that the *Akashiya* repeatedly stressed. This message, too, was meant to boost morale and male egos. As *Akashiya* articles admitted more than once, personnel had trouble finding marriage partners. This was a well-known problem. The paper blamed it on the specialized nature of their work. The fact that two-thirds of personnel stationed on the island came from other parts of the country did not improve their chances for marriage in Hokkaido. Neither did the fact that as the economy grew by double digits and well-paying private-sector jobs became plentiful in the 1960s, many people came to regard those who enlisted in the SDF as societal riffraff (*ochikobore*) who could not find better employment. Additionally, some parents objected to their daughters marrying an SDF man because of ideological reasons.[147]

To assuage such anxieties, Irikura and his fellow *Akashiya* staff deployed women to satisfy the male psyche. They frequently placed photographs of civilian women on the pages of the newspaper and other Northern Corps publications. The photos were not a ploy to get personnel to buy the paper; it was free. They may have been a way to encourage them to read the paper, though. If they did, they would have found that these women frequently spoke about their views of Northern Corps personnel. The women, who were purported to be representative Hokkaido females, often voiced a willingness, even an eagerness, to consider dating and marrying personnel. One such article in late 1966 described a gathering, sponsored by the Sapporo Friends of the Force Association, that brought together six single women ages of nineteen through twenty-six to discuss the "SDF as seen from the outside." Inevitably the conversation turned to—or was guided to—marriage, and participants made an assortment of heartening remarks about their readiness to be seen in public with a soldier in uniform and to consider marrying someone from outside of Hokkaido. One participant speaking for the group said, "We cannot stand a Beatles kind of guy. Of course, a disciplined, manly person is the most attractive. Therefore, we want a force member (*taiin*) who acts like a force member, and personnel dressed in their masculine uniforms are our favorite."[148] The Beatles had performed in Tokyo that summer and were already seen as symbols of an emerging counterculture and new form of youthful, rebellious masculinity, so the reference to the band as a counterpoint to the SDF is not surprising.

*Akashiya* editors sought to communicate the message that male personnel were desirable and women by then were to be desired in obvious and subtle ways. One method they regularly used was to place photos of women and of often uniformed male personnel interacting with these women on the top, left-hand side of the front page of the paper. The photos, for example, showed soldiers and women lounging in Ōdori Park (figure 3.9), strolling on a trail between the famous poplar trees on the campus of Hokkaido University, or as mentioned, chatting during a break while planting rice seedlings. *Akashiya* editor Irikura confirmed that these photos were almost all staged and/or chosen for the purpose of heightening heterosexual egos.[149] These front-page photos, which sometimes included only a caption, possibly accompanied by a short, fluffy article, were a constant feature of the paper in the 1960s. Inside the paper, a monthly page entitled "Camera News" or "Photo News" also regularly featured photos of women, often without captions, as if they were not necessary, and sometimes featuring upper-body nudity. In 1969, the front-page feature was replaced in the *Akashiya* (and around the same time in other regional corps newspapers, as discussed in chapter 5) with short introductions of women who were civilian base employees, force nurses, and uniformed personnel, replete with an appealing photo of each highlighted woman. In the *Akashiya*, editors initially dubbed this series "Butai no hana" (A unit flower).[150] Other similar names followed. Although it is next to impossible to know what the reception of force members was to such messages, we do know the intent of the messengers. Again, Irikura confirmed that boosting force morale, encouraging personnel to date and

**FIGURE 3.9.**   One of the many photographs in the *Akashiya* that feature Northern Corps personnel with local women. Like this one, which appeared in the July 25, 1962, issue, such photographs were often placed on the front page of the paper in the top left-hand corner opposite the masthead. This photograph was taken in Sapporo's central Ōdori Park. The article to the right reports on the corps's dangerous disaster-relief mission in response to the eruption of Mount Tokachi in south-central Hokkaido, which killed five miners. Used with the permission of the Northern Corps.

marry local women, and attracting readers were the anticipated outcomes of these efforts.[151]

The GSDF's establishment of the Women's Army Corps (WAC) in 1968 followed this same pattern. The creation of the corps provided women with access to a career field—the military—that since 1952 had been almost completely dominated by men, except for nursing. But defense officials were more motivated by a "desire to more 'efficiently' use male SDF soldiers in what they deemed to be 'manly' jobs'" by "placing women in so-called supporting jobs" than they were by feminist goals.[152] Until 1974, these supporting jobs involved clerical work. After that, other positions that were considered appropriate for women, such as medicine and dentistry, were opened to them. In 1986, almost all branches of the force were opened to women and by 2000 "all restrictions for women had *de jure* been lifted."[153] Despite these changes, SDF image-makers metaphorically mobilized WAC female personnel in many of the same ways they had previously deployed civilian base employees, force nurses, and other women. That is, they consistently used them to make the force more appealing for potential recruits and current personnel by imagining them as objects of heterosexual desire and as prospective marital partners who would prioritize motherhood and wifehood and become guardians of home.

An examination of *Akashiya* confirms such practical and symbolic deployment of women. When the first WAC personnel member arrived in Hokkaido in 1968 after three months of basic training in Tokyo, Irikura conducted an interview with her and her (male) Northern Corps commander. In that interview, the commander confirmed that one of the three main purposes of the WAC program was for women to replace men for office work so that male personnel could be sent to "frontline" (*dai issen*) positions. The other two purposes, he said, were giving everyone, regardless of sex, the opportunity to defend the country and boosting public support for the SDF, especially among women.[154] On the pages of *Akashiya*, top corps officers and sometimes the women themselves insisted that there were no differences in the opportunities given to and treatment of uniformed male and female personnel, but this was obviously not the case in policy, practice, or discourse.[155] The force, like most Japanese employers at the time, limited female members, most of whom had just graduated from high school, to clerical work, expected them to quit when they got married, and objectified them to boost internal male morale and shape external opinion. And just as the *Akashiya* staff had regularly featured civilian female base employees, force nurses, and other women in prominently placed photographs, they deployed these new WAC personnel in a similar manner.

One issue of *Akashiya*, from August 1, 1974, aptly illustrates such continuities. The front-page feature, now called "Zoom Up," introduced a WAC member, twenty-two-year-old Komatsu Makiko from Obihiro, who had joined the force three years earlier. A close-up photograph showed only Komatsu's face and shoulders. After completing basic training in Tokyo, Komatsu performed office work on the Asahikawa Base. She would soon, though, be quitting the force because she was getting married and, as the article put it, that meant she had "accomplished her mission." The feature concluded with, "Komatsu is 5'4 and weighs 116 pounds. It is unfortunate we don't have a photo showing her magnificent proportion."[156] Providing such information about a woman's body was typical for these articles. On page 4 of the same issue, the series "Photo News" included a photograph with not-so-subtle phallic connotations from the GSDF base in Rumoi, a small city north of Sapporo. The photo shows a female model in short shorts, sitting atop the cannon barrel of a tank with her long legs stretched along the cylinder. She is surrounded by several male personnel who are taking photographs of her posing. The caption reports that these personnel were among eighty who had gathered, including the regimental commander, to snap photos of her and another model who had been invited to the base for a day from Sapporo.[157] The GSDF regarded the women it employed as primarily serving the needs and desires of men, whether they were members of WAC, who were supposedly treated the same as their male counterparts, or were civilian base employees or models who were treated as obvious objects of sexualized fantasy. This sort of gendering was also an elementary part of the construction of the Northern Corps Shōwa farmer-soldier, one iteration of the wider SDF's and country's Cold War defense identity.

Persuading GSDF personnel based in Hokkaido that they were Shōwa farmer-soldiers, manly, and attractive was designed to boost recruitment, retention, and morale. Northern Corps leaders sought to instill this message in the minds of their members and then, through programs managed by matchmakers, to woo society one marriage at a time. Even a US military adviser took note that "SDF men marry[ing] local girls" was an effective strategy for the organization and its men to "obtain . . . the active support of the local inhabitants," to "win community support," and to "become part of the community."[158] Perhaps the SDF's efforts were successful after all.

Although the internal messaging of the Northern Corps may have bolstered the morale of its members and contributing to some marriages, just how successful was the organization in becoming a beloved Self-Defense Force? In Hokkaido, despite strong sympathies for the left among the citizenry, contemporary observers and participants alike came to regard Sapporo and the prefecture as a whole as unrivaled in their affinity for the armed forces. The Northern Corps's service activities, especially disaster relief, were key to this development. In 1970, Takashi Ota of the *New York Times* observed, that a "close relationship seem[ed] to exist between local citizens and the armed forces" in Sapporo.[159] A year later, the US consul in Sapporo observed, "The SDF is today an integral part of the Hokkaido community."[160] And the former Eleventh Division equipment battalion commander Kuboi, who served throughout the archipelago during his career from 1950 until his retirement in 1977, asserted in his memoirs that no other regional units in the country had "taken root in and become as heavily relied upon" by the surrounding community as the Northern Corps.[161] His colleague Irikura, another GSDF transplant to Hokkaido, expressed a similar view.[162] Perhaps these latter two views were the wishful thinking of veterans who wanted themselves as men and the organization with which they strongly identified to be accepted by the communities in which they lived. Yet, ample evidence supports their assertion that the Northern Corps succeeded in integrating itself into the socioeconomic fabric of surrounding communities and the broader region during these early Cold War decades. If this is true, then the SDF certainly transformed a society that, perhaps even more than those in other parts of Japan, was leery of the force and its men when they arrived in the early 1950s. Based on the experience of Hokkaido and examples from elsewhere, it is reasonable to conclude that other areas, rural as well as urban, also came to accept the SDF following similar patterns.

Did this process also change the SDF and result in military-society integration rather than just societal change? In the early 1970s, Leonard A. Humphreys reflected on his two-decade observations of the SDF in an essay entitled "The Japanese Military Tradition." "The SDF," he wrote, "fosters the image of a force ready to extend a helping hand to people during natural disasters. . . . They try to present an image of ready, friendly participation in local community activity offering their facilities for parades and festivals and their men and equipment for certain public works. They also seek recognition as a technologically modern military force with the latest equipment and the expertise to manage advanced conventional weapons and logistical systems well. All this is useful, but it is not the basis for a military tradition. That can only be found, at present, in the forerunners of the Self-Defense Forces," the imperial military.[163] Humphreys may have been right. Perhaps such public service and an emphasis on being a democratic defensive force dedicated to peace is a shallow, unstable foundation for a military tradition.

Yet, it does seem that even by the 1960s, the search for greater public acceptance and efforts to be useful to society had transformed the SDF just as they had reshaped society's attitudes toward the force. As previously discussed, some civilian and military officials periodically expressed resentment that the force's community-service activities led the public to forget its principal mission. In 1969, to cite another example, Northern Corps Lt. Gen. Hashimoto Masakata grumbled that all the service his troops engaged in for the snow festival distracted them from their core mission and was taken for granted by the public.[164] Over thirty years later, this tension continued. The year 2005 marked the final time that the GSDF's Makomanai Base hosted the Sapporo Snow Festival. The rationale for this decision was the planned reductions in the number of troops stationed there. The Eleventh Division was to become a brigade in accordance with a Defense Agency plan to modernize and prepare the SDF for new perceived threats, such as North Korea and China. Russia was no longer seen as much of a danger, so many personnel were being transferred to western Japan and Okinawa, and there was talk of closing some bases in Hokkaido. Deployments of personnel from Makomanai, Asahikawa, and Nayoro to southern Iraq from 2004 to 2006 also reportedly made it difficult for the corps to provide as much support for the festival as it had in the past.[165]

But just as the Northern Corps continued to assist the snow festival after Hashimoto's complaints in 1969, so too did it continue to do so after 2005. In short, it proved difficult for the corps to extricate itself from the festival, despite force reductions, evolving strategic priorities, and periodic grouching by top commanders. Since 2005, Eleventh Division members have continued to haul snow to and build the snow statues in Ōdori Park. Northern Corps soldiers still provide support for Makomanai Base's replacement site, a space on the other side of the city.[166] In short, sixty years of cooperation has created a relationship that is almost impossible to discontinue. Like other facets of Hokkaido's socioeconomic environment, the festival is so dependent on the GSDF, as the US Sapporo consular official observed in 1971 at the beginning of this chapter, that even today it would be impossible for this world-famous event to continue at its current scale without the force. By that same token, decades of involvement have made participation in the festival a tradition and source of pride for Northern Corps personnel. They, as well as former force members who live in Hokkaido and draw on years of experience building the statues, continue to be proud of the role they play in the success of the festival.[167] Conservatives may achieve their wish in transforming the SDF into a military in name and function along the lines of other global powers, but disaster relief and other forms of public service—expertise first developed domestically during the force's early decades and then refined in overseas operations since the end of the Cold War—will likely remain in some form as an unintended but enduring tradition of Japan's postwar, post–Cold War armed force.

## CHAPTER 4

# Public Service / Public Relations during Anpo, the Olympics, and the Mishima Incident

For many years since it opened in 2002, the GSDF Public Information Center on Asaka Base, located on the outskirts of Tokyo, has displayed over a half-dozen oil paintings by the artist Ono Hisako representing key events in the history of the force. Some of those events might be familiar to visitors: the founding of Police Reserve Force in 1950, Prime Minister Yoshida reviewing units in 1954, the first GSDF combined exercises with the US armed forces in 1981, the force's first United Nations peacekeeping operation in Cambodia in 1992, the Kobe earthquake disaster-relief mission in 1995, an international disaster-relief operation to flood-stricken Honduras in 1998, and Iraqi children standing around members of the force's Reconstruction and Support Group in Samawah in 2005. One of the paintings portrays the GSDF's involvement in the 1964 Tokyo Summer Olympic Games, a significant if perhaps less well-known moment.[1] Although popular memory has generally neglected the organization's contribution to the 1964 games, the SDF's backing was essential to their success. The International Olympic Committee (IOC) regarded the games as among of the best organized and executed ever, and organizers and media observers openly acknowledged the vital work provided by the force, particularly the GSDF. As Tokyo prepared to host the 2020 games, which were delayed until 2021 because of the coronavirus pandemic, SDF public-relations specialists at Asaka and the force's allies in the media sought to remind citizens of this history and tie it to the force's logistical support of the approaching Olympics.[2] As before, the SDF offered extensive support for the games in 2021.[3]

The SDF's involvement in the 1964 Olympics came in two forms: logistical support and the training of athletes. Ono's painting aptly captures that dual participation (figure 4.1). Representing the over seven thousand personnel who helped manage the Olympics, a force member stands in the right foreground on the side of a broad thoroughfare, his right hand holding a radio telephone to his mouth. He wears a formal green uniform with the official games badge—a red rising sun above five golden interlocking Olympic rings—sewn to his breast pocket. To his right are pictured two marathoners running down the road, surrounded by spectators waving Japanese flags. The leading runner is Japanese and a black African athlete follows a few steps behind. The Japanese runner undoubtedly represents Tsuburaya Kōkichi, who won the bronze medal and became the most famous of the twenty-one GSDF athletes who competed on the national team.[4]

Not only in official institutional memory but also according to many individual SDF personnel and some observers, the Tokyo Olympic Games were

**FIGURE 4.1.** Ono Hisako's oil painting depicting the 1964 Olympic marathon on display at the GSDF Public Information Center at Asaka Base, located near Tokyo. Photograph by author, 2019.

a defining moment for the force. Those three weeks in October 1964 seemed to transform the force's relationship with society. As Irikura Shōzō, the PRF recruit turned public-relations specialist discussed in chapters 1 and 3, stated, the Olympics allowed the organization and its members to "emerge from the shadows and shine" for the first time.[5] Likewise, Leonard Humphreys, a US Army attaché in the late 1950s and a MAAG adviser to the GSDF from 1962 to 1965, identified the games as a turning point in the SDF's campaign to gain acceptance.[6]

This deployment did indeed seem to mark a milestone for the SDF. For the force, the games were a huge success. Public service provided the force with a relatively noncontroversial and generally positive public-relations coup in its ongoing campaign against public alienation and ambivalence. Involvement in the Olympics, along with several high-profile disaster-relief missions in the early 1960s, earned the force a greater degree of legitimacy that boosted its reputation and helped it weather the turmoil of radical left-wing protests that swept the country—and much of the industrialized world—in the late 1960s. Though many on the left still saw the SDF as a constitutionally illegitimate, dangerous successor to the imperial military and as "puppet troops" embarrassingly overshadowed by US forces based in the country,[7] and though some conservatives regarded the SDF as not measuring up to the imperial military, by the mid-1960s a solid majority of citizens came to accept and support the status quo: the existence of a force providing self-defense for the country.

The decision to mobilize the SDF for the Olympics in 1964 and the decision not to do so in the face of the massive demonstrations that wracked the country in 1960 and in the final years of the decade created positive visibility and avoided negative exposure for the organization during a period that was marked by double-digit economic growth and Japan's return to the world stage through the Olympics, and was bookended by that turbulent political and social protest. This chapter uses the force's support of the Olympics—and how the force, its public-relations officers, the media, leftist critics, and others represented those endeavors—as a framework to examine the force's evolving relationship with society. It also evaluates the extent to which support for the Olympics and other actions and inaction during the 1960s altered an ambiguous relationship with a society that depended on, yet in many ways still only partially accepted, the defense force.

The decade of mobilization for—and not against—the people also changed the SDF. The organization and its personnel took pride in representing and supporting the country. Support for the Olympics was a highlight in ongoing public-service and public-relations outreach. It put the SDF in a spotlight that was overwhelmingly positive and enveloped by national pride as never before and rarely since. It solidified an esprit de corps tied to disaster relief, civil engineering, and other public service, as recounted in the previous chapter, that departed from that of the imperial military in spirit and substance.

The SDF's motivations for contributing to the Olympic Games were of course varied and complicated. The organization was not simply rendering public service for public relations. National pride may have primarily prompted institutional and individual actions. Like the general public, force leadership and personnel wanted to contribute to a national effort to complete Japan's reintegration into the international community by hosting the Olympics.[8] By the same token, they certainly wanted Japanese athletes to win many medals. Individual soldiers were also spurred on by more personal motivations, such as effectively representing the force and individual units and improving their prospects for promotion. But it is also clear that the force's leadership and rank-in-file personnel hoped that a byproduct of the organization's Olympic efforts, as of its disaster-relief activities, would be wider social acceptance. This would produce both abstract and concrete benefits, such as boosting internal morale, enlistment, and retention.

It is well known that the Tokyo Olympics helped to restore Japanese national pride. Writing decades after the games, prominent *Asahi* newspaper columnist Funabashi Yōichi noted that the Olympics provided Japanese with an opportunity to view the *hinomaru* flag, with its red disk on a white banner, for the first time since World War II without apprehension.[9] It also allowed them to hear the national anthem, "Kimi ga yo," without reservation. They could take pride that the flag was raised and the anthem played at the beginning of the games, because for the first time an Asian country—their country, once an international pariah, now accepted into the community of nations— was hosting the Olympics. Moreover, the sight (and the sound when Japanese athletes won gold) could be enjoyed without guilt, which heightened the pressure for Japanese athletes to excel.[10] The games also had immense significance for those who were raising the flag and playing the anthem—the SDF and its members. The Olympics gave the postwar military its first opportunity to make itself visible and heard by the entire country on a stage permeated by national pride. These dynamics contributed to military-society integration and the making of a defense identity that remained dominant, though contested, for the rest of the Cold War and beyond.

## Anpo, May 1960: "Not What the SDF Exists For"

Although no one seems to have noted it at the time, it was ironic that GSDF personnel descended on the streets of Tokyo in 1964. Just four years earlier, during the spring of 1960, Prime Minister Kishi Nobusuke decided to mobilize the force in response to the demonstrations against the renewal of the US-Japan Security Treaty, or Anpo as it is abbreviated in Japanese. Trouble had been brewing since the beginning of the year. In January, the government announced that it had signed a revised ten-year treaty in Washington. Kishi saw the revised treaty as one between equals that eliminated the subordinate independence of the 1952 agreement that Yoshida had submitted to. That treaty had not required the United States to consult with Japan prior to deploying its forces based in the country and had allowed the US military to intervene in Japan to suppress internal riots and disturbances. Kishi was confident that the 1960 treaty would open a new era in bilateral relations, but the treaty had to be approved by the Diet before it went into effect.[11]

As Kishi tried to persuade the Diet to ratify the treaty, opposition to further rearmament and fears that US military action in Asia might lead to Japan's direct military involvement on the continent sparked tremendous political resistance. The opposition was heightened by a profound distrust of the prime minister. Kishi had served as a bureaucrat in wartime Manchuria (Manchukuo). He had been listed as a class A war criminal by occupation authorities, but had escaped prosecution. As prime minister from 1957, he worked to overturn many occupation-era reforms, including constraints on the military, such as Article 9, and the economics-first policies of Yoshida. Revising and extending the treaty was part of these wider policy goals. Kishi was desperate to complete ratification of the treaty before the scheduled arrival of US President Dwight D. Eisenhower on June 19. According to constitutional rules, if the treaty was passed by the lower House of Representatives, it would automatically become law in thirty days even if the upper House of Councilors did not vote on it. So Kishi needed the lower body to approve the treaty by May 19. He accomplished the task that evening only by deploying several high-handed measures, most egregiously by having a force of five hundred policemen physically remove opposition politicians who were staging a sit-in in front of the speaker's office.[12]

The crisis in the Diet was matched by turmoil on the streets. Even before May 19, tens of thousands of demonstrators had taken to the streets, and the government's cavalier actions that evening further inflamed the situation. In the days and weeks that followed, the protests grew and as many as six million workers went on strike. By May 26, the number of protesters was said to have reached a half a million. On June 10, Eisenhower's press secretary, James Hagerty, arrived in Japan to coordinate the president's upcoming visit. As he left Haneda Airport to go to the US embassy, protesters mobbed his car and he had to be rescued by a US Marine helicopter.[13]

The protests led the government to consider something unprecedented: fully mobilizing the GSDF. Soon after the Hagerty incident, Kishi, supported by several cabinet ministers—including future prime ministers Ikeda Hayato and Satō Eisaku, who were disciples of Yoshida and mainstream conservatives—decided to invoke Article 3 of the 1954 SDF Law that gave the force the charge to defend against "direct and indirect aggression, and also maintain public order when necessary." This power was grounded in the original justification for the creation of the PRF in 1950: that an additional police force was needed to maintain public order and protect against an indirect invasion. But in 1960, the organization was no police force, if it had ever been one. Yet this domestic security rationale still had significant support among conservative politicians even though it had never been fully used.[14] As discussed in chapter 1, even when the force was called the Police Reserve Force, many political leaders and senior force officers were reluctant to deploy the force for that purpose. But with the backing of many members of his cabinet, Kishi decided to mobilize the GSDF so that Eisenhower could make his scheduled visit and sign the treaty. Late on the night of June 14, Kishi summoned Defense Agency Director Akagi to his residence, which was surrounded by protesters. Over a hundred thousand police had been deployed throughout the country and they appeared to be at a breaking point.[15] Kishi and others regarded the protests as "akin to an indirect invasion backed by the international communist movement."[16] Already other cabinet ministers and government officials had been pressuring Akagi to use the force to provide relief for the police. (There was even talk of asking the United States to mobilize its troops stationed in Japan, because the new treaty, which forbid precisely such intervention, was not yet in force.) Despite this pressure, Akagi attempted to rebuff Kishi. His concern was that deploying the force would irreparably damage the SDF's fragile relationship with society. "If we send them in," he argued, "they would have to be armed, with at least machine guns. They may end up having to use them. If that happens, many people may die. That would be Japanese killing Japanese and that is not what the SDF exists for. It exists to protect against foreign enemies."[17] Many civilian bureaucrats and uniformed officers within the Defense Agency backed Akagi's stance.[18]

The protests became even fiercer the following day as the cabinet wrestled with how to respond. An estimated hundred thousand members of Zengakuren (All-Japan Student Federation) gathered near the Diet. In clashes with police that evening, Tokyo University student Kanba Michiko was killed. The next day, on June 16, Akagi carried with him to a cabinet meeting a letter of resignation that he was prepared to submit if ordered to mobilize the GSDF. To his surprise, Kishi relented. He announced that he had decided to ask Eisenhower to cancel his visit.[19] The new treaty automatically went into effect on June 19, even as demonstrations continued to rage in the streets. The unrest only subsided after Kishi resigned as prime minister four days later. Kishi's success in renewing the treaty, along with his defeat and resignation, constituted a defining moment in the ascendancy of the country's military-defense identity. It marked the "consolidation of the low-key, minimalist approach to defense and national security begun by Yoshida."[20] Kishi's successors as prime minister, Ikeda (1960 to 1964) and Satō (1964 to 1972), returned to and further strengthened the doctrine of their mentor Yoshida by prioritizing economic growth over greater geopolitical autonomy and rearmament.[21]

Critics on both the left and the right criticized Akagi's decision. "The left-wing opposition argued that Mr. Akagi wanted to suppress the disorders but hesitated to do so because he was afraid to damage the image of 'the people's Self-Defense Forces'—an image which is necessary for the rebuilding of the nationalist, militarist spirit upon which a future military take-over must be based," the political scientist Martin E. Weinstein observed. "The rightist critics accused the Defense Agency bureaucrats of using the armed forces as a 'toy,' and of placing their own political ambitions above the safety and order of the country." Both sides, though amiss in their conspiracy theories, concurred that Akagi's decision was based on his "concern over the popular response to the use of the Self-Defense Forces for suppressing internal disorders."[22] The reluctance to mobilize the force against the people had grown stronger since the PRF was partially mobilized just days after the occupation ended.

Even as Akagi blocked Kishi's request to call out GSDF troops, he did have the force support the police behind the scenes by providing them with food, trucks, lodging, and other items, and he readied some armed troops to intervene if the police were overwhelmed and the situation got completely out of control, but he did not mobilize them against the protesters.[23] Yet, just a few years later, again motivated by similar concerns about the relationship of the force with the people, the government sent personnel into the streets, though for a radically different mission.

## Olympic Material Support

The SDF's support of the Olympics was extensive and varied. Its work began in earnest over two years before the summer games opened in October 1964. The month was chosen to avoid Tokyo's stifling summer heat and humidity and because meteorologists judged it unlikely to rain then. In 1962, three years after the IOC awarded Tokyo the games in 1959, the national organizing committee requested the assistance of the SDF. In response, the Defense Agency outlined a plan of support that involved all three branches of the force but was led by the GSDF. Force commanders mobilized the organization's unrivaled mechanical power and logistical expertise for the games to augment an intensive national effort to host athletes and visitors. As the games official report recounts, SDF assistance involved "7,500 personnel, 7 ships, 12 air-planes, 740 vehicles, and approximately 820 units of communication equipment, and three salute-guns." The GSDF Eastern Corps oversaw the Tokyo Olympic Support Command (TOSC), with the support of personnel from the three service branches—ground, maritime, and air—from across the country and cadets from the NDA. TOSC comprised seven groups: command headquarters, ceremonies, communications, medical services, air and ground transportation, Olympic Village management, and event support.[24] Personnel also participated in large numbers in the Olympic torch relay as it made its way through the archipelago from Okinawa to Tokyo after arriving from Athens. In Kyushu alone, eighty-nine members of the Western Corps served as torch-bearers.[25]

Providing logistical support for the Olympics gave the SDF an unsurpassed opportunity. The role of national military forces in providing security at the Olympics has become familiar, after the Black September Palestinian attack on the Israeli team during the Munich games in 1972 and since the September 11, 2001, attacks. But national militaries fulfilled key roles in ensuring the success of the modern Olympic Games well before these incidents and through involvement beyond just providing security. The Greek military helped to manage the marathon course at the first Olympics in 1896. The Wehrmacht, along with other entities of Hitler's Nazi regime, played a key role in orchestrating the 1936 Berlin games.[26] At the winter games in Squaw Valley and the summer games in Rome, both in 1960, the US and Italian militaries provided significant manpower and technical expertise.[27] And over twenty thousand German soldiers provided assistance at the 1972 games. Unfortunately, they were not instructed to devote much attention to security, which helps to explain the ease terrorists had in entering the Olympic Village.[28] Thus, in some ways the SDF's contributions to the Tokyo games were not extraordinary. But the Olympics were far more important to the SDF than to other militaries because for Japan's postwar force, the stakes were much higher.

Months before the games began, divisions throughout the country dispatched soldiers to Tokyo. One such member from Hokkaidō's Northern

Corps was Lt. Satō Noboru, who served in the Spanish section of the Olympic Village. SDF organizers may have selected Satō in part because he had already spent a year at the US Army Air Defense Artillery School at Fort Bliss in El Paso, Texas, which numbered him among the 13,790 SDF personnel to receive instruction in the United States from 1950 to 1963.[29] Before departing for Tokyo, Satō and 18 other Northern Corps personnel gathered at the American School on the US Air Force base in Chitose for three weeks of Spanish-language training conducted largely in English by a Mrs. Melendez, the wife of a US captain.[30] In this and other ways, the US military quietly aided the preparations for the games. It also returned to Japan what the Americans called Washington Heights, land in the central Tokyo area of Yoyogi that had been used for US military housing since the occupation, so that it could be transformed into the Olympic Village, a map of which SDF and US military officials are looking at in the photograph below (figure 4.2). In the village, Satō and his TOSC colleagues guarded the entrances, patrolled the village, and responded to the daily living needs of some 7,500 athletes, coaches, and officials from 110 different countries, which involved duties ranging from taking care of belongings to dealing with backed-up toilets.[31] Just as the Olympics united Japanese in celebrating the nation hosting the event, personnel gathering from units throughout the country to provide support fostered a greater sense of organizational

**FIGURE 4.2.** Left to right, GSDF TOSC officials Lieutenant General Umezawa, Colonel Yoshiide, Colonel Ōkouchi, and Colonel Tabata Ryōichi meeting with two US military officials, General Worthington and Colonel Palia, dressed in civilian clothes, about plans for the Olympic Village. Raymond Aka, a Japanese American civilian MAAG employee and translator, sits to the left of the two Americans. Undated photo. Used courtesy of Raymond Aka. Author's collection.

pride in their work. And personnel appearing in internal newspapers and the wider media boosted force morale.

Not all the SDF's responsibilities were removed from the limelight of spectators and television cameras. The duties of the ceremonial support group during the opening and closing festivities, in particular, put the force on full display. The SDF provided over half of the personnel for the 530-member band, 108 NDA cadets led each national team into the National Stadium carrying placards displaying the names of each country, soldiers hoisted the flags of the medalists, artillery experts fired cannons in salute, and most spectacularly, five ASDF Boeing F-86 Sabre jets traced the five interlocking Olympic rings in the clear blue sky to culminate the opening ceremony on October 10 (figure 4.3).[32]

Whether parading in full view or working behind the scenes, like personnel along the marathon route, members of the SDF appeared—often in their military uniforms—in front of millions of live spectators, newspaper readers, and radio and television audiences during the Olympics and in

**FIGURE 4.3.**  Force personnel in the stands of the Olympic Stadium watch ASDF pilots trace rings in the sky as a part of the Tokyo Olympics opening ceremony on October 10, 1964. Photograph by Kubota Hiroyuki, National Defense Academy Archives. Used with permission of Maki Katsura and the National Defense Academy.

the months and years leading up to the games. An estimated 90 percent of Japan's population of nearly a hundred million watched via television the opening ceremonies, the event during which the force was most visible.[33] Even TOSC's more mundane tasks, such as receiving training to transport Olympic athletes around the city, elicited media attention—both national and local—as Olympic fever gripped the country in the months before the games began. Once they began, an astonishing percentage of Tokyo residents—over 95 percent—indicated that they thought the Olympics were very or somewhat successful, according to a poll conducted by the national broadcaster NHK.[34]

## The GSDF's Olympic Athlete Training Program

Although many who witnessed the Olympics, whether in person or via television, may have beheld the supporting role of the thousands of SDF personnel, the starring performances of a few GSDF personnel who were members of Japan's Olympic team drew even greater attention and adoration. The media celebrated the feats of weightlifter Miyake Yoshinobu, who claimed Japan's first gold medal of the games. And it raved over Tsuburaya Kōkichi, who finished sixth in the ten-thousand-meter race and a week later won bronze in the marathon. This was Japan's only medal in track and field during the games and the country's first in twenty-eight years in that category.[35] Placing athletes on the Olympic team provided the SDF with an excellent opportunity to gain recognition and intense backing. In the heat of international competition, what citizens—including hard-core leftists who were opposed to the force's very existence—could restrain themselves from cheering for the force's athletes competing for Japan?

Before the 1964 games, neither the SDF nor its predecessor the imperial military had ever engaged in the systematic training of athletes. Probably because of its greater international and cosmopolitan character, the Imperial Navy provided more support for sports than the Imperial Army, but it did not allocate resources for training elite athletes. Nevertheless, Japan's first gold-medal-winning swimmer, Tsurata Yoshiyuki, who won the two-hundred-meter breaststroke at the 1928 Amsterdam and 1932 Los Angeles games, began to swim competitively after he joined the Imperial Navy in 1924.[36] The Imperial Army also provided some backing for sports but by the 1930s came to view competitive sports and their commercialization with suspicion. The only Olympic sport that soldiers participated in was equestrian events. This sport was also one of the few for which top officers had much respect. Prewar soldiers who participated in the Olympics, such as Col. Baron Nishi

Takeichi, who with his horse Uranus won a gold medal in show jumping at the 1932 Los Angeles games (and died during the defense of Iwo Jima in March 1945), succeeded more because of their status and wealth rather than because of active army support.[37]

The attitude of the reestablished postwar force toward athletics was a marked departure from that of its predecessor. This was apparent almost immediately in the PRF camps. The change occurred in part because of US influence. Remember Satō Morio's memories of playing baseball or softball daily on a beautiful diamond until weapons arrived and training began (chapter 1). Such support continued as PRF, NSF, and GSDF officials encouraged the participation of personnel in variety of sports and internal and external competitions. Although small of stature, Satō excelled at baseball and was chosen from his division to play on one of the top ground-defense teams in national tournaments.[38] Still, until Tokyo was awarded the 1964 games, the SDF had offered little official support for competitive athletics on the international level, and only one member made the Olympic team before the Tokyo games (in rifle shooting at Rome). Since the twenty-one GSDF personnel made the 1964 team, hundreds of members of the military have competed at the Summer and Winter Olympics, and over two dozen have medaled.[39] This involvement is another way that the GSDF was transformed by its engagement with society, and in this case, specifically with the Olympic Games.

In other countries, many militaries had for decades been engaged in training athletes for international athletic competition and especially the Olympics. Not surprisingly, soldiers had long dominated equestrian and shooting events, but military physical training programs and teams in Britain, the United States, the Soviet Union, and elsewhere systemically trained their soldiers for other sports, particularly in the 1950s.[40] US athletes affiliated with the US military at the 1956 Melbourne summer games, for example, numbered seventy-nine, forming a majority of the team, and won twenty-five medals, which if they had competed as a separate team would have placed them fifth behind Hungary, Australia, the United States, and the top medal-winner, the Soviet Union.[41] Beginning with the Tokyo games, the SDF joined its military counterparts in mobilizing its personnel for international sporting competition.

The initiative began in late 1960 when the new Defense Agency chief, Esaki Masumi, ordered the creation of facilities dedicated to the training of athletes. Japan had sent the third largest contingent of athletes to the 1960 Rome games after the Soviet Union and the United States but came away disappointed after only winning gold medals in gymnastics. Before the Tokyo games, Esaki boasted to other cabinet ministers that "the crack members of the 250,000-strong SDF will claim five or six gold medals."[42] To accomplish such goals, GSDF officials established the Physical Training School (Jieitai Taiiku Gakkō) on the grounds of Asaka Base in August 1961. The school had two principal missions—training physical-exercise instructors for the GSDF and preparing athletes for international competition. For the latter aim, the school focused on six sports—weightlifting, boxing, wrestling, shooting, canoeing, and track and field events—and only on male athletes.[43] (In the early 1960s, there were no female members of the SDF, except for nurses, a vocation deemed appropriate for women.) Staffed by dozens of coaches, the program recruited a handful of established athletes, such as Miyake, a Hōsei University student and winner of a silver medal in the bantamweight (56 kg) division in Rome, to join the force in exchange for financial and training support.[44] The program also drew on the ranks of the quarter-million members of the SDF. By March 1963, school officials selected sixty-eight athletes to undergo intensive training, including two others besides Miyake who joined the force specifically to prepare for the Olympics.[45]

The GSDF's entry into the training of elite athletes elicited considerable excitement and some concern. The opening of the Physical Training School, with its commitment to identify and train hundreds of young men with athletic talent in new facilities that might also be open to other athletes, was welcomed by the sporting world.[46] In 1961, that world was resource-starved, with slim government and educational budget backing and little corporate sponsorship. The country's economy had only returned to its prewar level in 1955 and was just beginning to experience a decade of double-digit growth. Some companies sponsored teams, like the volleyball squad of the textile manufacturer Nishibō that formed the core of the women's national team, which competed in industrial leagues. To be sure, some commentators expressed anxiety about what the force's entry into athlete development might represent. Leftists, including on the floor of the Diet, worried that the force would use sport and the Olympics primarily to burnish its image, and questioned sporting officials about whether the SDF was receiving preferential treatment. Some pundits questioned whether complete government funding (through the military) of sports training represented a violation of the modern Olympics founder Pierre de Coubetin's ideals of amateurism and the advent of state amateurism along the lines of the Soviet Union's training of athletes in its fierce international rivalry with the West. Still, within sporting circles, the greatest concern about the Physical Training School was that it would be closed after the games ended, because GSDF leaders would not make firm commitments about its future.[47]

Force athletes did not win five or six gold medals as Esaki had boldly predicted, but they met and, in the case of Tsuburaya, exceeded immediate pre-Olympics media expectations. Before the games began, the press focused primarily on the prospects of Miyake as well as of Tsuburaya, whose meteoric rise in 1963 from relative obscurity had captured the country's attention. On the third day of the games, Miyake captured Japan's first gold medal in the featherweight (60 kg) division with a world-record-setting lift. Miyake remained in the GSDF and won another gold medal at the Mexico City games four years later; he went on to become a coach and then, in the 1990s, the director of the Physical Training School.[48]

Tsuburaya's bronze in the high-profile marathon was much more dramatic than Miyake's gold and his background was one with which many of his compatriots (and fellow soldiers) could identify. Indeed, because he came from a humble background and was painfully shy, he became a sort of everyman. News accounts almost invariably reminded readers of his roots in Tohoku, the northern region of the main island of Honshu known for its grinding poverty, and frequently identified him as "the SDF Tsuburaya." They praised Tsuburaya for his serious demeanor and his good manners, which they often interpreted as deriving from his military training.[49] Born and raised in a large family with five brothers and one sister in rural Fukushima Prefecture, Tsuburaya joined the force in 1959, when all other employment options failed him. He was not a good enough runner to be hired by a company to join one of the few corporate-sponsored clubs or to compete on a university track team, and he was not a good enough student or from a family of enough means to go to college. Only several years after joining the GSDF did he become an athlete of national and then international stature.[50] As a result, the general public and SDF members linked his success directly to the armed forces. Like Miyake, Tsuburaya remained in the force after the Tokyo games and trained for the Mexico City Olympics. His preparations, however, were hampered by serious back problems and then an injury to an Achilles tendon. On January 3, 1968, as it became clear that his hopes were out of reach, Tsuburaya, isolated and depressed, weighed down by national anticipation that he might win another Olympic medal, and distraught that his onetime girlfriend had married someone else after his commander had not allowed him to get engaged to her before the Mexico City games, committed suicide by using a razor blade to slice a carotid artery in his room at the Physical Training School.[51]

Four years earlier, though, as the marathon—the final track and field event of the games—began at one o'clock on October 21, the eyes of the nation were fixed on Tsuburaya. A week earlier he had raised expectations by performing well enough to place sixth in what was thought to be his best event, the ten-thousand-meter race. The nation's intense, hopeful gaze is captured by Ichikawa Kon's official IOC documentary, *Tokyo Olympiad*. The film, which partially drew from the live television broadcast of the marathon that including aerial shots taken from SDF helicopters, provides glimpses of how tens of millions of people witnessed the race, whether along the route or via television.[52] The film introduces a dozen or so of the frontrunners one after another as they pass through the streets. The final runner introduced is Tsuburaya. The camera lingers on him for a few moments, in contrast to previous runners, then it cuts to a series of short clips showing spectators—including a man holding a child on his shoulders, a group of young women, and a close-up of an elderly woman—a cross section of an estimated 1.2 million fans lining the road cheering for Tsuburaya. The television announcer, too, repeatedly urges Tsuburaya onward: "Tsuburaya *ganbare, ganbare*" (Go, Tsuburaya, go).[53]

Their cheers were not in vain. Abebe Bikila, a sergeant in the Ethiopian army and gold medalist in Rome, entered the stadium first and repeated his Rome marathon victory in Olympic-record time. Several minutes later, Tsuburaya entered the stadium in second for one final lap (figure 4.4). Britain's

**FIGURE 4.4.**    Tsuburaya Kōkichi leading Britain's Basil Heatley in the final stage of the marathon as they approach the Olympic Stadium, where on the final turn of the lap around the track Heatley passed Tsuburaya to win the silver medal. The four uniformed figures in front of the car marked with the International Association of Athletics Federation (IAAF) banner may be GSDF personnel providing logistical support for the event, like the uniformed man depicted in Ono's painting. October 21, 1964. Used with permission of the Asahi Newspaper Company.

Basil Heatley followed a moment later and on the last turn sprinted past an exhausted Tsuburaya to take the silver.[54] Tsuburaya, though, had clearly given his all to win the bronze.

## Public-Relations Successes and Missteps

Late that afternoon, the Defense Agency announced that it would award Tsuburaya and Miyake with the SDF's top decoration in recognition of their Olympic medals. The agency appeared anxious to capitalize on the excitement of the moment, before the games ended and attention turned elsewhere, to remind people that the two athletes represented the force as well as Japan. The timing and apparent intent of this move did not go unnoticed. To some observers, the decorations seemed like a blatant attempt to take advantage of their accomplishments and an unnecessary distraction from the ongoing competition before the games closed a few days later on October 24. Even in the right-leaning daily newspaper *Yomiuri*, sports commentator Kawamoto Nobumasa forcefully criticized the agency for not having "at least waited until after the games were over" to bestow the honors. Civilian and uniformed leaders could take solace, though, in the fact that Kawamoto immediately pointed out, "If the agency was going give out decorations, it should give them to personnel who supported the games behind the scenes, such as the band members, helicopter pilots, and others. They are the people who really deserve to be honored."[55]

This minor controversy highlights the various ways that the SDF's contributions to the Olympics, both athletic and material, were represented by the force, the mass media, and critics of various political stripes. The force was best able to convert its public service into positive public relations when it was perceived as not trying to do that. Any move deemed an overt attempt to generate positive public relations risked provoking criticism that could erase or at least discolor the positive impressions created by the force's contributions. Ever since it was announced that the SDF would be training athletes and providing logistical support for the games, many newspaper accounts mentioned that the Olympics offered the force an excellent public-relations opportunity and that this was one of the primary motivations for the leadership's enthusiasm for assisting the Olympics.[56] As a result, the SDF had to proceed as if it was not trying to take advantage of the games to enhance its image at the same time it was attempting to do just that. This was a difficult balance to achieve. The strategy that the force generally opted for was to let its actions speak for themselves and hope others would speak favorably of them.

The SDF's challenge was complicated by the fact that its leadership and public-relations officials' appeals to the organization's rank and file to take advantage of the Olympics to burnish the external image of the force sometimes found their way into the mainstream media as well as into the hands of leftist critics. In internal newspapers and speeches, Defense Agency officials and SDF officers repeatedly reminded personnel that the Olympics provided the force, as one internal magazine put it, with the "best PR tactics ever."[57] They also sought to leverage the SDF's involvement to boost internal morale and, as discussed in chapter 3, to communicate to members a set of normative expectations about how they should behave in order to improve the force's relationship with the public.

The resulting media discourse was in general positive. Mainstream newspapers and magazines routinely reported on the Olympics-related activities of the SDF and usually did so in an objective, just-the-facts manner. When they strayed from this pattern, it was often to focus on some official playing a key organizational role, such as interviews with the officer in charge of TOSC, and such coverage tended to humanize the force and its members.[58]

A few other themes are apparent in reporting on SDF participation in the games. First, both media commentators and force officials frequently tapped into visual metaphors that had been used, as noted in the introduction, to describe the force since 1950. Since its establishment, critics of the force had regularly described it as a "hidden army" (*kakure no gun*) or "shadow army" (*hikage no gun*), and its personnel as *hikagemono*, literally "shadowy things." The multiple meanings of *hikage* made it a particularly rich word to use. These include a person who lives in obscurity; a social outcast; a person with a shady past; a ruined person; an ex-convict; and a kept mistress. None of these are positive connotations. Though it is difficult to know precisely what critics meant when they denigrated personnel as *hikagemono*, the term captures all three of their difficult relationships: alienated from and by society, stained by the imperial military past, and rendered an illegitimate and unequal partner to the US military.

In the context of the Olympics, critics, more neutral observers, and even allies adopted similar language. Newspaper accounts repeatedly mentioned that personnel were working in the shadows of the Olympics. So too did a book that celebrated TOSC's service. Within months of the Olympics, the publisher of the *Asagumo*, a daily newspaper similar to the *Stars and Stripes* that began publication in June 1952, issued *Tōkyō Orinpikku sakusen* (Tokyo Olympic tactics), a collection of experiences composed by TOSC participants. In the introduction, Japan Olympic Committee president Takeda

Tsuneyoshi, a former prince, lieutenant colonel in the Imperial Army, and Olympic equestrian participant at the Berlin games, wrote of his wish to "make widely known to the public the hard work and good humor of the SDF, which has been in the shadows."[59] Elsewhere, a magazine commentator, who praised the SDF for its "gold-medal level" service, stressed the importance of its personnel being "close-up" in "front" of the entire nation's "eyes."[60] Likewise, leftists objected to the SDF emerging from the shadows at the opening ceremony to visually assault spectators, who they asserted had no desire to see it and its so-called service.[61] If there was one thing that both allies and critics of the force seemed to agree on it was that the SDF making itself visible at the Olympics would have a powerful effect on society. Proponents of the SDF believed that the response to such images would be positive, but their repeated use of words like "shadow" likely reminded people of the force's complicated past.

A second theme identifiable in discussions about SDF involvement was media's, force officials', and critics' frequent use of the vocabulary of war to portray the logistical and athlete-training support of the organization. They applied words such as "deploy" (hahei), "mobilize" (shutsudō), and "tactics" (sakusen) to describe actions that were not nearly as dramatic as armed conflict.[62] One article even sensationalized a minor accident involving a communications jeep during the games as the "support force's first sacrifice."[63] Such wordplay seemed like a way for the media and the SDF to gesture toward but ultimately sidestep the sensitivity of the force's prominent role in an event that supposedly was all about peaceful international interaction and had little to do with the official duties of the SDF. Left-leaning critics, of course, did not shy away from what they saw as the militarization of the games and the potentially legitimizing effect on the force. In a discussion of the opening ceremony in the left-leaning daily newspaper Asahi, for example, three guest commentators—two movie directors and a painter—criticized the "military atmosphere" of the music and vast numbers of SDF participants in the program. They and others expressed concern about the remilitarization of society and Japan's image abroad. Despite these criticisms, the three took turns praising aspects of the SDF's performance, such as the maneuvers of the ASDF planes that created the interlocking vapor Olympic rings in the sky, and recognized that much of the program would not have been possible without the force's participation.[64] Criticism of SDF involvement was harshest before or just as the games began (as in the article discussed above), but largely dissipated—like the Olympic rings high above the stadium—once it was in full view. Confronted with the unfolding success of the games and Japan's Olympic team, it undoubtedly became all the more difficult to speak negatively of the SDF in an atmosphere rife with national pride.

## The Last Embodiment of Japanese Spirit?

A third theme in discussions about the SDF's involvement in the Olympics was, not surprisingly, the spiritual (seishin) strength supposedly embodied by the force, both support personnel and athletes. Numerous commentators suggested that personnel represented the lone embodiment of konjō, whose characters literally mean "root nature," but which functions like a synonym to seishin and can be translated as spirit, willpower, or simply guts. These pundits hailed SDF personnel as examples of a character trait that some commentators worried was disappearing among young people who had not experienced war and were growing up in a prosperous country that was making them soft.[65] Such anxieties reflected and contributed to a reevaluation or reconfiguration, in some quarters, of World War II's legacy and martial values, fueled in part by a rise in national pride prompted by rapid economic growth and hosting the Olympics. Because defining national character in terms associated with the wartime years, such as "the Yamato spirit" (Yamato damashii), the culture and characteristics of the ethnic Japanese people, and bushido, was still problematic in the early 1960s, commentators repackaged wartime ideas and rhetoric using new terms, such as konjō, that cast the war, military ideals, and their legacies in a more positive light.

Konjō and an amplified variant of the term, dokonjō (indomitable guts or willpower), seemed to be everywhere as the Olympics approached. It gained some currency during the war but it appears its use was not widespread. Likewise, journalists and authors rarely used the term during the early postwar decades.[66] That changed in the early 1960s. Daimatsu Hirobumi, the coach of the Nichibō company women's volleyball squad and the Olympic women's volleyball team, was primarily responsible for popularizing the word. The national team, which beat the Soviet Union to win the gold medal at the Olympics, had already achieved fame by upsetting the Soviet Union in the world championships in Moscow in late 1962. The following June, Daimatsu published Ore ni suite koi (Follow me), which became an instant bestseller and was reprinted forty-seven times within a year. In the book, Daimatsu repeatedly emphasized how the intense training he implemented instilled konjō in athletes and that it was this willpower that made the team a powerhouse. Daimatsu used the term frequently to explain his coaching philosophy and emphasized that his views originated in his wartime service as a soldier fighting and surviving through "sheer willpower" in China and Southeast Asia.[67] He wrote, for example, "Athletic competitions today are just like war. In sports today you either kill or are killed. It may not be proper to use the word kill but there is no value in finishing second."[68] Daimatsu's book appears to have unleashed a flood of books, newspaper and magazine articles, and television programs about konjō in the year before the Olympics. Suddenly author after author invoked konjō and argued that it was essential for success not just in sports but also in other areas, such as business, schooling, and parenting.[69] Various commentators debated the nature of konjō, and it was even discussed at the Diet. Ōshima Kenkichi, a triple-jump bronze medalist at the 1932 Olympic Games and national Olympic team official who oversaw athlete development, testified to a Diet committee in 1963 that konjō was both an innate and an acquired attribute.[70] Ōshima's testimony was the exception. In many discussions of konjō, commentators applied it only to the Japanese and implied it was a unique and inherent national character trait, as suggested by the title of the book *Konjō—the Vitality of the Japanese* (1964) by the psychologist Motoaki Hiroshi.[71]

In this way, konjō became a strand of what is called Nihonjinron essentialist discussions of the Japanese national character. Many a pundit touted konjō to explain Japan's sporting prowess and by extension its rising economic clout and cultural character. It became what the anthropologist Harumi Befu characterized as the claim of a "unique *geist*, or ethos, of the Japanese" similar to Yamato spirit, *kokoro* (heart), and *Nihon seishin* (Japanese spirit), some of the more familiar concepts used by some Japanese to describe supposedly unique national traits.[72] As such, it formed another thread that connected wartime declarations about the martial spirit of all Japanese, triumphant proclamations of economic nationalism in the 1980s, and other cultural claims that have emphasized superiority in the twentieth and twenty-first centuries.

Even as some commentators asserted that konjō was a trait particular to the Japanese people, some claimed that SDF personnel were especially endowed with it. A *Yomiuri* article, which focused specifically on konjō in a series about "present-day Japanese" that appeared two months before the Olympics, suggested that the SDF was one of the few institutions in modern society able to nourish this character trait. The article opened with an example of GSDF troops responding to a plea for help from Niigata officials to battle a fire threatening to ravage the city that summer. Residents, the paper reported, believed that the personnel succeeded in saving their city thanks to their "strenuous efforts" (*funtō dōryoku*) grounded in "konjō."[73] Likewise, some observers frequently praised Miyake and Tsuburaya for their willpower. After Miyake's gold-winning performance, one writer noted that he had heard several people say: "Young people need to join the SDF for a year or two. Unlike civilians, SDF members have konjō." Their assertion, he observed, was that the difference between Miyake's silver at Rome and his gold-winning performance in Tokyo was not just four years of training but more importantly the willpower he acquired in the force.[74]

Some commentators sought to distinguish the spirit supposedly embodied by the SDF from that associated with the imperial military. The Imperial Navy and especially the Imperial Army had increasingly substituted spirit for science, natural resources, strategy, and weaponry in the 1920s and 1930s, which contributed to the belief that Japan—technologically inferior, resource-poor, and with little planning and insufficient weaponry—could defeat the morally decadent, weak-willed, and spiritless Americans. The konjō of the SDF was different, claimed one newspaper commentator, because it was combined with more rational, modern societal values, which had been embraced in reaction to the war. A month before the games began, the article's title asked, "Why Are SDF Personnel So Strong?" The article introduced the GSDF athletes at the Physical Training School who would be competing at the Olympics. The reporter concluded, through rather circular reasoning, that personnel had tremendous willpower because they were in the force and cited the training of boxer Maruyama Tadayuki as an example. After Maruyama participated in an elite military training course, he became so tough he knocked a US military boxer out of the ring. According to the school's president, Yoshii Takeshige, the key to the school's success was that it instilled not just spirit (seishin) and konjō but the combination of these with modern science and coaching.[75]

As this example shows, SDF officials did their part to highlight—and encourage—konjō in their members, both the Olympic athletes and support personnel, for an internal and external audience. On January 2, 1964, the *Asagumo* welcomed in the new year by publishing a poem celebrating 1964 as the year of the Olympics and touted the "tenacious willpower" (*fukutsu no konjō*) of those who would "provide support for and compete in" the games and "raise the Rising Sun high in the sky."[76] In the same issue, as part of a two-page spread, the former Olympian Ōshima, who had emphasized konjō in his Diet testimony, served as one of several guest commentators. He stressed that especially for SDF Olympians the outcome hinged on their "willpower."[77] The caption of a photograph of Tsuburaya leading a pack of runners in the marathon, which served as an illustration for a discussion of personnel who would be serving in the TOSC, underscored the link most succinctly. The caption simply read, "The man with guts: Tsuburaya's powerful stride"

(*Konjō no otoko: Tsuburaya no rikisō*).[78] Not surprisingly, konjō continued to be a keyword in *Asagumo* coverage of preparations for the Olympics and of the games themselves.[79]

The actions of one GSDF Olympian athlete threatened to undermine the organization's reputation as the embodiment of guts. On the fourth day of the games, wrestling coach Hachida Ichirō expelled Kawano Shun'ichi, a light-heavyweight freestyle wrester, from the Olympic Village for what he called a "lack of fighting spirit" (*sen'i kakete ita*). Hachida was angry at Kawano's failure to attack aggressively in a third-round loss to an Iranian wrestler. He stated that Kawano's performance was "inexcusable" because, as an SDF athlete, taxpayers had funded his training. Kawano's banishment was short—the wrestling federation welcomed him back the following day— but his expulsion and Hachida's comments upset SDF leaders. Although they did not say so, his assertion that Kawano had wasted tax monies probably struck a raw nerve for personnel who had been regularly denigrated as tax thieves since the establishment of the force in 1950. The chief of the Defense Agency's Education Section protested that punishing an athlete for losing was "preposterous" and "unmodern."[80] The media, of course, made the most of the controversy. In a retrospective after the games, one columnist said that he felt bad about bringing it up but did so anyway.[81] The *Yomiuri* joked that Kawano's lack of fighting spirit was just like that of his employer and sponsor, the GSDF, which "only defended and knew nothing of attacking" (*mamoru dake de semeru o shiranu*), and it teased force leaders for lacking a sense of humor, just like the Imperial Army, in their response to the incident. Still, the editorial concluded, the SDF had profited from the games more than anyone thanks to positive impressions created by its support activities and the "'martial spirit,' which people are calling konjō," embodied by Miyake and Tsuburaya.[82]

## A Post-Olympic Honeymoon

Whether the SDF was the biggest winner of the Olympics is difficult to evaluate. Even so, that the Olympics resulted in an improved image for the force is amply supported by public opinion polls conducted before and after the games. A 1963 poll reported that just 23 percent of people knew something about the SDF's public-service activities. In 1965, 60 percent were aware of that service, a more than two-fold increase, which can largely be credited to the Olympics. More importantly for the SDF, the number of people who had a positive impression of the force rose to 57 percent in 1965 from 41 percent in 1963. When asked the reason for their positive opinion of the

SDF, respondents to the latter poll cited the force's support for the Olympics second only to its disaster-relief activities.[83]

Several natural disasters in the late 1950s and early 1960s provided the SDF with opportunities for action that was sincerely valued by the public and featured by the media. During these years, the force launched several major relief operations in the face of repeated storms, floods, and earthquakes. As mentioned in chapter 3, these were only the latest in a series of disasters to which the organization responded. In September 1958, a massive typhoon struck Ise Bay in central Honshu, leaving over 5,000 people dead or missing. Seventy-four thousand personnel engaged in rescue operations for two and half months, an effort so large it led the Defense Agency to cancel the annual anniversary parade and review of troops that fall.[84] Mobilization for this emergency, as well as the GSDF's search and rescue operations in response to storms that dumped over twenty feet of wet snow on Hokuriku, on the western side of central Honshu, during the winter of 1962–63, generated a lot of positive press coverage in print and in photographs like the one below (figure 4.5). As the US military adviser Humphreys, who accompanied the commander of the Eastern Corps to Hokuriku, recalled, the snowstorms were "a disaster but a happy disaster."[85] They were, in fact, not much of a disaster. No deaths were directly attributed to the storms. Residents of

**FIGURE 4.5.**   GSDF personnel work to clear a rail line after a series of huge snowstorms pounded Hokuriku (northwestern Honshu) during the winter of 1962–63. Used with permission of the Asahi Newspaper Company.

mountain villages were stranded and inconvenienced but were not in imminent danger. As the political scientist Tomoaki Murakami pointed out, the
Ikeda administration broadly interpreted SDF Article 83 in order to dispatch
the troops, because it did not "necessarily qualify as an 'emergency' in the
traditional sense."[86] The most serious threat was the snow melting quickly
and causing floods. The GSDF mobilized several divisions (about 5,700 soldiers), and sent in helicopters to deliver supplies, bulldozers to clear roads,
and trucks to dump millions of tons of snow into the rivers to be swept away.
An *Asahi* correspondent, who covered the story in part thanks to rides on
GSDF helicopters, reported that villagers greeted personnel warmly as they
passed, which surprised one soldier who was used to being frequently called
a "tax-thief."[87] Humphreys speculated "that there were many in Hokuriku
who remembered the GSDF soldiers in a positive way from that time on."[88]
His observation appears to be true on a national level according to the aforementioned polls. Natural disasters and the Olympics together were a boon
for the SDF's image.

Officials in the US Embassy in Tokyo noticed the shift in public attitudes,
too. In an update to the comprehensive report the embassy had sent to Washington in early 1964, embassy officials noted just months before the games
opened that "public attitudes [were] changing in the direction of still greater
acceptance of the JSDF" and that "barring unforeseen developments, the
JSDF should continue to grow in public esteem." The report attributed this
improved public image to "continued efforts of the force to de-emphasize
the military side of their mission and to emphasize disaster relief and other
civic action projects," such as support for the Olympics.[89]

The SDF's improved public image around the time of the Olympics is
also supported by anecdotal, force-filtered evidence. *Tōkyō Orinpikku sakusen*, the collection of games-related experiences of TOSC personnel, was
in part gleaned from articles that had appeared in internal corps newspapers like the Northern Corps's *Akashiya* and the Western Corps's *Chinzei*,
as well as in the Defense Agency–sponsored *Asagumo*. Several contributors
related post-Olympic incidents in which they felt they had been treated better by people as result of the games. One soldier wrote that as he returned
to Kyushu following the Olympics, he met a union activist and a leftist teacher
from Hokkaido on their way to protest the docking of US naval vessels carrying nuclear weapons at the port of Sasebo in Kyushu (which the US Navy
shared with the MSDF). This pair said that they "were forced to recognize the
valuable role fulfilled by the SDF at the Olympics."[90] Another soldier, Kami
Kazuhiko, told of stopping by a bar in the capital just before heading back
to his home base after the end of the games. After noticing the uniformed

Kami, one man began yelling "SDF banzai!" Kami wondered if the man was making fun of him or was simply drunk, but about ten other customers gathered around and complimented the SDF on making the Olympics a "fantastic" success. Thanks to the SDF's involvement with the Olympics, Kami felt "people looked at us differently," in sharp contrast to his experiences when people had turned a dog on him and ignored him when he asked for directions. "To not ever lose this respect," he concluded, "each member must continue to work even harder."[91] As indicated by the surveys, these isolated experiences may have indeed represented a significant shift in public attitudes toward the SDF, but their inclusion in the collection also represented top leadership's hopes and expectations. The stories clearly emanate a sense of self-congratulatory accomplishment and, as Kami's concluding comment suggests, issue a continuing challenge aimed at personnel to do what they must to maintain this newly acquired respect.

The post-Olympics favorability bounce was challenged by what came to be called the Mitsuya Incident, a political scandal involving SDF top-ranking officers. In February 1965, just months after the Olympics ended, a Socialist Party Diet member, Okada Haruo, revealed that the force in 1963 had secretly formulated contingencies in the event of a crisis on the Korean peninsula. General Tanaka Yoshio, a former Imperial Japanese Army officer who was then chairman of the Joint Staff Office, led the Mitsuya Kenkyū (Three Arrow Study) contingency planning group, as it was called, that was staffed by over fifty top officers. Because the tabletop exercises had allegedly (but not actually) proceeded without the authorization of civilian officials, Okada charged that the SDF was undermining civilian control of the military and raised the specter that the officers were plotting a coup along the lines of the infamous February 26, 1936, attempt to overthrow the government.[92] Although Okada's comparison was faulty and the SDF was right to have been planning for contingencies, as Sado Akihiro observed, the scandal only subsided after Tanaka and twenty-six officers were dismissed and the Defense Agency director, Koizumi, resigned in June 1965.[93] That the incident came to be considered a scandal highlights the continued distrust of a large segment of society.

Around the same time, defense officials surely relished an event that distracted the country's attention from the Mitsuya Incident and extended the afterglow of the Olympics by connecting the games to the SDF. On April 22, as the media focused on the Mitsuya scandal, the captain of the gold-winning women's volleyball team, Kasai Masae, announced her engagement to First Lieutenant Nakamura Kazuo, an GSDF infantry officer who had joined the PRF as part of the resurrected military's first recruitment drive in August

1950. Because the announcement served to remind the public of the link between the SDF and the Olympics,[94] and given that force officials were concerned that many women did not consider personnel to be suitable marriage partners and that some parents continued to object to their daughters marrying SDF men, this union between one of the country's most famous single women and a member of the force undoubtedly pleased its leaders. Their union was in fact facilitated at the highest level by Prime Minister Satō, who had introduced them to each other at his residence two weeks earlier. Furthermore, Kasai's description of what attracted her to Nakamura dovetailed with the message that the SDF was seeking to convey and had been credited to it in discussions about konjō. "Because people have depended on me up till now," Kasai said at the news conference announcing her engagement, "I wanted someone I could depend on."[95] Just over a month later, on May 31, with the prime minister, the defense chief, and coach Daimatsu in attendance, Kasai and Nakamura, he dressed as at the engagement announcement in his military dress uniform, were married at the Grand Hill's Hotel, next to the GSDF's headquarters, in a ceremony that was broadcast live on national television.[96] Asked about their upcoming honeymoon, Nakamura replied that they would be spending a week in the resort town of Hakone, but all other information, he joked, was "a defense secret."[97]

## A Recruitment Boost and Ongoing Challenges

A more substantive way that the SDF sought to take advantage of the Olympics was to bolster its recruitment efforts. More and better-qualified applicants and increasing enlistment and retention generated tangible, measurable benefits. In the wake of the games, enlistments spiked. But the increase in applicants and a high rate of enlistments in 1965 may have been in part the result of a brief post-Olympic economic downturn that narrowed the job prospects of high school graduates. As the economy returned to its double-digit growth and the Olympic glow faded, the SDF and especially the ground force once again faced serious recruiting problems in the late 1960s.

From the time of the SDF's establishment in 1954, the government supplied the force with a legal tool to assist its recruitment efforts. As mentioned in chapter 3, the SDF Law issued in June 1954 required regional and local government officials to cooperate with recruiters. Specifically, the law charged prefectural governors and mayors of cities, towns, and villages to cooperate with personnel liaison offices, located in each prefecture and many large cities, to publish and disseminate information concerning the time and duration of recruitment drives. As the political scientist Thomas M. Brendle found in his evaluation of recruitment in the 1960s and early 1970s, the extent of local cooperation beyond doing what was legally required varied widely from one area to another.[98] If prefectural and local officials were ideologically opposed or unsympathetic to the SDF, they likely assisted with recruitment as little as possible. And because force officials were reluctant to stir up controversy, "recruiters [were] prepared to conduct their affairs without civilian support when it [was] denied to them."[99]

This sensitivity about sparking controversy demonstrates that in many ways the task of recruiting, too, was ultimately contingent on fostering positive public opinion. Structural characteristics of the SDF recruiting system made this even more the case. The organization conducted (and still conducts) recruitment drives quarterly rather than continuously, which meant that applicants usually had to wait for a time before examinations took place, endure another wait until the results of the exams were announced, and then again wait until all enlistees were called up for induction and training. Unlike in many militaries, there was (and still is) no legal minimum commitment for service, and enlistees are free to quit at any time during the recruitment process or after joining the force. Many recruits therefore were influenced by public opinion and peer pressure during the waiting periods, developed other employment options, and did not face any consequences if they did not proceed to the next stage of the recruitment process or quit after joining. Article 18 of the constitution, which bans involuntary servitude, has been interpreted to mean that conscription is illegal, and memories of young men being drafted during the war made it publicly unacceptable. Of more relevance to the issue of retention, SDF personnel—including NDA cadets— are considered to be civilians, so they can resign at any time. In other words, the force cannot prosecute personnel for desertion because, legally, there is no such thing.[100]

As the Japanese economy began to grow rapidly in the early 1960s, the organization's long-running challenges with recruitment and retention became more severe. Throughout its history, the SDF has struggled with human-resource challenges. Rank-and-file enlisted personnel, who make up the overwhelming majority of the force, enter on renewable two- or three-year contracts. For most, as the historian John Welfield observed, "their objective was simply to learn a trade, save money and return to the private sector. It was difficult to recruit them. It was also difficult to retain them." During these early decades, around twenty thousand to thirty thousand of them left the force and re-entered civilian life each year.[101]

The GSDF, in particular, because it was larger and less popular than the other two branches, was constantly confronted by staffing issues. During the first half of the 1960s, the actual size of the ground force fell below 90 percent of its authorized strength as the number of applicants and of those accepted who entered the force fell drastically. In 1963, the branch only had enough soldiers to form twenty-one of its mandated twenty-three divisions. In response, the Defense Agency announced in early 1964 a plan to boost enlistment that included improvements in living conditions, more recruitment centers, and better technical training.[102] US military advisers noted the branch's austere environment: "A day's fare in a GSDF mess hall would hardly act as an enticement to the average young man in Japan today. The menu of the day may consist of fried bean curd, soy bean soup, and pickled vegetables for breakfast; slices of raw fish for lunch; fried fish and seaweed broth for supper. Each meal has, of course, the usual rice or wheat. The meal must be provided by the SDF at a cost not to exceed ¥113 (31¢) per member per day."[103] The last strategy, better technical training, was grounded in the realization that personnel quitting for better employment opportunities was an unavoidable reality, but that the organization's provision of skills that were attractive to private-sector companies might encourage potential recruits to join and stay several years before leaving the force.[104]

The positive publicity created by the SDF's support for the Olympics and its high-profile disaster-relief operations likely had a positive impact on recruitment, but the post-Olympic economic slump also probably helped boost enlistments. In 1965, when about 55 percent of the country's high school and college graduates were unable to find jobs, the force had greater success attracting more and better-qualified applicants. As the economy recovered the following year, the number of applicants plummeted to fewer than forty-eight thousand from around sixty-four thousand the year before.[105] Because the number of applicants dropped, the SDF accepted a much higher percentage of them than before, so the quality of personnel likely decreased. The increasing challenges of recruitment after 1965 are illustrated by what recruiters call "pure volunteers" and "persuaded volunteers." Pure volunteers came to SDF recruiters seeking to join, whereas persuaded volunteers applied as the result of visits and pressure initiated by recruiters. In the 1950s and early 1960s recruiting officials estimated that the ratio between the two was about equal, but in the late 1960s more than 90 percent of all applicants were persuaded volunteers.[106] Although pure volunteers did not always make better soldiers than persuaded volunteers, the quality of those who enlisted deteriorated. Recruitment pressures, Brendle found, prompted the force to lower its standards and "to admit less qualified people, such as the color blind or physically weak."[107] After 1965, the number of force members who quit rose, whereas it had steadily fallen during the first half of the decade. Recruitment and retention difficulties combined to create personnel shortages for the GSDF ranging from ten to fourteen percent throughout the 1960s.[108] Within a relatively short time, the SDF's human-resource challenges returned to their pre-Olympic severity and then got even worse.

As the quality of recruits suffered, media coverage highlighted the problem. Newspapers reported on the misdeeds of the few soldiers who committed crimes or got in other trouble and tied such trouble to the SDF's recruiting difficulties. Such coverage certainly did not improve the public's view of the force. These factors likely created a vicious cycle—recruitment struggles leading to lower standards and personnel getting in trouble contributing to a less favorable public image, which in turn led to further recruitment struggles. Although an economic downturn in the early 1970s caused by the worldwide oil shocks boosted recruitment, recruiters would continue to struggle to fill the force's ranks with quality personnel as the economy grew rapidly in the 1980s. Even when recruitment improved as a result of the long recession beginning in the 1990s, the belief that the SDF could only get societal dropouts (*ochikobore*) and was willing to employ them continued to linger. Such personnel were seen as unmanly men, who did not measure up to the standard of the defense force man, much less the archetype of postwar masculinity, the *sararīman*.[109] In the late 1990s and early 2000s, such lingering perceptions provided fodder for the writer Asada Jirō to publish a series of short stories loosely set in the late 1960s and 1970s. In one story a new recruit feels tricked by the recruiter and contemplates leaving as soon as he joins up. By the next morning, he feels a sense of identity and order and decides to stay, but still wonders if the electric fence around the base is designed less to keep out left-wing radicals than to keep new recruits from escaping.[110] In these stories, Asada captured the sense of masculine anxiety that troubled the force during the Cold War decades.

One step the SDF used to address these recruitment challenges was to welcome more women into the force in roles other than those of nurses. As discussed earlier, Defense Agency bureaucrats and GSDF officers, inspired by US military models, decided to try to make up for personnel shortfalls by establishing the Women's Army Corps in 1968. One top civilian defense official argued that the GSDF should seek to maximize its limited supply of male recruits by allocating them to "manly" positions handling "machine guns" and opening up office support positions to female recruits. These moves, Satō Fumika suggested, were designed to "'secure' the masculinized integrity and character of the military profession, while expanding the role of women in the SDF."[111] Other factors also motivated the decision. Leaders thought that the inclusion of women would win greater public support for the force and that female personnel, as one officer put it, would become mothers who would "bear children who would become soldiers."[112] Thus, even as the SDF opened a door to women, it did so for distinctly patriarchal reasons that were influenced by the lingering prewar ideology of "good wives, wise mothers" (ryōsai kenbo). In the end, the SDF admitted relatively few women into the force, and this only began to change slightly in the late 1980s.

## Experiential-Enlistment Programs

Another way that top defense officials sought to bolster recruitment and the organization's image was through "experiential enlistment" (taiken nyūtai). These programs allowed young people—almost all males—to experience life in the SDF by joining the force for a short period of time—from several hours to an extended number of days. Among the force's three branches, the GSDF organized the majority of such programs. In the 1950s, as mentioned in chapter 3, the force aimed these programs at teenage boys. By the 1960s, as the organization became associated with konjō, it began to provide "spiritual training" (seishin kyōiku) in the form of experiential enlistment for private companies that were seeking to instill this character trait in their employees, especially the white-collar sararīman. Although the SDF struggled to compete with other industries for employees, particularly during times of high economic growth, the programs gave it a tool to do so and to counter fickle public opinion. This initiative was rich with irony. As noted, force personnel often measured their manliness vis-à-vis the sararīman, the epitome of postwar masculinity. But through experiential enlistment, they provided training in how to be tough, determined, and manly to precisely that rival.

The force began to target company employees in part because of criticism of its focus on male teenagers. One of the goals of experiential enlistment was to increase the number of pure volunteers. In the early 1960s, bases across the country expanded their experiential-enlistment offerings by inviting teenagers to overnight camps during school summer vacation (from late July to late August).[113] In the summer of 1962, this effort sparked an outcry from the leftist high school teachers' union and the Socialist Party, which condemned it as a revival of wartime school military training. The controversy led the Defense Agency to deemphasize the program, though continuing it with different demographic targets. The SDF also began to reach out to women around this time. This was not to recruit them, but to instill in mothers and sisters, who would likely influence the career decisions of young men, positive impressions of the force.[114] Even if these efforts did not result directly in boosting recruiting numbers, the SDF hoped that they would improve the public's image of the force. These aims were also motivating factors for the organization as it began to offer employee training for companies in the early 1960s.

The motivations of company executives to have their employees—who were almost invariably males—participate were more complicated. The primary rationale was that experiential enlistment would help management effectively conduct spiritual education for employees. Based on his field work on employee training programs in the early 1970s, the anthropologist Thomas Rohlen estimated that about one-third of all large and medium-sized companies conducted spiritual training, and many of these included experiential enlistment as a part of that training.[115] Company executives hoped experiential enlistment would foster discipline, teamwork, and good manners in their employees. More practical concerns may have been at play, too. Managers probably recognized a good deal when they saw one. The SDF provided all the training, lodging, and clothing (that employees borrowed) for free. The only cost incurred by companies was inexpensive meals (about 50 cents a day in the late 1960s) at base cafeterias, which, like at the NDA, were nutritious though not delicious.[116] They certainly would not make trainees fat, which was apparently the concern of at least one company that had its employees undergo several days of training at a number of GSDF bases each year to slim their waistbands and make them more physically fit.[117] More typically, executives hoped their employees would gain technical knowhow through training and interaction with the SDF.[118] The force, which received some cutting-edge technology from US companies and interacted with the US military, was seen as a source of specialized expertise. One company, for example, was interested in its employees seeing a state-of-the-art warehouse logistics–management system, which the GSDF had recently purchased from a US company.[119] An additional rationale mentioned by senior managers was the recruitment of personnel who were leaving the force and entering the job market.[120]

Companies participated in experiential enlistment in a variety of ways. Some did so as part of new-employee or mid-career training for various lengths of time. In general, these trainings included activities such as Zen meditation at a Buddhist temple, a weekend in the countryside, an endurance walk, and a visit to Meiji Shrine in central Tokyo.[121] As for the SDF component, programs might consist of an entire week or multiple spiritual training sessions on a base. Typical activities included physical-fitness training, navigating obstacle courses, team exercises, listening to lectures from officers about the importance of Japan maintaining a strong defensive force, and sometimes even light weapons training.[122]

The number of companies participating in experiential enlistment appears to have risen dramatically as the Olympics approached, increased even more during the post-Olympic glow, and remained popular until the end of the decade, though signs of decreasing interest began to emerge. It appears likely that companies that began participating earliest were ones with managers who were force veterans and had personal connections with officials on nearby bases.[123] Others became involved when they decided that some of their best employees were former personnel. Participation appears to have increased and attracted significant media attention around the same time that the SDF came to be associated with konjō. A number of major corporations, such as Nissan, Canon, Fujitsu, Hitachi, and Sanyo began to participate before the Olympics, as well as many small companies.[124] Some companies hired in-house spiritual advisors, veterans of the prewar military and/or postwar armed forces who were in their fifties and sixties, to organize spiritual training for employees that was similar to that provided by the SDF, but most outsourced this training to the force.[125] The demand apparently became so great that bases could not handle all the requests, especially after the games. In 1965, the GSDF alone received requests for 150,000 workers to participate, which was too many to accommodate. That year, an estimated 90,000 employees participated in programs run by all three branches.[126] But corporate enthusiasm for spiritual education, and by extension experiential enlistment, probably reached its zenith by the end of the sixties. In 1969, the *Yomiuri* newspaper observed that the watchwords of employee training were now "initiative" and "fulfillment in work," and that far fewer companies thought it was essential to instill konjō in their employees.[127]

Yet, even as the enthusiasm for konjō and spiritual education waned, many companies continued to find a reason to turn to the GSDF for experiential enlistment. In the late 1960s, popular culture began to idealize the sararīman as a "gung-ho corporate employee" (*mōretsu shain*) as well as a "corporate warrior" (*kigyō senshi*). The former was a term first popularized by the media during the war as part of the effort to mobilize the entire population for the conflict, though this etymology went unacknowledged at the time. A business analyst observed that companies seeking to foster such attributes in employees continued to find experiential enlistment to be an attractive option. He did note that the program sometimes created concerns, as when employees, rather than a showing reluctance about holding a gun, asked to do so.[128]

Much of what we know about experiential enlistment comes from newspaper and magazine coverage. Journalists were generally quite critical in their reporting. A short editorial on the front page of the left-leaning

*Asahi* newspaper was among the flurry of articles about the programs in April 1963. (April is the month when huge numbers of newly hired workers join companies and begin corporate training programs.) In a disapproving tone, the commentary noted the rising popularity among companies of spiritual education and experiential enlistment and concluded by observing, "Employee training too, seems to be making a 'right face.'" This comment was an allusion to the military drill command that also suggested the training might shift political views in a rightward direction.[129] That same month, once again in the *Asahi*, the economist and University of Tokyo president Ogawauchi Kazuo criticized experiential enlistment as backward-looking because the SDF was a hierarchical, vertically structured organization rather than one that was horizontal and valued equality.[130] Even the right-of-center *Yomiuri* newspaper periodically poked fun at experiential enlistment.

Many journalists, Rohlen observed, criticized such programs as "unwanted and unwarranted echoes of Japan's pre-war education philosophy." Although Rohlen admitted that such judgment was not without some validity, he concluded that the private companies themselves were now "the prime focus of morality, whereas before [1945], the nation, in the person of the emperor, was central." Rather than rituals of nationalism, companies drew attention to their own symbols, and they urged their employees to "fulfill their responsibilities to the nation through loyalty to their company," as they had done to some degree during the Meiji period. Not all companies were sold on spiritual education. Rohlen estimated that only a third of companies conducted any sort of spiritual training.[131] Some corporate executives, such as Sony's president, publicly criticized spiritual education, though he, too, worried about the lack of konjō among new hires. His suggested solution was the establishment of more youth groups like the Boy Scouts.[132]

Although some companies found experiential enlistment beneficial enough to continue it throughout the 1960s, it is unclear if it produced recruiting success and an improved public image. It did not help that the force could not compete with the pay offered by private companies.[133] The programs, though, may have prevented the force's recruitment and image challenges from becoming even greater.

The popularity of the program had at least one unintended consequence. As the SDF tried to accommodate increased demand in the years after the Olympics, its status as a public entity made it difficult for it to turn down requests from any group that wanted to participate. In mid-1966, the *Yomiuri* newspaper reported that the GSDF was unable to prevent an unnamed extremist right-wing group from participating in a program at the Komakado Base in Shizuoka Prefecture. In a prescient query, the *Yomiuri* wondered,

"What ripple effects will this have?"[134] Little could the *Yomiuri*, the SDF, or anyone have known.

## The Mishima Incident

If people today are aware of the SDF's experiential-enlistment programs, it is perhaps because the force still offers them, though on a more limited scale.[135] Few are aware that their most famous participant was the writer Mishima Yukio, who as mentioned in chapter 2 reported on his visit to the National Safety Academy in 1953. It is unlikely that the request from the right-wing group to participate in experiential enlistment in 1966 had anything to do with him—he had not yet formed such a group—but a year later Mishima, who was already well known for his radical views, used his fame to persuade wary GSDF officers to allow him as an individual to receive training for a month and half.[136]

The anti–security treaty Anpo demonstrations of 1960 seem to have begun Mishima's transformation into a right-wing extremist. They reminded him of the February 22 Incident of 1936, when young military officers sought to overthrow the government and return power to the emperor in a Shōwa Restoration, an attempt by ultranationalists to inaugurate direct imperial rule in Japan and the rest of Asia. In the aftermath of the protests, Mishima penned a forty-page story, *Yūkoku* (Patriotism), which was published in early 1961 and glorified the actions of those emperor-obsessed rebels.[137] Mishima does not appear to have had any notable interaction with the SDF from the time he reported on his visit to the National Safety Academy in 1953 until his training in 1967. Though some officers were concerned about Mishima's right-wing views when he made his request, they accommodated his unusual wish to enlist alone rather than as part of a group and to do so for an extended period. GSDF officials decided, apparently, that they "could hope for no better public relations man than Yukio Mishima."[138]

Mishima began his training in April 1967. He spent forty-six days at three different facilities. Though Mishima "clandestinely enlisted," as he put it, using the pseudonym "Hiraoka" (his actual family surname), soon after the six weeks ended, he published a detailed account of his experiences in an eight-page spread in the *Sunday Mainichi*, a popular weekly news magazine.[139] In the article, Mishima aestheticized and fetishized the corporeal experiences of military training—holding a rifle and "weapons of every kind" and the harsh physical exercises and extreme environmental conditions—and contrasted them with modern life. He declared that the only way to really understand military life was to experience it "bodily" while "pouring out sweat."[140] By coincidence, he stayed in the same barracks at Camp Fuji that he had as a teenager when he underwent military training during the war. He drew another parallel to the war years; he favorably compared the personnel he trained with to the tokkōtai (kamikaze) pilots who had sacrificed their lives for the country. More generally, he expressed admiration for the GSDF as an organization and the officers and the enlisted men with whom he associated. They were, he wrote, to be respected as role models to other men, and were attractive as men not for women, but simply as men in a broader sense, or to use a phrase familiar both inside and outside the force, they were "men among men." Force personnel, he continued, had "more mutual respect, humor, and compassion than any group with which" he had "ever belonged."[141]

Mishima seems to have found a form of muscular and martial masculinity that he had been seeking for some time. He described training with the SDF as instilling a "certain kind of refreshing manliness."[142] Mishima had become obsessed with exhibiting a hypermasculinity that was designed to compensate for his perceived personal and national weakness. In 1955, motivated by an "intense physical inferiority complex," he began bodybuilding and sculpted his body over the next decade into a finely muscle-bound form, which he often put on display in homoerotic photographs.[143] Weightlifting was only a prelude to other physical activities closer to violence, such as boxing, kendō, and karate.[144]

But for Mishima, this yearning for manliness was not just personal. It was societal. On a national level, "Mishima passionately believed," biographer Damian Flanagan observed, that "Japan's glorious samurai traditions, its manliness and heroism, had been suppressed as something of which to be ashamed. Instead, the so-called Peace Constitution had turned Japan into an effeminate, anodyne, culturally barren society."[145] John Nathan, one of Mishima's contemporary literary translators, recalled that Mishima's "professed reason for enlisting was concern about national defense" and that he wanted the force to "assume its rightful place as a 'national army.'" Mishima regarded the SDF as a "metaphor, at once a victim and a living example of the hypocrisy of postwar society: here was an army pledged to defending a constitution which forbade its existence, an army obliged to refer to tanks as 'special vehicles' because Japan had renounced its 'war potential.'"[146] Mishima hoped to inspire force personnel, who he thought had—like Japanese society more widely—been emasculated, to restore the legitimacy of the organization by assuming their role as men who could and would fight and die for their country.

To do this, Mishima hoped that GSDF personnel would follow his example and embrace what he defined as the way of the warrior, bushido. Although Mishima probably did not intend to die when he began training with the force, Nathan believed that through this process he began "preparing to become a samurai," which "meant preparing for death."[147] Indeed, Mishima seems to have become enamored with achieving a heroic death and with *Hagakure* (In the shadow of the leaves), a collection of commentaries by a Tokugawa-era samurai, Yamamoto Tsunetomo. The text is best known for its famous line: "The Way of the Samurai is found in death."[148] After his initial experiential enlistment in 1967, Mishima published a book-length commentary on the text.[149] *Hagakure* remained largely unknown for over two centuries after Yamamoto completed it. During the 1930s and 1940s, it came to be used by government educators and ideologues to instill bushido in soldiers and increasingly in the wider population as the country engaged in a desperate total war culminating in banzai charges, kamikaze attacks, and civilians of all ages and genders preparing to die defending the homeland. Mishima probably first read *Hagakure* as a teenager during the war. Like Yamamoto, a warrior who in the late seventeenth century had no wars to fight, Mishima bemoaned living in an age of peace but declared, "The samurai's profession is the business of death. No matter how peaceful the age in which he lives, death is the basis of all his action."[150]

By that fall in October 1967, Mishima decided to create his own paramilitary force. He called it Sokoku bōeitai (Fatherland Defense Corps) and declared that it would aid the GSDF should it have to face an internal insurrection by radical leftists. Mishima proposed that the corps, which he envisioned as numbering some ten thousand men, receive training from the GSDF each year for ten days to a month to be prepared for such an emergency. On February 26, 1968, thirty-two years to the day since the failed 1936 coup attempt, Mishima and eleven university students signed a blood oath pledging "in the spirit of true men of Yamato to rise up with sword in hand against any threat to the culture and historical continuity of the Fatherland."[151] Like radical civilians in the 1930s who received assistance from sympathetic high-ranking army officers, Mishima sought financial, material, and moral support from senior GSDF staff. Unlike them, he was to be disappointed. The force, he felt, gave him insufficient moral and material support. His group, however, continued to receive training each spring and summer when university students, who formed the core of his group, were on academic break. Mishima also maintained friendships with a few senior officers. Among them was Col. Yamamoto Kiyokatsu, the director of military intelligence at the GSDF Research School, who regularly gave lectures to Mishima and his cadets.

Yamamoto apparently believed that Mishima's group might act as a valuable partner to the SDF in combating radical leftists, though later he became concerned about Mishima's volatility.[152]

Even as Mishima benefited from his association with the GSDF, he gradually became disenchanted with the force. One manifestation of this was his reaction to the suicide of the runner Tsuburaya in early January 1968. In an op-ed published in the *Sankei shinbun* newspaper a week after the suicide, Mishima criticized a comment made by an officer who blamed Tsuburaya's suicide on a nervous breakdown. Such a statement, he wrote, denigrated a "moving, beautiful death," and such an "ugly conceit expressed by those still living" was "hard to tolerate." Death, he continued, was Tsuburaya's only acceptable option as a "military man." Otherwise, he would have had to "kill his spirit," which would have been even worse. Mishima praised Tsuburaya for using a razor blade to take his life rather than a gun, which he could have easily obtained, or poison, asserting that this, too, was the mark of a true samurai.[153]

Probably because of this growing disenchantment and a lack of material and moral support, Mishima abandoned his plans to establish a massive defense corps in March 1968. The personnel, logistical, and financial challenges were too daunting. Instead he decided to create a hundred-man private paramilitary, which he thought he could finance entirely on his own.[154]

By that fall, as protests against the Vietnam War, the ongoing US occupation of Okinawa, and the conservative establishment wracked university campuses and city streets, Mishima prepared to form the group. On November 3, he announced the establishment of the Tate no kai (Shield Society), less than two weeks after leftist demonstrations rocked Tokyo on International Anti-War Day (October 21). Mishima hoped that the protests on that day the next year, unlike the 1960 Anpo protests, would prompt the government to mobilize the GSDF. Such a mobilization, he hoped, would spark a political crisis or coup d'état, and the Shield Society would then play a key role in bringing about constitutional revision, including scrapping Article 9. He had a reason to be optimistic. After the Anpo demonstrations, the Diet had revised some laws to make it easier for the GSDF to be deployed against internal disturbances. The ground force reorganized to create more mobile and mechanized divisions that would be used to counter threats to internal security, and it had concentrated these troops near Tokyo and other industrial cities.[155] Moreover, as leftists radicalized in the years after the Anpo demonstrations, protests became larger and more violent. In 1968, leftists and labor unions in Hokkaido even protested against the Northern Corps's support of the Sapporo Snow Festival. On October 21, 1968, an estimated 170,000 people demonstrated across the country. In Tokyo, some of the protests turned violent. In one of the day's most dramatic scenes, radical students unsuccessfully attempted to ram through the front gate of the SDF headquarters in the Roppongi neighborhood.[156] In response to the demonstrations, officials secretly put the GSDF's domestic security units on alert.[157] Mishima expected and hoped that the 1969 protests would be even more chaotic.

It initially appeared that Mishima's dream scenario might come to pass in October 1969. It was rumored that the GSDF had put 20,000 soldiers on alert in the Tokyo area and readied another 50,000 elsewhere. Huge numbers of protesters took to the streets—around a half million nationwide—and the demonstrations became more violent, "possibly the most violent . . . in the entire . . . antiwar movement."[158] But Mishima was to be disappointed. In response to the Anpo protests, "the police [had taken] a variety of measures . . . to avoid a repeat of 1960." These measures included "new rules and tactics to combat street protests" and to "systematically close down, occupy, and collapse public space."[159] In Tokyo, the government deployed 32,000 police from across the country, including 4,500 specially trained riot policemen. Furthermore, months of unrelenting police pressure, including preemptive arrests and a massive spying operation, along with waning public support for an increasingly radicalized protest movement, made mobilizing the GSDF unnecessary. A year later, in the manifesto he issued the day of his death, Mishima despaired that in 1969 the state had "gained the confidence that it could defend the political system with the police force alone."[160] There would be no crisis that the Shield Society could take advantage of to participate in a coup and bring about constitutional revision. Mishima's hopes that force personnel would play a role their own liberation also dissipated. After Defense Agency Director Akagi refused the prime minister's request for the GSDF to mobilize in 1960, his decision came to be regarded as a "success story" by agency bureaucrats and gave them more confidence in resisting any attempts to do so by future politicians, who despite loosening the restrictions on the SDF participating in suppressing domestic disturbances, became "more cautious" about relying on the force for the maintenance of internal order.[161]

A week after the disappointing October Anti-War Day protests, Mishima considered his options. The SDF, he argued, "could not be expected to stand up and fight for its rights as a national army."[162] Nevertheless, he and his Shield Society continued to receive training, attend lectures, and have private meetings and other interactions with senior officers and top government officials, including the new Defense Agency chief, Nakasone Yasuhiro.[163] Despite this interaction, Mishima's disillusionment with the SDF reached new heights that only became obvious the day of his suicide a year later.

On that cold, clear day, November 25, 1970, Mishima arrived with four members of the Shield Society at the GSDF Ichigaya Eastern Corps headquarters for a prearranged meeting with Gen. Mashita Kanetoshi, a corps commander who had been Imperial Army officer and joined the force in 1952. The general assumed that Mishima was there to discuss plans for the continued training of his group. Without warning, Mishima and his men took the general hostage and tied him up. Mishima then fought off with a sword attempts by other officers to enter the office, wounding several of them and leaving marks on the doorframe that can still be seen there. He then demanded that members of the Eastern Corps be assembled in the courtyard below to hear him speak. By noon, a thousand men had gathered below the office balcony. As Mishima stepped out to address them, his men unfurled banners proclaiming his call to arms and scattered leaflets urging the SDF to join them in overthrowing the government in a Showa restoration that would emulate the one military rebels had attempted in 1936 (figure 4.6). Trying to make himself heard over the roar of media helicopters circling overhead and the jeers of the assembled soldiers, Mishima was able to deliver only portions of his prepared speech.[164] Distributed beforehand to newspapers, the manifesto was published that day.

The manifesto is almost entirely about Mishima's interactions with the GSDF and his frustrated hopes regarding it and its men. The statement immediately addresses that relationship by placing it in Confucian terms:

> We of the Shield Society were raised by the SDF, and it could be said that the SDF is our father and brother. So why have we repaid that debt with this act of ingratitude? Looking back, during the four years— three years for my students—we spent as reservists within the force, we received an education that contained not a hint of mercenary self-interest, and we in turn loved the SDF. Here we saw the dream of a "true Japan" that no longer exists outside the forces, and here we finally knew the tears of true men, unknown since the end of the war. The sweat we shed here was pure, as we ran about the plains of Mount Fuji with comrades who shared our patriotic spirit. On this point, there can be no doubt. To us, the SDF is our homeland, and the only place in today's listless Japan where we could breathe a rigorous, bracing atmosphere. We received incalculable love from the instructors and assistant teachers. Why, then, have we come to take this action? Although it might sound implausible, I declare that we have done it precisely because we love the Self-Defense Force.[165]

**FIGURE 4.6.** The writer Mishima Yukio stands on the balcony at GSDF headquarters in the Ichigaya neighborhood in central Tokyo and speaks to assembled troops below. Mishima's manifesto is written on a sheet hanging from the balcony. November 25, 1970. Soon thereafter, Mishima committed ritual suicide in the room directly behind him of the top commander, whom Mishima and his followers had taken hostage. Used with the permission of the Asahi Newspaper Company.

Mishima's affection for the SDF, though, was mixed with ambivalence. He recounted how he "watched postwar Japan . . . become infatuated with economic prosperity and [forget] the foundation principles of the nation." He believed that the SDF was "the only place where the true Japan, true Japanese people, and the true soul of the warrior spirit remain[ed]." But because "it [was] clear that legally the SDF [was] unconstitutional" and because "the fundamental issue of the nation's defense [had] been weaseled around with an opportunistic legal interpretation, . . . having a military that [did] not use the name 'military' [had] become the source of corruption of Japanese souls and the degeneration of morality." Mishima explained, "[As a result], the military, which should hold the loftiest honor, has been the subject of the basest of deceits. The SDF continues to bear the dishonorable cross of a defeated nation. The SDF is not a national military, has not been accorded the foundational principles of a military, has only been given the status of a physically large police force, and even the target of its loyalty has not been made clear. Postwar Japan's long slumber enrages us. We believe that the moment the SDF awakens will be the same moment Japan awakens."[166]

In the end, Mishima expressed a sense of betrayal toward the SDF. He described his dismay that the demonstrations in October 1969 did not lead the government to mobilize the GSDF, which he and members of the Shield Society believed would have provided an opportunity for the force, "the bastard child of the constitution," to bring about constitutional revision so that it could become a "national military with honor." He vented his frustration with the force. "Ever since that day [in October 1969], we have been watching the SDF carefully. . . . If, as we had dreamed, the soul of the warrior still remained in the SDF, how could it ignore this situation?" Why, he asked, did the organization protect "the very thing"—the constitution—"that negated it?" He questioned the manliness and the spirit of its personnel: "If you are men, how could a man's pride allow this? . . . From nowhere in the SDF did we hear a man's voice rise in response to the humiliating order to protect that which negates you." Instead, he declared, the SDF had been "castrated without even the right to make personnel decisions, manipulated by treacherous politicians, [and] used as a pawn for party politics." Even with the return of Okinawa from US occupation in two years, he bemoaned, there still would not be "a truly autonomous Japanese military" to protect Japanese territory. Rather, "the SDF, as leftists" said, would "be nothing more than mercenaries for America." In conclusion, Mishima declared in the written manifesto and tried to proclaim in similar words over the sound of circling helicopters overhead and jeering personnel below, "Is there no one here who will throw their bodies against this degenerate constitution and die? If there is, stand with us and die with us now. We have undertaken this action in the fervent hope that you, gentlemen [*shokun*], who have the purest souls, may be reborn as individual men and as warriors."[167]

Met with indifference, irritation, and heckling by the troops gathered below, Mishima gave up. After shouting "Long live the Emperor" three times in the direction of the Imperial Palace, he retreated back into the office where he and Morita Masakatsu, his top lieutenant, committed ritual suicide. Mishima first stripped himself naked except for a loincloth. He then pierced his left abdomen with a short sword and pulled it to the right, and Morita, acting as the appointed *kaishaku* assistant tasked with beheading the person committing seppuku, cut off Mishima's head with a long sword. Next Morita repeated this process assisted by another student, who beheaded him in a single sword stroke. All the while the tied-up General Mashita, who had acted as a *kaishaku* for a senior officer at the end of the war, watched.[168]

As in the responses to the rioting of the late 1960s and the Anpo demonstrations of 1960 and earlier, government officials were cautious about mobilizing the GSDF. When Defense Agency Director Nakasone learned of the incident, he instructed the Eastern Corps to "encircle the area and, if necessary, . . . deal with it themselves but [insisted that], insofar as possible, violence should be avoided and the police should be to the fore." He later explained, "[I felt] social impact [of the incident] would be enormous. Consequently, I wanted to deal with it quietly, and insofar as possible, to put the police in the front line and leave use of the Defense Forces until the last."[169] Like Defense Agency Director Akagi ten years earlier during the Anpo protests, Nakasone was committed to protecting the reputation of the SDF by not mobilizing it and preventing a civilian-military clash.

Though personnel recognized the contradictions of the SDF that Mishima criticized, his final act failed to alter the defense identity of the force. As illustrated by the cold reception he received from the soldiers who were assembled in the plaza below the balcony, most personnel found Mishima's appeal to overthrow the constitution in the name of the emperor to be anachronistic and in opposition to their Cold War defense ethos. They took seriously the Ethical Principles they had sworn to follow: "To defend the peace and independence of [the] country, . . . to obey the laws, maintain unity and solidarity, maintain strict discipline, continually cultivate virtue, respect character, train mind and body, sharpen [their] skills, abstain from political activities, . . . and thus reply to the responsibilities entrusted to [them] by the people."[170] Nakasone, though a staunch conservative who had carped at Japan's subordinate status to the United States and argued for a more independent military posture for decades, reflected this view. As he wrote later, "on a personal level [I] could understand Mishima's feelings," but he abhorred his actions. He asked the NDA president, Inoki Masamichi, a Kyoto University professor of political thought who came from the same liberal-conservative mold as Maki, to draft a statement that unequivocally condemned the incident. "For someone arbitrarily to use the Self Defense Forces for a specific political purpose" it read, "would be to turn them into a private army. However pure the motives, and no matter that the actions put the perpetrator's own fate on the line, such a destructive philosophy must be firmly rejected."[171] As suggested by this statement, which became the SDF's official statement, the government's response placed blame on those outside the force rather than on its senior officers who had interacted with Mishima.[172] As a result, the SDF did not levy disciplinary action against any of the officers who had associated with Mishima. Doing so would have been awkward because Mishima had met several times with Nakasone and had participated in a panel discussion with Inoki. General Mashita resigned from the force in December, taking full responsibility for the incident, which he was not in fact responsible for.[173]

The Mishima Incident, as it came to be known, dented public support for the SDF. According to polling data, the percentage of citizens who thought the "SDF was necessary" dipped from 75 percent in 1969 to 71 percent in 1971, but public support for the force largely recovered by the mid-1970s. The percentage of those who thought the SDF should be strengthened and the percentage those who thought it should be weakened or eliminated swung more dramatically—by 20 to 30 points—in opposite directions, but these numbers, too, returned to about the same level by mid-decade.[174] In the end, the incident did not do much to change the support the force had achieved since the early 1960s. About three-fourths of people supported the SDF's existence and one-quarter did not. Public support for the force was in many ways support for the status quo—for the Cold War defense identity.

It is difficult to determine why the incident did not more seriously stain the image of the SDF. One reason may be that the media almost universally explained the incident as a vain act of literary theater rather than as a serious security threat. Reporters and especially the commentators they turned to generally dismissed Mishima's political views and emphasized his cultural and aesthetic motivations.[175] Such an interpretation—and the improbability that the SDF would heed his call to join him in overthrowing the government—served to minimize the fact that some personnel harbored sympathy for his views.[176] The reaction of the assembled rank-and-file troops also served to discourage concern about officers who were sympathetic to Mishima's ideas. The media and by extension the public believed that the reaction of the assembled troops was identical to that of everyone else—disbelief and ridicule for a figure, famous as he was, whose ideas and actions seemed to be decades behind the times.

Especially given other developments in the early 1970s, it seems counterintuitive that the Mishima Incident did not damage the SDF's reputation in a more severe or sustained way. In the late 1960s, progressives scored a series of electoral triumphs in prefectural and city elections. Many of these new governors and mayors withdrew permission that allowed local bases to use public streets as routes for the parades that celebrated the SDF's anniversary each fall. In response, local bases began to hold the parades inside bases and invite the public to them, as they did for other events. Also, in the early 1970s, leftists fighting the SDF's legal legitimacy scored their biggest victory when a district court ruled that the SDF was unconstitutional (the decision was overturned by a higher court three years later). But the Mishima Incident was far less alarming than the extremism of the 1930s that exploded within the military. (In the late 2010s, extremist elements also emerged in the German and US militaries.[177]) The repercussions were also probably not as severe because, though most Japanese agreed with Mishima that the SDF was riven with constitutional, geopolitical, and societal contradictions, they were comfortable with them. They had come to embrace the SDF's role as a military and as a defense force—a deputy to US forces based on Japanese soil, constrained by public opinion, and of questionable constitutional legitimately—and they appreciated its response to natural disasters and its other public service.

For these reasons, the transformative effect of the SDF's mobilization for the Olympics on society and the force itself was ultimately not fleeting. Although the SDF's support for the Olympics did not permanently insulate it from shifting public opinion, its logistical and athletic involvement in the world's largest sporting event on a huge national stage solidified the practice of the armed forces' engagement in public service. Thereafter, the SDF's service and other prominent outreach activities became less controversial, and this allowed the force to prevent its image from suffering even more than it might have during the upheavals of the late 1960s and early 1970s. For example, despite the social, political, and legal challenges in the early 1970s, its support for the Sapporo Winter Olympics in February 1972 attracted little criticism and controversy. In part this may have been because the games were held in Hokkaido, which by then had developed a friendly relationship with the SDF thanks to the force's public service and outreach efforts (described in chapter 3), but the reaction also reflected broader national trends. Geopolitical and domestic changes after the end of the Cold War would lead to a more dramatic shift in public views of the SDF, but in the 1960s the decisions to deploy and not to deploy personnel on the streets of Tokyo bolstered the force's efforts to integrate itself into a society in which a majority of people had come to accept it in its current form.

Although this was the case on the main islands, it was not so in Okinawa, which in 1972 was returned to Japan after twenty-seven years of occupation by the United States. There, the brutal treatment of Okinawans by the imperial military during the Battle of Okinawa made many Okinawans extremely suspicious of the arrival of the SDF after reversion. Winning over Okinawans in the 1970s proved to be a task even more difficult than wooing Japanese on the mainland during the previous two decades.

# CHAPTER 5

# The Return of the "Japanese Army" to Okinawa

On May 15, 1972, twenty-seven years after the end of the war, the US administration of the Ryukyu Islands finally came to end with their reversion to Japan. At the Budōkan Hall, an indoor arena built for the Tokyo Olympics, Prime Minister Satō Eisaku and US Vice President Spiro Agnew presided over a ceremony attended by around ten thousand people. Satō dabbed tears from his eyes as he celebrated the success of one of the main goals of his ten-year tenure as prime minister. Agnew declared that Okinawan reversion marked the beginning of a new era during which Japan and the United States "[could] expect an even greater community of interests."[1] Outside, fifty thousand riot police watched over tens of thousands of demonstrators who protested the terms of reversion, especially the extensive US military bases that would remain on the islands.[2]

In Okinawa, the response to reversion was even more complicated because it was more personal. The day's heavy rains, which triggered minor flooding and landslides and led to the cancelation of most commemorative celebrations, seemed to capture the mood.[3] The weather did not stop over 5,000 demonstrators from gathering in Yogi Park in the capital Naha to protest the unchanged status of the US bases and the disposition of the Self-Defense Force to Okinawa. After some speeches, the crowd marched down Kokusai (International) Street to the new prefectural office (figure 5.1). As they proceeded, some protesters ripped down banners, signs, and Japanese

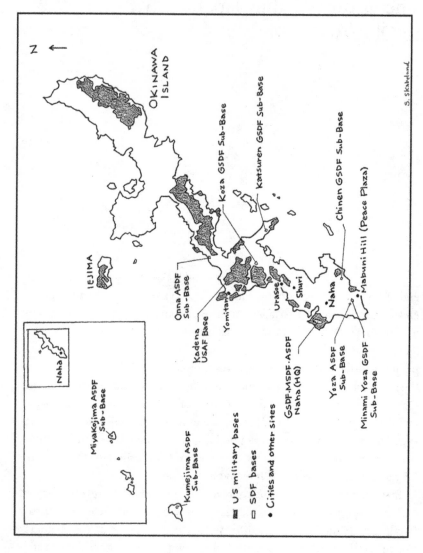

**MAP 2.** Okinawa Island, 1973. Map by Seiko Todate Skabelund.

flags that merchants had used to decorate the street and clashed with police. Yara Chōbyō, the governor of the restored prefecture, spoke at an official ceremony held at the Naha Civic Hall and attended by an estimated 1,300 people. Yara, who as the head of the powerful Okinawa Teachers Association had led the Ryukyu reversion movement since the 1950s, acknowledged, like Agnew, that the day marked the start of a new era, but he lamented how little things would change for Okinawans because of Japanese and US interests. He declared, "[The] terms of the reversion do not necessarily reflect [the] sincere desires of the prefectural people [of Okinawa] . . . and many problems are in store for us."[4] After two decades of intense activism, often suppressed by US authorities, such ambivalence about reversion and outright anger in Japan, on the day the long sought-after goal was achieved, were a striking reversal. It was ironic that the protesters tore down Japanese flags, because the *hinomaru* flag had been the symbol of the reversion movement and its display had been at times outlawed by the Americans in an effort to combat the movement.[5] Disenchantment with the terms of reversion even led a few activists to call for Okinawan independence. As Yara predicted, many problems were in store, because, although reunification with Japan had finally been achieved, many Okinawans, including reversion's most ardent proponents like Yara, found its terms to be extremely bitter.

Many problems were store for the SDF, specifically. The three challenges that the reconfigured postwar military had faced for over two decades on the mainland—society regarding the force as illegitimate, commensurate with the discredited imperial military, and a surrogate of the US military—confronted the force and its personnel as never before in Okinawa, with some inflections. Although a powerful pacifist ethos challenged the emergence of a military organization in 1950s and 1960s Japan, an even more intense pacifism in Okinawa confronted the return of Japanese armed forces to the islands.

In particular, associations with its predecessor the imperial military plagued the SDF. Unlike Japanese elsewhere, Okinawans had not just suffered as a consequence of the so-called "stupid war" started and waged by the military but had also suffered at the hands of the military itself, which had executed some Okinawans and driven many others to their deaths. Unlike mainland Japanese, Okinawans endured twenty-seven years of harsh, direct rule by the United States rather than a seven-year, relatively lenient, indirect occupation. Moreover, Okinawa's prolonged occupation was enabled by the emperor, who had suggested to MacArthur that US control of Okinawa could continue so that Japan, minus Okinawa and the Amami Islands, could regain its independence. Little economic development took place during the

**FIGURE 5.1.** Protesters marching against the terms of reversion, including the stationing of the SDF on Okinawa, in central Naha on May 15, 1972. The banner in front calls for Okinawa to be returned without nuclear weapons and bases and for the SDF to not be stationed on the islands. It also expresses opposition to forced acquisition of land for military use and the United States' war in Vietnam, specifically its blockade and aerial bombardment by planes based in Japan. Used with permission of the Asahi Newspaper Company.

US occupation, even as mainland Japan was rapidly recovering from the war and becoming the world's second largest economy. International events mattered, too. As in the early 1950s, fire raged across the sea, this time in Vietnam. Unlike the Korean War, which made many citizens more sympathetic to rearmament, opposition to the conflict in Vietnam was fierce, fueled in part by a global counterculture movement, and led Okinawans to become all the more suspicious of militaries—both the United States' and Japan's. All these elements combined to create a perfect storm of hostility toward the SDF in Okinawa.[6]

Fortunately for the SDF and its personnel, the organization had developed strategies over the course of the past two decades to navigate such a severe storm. To counter opposition, personnel used many of the same methods they had utilized and continued to use on the mainland. As in Hokkaido and elsewhere, the SDF and especially the ground force, which made up a sizable portion of the force on the islands, increased its visibility in some areas to win over society and reduced its visibility in other respects to avoid stirring up greater controversy. Some of its tactics—civil engineering projects, disaster relief, alliances with support and business groups, and encouraging marriages of personnel to local women—were familiar. The force employed and publicized some of its tactics more frequently and prominently in Okinawa, such as the emergency transport of patients from remote locations and the demolition of unexploded ordnance from the war. In other ways, the SDF maintained—or was forced to maintain—a lower profile. Because of local politicians' reluctance to request assistance from the force, it had fewer opportunities to provide service in the form of disaster relief and civil engineering, despite its desire to do more. Also, commanders did not encourage their troops to wear their uniforms in public until the late 1990s.[7]

The SDF also tried to minimize the visibility of its relationship with the US military. The force was mainly stationed on slivers of former US bases returned to Japan that were immediately adjacent to them. The physical proximity of the SDF to US bases was and continues to be more pronounced in Okinawa than on the mainland (and not just because of the small size of the prefecture). This made differentiating the force from the Americans even more of a challenge. The imposing size of US forces mattered, too. The SDF presence pales both in land area occupied by bases (30 to 1) and troop numbers (4 to 1).[8] Because US bases were subject to tremendous resentment, SDF personnel generally kept interactions with the Americans to a minimum, at least in the public eye.

The SDF's relationship with the imperial military was even more complicated. Because former imperial military officers led the force, they tended to emphasize and honor its ties to and identify with the pre-1945 military even when it was inadvisable to do so. But in general, the SDF attempted to distinguish itself from the prewar military in Okinawa to bolster its public support.

In the end, the storm was an initially intense and sustained tempest followed by spasmodic bursts of protest and ongoing irreconcilable hostility that brewed among a segment of the population. Indeed, within several years of reversion, a majority of the population came to grudgingly accept or at least resigned themselves to the presence of the SDF. Fierce opposition still lingered with far more intensity than on the mainland, but over time it came to be increasingly directed at state symbols more abstract than the force and its personnel.

As on the mainland, this process not only changed society but also transformed the SDF, including the GSDF. As the force continued its efforts to gain legitimacy and integrate itself into society, it further embraced and reinforced some of the nonmilitary roles that often received more attention than its primary mission of protecting national security. The public-service activities that the SDF used in part for public-relations objectives became an essential part of its work on Okinawa, as on the mainland, and contributed to an evolving Cold War defense identity. Yet because military-society integration proved to be more of a challenge in Okinawa, this identity was less pervasive and more contested within both the SDF and society. This remains the case to this day. To cite one example, as the SDF was preparing in 2019 to build bases on small islands south of Okinawa in the East China Sea near the disputed Senkaku (Diaoyutai) Islands, it encountered significant local opposition.[9]

## The Betrayals of Okinawa and SDF Deployment Plans

The disposition of the SDF was another expression of a long, complicated, and contentious history of interactions between Japan and Okinawa. That relationship can perhaps be best understood through the concept of "disposal" (*shobun*). Japanese political thought, the historian George H. Kerr wrote in 1958, does not regard "Okinawa to be a vital part of the nation's body; it is expendable, under duress, if thereby the interests of the home islands can be served advantageously."[10] For many Okinawans, the arrival of the SDF was another example of *shobun*, of being treated as disposable. When Satō and President Richard Nixon jointly announced the islands would be returned to Japan, Okinawans celebrated. But it became clear that the burden of US bases would be only slightly reduced. In fact the percentage of the US military's bases located on Okinawa doubled, to 75 percent on just 0.6 percent of the total national land mass as the burden on the home islands decreased. Okinawan joy turned to resentment and even to regret about reunification for several years after reversion. The deployment of the SDF, among other things, stoked bitterness. This was especially the case as the 120,000 Okinawans who died in the Battle of Okinawa began to be memorialized not as heroes (as they had been previously), but as having been betrayed, sacrificed, and even murdered by members of the Japanese Army, which critics tied to its successor, the SDF. This anger led the Defense Agency to take a cautious approach as it planned for the deployment of the SDF, and the organization began to employ some of its public-relation strategies even before reversion was realized.[11]

Okinawa's long relationship with Japan, as Kerr suggested, has been marked by repeated mistreatment. In the fifteenth century, the Ryukyu Kingdom thrived as an independent trading state leveraging its geographically advantageous position on the eastern edge of the East China Sea, roughly equidistant from the Japanese archipelago, Taiwan, and the continent. In 1609, less than a decade after the Tokugawa clan reunified the archipelago, warriors from the Satsuma domain in southeastern Kyushu, who were concerned about growing European pressure and greedy for trade, conquered the kingdom. Satsuma leaders eventually allowed the kingdom to maintain the appearance of sovereignty so that the domain and by extension the Tokugawa shogunate could take advantage of Ryukyuan trade with the Ming Dynasty and later the Qing.[12] In 1879, as the new Meiji government experienced even greater pressure from the Western imperial powers that had contributed a decade earlier to it overthrowing the Tokugawa regime, Meiji leaders moved to exert even tighter control over the Ryukyu Islands. They abolished the kingdom, incorporating the islands as the "last and least of its [Japan's] prefectures," and called them Okinawa, which refers both to the main island and to the entire island group.[13] Over the next half-century, Imperial Japan subjected Okinawa to a regime of assimilation (*dōka*) and emperor-centered moral education (*kōminka*) that led many Okinawans to identify as Japanese even as they were treated as second-class subjects.[14] Given that treatment, not surprisingly, many Okinawans resisted nationalization. Government officials, as they did in the metropole, sought to nourish nationalism in young people through military conscription and organized village youth associations, but encountered more "robust resistance" than on the home islands.[15] Such prewar opposition to authority, compounded by wartime experiences, continued into the postwar and post-occupation eras.

Okinawan misgivings were further confirmed in the spring of 1945 during the two-and-a-half-month-long Battle of Okinawa, aptly known as the "Typhoon of Steel." An estimated 150,000 civilians, over a quarter of the prefecture's population, perished in the battle.[16] Among those civilians was a daughter of Yara, the future governor. Indeed, almost all Okinawans lost a family member during the campaign. The dead included thousands of women and children, many of whom the Japanese Army coerced into committing suicide. Japanese soldiers also executed hundreds of civilians on suspicion of being traitors, often for speaking in the Okinawan dialect, which was unintelligible to most mainlanders.[17]

Further betrayal at the hands of the Japanese government came six years later when it agreed in secret bilateral negotiations in 1951 to allow the United States to continue its rule of Okinawa as it brought the occupation of the mainland to an end in 1952. A secret message from Emperor Hirohito to MacArthur in 1947 is believed to have played a key role in this decision. The emperor expressed in the memo "hope . . . that the United States [would] continue the military occupation of Okinawa and the other islands of the Ryukyus" as part of a "long-term lease—25 to 50 years or more—with sovereignty retained in Japan" in exchange for a peace settlement.[18] This document gave US officials leverage to sever the islands from the mainland and transform them into an advance base in the Cold War, a US "keystone of the Pacific."[19] In the meantime, the US military directly ruled the islands for five years, until the civilian United States Civil Administration of the Ryukyu Islands (USCAR) was established in 1950. Massive US military bases continued to sprawl across Okinawa.

Despite this history of repeated abandonment, Okinawans came to support an end to US rule and reunification with Japan. Through the San Francisco Treaty in 1952, Prime Minister Yoshida, concerned about Cold War geopolitical imperatives, allowed US rule of Okinawa to continue indefinitely, while securing recognition that Japan retained what was termed "residual sovereignty" over the islands. Part of the reason for Okinawans' desire to return to Japan was that they were attracted by the ideas of the peace constitution. They decried their separation from Japan and brushed aside efforts by US authorities to weaken the growing support for reunification, which included USCAR attempts to nourish a distinctive Okinawan identity.[20] As Okinawans struggled to recover from the wartime devastation and suffered from widespread unemployment and economic malaise, the reunification movement gained support. From the mid-1960s, the US war in Vietnam and the use of US bases in Okinawa to prosecute it further strengthened pacifist sentiments, which were grounded in memories of the Battle of Okinawa. At the same time, Okinawans became increasingly dependent on the growing US bases for employment and economic activity. They also received no or utterly inadequate payment for land that had been forcibly requisitioned for US bases before 1952. Reunification with Japan, Okinawans believed, would bring about the closure of the bases, the departure of the US military, and the enjoyment of new social and economic opportunities available on the mainland.[21]

Reversion finally arrived in 1972. Pressure exerted by Satō, who proclaimed in 1965 that the "postwar era [would] not end until the return of Okinawa to the homeland [was] realized," increasing civil unrest on the islands and in Japan in the late 1960s, and unfavorable international opinion about a seemingly never-ending occupation led President Nixon to agree in November 1969 to return the islands.[22] A subsequent agreement reached in June 1971 granted the United States the use of military facilities and areas on the islands in line with the US-Japan Security Treaty. Okinawans were neither included in the negotiations nor even consulted. Satō touted the agreements as achieving his stated goal of reversion "without nuclear weapons, and on par with the rest of Japan" (kaku-nuki, hondo-nami).[23] This meant that all nuclear weapons would be removed from the islands and the US presence would be reduced to mainland levels. Yara and many other Okinawans did not think this goal had been achieved, much less what they wanted—the elimination of all bases. The initial euphoria that greeted the reversion announcement in 1969 soured as the terms became clear. In the end, neither the terms nor their application met Satō's professed objectives. Rather, the deal was in fact, as Fukuchi Hiroaki observed, "nuclear concealing and base reinforcing" (kakukakashi kichikyōka), as secret agreements by Satō allowed for the storage and transfer of nuclear weapons.[24] The unchanged status of the bases and the continued presence of some forty thousand US service members were no secret. When the public realized that its wishes were being betrayed, many Okinawans switched from being simply proreversion to supporting reversion free of any military bases, and some Okinawan nationalists argued that the islands should pursue independence.

This was the context into which fierce opposition to the deployment of the SDF emerged. Few people had paid much attention to the SDF until the specifics of the reversion began to be discussed. As a US Army analyst observed in June 1970, "[The] SDF entry has been overshadowed by more pressing issues."[25] By then, that was no longer the case. In mid-1969, Nixon announced at a press conference in Guam what became known as the Nixon or Guam Doctrine. He called for US allies, particularly those in Asia, to take more responsibility for their own defense. "Asian hands," he declared, "must shape the Asian future."[26] This was Vietnamization, the policy of gradual withdrawal of US ground forces from Vietnam. For Japan, "Asian hands" meant that the SDF would be tasked with the defense of Japan, though US bases would remain, especially in Okinawa, to project US military power into the rest of Asia. Thus, as negotiations over the terms of reversion proceeded, Okinawans came to realize that the government would dispatch the force to the islands, something which was formally agreed to in the agreement signed in June 1971. This prompted Yara to link the stationing of the SDF with the issue of US military bases. "Okinawans have no choice but to be opposed to the disposition of the SDF," he declared, "given that there is no plan to reduce the U.S. bases" on the islands.[27] He and other critics of the Vietnam War and of the US military using bases in Okinawa to prosecute the war feared that the conflict might draw in Japanese forces stationed there.

Distrust of Tokyo in Okinawa was further heightened by developments emanating from the Defense Agency. In January 1970, Satō had appointed Nakasone Yasuhiro as its director. Nakasone was a veteran of the Imperial Navy and a hawkish conservative who was known from the time he was first elected to the Diet in 1951 for his opposition to Yoshida's mercantilist economics-first strategy and for his support of Japan assuming greater autonomy for its defense. On October 20, 1970, under his direction, the agency issued its first ever white paper and the following day announced the Fourth Defense Build-Up Plan, which triggered foreign and domestic concerns that the country was once again on the path to becoming a major military power.[28] Other government ministries and agencies had annually issued such reports for many years, but the Defense Agency had never done so because of the political sensitivity of security issues. Perhaps doing so in 1970 was premature; it did not do so again until 1976, after which it has continued to do so every year. Two weeks before the publication of the report in 1970, Nakasone confirmed during a visit to Okinawa the need for US bases to be maintained, criticized those opposed to the terms of reversion, and confirmed that SDF personnel would be dispatched to the islands as a part of reversion.[29] His actions and words further alarmed many Okinawans, and his visit was met by large protests.[30]

As plans for the disposition of the SDF to Okinawa proceeded, observers accurately anticipated the problems it would encounter in its relationships with society, the US military, and the former imperial military, and recommended possible strategies to deal with them. US Army officials predicted, "Land for JSDF use is [the] most difficult problem connected with JSDF entry. Okinawans assume JSDF will be established only on existing U.S. base area."[31] To sidestep conflict over land issues, this was precisely the strategy the force used. The bulk of SDF units that entered Okinawa after reversion—units from the GSDF, the ASDF, and the MSDF—took over part of a US base that included sections of the Naha port and airport. This land was central-government property.[32] That allowed the SDF to largely avoid complicated land issues, which continued to trouble the US military's relationship with local property owners. The force established a handful of sub-bases elsewhere but was unable to acquire or rent land for training facilities. As a result, it was forced to send its personnel to Kyushu for training. Until it began to conduct joint exercises with the US military in the 1980s, the GSDF did not conduct training on US bases or training grounds on Okinawa.[33]

US Army intelligence officers also recommended that public interaction with the US military, despite the close physical proximity of US and SDF bases, be kept at a minimum. The same memo stressed, "[The] JSDF should maintain identity apart from U.S. forces on Okinawa. If bases occupied jointly, uniqueness should be emphasized by separate access roads and color of buildings." The "JSDF," the memo continued, "should in no way appear to be under U.S. operational control."[34] Needless to say, the SDF, which did not want to seem either too closely connected with or subservient to the US military, paid close attention to appearances. But the small size of islands, the fact that the majority of US bases are located on the southern half of the main island of Okinawa, the painful history and land acquisition for those bases, and the difficulty the SDF encountered in acquiring land for bases that had not been part of US bases and were thus right next to US facilities hampered the force's efforts to distinguish itself from the US military, as aptly illustrated by the photograph below (figure 5.2).

Associations with the former imperial military created even more serious challenges. It was this issue more than any other that generated dislike for the SDF. Experiencing one of the most long and brutal battles of the war led Okinawans to value peace. In the early postwar decades, it had not necessarily led them to feel hostility toward the imperial military, and by extension, the SDF, or toward the Japanese government and emperor. Thanks to the publication of the book *Tetsu no bōfū* (Typhoon of steel) in 1950, many Okinawans were well aware that the Imperial Army had ordered islanders to commit group suicide and had executed those suspected of disloyalty.[35] This account and others on the topic over the next two decades, however, rarely criticized the Imperial Army and usually characterized these incidents as unfortunate tragedies that occurred in the extreme circumstances of the battle.[36] In the 1950s, most Okinawans were so concerned about simply making ends meet that such knowledge, the pacifist sentiments it engendered, and memories of the war did not become a political or social force. By that

**FIGURE 5.2.**    GSDF personnel of the Okinawa Brigade celebrate the opening of the GSDF Naha Base on October 11, 1972. Notice the English "entrance" sign on the other side of the fence, perhaps indicating that the base is immediately adjacent to a US military base or has frequent US military visitors. Used with permission of the Asahi Newspaper Company.

same token, as the US military drastically expanded its bases on Okinawa, opposition emerged not primarily because of pacifism but because how the Americans forcibly took the land without proper compensation.[37] But by the late 1960s, things had changed. Okinawa, though impoverished compared to the mainland, was more prosperous than before, which allowed for a greater political and social consciousness to emerge. War again raged nearby—in Vietnam rather than in Korea—but this time Okinawans as well as mainland Japanese had the leeway and freedom to vigorously oppose the war for victimizing other Asians and their islands that were being used to prosecute it. As support for returning to Japan grew, so too did pacifism, specifically the desire to be subject to Japan's peace constitution and free of US bases that were being used to bomb Vietnam.

From around 1969, the mounting reversion and pacifist movement began to be colored by a much more critical stance toward Japan. Scholars, journalists, and activists began to revisit the war and prewar years, to carefully document the past as never before, and to share it with a new generation. This new research no longer excused the Imperial Army, the government, or the emperor for their actions. In the case of the emperor, this new war memory condemned him for his inaction in not bringing the conflict to an end sooner and for sacrificing Okinawa. The most important contribution to this emerging discourse was *Minikui Nihonjin* (The ugly Japanese), a scathing critique by Ōta Masahide, a professor at the University of the Ryukyus who would be elected prefectural governor from 1990 to 1998. The book, which was published in 1969 and widely read on Okinawa and the mainland, detailed Japan's multiple betrayals of Okinawa: the invasion of the Ryukyu Kingdom by Satsuma, Imperial Japan's discriminatory policies, sacrificing Okinawa for the defense of Japan during the war, and sacrificing the islands again to assure Japan's independence and bolster its security after the war.[38] As the historian David Tobaru Obermiller observed, the book "increased Okinawa consciousness that reversion would once again expose Okinawa to second-class citizenship."[39] Ōta's critique of Japanese discrimination, though, did not necessarily contribute to less support for reversion. Rather, because the "reversion movement was directed not only against alien rule but also against the Japanese government and people that had discriminated against Okinawans," his book "indicted [the Japanese] and pressed [them] to atone for their discrimination against Okinawans" through the return of Okinawa to Japan.[40]

Local schoolteachers who were union members of the Okinawa Teachers Association also produced compelling research documenting Imperial Army atrocities against Okinawans. As they conducted their research, they published their findings in popular magazines and local and mainland newspapers in the year before reversion. Specifically, the teachers detailed the coerced group suicides, massacres, and executions. Ultimately, the teachers published their findings as a booklet, *Kore ga Nihon gun da* (This is the Japanese Army), nine days before reversion (figure 5.3). (School teachers in Okinawa continued to use the booklet for years and it was reprinted many times.) As the booklet's title indicates, it asserted that these actions showed the fundamental character of the imperial military. The title also had a double meaning, claiming that the SDF was now the Japanese military. Indeed, the chief author of the booklet declared in the introduction that the "atrocious actions of the Japanese Army" described on its pages were "not unrelated to the stationing of the SDF on Okinawa." To the contrary, "because the Battle of Okinawa live[d] on for the citizens of Okinawa Prefecture, the Self-Defense Force [was] the Japanese military."[41] This charge was repeated again and again in such writings. The deployment of the SDF was not only compared to the "return of the Imperial Army" but also, invoking an earlier example of disposal, to the invasion of Ryukyu by Shimazu clan samurai from the Satsuma domain in 1609.[42] As local newspapers featured story after story with headlines like "Over 780 people massacred by the former Japanese military" that recounted wartime atrocities in the months before reversion, opposition to the SDF grew as anxiety about impending political, economic, and social dislocation replaced excitement about Okinawa's return to Japan.[43] Such newly reconstructed war memories heightened the growing dissatisfaction with reversion and fueled a series of major strikes and protests in the islands and on the mainland in 1971 and 1972. By early 1972, an estimated 56 percent of Okinawans opposed the stationing of the SDF.[44]

The intensity of the opposition seems to have caught the central government off guard. The SDF did not start organizing ground, maritime, and air units to be sent to Okinawa until early 1972, just months before their deployment. Nakamura Ryūhei, a top GSDF commander at the time of reversion, blamed this belated preparation on the difficult political situation the force found itself in. Okinawans were opposed to its disposition, the central government was cautious about proceeding with deployment, and US military officials wondered why the SDF was so slow in preparing for its deployment.[45]

Another response to the opposition was Defense Agency and SDF officials emphasizing the nondefensive aspects of the force's mission and the benefits it would bring to Okinawa. In February 1972 newspapers reported that the agency announced that troops arriving after reversion would only carry light weapons and bring "plenty of civil engineering machinery, such as bulldozers, cranes, SP compressors, buckets, etc., to have it play a positive role in development of the underdeveloped basis for the Okinawan people's livelihood, including road construction work, etc."[46] This was part of an attempt to highlight the differences between the SDF and the imperial and US militaries. SDF leaders also emphasized patience. "It will take one or two years at least . . . [after reversion] until the Okinawans really understand that [the SDF] is neither the Japanese Army, which existed before WWII nor the U.S. forces," declared Maj. Gen. Ogata Jirō of the Western Corps, "but the Self-Defense Forces."[47]

The Defense Agency realized that public relations would need to be a key component of the SDF strategy to gain Okinawan public support, as had been the case during the previous two decades on the mainland in places like Hokkaido. In September 1971, the agency sent Matayoshi Kōsuke, a native of Yomitan village in Okinawa, from the mainland to serve as the director of the Okinawa Provincial Liaison Office (Chihō renrakubu) in Naha. Matayoshi's superiors chose him because he was from Okinawa, but they probably did not recognize at the time the value of his personnel connections. One of

**FIGURE 5.3.** Cover of *Kore ga Nihon gun da* (This is the Japanese Army), 1972. Used with permission of the Okinawa Prefectural Library.

his teachers in high school was Yara, the future reversion activist and governor. A 1941 graduate of the Imperial Army Academy, Matayoshi served in the infantry in Niigata, Sendai, and the Kurile Islands, and was stationed in Hokkaido as a captain when the war came to end. After defeat, he returned to Okinawa, became a teacher, and again interacted with Yara, who was the principal of the high school where Matayoshi taught English and physics. It was around this time that Yara began to become involved in the reversion movement. Matayoshi went in a very different direction. In 1955, he left for the mainland and joined the GSDF. When he returned to Okinawa to oversee the Provincial Liaison Office in 1971, he sought to increase the visibility and change the image of the SDF. One of his tactics was to arrange for Okinawans who were SDF members to interact with local society and be seen in uniform while they were visiting family members on the islands. Okinawans were not used to seeing fellow islanders in uniform and these personnel were sometimes asked if they were members of the fire department, or even military personnel visiting from Taiwan or the Philippines. One member whom Matayoshi used to soften the image of the SDF was Tameyoshi Yaeyako, the first Okinawan member of the Women's Army Corps, which the GSDF had established in 1968. Matayoshi enlisted Tameyoshi to assist him during her visits to Okinawa to see family.[48] In addition to the Naha office, Matayoshi established eight other branch offices throughout the prefecture. He and his colleagues collaborated with support groups to boost recruitment, provide employment assistance for personnel leaving the force, and encourage local governments to request disaster relief and civil engineering projects.[49]

Matayoshi tried to make the most of his connections with Yara and other political and economic figures, though the governor never relented in his public opposition to the SDF. That said, former *Okinawa taimusu* reporter Kuniyoshi Nagahiro credited Matayoshi's approach with persuading Yara and other politicians to not pursue even more confrontational measures.[50] Despite the tremendous and widespread opposition, for example, the Government of the Ryukyu Islands legislature (before reversion) and prefectural assembly (after reversion) never passed a resolution against the SDF's disposition. Matayoshi's efforts to prevent this from happening came close to being derailed when Nakasone, during his visit to Okinawa in October 1970, dismissed the opposition to the SDF's deployment as being isolated to Yara because the legislature had not passed such a motion.[51] Nakasone's belittling of Yara angered activists but, perhaps because of Matayoshi's intervention, did not result in a resolution condemning the stationing of the force.[52]

Concern about relations with society was also a key consideration in the selection of other senior officers. In early 1972, the Western Corps, which was headquartered in Kumamoto in Kyushu, finally established the Interim First Combined Brigade to be stationed in Okinawa. The ASDF and MSDF formed similar units around the same time, but the GSDF's was the most prominent. The force appointed Col. Kuwae Ryōhō to command the brigade, which was dubbed the "Okinawa unit" (Okinawa *butai*). Kuwae was chosen because, like Matayoshi, he was a native of Okinawa and an experienced military officer who had served in both the Imperial Army and the GSDF.[53] Or to put it bluntly, as an *Okinawa taimusu* reporter did, the GSDF chose Kuwae "as a tactic to make it more difficult for Okinawans to oppose its deployment."[54]

As a junior high school student in the 1930s, Kuwae, inspired by fictionalized and romanticized stories of military academy life that appeared in the monthly boys' magazine *Shōnen kurabu* (Boy's club), left Okinawa for a regional cadet school in Hiroshima. After he graduated in the same class at the Imperial Army Academy as Matayoshi in 1941, Kuwae served in Manchuria and was stationed in Micronesia when Japan surrendered. Back home, one of his younger brothers and his grandmother had perished in the Battle of Okinawa. In 1952, he joined the PRF and went on to serve as a regimental commander in the Northern Corps in Hokkaido and twice as an instructor at the National Defense Academy. In the Okinawa unit, he was the sole Okinawan among a hundred officers. (Because Matayoshi served in the liaison office, he was not considered to be part of the Okinawa Brigade.) This background, plus his long experience serving as an officer in both the prewar and postwar forces, made him invaluable to the SDF in Okinawa. Kuwae recognized this, and even though he was so frustrated by personnel issues as the SDF was being dispatched to Okinawa that he considered leaving the force, he did not do so because he knew it would severely compromise the mission if its sole Okinawan officer resigned.[55] Yet during his service as well as in his writings immediately after retirement, during his subsequent political career as a representative in the prefectural assembly, and in an oral history interview conducted near the end of his life, Kuwae appears to have never publicly expressed any ambivalence about the imperial military's or SDF's role in Okinawa.

After his selection as brigade commander in early 1972, Kuwae turned to carefully choosing 760 men for the unit. (No WAC personnel were part of the initial brigade, and the first female force member was not assigned to Okinawa until 1987.)[56] Kuwae included as many Okinawans as possible. He tried to personally interview and vet those selected. Despite US occupation authorities in the islands not allowing the Japanese government to conduct any official recruitment activities on the Ryukyu Islands from 1954 onward, an average of a couple hundred young men from Okinawa applied to join the SDF each year and about 25 percent of them were admitted annually.[57] Applying to join the SDF required Okinawans to be in Japan when they did so, which meant obtaining a passport issued by US authorities and traveling to the mainland. All these recruits served as enlisted personnel and, like many enlisted men, they likely left the force after a tour or two of several years. In 1970, US Army officials estimated that "200 plus" Okinawans were serving in the three branches of the force, and expressed the hope that early units deployed to the islands would include as many Okinawans as possible.[58] In the two years before reversion, this number may have increased as it became easier for Okinawans to go to the mainland to join the organization and as some Okinawans on the mainland saw the SDF as a way to return to Okinawa and have a steady, well-paying job there.[59] Almost all Okinawans in the SDF were in the ground force. Kuwae selected around 220 of them to serve in his unit.[60] Although adjusting to Okinawa was certainly easier for these men and they may have helped the SDF gain acceptance in society, they, too, surely encountered considerable suspicion in some quarters.

Okinawans in the SDF were not immune to the opposition that arose over the force's impending deployment to the islands. In April 1972 a month before reversion, five SDF personnel, including a ground force member from Okinawa, Yonemine Hitoshi, surprised Defense Agency officials when they appeared in uniform at the agency's main gate and, among other demands, called for the cancelation of the deployment of troops to the islands.[61] (Yonemine, who was stationed at the Ichigaya GSDF headquarters in Tokyo, had not been selected to be part of the Okinawa Brigade.)[62] The five were accompanied by former ASDF staff sergeant Konishi Makoto, who had already become notorious as the "antiwar SDF officer" (hansen Jieikan) because of his discharge from the SDF for very publicly opposing the Vietnam War and the renewal of the US-Japan Security Treaty in 1970. Specifically, Konishi had objected to the SDF's internal security training to prepare troops for the protests against the war and the expected renewal of the treaty—precisely the kind of training that Mishima vainly hoped the SDF would apply against leftist radicals, which would lead to a constitutional crisis, the revision of Article 9, and possibly a coup. In response to the five members' demands that the SDF not be deployed to Okinawa, the agency dismissed them for criticizing their superiors, a violation of Article 46 of the SDF Law.[63]

To fill the remaining positions in the brigade with men other than those from Okinawa, Kuwae and his fellow officers put a premium on selecting men of high quality who wanted to serve in Okinawa. In the end, many of those chosen were already members of the Western Corps who were serving in and usually were from Kyushu. The corps appears to not have avoided selecting natives of Kagoshima Prefecture, which had been Satsuma domain before the Meiji Restoration and had conquered the Ryukyu Islands in 1609. Many natives of Kagoshima and other Kyushu prefectures were serving in

Hokkaido and were anxious to serve in Okinawa so they could transfer to the Western Corps and serve in Kyushu once their service in Okinawa came to an end.[64]

Kuwae also seems to have preferred another group of islanders, natives of the Amami Islands, which lie between Kyushu and the Ryukyu Islands. Katsu Hidenari was among forty to fifty GSDF personnel who were from the islands, all of whom were selected to go to Okinawa. When he was nineteen years old in the late 1960s, he left Tokunoshima Island to join the SDF and was stationed in Osaka in early 1972. Asked repeatedly if he would volunteer to serve in Okinawa, he decided to do so because he was concerned that not enough personnel would. He arrived with one of the first groups to be deployed in July and was assigned there for ten years, long beyond the expected three-year deployment. Katsu remembers being in a liminal position, which in some ways gave him greater credibility and made living in Okinawa easier. He was used to small-island life and had some relatives in Okinawa who had moved there from Tokunoshima. On the mainland, he was regarded as an islander—thus the expectation that he would volunteer to serve in Okinawa—but in Okinawa he was neither regarded as an outside mainlander nor as an Okinawan, which made him suspicious to those opposed to the SDF, who regarded him as someone betraying his people. Some Okinawans mistakenly thought he was from Kagoshima Prefecture, which administratively oversaw the Amami Islands. In response, he declared that he was not from Kagoshima but from the Amami Islands, which had once been a part of the Ryukyu Kingdom after the latter conquered them in the fifteenth century. Therefore, he stressed, he was not a descendent of the Satsuma samurai who had invaded the Amami and Ryukyu Islands. Instead, like Okinawans, his ancestors were on the receiving end of the invasion as the Shimazu clan fought its way southward. In addition, like Okinawans, the Amami islanders had endured a US occupation longer than that of the mainland, though only until 1953. Katsu felt his background helped him and other personnel from Amami to more easily gain the trust of local residents with whom they interacted.[65]

Matayoshi's work in Okinawa, Kuwae's appointment, and the selection of many men from Okinawa and Amami to serve in the Okinawa unit appears to have done little to placate criticism of the imminent deployment from many Okinawans and mainland leftist groups. A logistics error illustrates the sensitivity of the issue in the months before reversion. An outcry erupted in March 1972 when it was discovered that the ASDF had sent a relatively small shipment—about 120 tons of equipment—to Naha two months ahead of reversion, without proper authorization from the Defense Agency and without consulting US authorities. This angered those opposed to the stationing and was mentioned by the five personnel who protested the deployment the following month. It was also cited by leftist politicians who were concerned about civilian control of the military. The government apologized, two ASDF officers offered to resign, and the shipment was returned to Japan.[66] This embarrassment and political pressure from Okinawans and the mainland led the Defense Agency to reduce the number of personnel to be deployed to 2,900 from 3,200 and to announce that it would slow down the deployment in the months after reversion.[67]

Meanwhile, at the GSDF Kita Kumamoto Base, Kuwae and Western Corps officials sought to educate Interim First Combined Brigade personnel about Okinawa and the particular challenges they would face there. Some clues to the content of this preparatory training can be gleaned from articles in the Western Corps's newspaper, *Chinzei*. (The paper's name, which is an appellation for Kyushu dating from medieval times, suggests how the Western Corps subtly sought to create a sense of identity through historical branding.) The March 25, 1972 issue, which highlighted the formal establishment of the brigade on a rare snowy day in Kumamoto on March 1, included a one-page introduction of Okinawa—its geography, dialect, size and population, culture and customs, and climate. The article provided a short overview of its history, mentioning briefly and in general, vague terms the Battle of Okinawa and the long US occupation. There was of course no mention of the imperial military's treatment of civilians.[68]

That said, as they prepared their men for deployment, Western Corps commanders recognized that gaining public support in Okinawa would be a challenge. In the same *Chinzei* issue, corps commander Gen. Horie Masao published a directive (*kunji*) he had made earlier that month in which he stressed the corps's commitment to doing "everything possible to prepare" the Okinawa unit. Horie urged unit personnel to gain an understanding of the "unusual experience of living through one of the most severe battles of World War II and under foreign rule for the last twenty-seven years."[69] Brigade members, he said, "by becoming citizens of Okinawa Prefecture can help other Okinawans come to a correct understanding of the U.S. forces stationed there."[70] Horie's statements indicate the degree of the collusion that Japanese officials engaged in with the Americans to maintain the indefinite operation of the US military bases. His assertion that brigade members needed to educate Okinawans about the "correct" reasons for the stationing of US forces also reveals a patronizing attitude that contradicts his empathetic suggestion that personnel seek to understand the Okinawan experience of surviving the Battle of Okinawa and living under foreign occupation for decades. Perhaps, in private training sessions, commanding officers made some mention of the controversies related to the government's and imperial military's treatment of Okinawans, but it is unlikely that they received any serious attention. One would hardly expect such an acknowledgment from former Imperial Army officers like Horie and Kuwae, even though the latter was Okinawan. Rather, they glorified the sufferings of Okinawans, with little detail and no mention of responsibility, and made assurances that the SDF was dedicated to preserving peace.

At its core, differences between how the SDF and its conservative allies remembered the Battle of Okinawa and how many Okinawans and their pacifist allies did so are essential to understanding the divide over the disposition of the force. A lecture to the brigade delivered by an Okinawan, Kinjō Kazuhiko, who left Okinawa during junior high school, graduated from Tokyo University of Education soon after the war, and then taught at the high school and university level—one of many Okinawans who left the islands before the war and never returned—sheds some light on this issue. In March, Kinjō came to Kumamoto from Tokyo to deliver a lecture to the Okinawa unit and conduct cultural training for them and their families. In his lecture about Okinawan history, Kinjō focused on the Battle of Okinawa. According to an article about the talk in the first issue of the brigade newspaper, Kinjō stated that Okinawans had "bravely and determinedly fought, throwing their lives away for the defense of the mainland."[71] In short, Kinjō depicted Okinawans as tragic heroes who had sacrificed themselves in the name of the nation.

Kinjō had published several accounts about the experiences of the male Imperial Blood and Iron Youth and female Himeyuri (Lily Corps) auxiliary nurses in the battle.[72] Like many Okinawans, he had a strong personal connection to the battle. Two of his younger sisters were among the Himeyuri nurses, over two hundred teenagers at two of Okinawa's elite girls' middle schools who were drafted into service and quickly trained in nursing. The girls served alongside soldiers as they moved southward, often taking refuge in the many caves of the island, fleeing from advancing US troops. Kinjō was unsure how his sisters perished. Like many female and male students drafted into service, they may have been encouraged to commit suicide by Japanese soldiers. Kinjō, however, did not speculate whether this was the case or not. Indeed, in his most in-depth account of the battle, he did not criticize the actions of the Imperial Army, but simply reconstructed what appears to have happened while offering little in the way of analysis or commentary.[73] As mentioned, this was typical of much of the writing and popular sentiment about the battle during the 1950s and 1960s, which tended to glorify

Okinawan loyalty and sacrifice and rationalize it as an unavoidable tragedy of war.[74] As reversion approached, new interpretations, critical of Japan, such as Ōta's *Minikuni Nihonjin*, gained ascendancy. Rather than portraying Okinawans as heroes who had valiantly sacrificed themselves on behalf of Japan, these new interpretations identified them as victims who were driven to suicide, sometimes killed by their own Japanese soldiers, and discarded by the emperor. This was certainly not the interpretation that Kinjō shared with his audience of SDF personnel in Kumamoto.

Even as SDF officials were preparing personnel in Kyushu for the challenges they would face in Okinawa, their allies on the islands were employing a variety of techniques to improve the image of the organization. One tool was the Taiyū-kai (Force Friends Association), the support group mentioned in chapter 3 that had been established on the mainland in the late 1950s and was established on the islands by an Okinawan, Ishimine Kunio, in 1969. After the war, Ishimine worked as a truck driver on US bases and then as a teacher before going on a short-term visa to the mainland, where he joined the GSDF from 1957 to 1959. He then returned to Okinawa, where he went to work for a bank. Just a month before reversion in April 1972, Ishimine and his fellow Force Friends Association members helped organize an art exhibit of work produced by SDF personnel at the Orion Beer Hall in Naha. (Orion was and is an Okinawa brewer of the islands' best-selling beer.) An article in the *Chinzei* reported that visitors to the exhibit were startled that the art was created by personnel and that it communicated the "actual character of the SDF."[75] In an accompanying commentary, the Okinawan artist Ōmine Shinichi praised the artwork and wrote that it should not be judged by the fact it was by created by SDF personnel.[76]

Yet that was the point of the exhibit. As the author of the first *Chinzei* article suggested, the objective of the exhibit was to normalize and humanize SDF personnel and to portray them as sophisticated, cultured men, endowed with ability in the arts (*bun*) rather than just the military (*bu*) arts. Although the two most prominent local newspapers, the *Ryūkyū shinpō* and the *Okinawa taimusu*, do not appear to have covered the exhibit, Ishimine remembered being pleased with the number of attendees and their conclusion that force personnel were so artistically talented. His involvement, though, came at a cost. When anti-SDF activists discovered that he had helped organize the exhibit, they hounded him with phone calls at work to such an extent that he decided it was unfair to his employer the bank to continue working and resigned. Fortunately for him, his volunteer efforts led Matayoshi to offer him a position at the Provincial Liaison Office, where he worked until his retirement in 1990.[77]

Despite the SDF's efforts to prepare its personnel and to counter opposition to its disposition in the months and weeks before May 15, 1972, grievances about the past and concerns about the future generated distrust of and resistance to the SDF as it prepared to establish bases on Okinawa. As the terms of reversion became clear, enthusiasm turned to anxiety and critical views of the Imperial Army gained even wider currency. This led some Okinawans to question whether returning to Japan was a good idea. Many identified the SDF as a new "Japanese Army" and as a deputy to the US military that had long occupied the islands and which was now bombing their fellow Asians in Vietnam from bases in Okinawa. These dynamics all created opposition to the SDF that was much more intense than anything the organization had faced on the mainland during the previous two decades. To counter this familiar but in some ways unprecedented opposition, the SDF drew on a preexisting model but adjusted to try to meet the specific circumstances of Okinawa in the 1970s.

## Weapons of the Weak: Okinawan Pacifist Resistance

As daunting as the challenges faced by the SDF in Okinawa in 1972 may have been, it is important to remember that it always had the advantage over those opposed to its disposition. Once the terms of reversion were agreed to by the Japanese and US governments, there was little chance they would be reversed or modified. The SDF was to be dispatched to bases, and once it had arrived the Japanese government was not likely to have it pack up and return to the mainland. At best, implementation would be slowed down. When a small advance group arrived in February 1972, protesters plotted ways to force its retreat from the island by trying to persuade every shipping and bus company and hotel to refuse them service.[78] But this was next to impossible. Despite the widespread rage against the huge US bases, there seemed to always be companies and individuals willing to do business with the Americans. The same was true regarding the SDF.[79] As a result of such realities, from the beginning the opposition was not fueled by optimism but by disappointment and frustration.

Opposition to the SDF was more intense on Okinawa for decades not only because of the islands' distinctive history but also because the international and domestic context was different. Deep political divisions splintered countries around the globe in the early 1970s, including Japan. Protesters demonstrated against the Vietnam War and the automatic extension of the US-Japan Security Treaty. Extremists, particularly on the left but also on the right like Mishima, splintered from more moderate movements and engaged in more radical and violent protests during these years. Clashes between students and riot police, which virtually closed college campuses in 1969, diminished but persisted. Citizen movements, which emerged in the late 1960s, joined forces with older partisan politics, bringing attention to environmental concerns and oppressive state power. By the mid-1970s progressive politicians led over 150 cities, towns, and prefectures—including the seven largest cities.[80] Sometimes these regional and local leaders implemented policies that hampered the activities of the SDF, for example, by preventing them from holding parades on public streets. Meanwhile, pacifists challenged the SDF's constitutionality in court, though whatever victories they enjoyed—as when the Sapporo District Court ruled the SDF to be unconstitutional in the Naganuma Case in 1973—were fleeting and bore more symbolic meaning than practical consequences. In these struggles, progressives on Okinawa and the mainland, including public intellectuals such as Ōe Kenzaburō, the writer discussed in chapter 2 who criticized Defense Academy cadets, inspired and aided each other.[81]

The most visible expressions of opposition to the SDF's deployment to the islands were frequent public protests in Okinawa from 1971 until 1974. Demonstrators also took to the streets in Kumamoto, Tokyo, and other cities. All these protests need to be understood within the context of intense and sometimes violent anti–Vietnam War, anti–security treaty, and prereversion demonstrations that shook Okinawa as well as Tokyo and other cities on the mainland from the late 1960s. Around 1970, as the terms of reversion were announced, protests for reversion morphed into protests against the terms of reversion; many of those who had led the reversion movement now began to protest its conditions. In Okinawa, the most violent expression of anger over the reversion terms erupted in Koza in December 1970, when a riot broke out a few blocks from Kadena, the largest US Air Force base, after a pedestrian was injured in a collision with a car driven by a US soldier.[82]

Among the protests against the terms of reversion, those that primarily targeted the SDF reached their greatest intensity in 1972. The organization that led the movement for reversion, the Okinawa ken Sokoku Fukki Kyōgikai (Coordinating Committee for the Reversion to Our Homeland and the Restoration of Okinawa Prefecture), made preventing SDF disposition one of its principal objectives. Its leaders reemphasized that they wanted reversion to mean a return to the peace constitution, pacifism, and life without military bases—US and Japanese. This group became the chief organizers of protests, which brought attention to its complaints, were an irritant to the SDF, and hampered deployment. On the night of February 16, protesters "hurled Molotov cocktails" into a building that housed the Japanese government's office responsible for preparing for "Okinawa's return to Japan." Handbills left at the site proclaimed, "We will prevent by force the stationing of the SDF on Okinawa."[83] Opponents engaged in violence a few other times as well. In July 1975, two young radicals threw a firebomb and firecrackers at Crown Prince Akihito while he was visiting a monument dedicated to the Himeyuri student nurses during his trip to Okinawa for the Ocean Exposition. The crown prince was not hurt.[84] Such violence was the exception, though. Protests, which were almost always peaceful, continued after reversion and reached their height during the last three months of 1972, when the bulk of SDF personnel, including the large main group led by Kuwae, arrived. An estimated 8,000 protesters turned out to greet Kuwae's unit on its arrival in October. Katsu, the SDF member from the Amami Islands, remembered demonstrations occurring every Saturday during these months.[85]

A less visible form of resistance with a longer impact was "peace education" (heiwa kyōiku), taught in Okinawa's schools. Most teachers were members of the Okinawa Teachers Association. During the 1950s and 1960s, teachers supplemented the curriculum with lessons that promoted reversion, instructed students how to prepare to become Japanese citizens, and critiqued US military rule and bases. Reflecting broader political trends, by the 1970s, these sorts of lessons focused increasingly on the evils of war and nationalism and the continued disposal of Okinawa. After reversion, teachers concentrated on issues such as the atrocities committed by the imperial military during the Battle of Okinawa, the emperor's responsibility, the unchanged status of US bases, and criticism of the SDF as a violation of the constitution and for its deployment in Okinawa. The discussion and criticism of the force in school curricular materials continued until at least the early 1980s, but schoolteachers probably continued to draw from such materials for many years, which contributed to a lingering suspicion of the force.[86]

Two constant voices of criticism were Okinawa's main newspapers, the Okinawa taimusu and the Ryūkyū shinpō. The two papers dominated the newspaper market in the 1970s, maintaining about a 98 percent market share.[87] Thanks to that dominance, made possible in part by Okinawa's geographic remoteness, the two papers had an oversized influence on public opinion unequaled by local newspapers in other prefectures, a position they maintain today, though to a lesser extent. During the US occupation, people regarded Japanese newspapers such as the Yomiuri, the Mainichi, and the Asahi almost as foreign publications. After reversion, the mainland papers continued to cost more and arrive later in the day than local papers, and they still contained almost no coverage of Okinawa. They therefore had difficulty establishing much of a readership. Conservatives established new local newspapers and magazines, like the *Okinawa keizai shinbun* and the *Okinawa gurafu*, but these publications failed to attract many readers and often collapsed within a few years.[88] By the late 1960s, both the left-leaning *Okinawa taimusu* and the populist center-right *Ryūkyū shinpō* had adopted a proreversion and increasingly antibase position.

The *Okinawa taimusu* and the *Ryūkyū shinpō* were also unstintingly critical in their coverage of the SDF. As reversion approached, they reported on the research of academics and schoolteachers that detailed the crimes committed by the Imperial Army during the Battle of Okinawa and frequently criticized the looming deployment of the force. Like shifts in the wider reversion movement, such articles were symptomatic of the emerging critical view of reversion that objected to Tokyo's collusion with Washington to maintain the status quo of US bases and to continuing mainland discrimination against Okinawa. The *Ryūkyū shinpō*, to cite one example, editorialized: "Soon an unmistakable 'military force' will be coming to Okinawa. No matter how the style will differ from that of the past, its military function will be undeniable. Those who in the past commanded forces which pointed rifles at Okinawans, forced them out of the [caves], and made them commit suicide are still commanders of these forces."[89] For its part, the *Okinawa taimusu* was unrelenting in its reporting on the force. Starting on January 1, 1972, for example, the paper began a thirty-two-article series probing almost every aspect of the SDF's relationship with society. In addition to offering consistently critical coverage of the force, the *Okinawa taimusu* and the *Ryūkyū shinpō* chose not to cover some stories that the SDF would have liked them to.

As reversion approached, the press's influence went beyond its coverage. All of the major media companies in Okinawa except the national broadcaster NHK agreed not to run any SDF-related advertisements, including recruitment ads, not to allow the participation of personnel at events sponsored by the companies, and not to facilitate their news coverage by accepting help from the SDF, such as by using ASDF planes to take aerial photographs.[90] Mainland papers rarely had taken such steps.

Yet, in the long run and paradoxically, the media's coverage of the SDF, even if often biting, may have worked in its favor. At his final news conference before his retirement from the GSDF in 1976, Kuwae thanked the *Okinawa taimusu* and the *Ryūkyū shinpō* for their reporting, which he thought had been much more comprehensive than anything the SDF had received on the mainland. He insisted that he was not being sarcastic. He recalled that initially protesters had yelled "Go back home, Japanese Army!" but within a relatively short time began to yell "Go back home, Self-Defense Force!" To him, this was progress. Thanks to the visibility made possible by the media,

Okinawans had become familiar with the force. Stories about the SDF's public service had led many citizens to realize that it was not a group of "monsters, snakes, and killers," as it was made out to be.[91] It is hard to know if Kuwae's analysis was correct or not, but the detailed reporting by the press certainly may have had unintended consequences.

Most local elected officials were also opposed to the SDF, especially during the first six years after reunification. Progressive critics like Yara, who were known as reformers, won overwhelming victories in the first postreversion elections for governor and the prefectural assembly in June 1972. They also dominated many municipal elections. Reformers emphasized antibase pacifism, Okinawan identity, and local autonomy, whereas conservatives stressed economic development guided by national government policies.[92] The former were part of the national wave of progressive politicians elected in the late 1960s and early 1970s on the mainland. Okinawan progressives, though, often took more aggressive stands against the SDF than their allies on the mainland. They had the public support to do so. Okinawan elected officials did not have many weapons they could use to combat the SDF, but they did what they could.

One weapon some mayors wielded was directing municipal government offices to refuse to register personnel living on base as residents by claiming they did not have the legal authority to do so. Japanese citizens are required to complete a resident registration (*jūmin tōroku*) in the municipality in which they live. Taira Ryōshō, the mayor of Naha, who served until 1984, was the first to take this stand, soon after reversion. His reading of the resident registration law was grounded in the pre-1945 view that military bases were "sacred ground" over which local officials had no jurisdiction.[93] The inability of personnel to register as residents made it difficult for them to enroll their children in school, get a driver's license, or receive other government services, including garbage collection.[94] Around five hundred personnel were unable to register as residents in Naha and several other cities and towns by the time the problem was resolved.[95] The strategy spread beyond Okinawa. The progressive mayor of Tachikawa, a city west of Tokyo, who was angry that an airfield used by the US Air Force since the occupation would be turned over to the SDF rather than reverted to civilian use, imitated Taira's action, and progressive politicians throughout the country voiced their support for Taira. The dispute finally ended in February 1973, when the central government confirmed that the jurisdiction of local governments did indeed include bases.[96] Nevertheless, some local Okinawan officials continued to make things difficult for personnel. In some municipalities, such as Urasoe, city employees refused to help personnel if they were dressed in uniform. SDF veteran Tanaka Kisaburō recalled that when he arrived in 1976 he had no trouble completing the resident registration at the Urasoe city offices, which he credited to being dressed in civilian clothing and being accompanied by a member who had already navigated the local bureaucracy. High school officials, though, made enrolling one of his children difficult. He experienced no troubles registering another child for junior high.[97] Although the resident registration stand-off was resolved after several months, personnel continued to periodically have problems, as illustrated by Tanaka's experience, in their dealings with prefectural, municipal, and school administrators.

Municipal and prefectural offices refusing to cooperate with SDF recruitment activities was another form of official resistance. On the mainland, some local governments refused to cooperate when they were controlled by Socialists, but in Okinawa such noncooperation was much more widespread and long lasting. The repudiation of recruitment did not change on the prefectural level until conservatives won the governorship in 1978. Not a single city, town, or village cooperated until 1979. Naha, which was the largest city as well as the capital, only began cooperating a decade later. In 2019, around eight municipalities still continued to refuse to do so.[98] Because Okinawa's population was relatively small, recruitment was more important to the SDF as a way to bolster local support than as a source of manpower. Thus, local governments refusing to cooperate was seen as an effective way of combating acceptance of the SDF.

Another tool that local governments used was less significant but attracted a lot of attention. On the national holiday Coming-of-Age Day (Seijin no hi) held each January 15, young people who have turned twenty years old during the past year participate in receptions held by local governments. Before the first postoccupation Coming-of-Age holiday in 1973, the Naha Board of Education did not invite any twenty-year-old SDF personnel to the event. By the next year, the practice had spread to other municipalities. These snubs became the focus of a fierce debate that recurred year after year. In 1979, a change that transferred sponsorship for the event in Naha from the board of education to four districts within the city appeared to resolve the problem there.[99] But that was not the case. Activists continued to object to personnel attending and especially to them attending in uniform rather than in other formal wear. They argued that uniforms were a form of propaganda and protested the events.[100] This pattern was typical. Often, after local governments reversed official barriers, activists filled the gap. The protests opposing personnel participating in Coming-of-Age Day continued until 2001, when opponents changed strategy and opted to resist in a less confrontational manner by holding an annual symposium to consider problems related to the SDF from a wider perspective.[101]

An additional resistance strategy was university officials refusing to allow personnel to enroll and take courses. As early as 1954, a number of public and private universities on the mainland resisted accepting researchers affili-ated with the SDF because they did not regard the force as constitutional, did not want to cooperate with rearmament, and did not want to support militarism as they had done during the war.[102] In the late 1960s, the refusal to admit force personnel, including Defense Academy graduates, again became an issue at many public universities in Tokyo and elsewhere.[103] Student and union activists also exerted pressure on universities to not allow personnel on campus, just as they had tried to block them from attending coming-of-age ceremonies. Ministry of Education officials criticized such decisions at private and public institutions as "discrimination" and worked to reverse them.[104] Despite that, university rejections of personnel continued, but by 1970 they largely came to an end on the mainland. In 1975, the phenomenon reappeared in Okinawa. Students and the university employee association at the University of the Ryukyus objected to the admission of an ASDF mem-ber and an MSDF member. In the former case, some students went on a hunger strike, occupied a campus building, and prevented the airman from attending classes.[105] In the latter case, the university president ruled that the sailor be admitted because not doing so would be a violation of equality before the law and equal access to education.[106] In the end, ongoing protests led the sailor to give up, and the next year the MSDF transferred him back to the mainland.

Participation of SDF-sponsored teams in athletic events also proved to be a controversy, which continued well into the 1980s. In conjunction with the one-year anniversary of reversion, the government held a special National Athletic Festival (Kokumin Taiiku Taikai, abbreviated as Kokutai) in Oki-nawa in May 1973. In response to a request from the Okinawa Teachers Association, Saga Prefecture agreed not to send an SDF baseball team as its representative. The Ministry of Education intervened, asserting that sports ought to be free of politics. The prefecture reversed its decision.[107] In the end, the team participated amid protests.[108] Until the 1990s, the participa-tion in sporting events of SDF teams or individual personnel periodically led to similar controversies, with mixed results—sometimes the SDF athletes participated, sometimes they did not. Katsu, the SDF member from Amami, remembers being able to participate as an individual in judo competitions off base without any problem, but he made sure not to bring attention to the fact that he was a member of the SDF so as to not trigger controversy.[109]

This sort of opposition was almost unheard of on the mainland during the 1950s and late 1960s, when hostility to the force there were at its height. Although other sources of controversy, such as preventing SDF personnel from enrolling in university classes, had precedent on the mainland, in many ways the opposition the SDF experienced in Okinawa was beyond anything it and its personnel had previously encountered.

## Strategies of the Strong: The SDF's Counteroffensive

To combat opposition on Okinawa, the SDF turned to many of the same strategies it deployed on the mainland, which had become practices it was proud of and part of its identity. Even before reversion, national and regional commanders began to put these in place by emphasizing that the force would be focusing on disaster relief and civil engineering, and by selecting Matayoshi and Kuwae, the two Okinawan officers, to act as the face of the force. The organization communicated to personnel that they should contribute to the development of Okinawa, seek to differentiate the force from the imperial military and keep their distance from the US military. Defense officials stressed the importance of public relations and integrating the force and personnel into wider society, a challenging task given the paucity of personnel from Okinawa and the widespread, deep-seated dislike they faced. Officials were confident that eventually time would dissipate much of the opposition. Still, they wanted to accelerate that process and transform antipathy or at least apathy into acceptance and support. From May 15—the day of reversion—the SDF assertively deployed strategies it had developed over the last two decades in its sustained influence campaign on the mainland.

As on the mainland, public relations and recruitment efforts were interrelated. In the face of local authorities refusing to cooperate in recruitment efforts, SDF officials had to rely on local allies. One was Ishimine, the Okinawan who returned to the islands to work for a bank after serving in the GSDF and helped establish the Force Friends Association on the islands in 1969. He recalled engaging in recruitment activities before reversion. Prevented from using schools to spread the word, he and other volunteers went door to door and organized evening gatherings in poorer urban and rural areas where they would show filmstrips produced by the Defense Agency. Concerned about disruptions by opponents, Ishimine sometimes hired local toughs who were skilled in martial arts to act as guards.[110] He coordinated his activities with Matayoshi and took along Okinawan SDF personnel like Tameyoshi Yaeyako, dressed in their uniforms, who were visiting from the mainland. Without the cooperation of local governments and schools and prevented from using the two major newspapers to advertise, the Provincial Cooperation Office struggled before and after reversion to spread the word about the SDF as an employment option. One way to get out the word was recruitment posters—which in the 1970s emphasized the force's contribution to peace and support for society.[111] But finding people who would agree to post them was a challenge, as was defacement and theft of the posters. It is impossible to determine how these messages were received, but enlistments did grow over time. Fifteen Okinawans joined the force in 1972, 61 in 1973, and 129 in 1974.[112] During the first ten years, an average of 610 Okinawans applied and 145 were accepted annually.[113] These enlistments enabled the percentage of Okinawans serving in the SDF who were stationed in their home prefecture (which represented most Okinawans in the force) to reach 5.4 percent by 1979.[114] By 2019, that number had reached about 40 percent, still much lower than other prefectures, despite the lack of other employment opportunities in Okinawa.[115]

As in other regions, the GDSF's internal newspaper played a role in public-relations efforts by trying to shape the attitudes and behavior of personnel, and by extension, to influence wider public opinion. The latter objective was pursued indirectly as staff of the regimental newspaper *Shurei* reached out to *Okinawa taimusu* and *Ryūkyū shinpō* reporters and editors and other shapers of public opinion to solicit positive coverage of the force, much as the *Akashiya* editor Irikura did with newspapers in Hokkaido. This was clearly an uphill battle in Okinawa. The brigade also tried to assume an Okinawan identity by adopting iconic Okinawan names and imagery. The *Shurei* appropriated the name of the famous gate Shurei-mon, which was built as a ceremonial entrance to Shuri Castle in the late sixteenth century, destroyed during the Battle of Okinawa, and then rebuilt in 1958.[116] The unit also appropriated an image of the gate for its unit patch and eventually changed the newspaper's masthead to a likeness of the gate.[117] The paper's original masthead included a background of shells, placed below a more specific symbol of Okinawa, the hibiscus flower. The hibiscus, as the historian Gerald Figal noted, played a key role in the tropicalization of the Okinawan landscape and its portrayal as a tourist playland.[118] From the mid-1970s to the early 1980s, the paper also ran a comic strip entitled "Shurei-kun," which was also the name of its protagonist, a male brigade member.[119] Whether Shurei-kun was from Okinawa or the mainland was unclear, but the comic allowed its audience—force members stationed in Okinawa—to imagine themselves as Shurei-kun, perhaps even as Okinawan, regardless of their ethnic background. The character participated in humorous scenarios, usually in military work settings, but also in after-work situations, including interactions with local women.[120]

Like other internal papers such as the *Chinzei* and the *Akashiya*, the *Shurei* sought to shape personnel, boost morale, and foster positive relations with local society. Indeed, in the inaugural issue published on June 1, just weeks after reversion, the paper reprinted a new directive from corps commander Horie urging personnel—nearly all of whom were not from Okinawa—to "achieve unity and become integrated with the people of Okinawa prefecture as quickly as possible."[121] In the same issue, Kuwae urged brigade members to help "build a bright and prosperous Okinawa" that would reap the benefits of being part of Japan, which now had the "world's second largest gross national product."[122] Referencing the second character of *Shurei*, in yet another piece Kuwae counseled his men to show propriety (*rei*) by respecting and always offering courteous greetings to everyone they encountered.[123] Although the challenges the SDF faced in Okinawa were daunting, its playbook was familiar.

As in Hokkaido and other rural areas in the 1950s and 1960s, GSDF officials expected that civil engineering projects and agricultural aid would reap significant good will. Things did not work out as they expected. Opposition to the SDF made using these considerable resources tricky. It may have not helped that the US military had tried to use a similar strategy during the twenty-seven years of US rule. A couple of examples illustrate the challenges. Soon after reversion, the conservative mayor of Chinen announced that because of village financial constraints he intended to ask the battalion to help grade the field of a local junior high school. Predictably, the teachers union objected. In midst of the disagreement, a village youth group volunteered to do the work. Two years later, the mayor of the village of Ōzato asked the GSDF for help cutting the sugarcane harvest, but when progressives objected, the request was revoked.[124] These two incidents were typical of the opposition the force encountered in trying to use civil engineering and agricultural aid to improve its reputation. In fact, the brigade rarely performed such work. It could not do so unless local elected officials requested the help. Most would not even consider doing so, and the few who did often faced a backlash.

SDF officials also expected that disaster-relief operations would help them prove the value of the force. Surely opponents of the force could not very well refuse to call on it for help in the case of emergencies. Individual members appear to have anticipated the opportunity as well. A few months before reversion, one member, Sergeant Second Class Shinjō Masahira from Okinawa vowed, "[I will] devote myself to the relief of typhoon victims. . . . I think I will be able to communicate with the residents not only with [my] mouth but with the whole body."[125] Unfortunately for the brigade, despite the islands lying in the heart of what is known as Typhoon Ginza, which usually gets hit by an average of seven hurricane-strength storms a year, the built environment rarely sustained serious damage because Okinawans constructed their homes and buildings to weather such storms, especially after US occupation authorities encouraged them to do so following an extremely powerful typhoon in the late 1940s that destroyed large swaths of the islands. Regardless, except in the most serious emergencies, requesting the SDF's help was politically sensitive. It was only after conservatives captured the governorship and more mayoral offices in the late 1970s that local political leaders began to request that the SDF be mobilized, but such opportunities were still rare. In addition, because of Okinawa's distance from the mainland, the brigade was not mobilized for disaster relief elsewhere until 2011, when top commanders dispatched it with units from across the country to respond to the Great East Japan Earthquake.[126]

In the absence of opportunities to perform disaster-relief operations in which it could demonstrate its mettle, the brigade found a niche providing emergency flights to transport patients from outlying islands without medical facilities to hospitals in Naha. The US military had previously provided this service. The ASDF conducted its first evacuation flight in December 1972, and for the next decade it averaged about a dozen per year, including many at night, which were riskier. At some point and in some areas, the ASDF came to divide this work with the Coast Guard, but it still performed most medical evacuations. Because the flights helped a single individual at a time, they were rarely newsworthy on their own and often did not get covered by the *Okinawa taimusu* or the *Ryūkyū shinpō*. Neither Yara nor his progressive successor as governor publicly thanked the SDF for this service, because they did not want to legitimize the force, though they surely appreciated its assistance.[127] It was up to the *Shurei* and private conservative publications to try to bring attention to the flights, though that was difficult given their limited readership. In 1974, the *Shurei* began to publish a running count of the total number of emergency air flights (*kyūkan kūrin*) each month, which included the date, time, destination, age and sex of the patient, and reason for the evacuation. The brigade also constructed a sign, which has a similar design to that of Shurei-mon gate and stands at the entrance of its Naha Base, that keeps a running tally of the number of emergency medical flights and unexploded bomb-disposal missions since reversion. On July 5, 2019, when I visited the base, the former had reached 9,501, approximately one flight every two days for forty-seven years.

The brigade also completed bomb-disposal missions with great frequency. The Battle of Okinawa had littered the landscape, especially the central and southern part of the island of Okinawa, with unexploded ordnance. During the occupation, the US military disposed of unexploded shells, removing several thousand tons.[128] After reversion, the GSDF, which had experience disposing unexploded bombs on the mainland, collaborated with the Americans. Within a few years, the Okinawa Brigade took over responsibility for the extraction, defusing, transport, and disposal of munitions. In late 1972, the GSDF estimated that thirty thousand (with a total weight of ten thousand tons) or 5 percent of the approximately six hundred thousand (or two hundred thousand tons) had been found. By 2019, the brigade's bomb squad had removed around two thousand tons of unexploded ordnance, an average of more than two pieces of unexploded ordnance per day since reversion. Officials estimate that it will take another seventy years to remove the rest.[129]

As development and construction accelerated on the islands, the unearthing of explosives increased in frequency, sometimes with tragic consequences. In March 1974, construction work caused an antitank mine buried by the Imperial Navy to explode in Naha, killing four people, including the three-year-old daughter of a brigade member who was playing on a swing at an adjacent nursery school.[130] Over the next decade, the brigade bomb-disposal unit responded annually to several hundred calls to deal with explosives. It did not require much imagination to contemplate the bombs' metaphorical meaning, especially when they exploded and killed people. The day after the accident in 1974, the *Okinawa taimusu* called them the "nightmare of war that rises again [*yomigaeru senso no akuyume*]." "The odious wounds of war are one after another unearthed," the paper opined, "the war is not over, the postwar is not over, . . . thirty years later Okinawa still hangs on a cross."[131] The paper did not extend the analogy further to suggest that the SDF was making amends for its predecessor, and in fact the coverage may have ironically, worked to undermine the SDF's public-relation hopes. Despite bomb-disposal personnel's brave service, news reports of their work may have served to remind Okinawans not only of the battle but also of the mistreatment of Okinawans by their military predecessors during the battle. The *Shurei* published a running total of this work, divided into the weight and type of each kind of ordnance, to bolster personnel morale and to try to generate, even if indirectly, positive public opinion. In articles about bomb-disposal incidents, the paper emphasized the bravery of the personnel and the gratitude of Okinawans. When the *Ryūkyū shinpō* and the *Okinawa taimusu* covered the work of the bomb-disposal unit, they did so in decidedly more neutral language.

Unfortunately for the SDF on Okinawa, much of its public service and the broader social context in which it existed did not lend itself to crafting a military-defense identity. Although the SDF did all it could to internally and externally publicize the emergency medical flights and bomb-disposal operations it performed, these missions, which were highly specialized and performed by a select group of highly trained personnel, did not translate as readily as disaster-relief operations into the sort of force identity that had emerged on the mainland. Local commanders recognized this and argued unsuccessfully, for example, for the regiment to be allowed to participate in the disaster-relief operations after the Great Hanshin Earthquake hit the Kobe area in 1994.[132] The intense and persistent resistance from local society also hampered efforts to create a sense of group identity, though the outside pressure may have contributed to greater internal solidarity and the need to collaborate with outside support groups. The transience and unpopularity of an assignment to Okinawa, particularly in the early years, may have also undermined efforts to create a sense of force identity. Finally, crafting a sense of military manliness was surely complicated by the ubiquity, unlike in Hokkaido, of US servicemen; pressure from society to completely distance the force from the imperial military; and the relative lack of mainland salaryman culture on the islands. These dynamics, which had helped the GSDF create a sense of internal identity elsewhere, were less useful in Okinawa.

In addition to proactively engaging in public service, the SDF pursued a variety of forms of public outreach to gain greater acceptance and achieve military-society integration. These efforts were generally similar to those it pursued on the mainland, though the intense and ongoing hostility it encountered led it to proceed cautiously. It also participated in fewer activities because officials understood that a cautious approach was imperative. For example, the force had provided logistical aid for the National Athletic Meet on the mainland every year since 1957, but it did not do so for a special, smaller version of the event when it was held in Okinawa in 1973, nor did it do so when the national meet was held on the islands for the first time in 1987. Doing so would have surely prompted protests beyond those targeting participation of SDF athletes. The only major event for which the SDF provided support for during its first decade on Okinawa may have been the International Ocean Exposition held from July 1975 to January 1976. But it did so entirely behind the scenes, apparently attracting no attention and leaving almost no evidence of its participation.[133] The newspapers, for example, appear to have not noticed or mentioned its work.

It was easier for the SDF to do outreach within its bases, though doing so was probably not as effective as doing it outside because the circumscribed location limited its reach. On-base events, though, did allow the force to exercise greater control and largely avoid controversy. From the time of reversion, the brigade hosted events open to the public inside its bases. One of the earliest on-base events was organized at Naha Base in March 1973 and included the opening of a public-relations center. The program included marching troops, a band performance, skits, an art exhibit, and a karate demonstration. The brigade estimated that about four thousand people attended. Many of them appeared to have been SDF family members. In fact, the caption of one photograph featured in the *Shurei* showing a crowd of people lounging on the grass asked, "Can you see yourself here?" This seemed appropriate given that most readers of the *Shurei*, like most attendees, were force personnel or their family members.[134] Family and friends of the force probably also made up the preponderance of attendees at SDF events on the mainland during the early decades of the force, but this trend was probably much more pronounced in Okinawa given the local dynamics. Predictably, the *Ryūkyū shinpō* and the *Okinawa taimusu* did not cover this event or most on-base events.

As in Hokkaido and elsewhere, the SDF made a concerted attempt to woo society by encouraging its personnel to court local women. Ōta, the University of the Ryukyus professor and future governor who published the blistering account of Japan's treatment of Okinawa in 1969, evaluated these marriages as the "most successful method the SDF used to gain social acceptance in Okinawa."[135] As in Hokkaido but even more so, the force was motivated to encourage these marriages for at least two reasons. First, its leaders recognized that marriages with local women would lead to greater legitimacy, one woman and one (extended) family at a time. Second, despite its subtropical locale, Okinawa was generally not a popular location to be stationed, and it helped the SDF if mainlanders were willing to put down roots and extend their assignments there. Most personnel posted to the islands were from Kyushu, and many hoped to return home as soon as possible. Tanaka, the veteran who experienced trouble enrolling one of his children in high school in Urasoe, and Yanagita Mitsuhara, a fellow native of Kyushu who served in Okinawa at the same time in the late 1970s, recalled that the islands were not a popular place to be stationed. Both men complained of water shortages, poor food, and cultural differences. By the late 1970s, they remembered, opposition to the SDF had dissipated but had not disappeared. Bikes were stolen, car tires deflated. Commanders told personnel to not commute in uniform for fear of them being the target of harassment.[136]

In the face of these challenges, the force sought to bring personnel and local women together. In March 1973, the ASDF hosted a dance on its base in Naha, but only twenty local women attended and the dance sparked negative publicity, as did later dances organized by the GSDF.[137] As signaled by that reaction, it would have been unthinkable for the prefectural or any municipal government to partner with the force to organize events designed to intro-duce local women and personnel.

Rather, as it did elsewhere, the SDF took more subtle steps. Like the North-ern Corps's *Akashiya* during the 1950s and 1960s, the editors of the regimen-tal *Shurei* and regional Western Corps *Chinzei* regularly featured eligible local women, who worked for contractors on base. (Among the dozens of such articles I located in the *Shurei* from the mid-1970s to the early 1980s, not one of them featured a female personnel member, which probably reflected the fact that few women were assigned to Okinawa at the time. Several of the women featured, though, mentioned that they had considered applying or wished they had applied to the WAC.) Despite the widespread and deep-seated antipathy for the SDF in Okinawa, local women may have agreed to be featured in these articles and been interested in a possible match with personnel because of the relatively high and steady income of force mem-bers, and perhaps because they were anxious to create an avenue to leave the islands. For a time, the articles in the *Shurei*, like those in the *Akashiya* and other GSDF papers around this time, had a flower theme. Each "Oki-nawan Flower" (Okinawa no hana) article associated a young woman with a certain tropical flower such as the *deigo* (Indian coral bean) and *bougain-villea*, which became the subtitle of an article (figure 5.4).[138] Conveniently, *hana* also means beauty, youth, and bride in Japanese. Like those in other papers, the articles were composed of a photograph of the woman and an introduction to her that often noted her height and weight, and frequently concluded with comments from the woman about what sort of man she was interested in. The series in the *Chinzei*, which was titled "Nadeshiko," the name of the wild pink *Dianthus superbus* that also refers to an ideal Japa-nese woman, featured women in both Okinawa and Kyushu. One article introduced a nineteen-year-old employee of a credit union on Naha Base. "When asked if she had a boyfriend," it stated, "she avoided the question by just smiling. Looks like force personnel might have a chance." "The beautiful hibiscus," the piece continued, metaphorically invoking the flower symbol-izing Okinawa and emblazoned on the banner of the *Shurei*, "is a flower with which many personnel are familiar."[139] The inclusion of these articles probably had several purposes. They functioned as a form of matchmak-ing, which, as on the mainland, was common in Okinawa. Any marriages that may have resulted from their inclusion would benefit the force's goal of gaining greater societal acceptance and help with staffing the force. And the articles, like those in the *Akashiya* and other unit newspapers, sought to boost the masculine morale and egos of the paper's readers, who were of

県立糸満高校を卒業して昭和四十八年六月から南与座分とん地で勤務する上原操子さん。

自衛隊で勤務するようになった動機は―救父（糸満市役所勤務）の勧めに応じて、航空自衛隊を希望したがどうした訳か陸上自衛隊に決ったという。事務官として机についた仕事よりは〝笑顔と親切〟をモットーに売店で撮影する方が好き」とこぼれるような笑顔が返ってきた。

家庭は母（父は昨年病死）と六人の兄姉がある。〝末子のためわがままと甘えの弱い面が多くある〟と自分を評する。

分とん地の隊員については……「皆やさしく、親切にしてくれるが、時には営業時間等で無理をいう人もある。仕事に熱中する隊員にたまらない魅力を感ずる」と働き者で有名な糸満女性の片鱗をの

休日にはデートの申込みもあるが母を心配させたくないと、趣味の「編物、読書」で過ごす事が多い。とか―母おもいの印象を受けた。

ぞかせる。

理想の男性像は―「亭主関白でも絶えず微笑をたやさない、南与座のカトレア」の印象を与えてくれる。

控目ではあるがしさを漂わせる。カトレアは一輪でも見事にその美れるん話しているときに〝南与座の上原さんと話しているときに〝南与座のカトレア」とか「〝男性の長髪、分とん地では見られませんが、自衛官の長髪程見苦しく、横にならないものはないですネ」と語る。

がまわれないが強りに減少してくれる人」と顔を染めた。〝嫌いなものはたづねると

沖縄の花「カトレア」

分とん地勤務
上原操子さん

**FIGURE 5.4.** One of the articles from the "Okinawa Flower" series that appeared monthly in the *Shurei*. The young woman featured in this article, which appeared on July 25, 1974, and which used a cattleya, an orchid, as its flower theme, is Uehara Ayako, who worked at a GSDF sub-base on the island. Used with permission of the Okinawa Fifteenth Brigade.

course almost all male. They seemed to signal to personnel that they could gaze at these women on the pages of the *Shurei* and desire them, and that they themselves might be desired in return.[140]

As highlighted by the inclusion of women from Kyushu in the *Chinzei*, this sort of encouragement was not limited to Okinawa or, as mentioned in chapter 3, to Hokkaido. Given the persistent stigma associated with the postwar military, the SDF sought to encourage and facilitate the marriage of its personnel no matter where they were stationed. Indeed, the SDF opened marriage consultation centers, through which it worked with local groups to match personnel with women in surrounding communities, in all 153 of its bases in mid-1973.[141] But even more so than in Hokkaido, getting Okinawan women to marry personnel had added benefits for human resources and public relations.[142] Katsu, the SDF member from Amami, apparently remained immune to all these efforts. Despite a ten-year stay in Okinawa from his early twenties, he remained single, a status he credited to his constant drinking.[143]

The precise effect of such strategies is impossible to determine, but within two years of reversion, forty Okinawan women had married personnel stationed in Okinawa, almost all of whom were from the mainland. The news was apparently notable enough that the *Okinawa taimusu* featured the story in June 1974. Its reporter began the article by noting that the SDF had put most of its effort into "collaborative activities to improve people's livelihood," such as emergency medical flights. But its biggest coup, the reporter exclaimed, were the forty marriages. Some of these unions had already led to the birth of what the article called *nisei*, presumably future second-generation personnel. "We have never had so many marriages in other prefectures," a force spokesperson stated, "We expect," he optimistically predicted, "that the numbers will continue to rise." In response, pacifists and unionists bemoaned, "'Little by little the opposition of prefectural citizens is being broken down as the force attempts to SDF-ize [*Jieitai-ka*] the entire prefecture.'"[144] Apparently, some Okinawans feared that, like US soldiers, SDF personnel would "take away" the islands' young women.[145] They indicated that they were working to organize a "movement against women becoming SDF brides" (*o-yome ni ikanai undō*) but the issue, as the reporter put it, was one "in the realm of the delicate relations between a man and woman," perhaps implying that it was inappropriate to interfere with romance, or perhaps that trying to do so would likely not yield the desired result.[146]

In its first issue after the *Okinawa taimusu* broke the story, the *Shurei* staff seemed to revel in the news. Under the headline "Hot topic ♥♥♥ marriage," the writer joked that he—the writer was probably a man—had assumed that "Yamatonchu [a Japanese resident of Okinawa] would not even cast an eye at Uchinanchu [Okinawans]," but was "relieved that [was] not true." In case anyone was thinking of trying to interfere with love, he invoked the constitution's Article 24—which was ironic, given that detractors argued that the SDF was unconstitutional: "Marriage shall be based only on the mutual consent of both sexes." The author concluded by thanking all those outside allies of the force who in a variety of ways, such as matchmaking, were helping to "build the foundations of defense."[147]

Eight years later in 1982, SDF supporters were surely pleased and detractors disappointed by a story about marriages between personnel and local women that appeared as one of a *Ryūkyū shinpō* series of articles at the time of the tenth anniversary of reversion. Based on SDF sources, the reporter estimated that since reversion around 410 local women had gotten married to personnel from the three branches of the force, a statistic so high it surprised several progressive activists. After citing these statistics, the reporter devoted most of the article to the experience of a recently married couple, who went unnamed, that aptly illustrates many of the family and societal dynamics of such marriages. The twenty-six-year-old woman, who had "grown up in Okinawa where anti-war, anti–Self-Defense Force feelings are strong," reflected that she "really hated" the SDF until she met the thirty-three-year-old sergeant who became her husband, but that her views changed as she observed the "pride he had in his work" and "learned about things [she] did not know." The relationship, though, was difficult for her family. Her parents were initially opposed because of the sergeant's occupation and because he was from the mainland, which they feared would lead her to leave Okinawa. An older brother who was a teacher involved in union activities refused to meet her then fiancé but in the end accepted her decision to get married. Not everyone did. One friend told her, "I'll continue to be your friend just like I have, but I will not be friends with your husband." In a decision that certainly further pleased the SDF, the sergeant had recently filed a request to "permanently reside" in Okinawa.[148] This example shows how such marriages influenced society one wedding, one family, and one network of friendships at a time, almost always positively for the force.

More broadly, as on the mainland, the SDF in Okinawa sought to nourish support groups for familial, ideological, political, and financial purposes. These included veterans of the SDF (Force Friends Association), family members (Fathers and Brothers Association), defense proponents (the SDF Cooperation Society and the Defense Association), conservative parties (the Liberal Democratic Party), and business interests. As elsewhere, many supporters were members of multiple groups as common interests led to significant crossover and collaboration. The GSDF veteran Ishimine, who helped found the Okinawan branch of the Force Friends Association and served as a volunteer recruiter, used his involvement in the Boy Scouts, the Lions Club, the Rotary Club, parent-teacher associations, and even a choral group, as well as business and political connections to be, as he put it in his self-published account of his life, a "bridge" between the SDF and Okinawan society.[149]

Some boosters of the SDF were likely motivated in part by financial considerations. One of the SDF's most prominent supporters was Kokuba Kōtarō, a titan of the local construction industry. After two years of service in the Imperial Army and gaining experience working on the reconstruction of Tokyo and Yokohama after the Great Kantō Earthquake of 1923, Kokuba returned to Okinawa and founded Kokuba gumi in 1931. For the next half-century, his firm built various facilities for the imperial military, the US military, and the SDF. Among its major projects was the expansion of the Oroku (later Naha) airfield (for the imperial military) in 1941, the enlargement of Camp Hansen (for the US military) from 1958 to 1962, and the International

Ocean Exposition in 1975.[150] During Defense Agency Director Nakasone's visit to Okinawa in early October 1970, he invited a group of businessmen including Kokuba to Tokyo in conjunction with the annual celebration of the SDF's anniversary on November 1. Nakasone arranged for the group of nearly forty to fly for free on an ASDF propeller transport plane (though Kokuba was the only businessman to take him up on the offer, whereas the others took a Japan Airlines commercial flight), put them up at the Grand Hill's Hotel adjacent to the Defense Agency in Ichigaya, arranged for them to be seated in a prime location for the parade, and hosted a fine dinner in their honor.[151]

After the group's return to Okinawa, Matayoshi and Ishimine immediately sought to capitalize on the trip by establishing the SDF Cooperation Association (Jieitai kyōryoku kyōkai) and the Okinawa Defense Association (Bōei kyōkai), both of which Kokuba led for many years after.[152] Among the members of the group was the president of Orion Beer, which helps to explain why the Orion Beer Hall hosted the exhibit of artwork by SDF personnel mentioned earlier in this chapter. Kokuba provided funding for the establishment of the short-lived *Okinawa keizai* newspaper and the glossy monthly magazine *Okinawa gurafu*, which featured many positive stories about and photographs of the SDF's public-service and outreach activities. One of his younger brothers, Kōshō, who had been elected to the Diet as a member of the LDP and served as the vice minister of the Okinawa Development Agency during the 1970s, succeeded him as president of the Defense Association, serving until he passed away. Such an intermingling of economic and political interests was common among many who did business with and supported the SDF as well as the US military.[153]

In December 1978, allies of the SDF like the Kokuba brothers gained the political upper hand when Nishime Junji overwhelmingly defeated the reformist candidate for governor. That victory, the political scientist Takayoshi Egami noted, "marked a turning point in Okinawan politics."[154] SDF veterans Tanaka and Yanagita, who were serving in Okinawa at the time, remember the election as important for the SDF, too.[155] During the campaign, Nishime insisted that Yara and his reformist successor Taira Koichi, who retired because of illness, had prioritized ideological issues over economic development. After defeating the reformist candidate, Chibana Hideo, Nishime immediately embraced the SDF, praising it for its public service and for protecting Okinawa and Japan. He attended the force's anniversary ceremonies, the first to be held off base; issued the first written expression of gratitude for its emergency flights; and directed prefectural officials to begin collaborating in recruiting activities, including those for the Defense

Academy.[156] "[T]he fundamental policies of the prefectural administration clearly changed from anti-war, anti–U.S. military base, and anti-national government," Egami observed, "to pro–U.S. military base, pro-SDF, and pro-national government."[157] In turn, the central government further expanded economic assistance after Nishime was elected, which helped grease the skids for greater acceptance of the SDF.[158] Although many progressives and activists continued to protest personnel participation in events such as coming-of-age ceremonies and athletic competitions, conservative control of the prefecture and more municipal governments was a boon for the SDF. Politics shaped society, and vice versa.

Indeed, social change was evident well before the elections of 1978. As early as 1975, three years after reversion, the SDF appears to have achieved what might be best called gradual acclimation when a majority of Okinawans indicated they thought the force was necessary. According to polling by NHK and the *Ryūkyū shinpō* in 1972, 1973, and 1974, 22 to 29 percent Okinawans thought the SDF was necessary and 39 to 60 percent though it was unnecessary. In 1975, according to NHK, for the first time a significantly greater number of people thought it was necessary rather than unnecessary, 47 percent to 35 percent. This trend continued. Journalism professor and future governor Ōta's analysis of this polling data confirmed this conclusion. He described the years from 1971 to 1974 as characterized by "opposition to the stationing of the SDF on Okinawa" and "opposition to the SDF," and from those 1975 onward as characterized by recognition that "the SDF is necessary."[159] Calling this recognition "acceptance" would be inaccurate, though. "Resignation" is probably a more appropriate term. Another contributing factor to this shift in attitudes was Okinawans, like Japanese on the mainland, becoming more focused on economics and less on ideology from the mid-1970s.[160]

These polling results certainly were heartening for Kuwae, and perhaps emboldened him. For several years, his Okinawa unit had tried to show that the SDF was different from its predecessor, that regardless of what their critics said the pre-1945 "Japanese military" had in fact not returned. Kuwae and some other senior SDF officers who had served in the imperial military at times expressed views that undermined this effort. For example, Kuwae sparked controversy when he declared in late 1972 that Imperial Japan was justified in going to war and that its objective for doing so was to free the colonized people of Asia.[161] After the incident, it appears Kuwae became more cautious about what he said, especially regarding the Imperial Army. Still, he found ways to nourish in personnel a link to and respect for the Imperial Army by having brigade members participate in cleaning memorial sites and recovering bones from battlefield sites, activities that both connected the force to and differentiated it from the prewar military. By the mid-1970s, he apparently decided he was going to do something riskier. Kuwae resented the fact that since reversion prefectural officials had never invited SDF officials to participate in Okinawa's Memorial Day ceremonies, held on June 23, the day organized resistance during the Battle of Okinawa came to an end with the predawn suicides of generals Ushijima Mitsuru and Chō Isamu. The main site of the memorial services each year was near Mabuni Hill, within which was a cave where the Thirty-Second Army Command had established its headquarters as it had retreated to the southern edge of the island. Each year beginning in 1972, Kuwae visited the site on Memorial Day, alone and in uniform, before the official ceremonies began. He was frustrated that he and other officers were not invited to the official ceremony, that he had to go early to avoid sparking a controversy, and most of all that the dominant narrative in Okinawa placed blame on the army for the deaths of civilians rather than celebrating both as having fought together bravely to the death. As early as 1975, Kuwae planned a group march to Mabuni, but he postponed it because he did not want it to distract from the International Ocean Exposition.[162] In 1976, he decided to wait no longer.

At 11 p.m. the night before Memorial Day, around a thousand ground force personnel departed from the Naha and Chinen bases. They marched twenty and eighteen miles, respectively, and converged at Mabuni on the Peace Plaza (Heiwa no hiroba) above the cliffs overlooking the ocean by 4:30 a.m., about the time when Ushijima and Chō had committed suicide thirty-one years before (figure 5.5). There Kuwae delivered a speech during which he by the light of a flashlight read the wills of one member each of the Imperial Blood and Iron Youth and the Himeyuri Corps.[163] After a bugler played the prewar military tune "Kuni no shizume" (Guardian of the country), the personnel observed a moment of silence. Within twenty minutes they had boarded trucks and returned to their bases.[164]

As Kuwae anticipated, reaction to the march was mixed. Predictably, the *Ryūkyū shinpō* and the *Okinawa taimusu* published headlines like a "Strange Army March in the Middle of the Night" and the "Sound of Army Boots on Hallowed Ground," and made comments such as "What was the 'army' thinking, and what might they have been praying for?"[165] Several days after the march, the *Ryūkyū shinpō* provided an overview of reactions. Governor Taira, who had only been in office for a few days, exclaimed his dismay. Prefectural officials expressed disappointment that they had not been consulted about the march and use of the park. The spokesman for a pacifist group accused the brigade of showing its true colors by "trampling on holy ground." Many people interviewed on the street, including some who had

**FIGURE 5.5.** *Shurei* coverage of the Okinawa Brigade's 1976 early morning march to the Peace Plaza on Mabuni Hill, the site of Okinawa's Memorial Day commemoration held each year on June 23. Colonel Kuwae Ryōhō is the white-helmeted figure to the right. This article appeared on July 18, 1976. Used with permission of the Okinawa Fifteenth Brigade.

lost family members in the Battle of Okinawa, expressed shock and anger. But some withheld judgment about the SDF's motives and said personnel should be free to pay their respects to war dead.[166] In his account of his service in Okinawa, Kuwae claimed that villagers whom the troops encountered as they marched through the night lent personal words of encouragement and that despite the "sensational" local coverage, there were no protests or angry letters to the editor in response to the march.[167] This indeed seems to have been the case, but that likely indicated resignation rather than support for the marchers' actions.

Although the march probably did not impact the slim majority of acceptance that the SDF had gained, it is telling in other ways. It speaks to the fundamental divide that lingered in Okinawa for the next several decades even as acceptance of the SDF, however grudging, rose to around 70 percent by the turn of the century, about the same level as on the mainland. At its core, opposition to or recognition of the SDF was about war memory, ideology, and identity, about whether to regard the force as equivalent to the imperial military, and about whether it was a threat to peace or a necessary guarantor of security.

Some Okinawans refused to blame the Imperial Army, the Japanese government, or the emperor for the tragedies of the battle. An increasing number came to believe that the SDF was not the same as the imperial military and was necessary for Okinawa's and Japan's security. Then there were outliers like Kuwae and Kinjō, the teacher who presented to brigade members in Kumamoto before they departed for Okinawa. For Kuwae, the Battle of Okinawa was also an intensely personal question, on several levels. When he and Matayoshi graduated from the military academy in 1941, Ushijima—the commander of the Imperial Army on the islands—was serving as the director commandant of the Army Academy, and by all accounts, he was a highly revered officer and gentleman.[168] Moreover, when Kuwae was transferred from Manchuria to Micronesia, the rest of his unit was sent to Okinawa, where his onetime comrades died resisting the Americans. As mentioned, his younger brother and grandmother also perished in the battle.[169] For this reason, Kuwae regarded Okinawa as "sacred ground" and could not countenance claims that soldiers and civilians had died meaningless deaths "like dogs."[170] Blaming the military for the civilian dead, either directly or indirectly, was unacceptable. The issue was also not just about the past. When Kuwae spoke of the "military, government, and people—as one—defending the country," as he did in his address to his men after the march, he was not just referring to events thirty-one years earlier but also to his aspiration for the present day—his hope for military-society integration.[171]

A few months later, Kuwae retired from the GSDF as planned and turned his attention to supporting the force by assuming leadership of and being involved in several support organizations. At his final press conference, in addition to thanking the *Okinawa taimusu* and the *Ryūkyū shinpō* tongue-in-cheek for their coverage, he reflected on the accomplishments and disappointments of the force. He expressed regret that he had been unable to secure more land for the GSDF to train on the islands, which forced the regiment to go to Kyushu for training. In terms of successes, Kuwae declared that the SDF had achieved acceptance in Okinawa much more quickly than the organization had on the mainland. This, he believed, was his biggest victory.[172]

Six years later, on the afternoon of December 11, 1982, a Saturday, the SDF held the first parade it had ever organized off base in Naha to celebrate the tenth anniversary of its deployment there.[173] It was a simple affair. The only entry, a 150-member band composed of personnel marched down the middle of National Route 58 in central Naha. The parade lasted only forty minutes. The brigade band had previously performed in the community at various events and had participated in larger parades organized by other groups, such as the Jaycees.[174] But the brigade had never organized its own parade off base. Given that conservatives had held power in the prefecture and most municipal governments for several years, and that polling showed that well over half the population thought the SDF was necessary, force commanders had reason to be confident that such a parade would not spark a backlash. But this assumption was, as the historian Arasaki Moriteru observed, "premature."[175] The parade prompted a response that the prefecture had not seen for years. An estimated 1,500 demonstrators turned out to harass, obstruct, and drown out the band's music with their shouts of "Army, get out of Okinawa" and "Go home, killers." Unlike Kuwae's march to Mabuni, the preannounced celebration held on a weekend gave critics of the force plenty of time to organize and marshal their forces. Supporters of the force turned out, too. They waved small Japanese flags and applauded, but it appeared many supporters were other personnel and people affiliated with the SDF. And they were overwhelmed by the organized crowd of union members, academics, and pacifists.[176] Ironically, what was essentially a military parade could not have taken place without the protection of the police. Not only was the parade premature, it was also anachronistic. It had been nearly a decade since the GSDF had held a parade on public streets almost anywhere in the country. The SDF had opted for on-base parades after progressive mayors on the mainland had thrown up bureaucratic roadblocks in the early 1970s. On that Saturday afternoon in 1982, the SDF, it seems, had not yet arrived at the future it imagined and had deployed an antiquated attempt at spectacle from the past.

The SDF had gained much wider acceptance, but the demonstration against the parade was not the last gasp of resistance. Opposition to the force continued in the 1980s, usually in the form of protests against the participation of personnel in athletic meets and coming-of-age ceremonies. Yet the nature of that opposition changed. Resistance once directed at the force came to be leveled at the central government and became more impersonal and abstract in its expression. This trend was illustrated by one of the dramatic acts of protests in the late 1980s. On October 26, 1987, activist Chibana Shōichi lowered and burned a Japanese flag at the opening ceremony of the National Athletic Meet's softball tournament. By the 1980s, protests came to target the flag and the national anthem, which in part was provoked by Ministry of Education directives that students and teachers must pay homage to the flag and sing the anthem at school events, as well as to efforts to remove or water down references to imperial military excesses, including its actions during the Battle of Okinawa, in officially approved school textbooks. As was the case for Chibana, such opposition was grounded in memories of Imperial

Army atrocities, but opponents no longer saw the SDF as equivalent to the Japanese Army. Instead, they suspected that its existence might tempt those in power to use it to take Japan (and Okinawa) to war again. Chibana, for example, did not mention the Self-Defense Force in his account of his activism.[177] Likewise, other critics of the situation in Okinawa—both Japanese and international—have rarely mentioned the SDF in their critiques since the 1990s. Critics in Okinawa also less often targeted the emperor. This may have been in part because Emperor Akihito, before and after he ascended to the throne in 1989 made repeated attempts to address the marginalization of Okinawa, including but going well beyond his visit to the islands in 1975 when he was the target of firebombs.[178] Increasingly, opposition anger was almost entirely fueled by problems related to the US bases and the Japanese government's collusion. In 1995, that anger at Tokyo combined with an outburst of particularly intense hostility toward the bases after three US servicemen raped a twelve-year-old girl.[179] By then, support for and opposition to the SDF were roughly at the same levels in Okinawa as on the mainland, though what opposition remained was (and is) certainly more intense and entrenched on the islands.

Thus, the SDF's strategy of military-society integration or begrudging acceptance of the force might be judged a limited or contested success. The force's application of seemingly tried-and-true strategies with some tweaks yielded acceptance that its existence was necessary. By keeping a low profile while also being visible through its public service, it sought to demonstrate that it was not a Japanese army. Instead, it was a defense force against dangers of all kinds. As a result, Okinawans came to recognize, though with misgivings, its existence.

This process obviously changed Okinawan society, but it also changed the SDF as it incorporated roles and tasks it had assumed on the mainland in Okinawa as well. The prognosis of an US Army official offered (in the usual terse military telegram diction) before reversion seems to have been prescient: "Bitterness toward Japanese military from war experience still underlies Okinawa attitudes. . . . At same time, substantial portion of population apparently accepts JSDF entry as necessary reversion development. Conservatives will attempt to reinforce this view. Leftists will doubtless continue to oppose entry, but this opposition is not likely to assume critical proportions if operation is carried out with careful attention to political factors. . . . JSDF will require 'PR' effort to demonstrate to public its potential contribution to people's welfare and Okinawan economy." "Okinawans," the report continued, "have not had Japan's 20 years to become inurred [sic] to JSDF," but "following [established] measures should ease entry and promote public image." Although in the end those established measures were not precisely the same as those used on the mainland, and the breadth, depth, and intensity of the opposition complicated these efforts, they did, as the report predicted, "work to establish in Okinawa the 'new look' image the JSDF [had] developed" on the mainland.[180] That new look was not just about appearances but also, as on the mainland, brought about some substantive changes to the priorities and role of the force.

To achieve this new look and acceptance in Okinawa, the SDF strove to avoid being associated with the US military. This was not easy. Many SDF bases were located on land vacated by the US military that was immediately adjacent to US bases. Okinawans complained that on SDF bases the only thing that had changed was "the color of the uniforms."[181] But the force endeavored to create a separate, distinct identity and to demonstrate it was not a military entity like the US forces that were actively engaged in fighting wars and that had a well-deserved reputation for being poor, demanding, and even dangerous guests. In some ways, being in the shadow of the US forces, while avoiding association with the entity that cast the shadow, may have worked as a successful strategy for the SDF. In 1975, one commentator accused the force of hiding in that shadow and predicted that if it stopped doing so, opposition would grow.[182] But by the time the SDF began to engage in joint training exercises with US troops in Okinawa in 1983, the urgency of maintaining a distance from the Americans had lessened.

Most importantly, the SDF in Okinawa tried to create an identity distinct from that of the imperial military. That association, rather than its questionable constitutionality (as on the mainland), generated the most intense opposition to its existence and presence. From the time of reversion, personnel stressed through word and deed that they were not the "Japanese Army" that opponents claimed had returned to Okinawa. This messaging was complicated by the fact that many of the Okinawa Brigade's top leaders had served in and retained a lingering loyalty to the pre-1945 military. But by the 1980s, almost all the senior officials who had once served in the Imperial Army, like Kuwae, had retired from the force, and its top leaders were increasingly graduates of the NDA. That leadership transition, the beginning of training exercises with the US military, and the success in achieving a greater level of military-society integration in Okinawa and on the mainland were benchmarks in the struggle of a force and its personnel to gain legitimacy. As the Cold War came to an end, a new era in that story began. More than thirty years later, it continues to unfold.

# Epilogue
## Whither the SDF and the Cold War Defense Identity?

Seven decades have elapsed since the reestablishment of Japan's postwar military, and three since the end of the Cold War. In some ways, little has changed since its formation and since the latter historic geopolitical milestone. Just as scholars and the public regard the postwar era as not yet having come to an end for Japan, the Cold War, too, seems to live on. Disagreements over war memory and territorial disputes, which went largely unaddressed during the Cold War, continue to complicate Japan's relations with its Asian neighbors. Structurally, Japan's security arrangement remains the same; seventy years on, the US-Japan Security Treaty is the fundamental organizing principle for transpacific and intra-Asian geopolitics. Tens of thousands of US troops continue to be stationed on Japanese soil. Article 9 endures. Although it has been reinterpreted, it has never been revised. Perhaps as a result, Japan has not been directly involved in a war since 1945, after repeatedly going to war from 1868 to 1945. That said, the three branches of the SDF, rearmed with highly sophisticated weaponry, form a well-funded, modern, technologically advanced military force. Just as Cold War dynamics continue, so too do elements of the Cold War defense identity. The GSDF in particular is highly regarded for its nonmilitary humanitarian activities, such as disaster relief—both in Japan and abroad—and continues to engage in public service and outreach. In many respects, elements of the Cold War identity persist as an ongoing postwar identity.

As I have recounted, that identity took shape during the force's first four decades of existence, which matched the duration of the Cold War and were in many ways shaped by the force's relationships with society, the imperial military, and the US military. As the SDF (particularly the GSDF) sought legitimacy from society, it embarked on a campaign of public service and public relations in local communities and across the archipelago, in rural and urban areas, first on the mainland and then on Okinawa. It pursued these strategies with caution, but it often sought to be as visible as possible and let its actions do the talking. At the National Defense Academy and in the wider force, leaders as well as cadets and rank-and-file personnel shaped its character, esprit de corps, and traditions, often in relation to its imperial military predecessor and the US military. By the end of the Cold War, as the force had made considerable progress in achieving a relatively high degree of military-society integration, transitioning to leadership trained in the postwar academy, and deepening its collaboration and training with the US military, it had become thoroughly imbued with and accepted by society—supporters and opponents alike—for its Cold War defense identity.

So how have the relationships that shaped the SDF during its formative decades changed since the end of the Cold War? As it came to an end, the United States increased its longstanding demands on Japan to shoulder more of a burden for its defense and to assume a greater role in international affairs, within the framework of the bilateral alliance and the United Nations. The countries' militaries had already begun to conduct joint combined exercises between different branches in the early 1980s. Still, Japanese officials were surprised when US policymakers asked the SDF to participate in an allied naval coalition to protect oil shipments in the Persian Gulf in response to the Iran-Iraq War in the mid-1980s. Nakasone, who was the first antimainstream, or in other words, the first anti–Yoshida Doctrine conservative to become prime minister (from 1982 to 1987) since Kishi in the late 1950s, backed the proposal. Nakasone, long a hawkish advocate of autonomous defense, including during his tenure as Defense Agency director from 1970 to 1971, favored termination of the security treaty and "a 'genuine' alliance with the United States on the basis of equality. Moreover, he wanted Japan to establish, as he put it, 'a constitution independently drawn up by the Japanese people,'" which would abandon Article 9 and make possible a more international, active role for the SDF.[1] In this instance, as with his wider agenda, he was largely unsuccessful. Other conservatives within the LDP, including Gotōda Masaharu, the former police official who had played a key role in helping to establish the Police Reserve Force and the National Defense Academy (see chapters 1 and 2) and who continued to embrace the Cold

War defense mentality, strongly opposed and blocked the plan.[2] A few years later, with the Cold War over, the United States again asked Japan to participate in an ad hoc coalition, this time to respond to the Gulf War of 1991. Again, opposition from within the LDP prevented the SDF from participating. Instead, the government opted to provide financial support, but world leaders and the global media criticized this as "checkbook diplomacy."[3] This criticism prompted the LDP to push through a law to allow the SDF to join United Nations peacekeeping operations, and this in turn led to the force's first overseas mission, when six hundred GSDF engineers were sent to Cambodia for six months in 1993. Repeated participation in peacekeeping operations and international disaster-relief missions followed, which allowed the SDF and particularly the GSDF to leverage and refine the experience and expertise they had acquired in domestic operations over many decades.

Japan's response to the September 11, 2001, attacks, a decade after the first Gulf War and the end of the Cold War, was unprecedented, yet its contributions were grounded in its longstanding practices and identity. When President George W. Bush asked for allies to "put boots on the ground," Prime Minister Koizumi Jun'ichirō, with widespread political support, dispatched the GSDF to southern Iraq to provide relief and reconstruction in 2004.[4]

In 2006, the Diet passed a law making the Defense Agency the full-fledged, cabinet-level Ministry of Defense. Around this time, Japan was coming to regard China and North Korea as serious threats that the SDF could not manage without closer cooperation with the US military. These concerns, and the interpretation of Article 9 as only allowing the SDF to use armed force defensively and not to protect allies like the US military, led Prime Minister Abe Shinzō to draft a new law that reinterpreted the constitution to allow for collective self-defense in 2015. Opposition was fierce. Legislative deliberations sparked the largest protests since those against the US-Japan Security Treaty in 1960, but the Diet passed the law. During the 2017 to 2021 presidency of Donald Trump, who cared little about traditional US alliances, Abe and other Japanese leaders became concerned about whether the United States would actually defend Japan, and that led to an increased urgency to revise the constitution.[5]

In the context of these international changes, domestic politics and developments since the end of the Cold War have brought about a significant shift in the SDF's relationship with society. By the mid-1960s, the force had secured a recognition that it was necessary from over 70 percent of the population. Despite the antiwar protests of the late 1960s and the Mishima Incident in 1970, that acceptance remained resilient. Subsequently, international relations, internal politics, the ascent of leaders educated at the NDA, and the SDF's ongoing public service and outreach continued to weaken the military-civilian divide. Even before the end of the Cold War, longstanding political opposition to the force was starting to soften. In 1984, the JSP recognized that the force was created by constitutional means but maintained its stance that the SDF violated the constitution. When the Japan Socialist Party joined the long-dominant LDP to form a coalition government in 1993, its leader, Murayama Tomiichi, became prime minister and recognized the existence of the SDF, undermining one of the core principles of the party. The following year, national- and local-level JSP misgivings about the SDF and force commanders' wariness of overstepping their authority out of concern for the political repercussions contributed to a delayed response by the force when Kobe was hit by the Great Hanshin Earthquake. As a result of this belated response, in the aftermath of the earthquake and relief effort "discussion of emergency response [by the SDF became] no longer taboo and virtually everyone came to accept a role for the military in disaster relief."[6] Moreover, the GSDF's lengthy and well-publicized service in Kobe, in international peacekeeping operations, and in other domestic disaster-relief activities, along with a prolonged economic downturn as the country's bubble economy burst, contributed to a substantial boost in recruitment in the 1990s.

But the force's improved reputation in those years paled in comparison to what it achieved after its response to the triple (earthquake, tsunami, and nuclear) disaster in northeast Honshu that began on March 11, 2011. Those events—3.11—proved to be a tremendous public-relations victory for the organization. The force dispatched a hundred thousand personnel, most of them GSDF soldiers, to respond to the Great East Japan Earthquake. They, working in close coordination with the US military as a part of what was dubbed "Operation Tomodachi" (friendship), helped rescue over nineteen thousand civilians. Scenes of GSDF helicopter pilots attempting to drop water on the highly radioactive reactors at the Fukushima No. 1 nuclear plant made them heroes to a disheartened nation.[7] Observers agree that the operation, as the political scientist Sheila Smith put it, "proved to be a critical turning point in the Japanese public's views of their military." Favorable views of the SDF jumped to over 90 percent in 2012 from 80 percent in 2009.[8] The SDF is now regarded as one of the most respected and trusted institutions in the country.[9] In the spring of 2021, it was not surprising that the government mobilized SDF medical doctors and nurses to help with a COVID-19 vaccination campaign as the Olympics approached to try to prevent a wave of infections.[10] The force's improved reputation certainly has had a positive impact on its individual members. Force personnel—both male and female—apparently became popular as prospective marital partners, with personnel appearing on television specials throughout the country—including in Okinawa—that tout their social and economic attractiveness. "[A] new word, *J-kon*, for 'marriage to a member of the Jieitai [SDF],' has . . . [even] entered the Japanese lexicon."[11] This is a striking departure from the early decades of the force, when personnel were called "tax thieves" on the street, when juvenile delinquents were recruited into its thinning ranks, and when its male members had a hard time getting women to regard them as worthy romantic interests and as acceptable prospective sons-in-law.

Even more substantive changes may be coming. The popularity of the SDF may contribute to growing public support for revising or amending Article 9. The SDF's response to 3.11, its contribution to United Nations peacekeeping operations, and the rising geopolitical tensions in Northeast Asia all bolstered support for Prime Minister Abe's wish to remove any doubt about the constitutionality of the SDF. In 2017, he expressed his desire for the constitution to be revised by the "2020 Tokyo Olympics, arguing that, just as the 1964 Olympics had been a new beginning for postwar Japan, so too would the 2020 Olympics be a moment of rebirth for the nation."[12] Although almost all citizens recognize the legitimacy of the SDF as it exists today, there is wider public and political discomfort with changing the constitution and transforming the force into even what Abe and others have called a self-defense military (*jiei-gun*), as signaled by massive protests against reinterpreting Article 9 to allow for collective defense in 2015. In the end, Abe was unable to achieve his ambitious timeline, and illness and disapproval of his handling of COVID-19, which led to a postponement of the Olympics until 2021, led to his resignation in September 2020. Although his successors as prime minister, Suga Yoshihide and Kishida Fumio (from October 2021), seem unlikely to push forward these still controversial revisions, the Self-Defense Force may eventually become a military in name and unbound from its current constitutional constraints.

So, how have these changes over the last three decades impacted the military-defense identity that took shape during the Cold War? Although societal views of the SDF, its proper role, and its personnel have shifted dramatically in the last thirty years, how has the identity of the SDF, organizationally and on a personal level, evolved? Not surprisingly, it appears that there is widespread support among officers and rank-and-file enlisted personnel for the force to play a greater, less constrained military role, but many members are also concerned about the risks involved, both personally and for the country, and many remain attached to the identity, values, and traditions forged during the Cold War decades. Force personnel continue to be dedicated to democratic principles, including civilian control of the armed forces, and have thoroughly internalized the idea of being an SDF for the people. The force's expertise in disaster relief, in particular, is a tremendous source of pride for the organization and its personnel, though, as during the Cold War, some personnel express impatience that some people still seem to regard it as their primary mission. Likewise, as signaled by the reluctance of the Northern Corps to further scale back and end its longtime support for the Sapporo Snow Festival, even nonemergency public-service activities have become a core part of the force's esprit de corps and its connection to society. The reinvented postwar military-defense masculine identity shaped during the Cold War decades has also been complicated by the inclusion of female personnel within the force, but their numbers—both in the officer corps and among enlisted troops—remain comparatively few.

The SDF's relationships with the US military and the imperial military remain a challenge for the organization and its soldiers. The continued large presence of US troops on Japanese soil, highly visible during Operation Tomodachi despite US efforts to not overshadow the force, and made more personal through more intensive and frequent joint training exercises, continues to complicate SDF military masculinity. Though some personnel may be sympathetic to right-wing nationalist critiques such as Mishima's, which still resonates today and is echoed by some rightists, most reject—as they did in 1970—extreme measures that do not align with democratic ideals. Even though the war is over three-quarters of a century in the past, "tension between efforts to disassociate [the SDF from its predecessor] by demonizing the Imperial Army and the desire to re-create a military tradition and uninterrupted history that allows service members to identity with and be proud of their predecessors" persists.[13] As evidenced by the efforts in the early 2010s of administrators and veterans of the National Defense Academy to mobilize memories of Maki to protect the liberal democratic ideals of the academy against rightists, moderate leaders are seeking to position those ideas as core to the identity and tradition of today's defense force. In contrast, right-wing veterans, politicians, and commentators such as Tamogami Toshio, the former ASDF chief of staff who was fired for expressing his extreme views, have argued the force should align itself with imperial military traditions, including bushido. From around the time of the SDF's deployment to Iraq in 2004, the samurai and, to a lesser but still notable extent, the imperial military man have become more prominent as martial figures held up as models for force personnel.[14]

As this overview signals, although elements of the SDF's Cold War defense identity survive, many of the values and priorities of the force have changed in the last thirty years to become what we might call a postwar, rather than a Cold War, defense identity. Fortunately, Japan, unlike the United States, has not been involved in any military conflicts since World War II, so the current postwar era cannot be confused with other postwar eras. Unfortunately, Japan, has not adequately addressed issues related to the war; it has achieved much less in this area than Germany. Three-quarters of a century after World War II, problems associated with the war—disagreements over war responsibility, discord with Japan's Asian neighbors, and the nature of the reconstituted military—continue to plague the country's internal and international politics. Thus, the country remains uncomfortably stuck in a seemingly never-ending postwar (*sengo*) era. It is not yet clear how the SDF will change, how its relationship with society, the imperial past, and the US military will evolve, how the force's identity will influence and be influenced by those changes, and how these processes will contribute to the end of the postwar era, whatever form that takes, and to the dawn of a new historical era.

Regardless of what the future holds for the SDF and its individual personnel, the force's long pursuit of legitimacy poses the question: How much legitimacy is enough? Was the level of acceptance achieved on the mainland in the mid-1960s and on Okinawa by the late 1970s enough? Is the even more favorable and deep-seated support of over 90 percent of the population the force secured after the triple disaster of March 11, 2011, sufficient? The force's newly obtained legitimacy may not translate into sufficient political support to bring about the revision of Article 9 and a change in its name, mission, and identity. In fact, support for its defense identity, which is grounded in the Cold War security posture of defensive defense, may serve to undermine efforts to revise the constitution and transform the force into a military. Of that, only time will tell.

# Notes

## Introduction

1. Satō Morio, interview by author, September 17, 2003, Sapporo, Japan; Satō Morio, interview by author, February 16, 2004, Sapporo, Japan.

2. For example, reporter Sam Jones observed, "Until a few years ago, many Japanese commonly referred to the military as a shiseiji (illegitimate child) fathered by the allied occupation forces." "Japan's Military Forces Winning Public Approval," *New York Times*, November 15, 1970, 3. Journalist John K. Emmerson similarly wrote, "In the beginning, the SDF was in fact the 'child of the United States,' not only in historical origin but through the technical, organizational, and financial assistance received from the United States throughout its formative years." John K. Emmerson, *Arms, Yen and Power: The Japanese Dilemma* (New York: Dunellen, 1971), 138. In 1970, the British chargé d'affaires D. R. Ashe in Tokyo observed, "That membership [in] the armed forces still fails to carry much glamour or social prestige and that they suffer from considerable difficulties in recruitment still testify to their peripheral place in Japanese society. They are far from being outcasts now, but politicians continue to draw their own conclusions about the extent to which public opinion, event twenty-five years after the defeat of the Imperial forces, would welcome manifestations of official approval or recognition." Ashe quoted in Hugh Cortazzi, ed., *The Growing Power of Japan, 1967–1972: Analysis and Assessments from John Pilcher and the British Embassy, Tokyo* (Folkestone, UK: Renaissance, 2015), 154.

3. Ivan Morris, *Nationalism and the Right Wing in Japan: A Study of Post-War Trends* (Oxford: Oxford University Press, 1960), 207.

4. James Auer, *The Post-War Rearmament of Japanese Maritime Forces, 1945–71* (New York: Praeger, 1973), 183.

5. Constitution of Japan, https://japan.kantei.go.jp/constitution_and_government_of_japan/constitution_e.html, accessed January 19, 2021.

6. Mishima Yukio, "Mishima's Manifesto," trans. Christopher Smith, https://www.japaneseempire.info/post/mishima-yukio-s-manifesto, accessed October 15, 2021. The Japanese original was published as Mishima Yukio, "Mishima Yukio no 'geki' zenbun," *Asahi shinbun*, November 26, 1970, 4.

7. Frank Gibney, "The View from Japan," *Foreign Affairs* 50, no. 10 (October 1971): 108.

8. Hanmura Ryō, *Sengoku Jieitai* (Tokyo: Kakugawa shunju, [1971] 2000). The 1979 adaptation of the story was remade as a motion picture, *Sengoku Jieitai 1549*, in 2005 and as a television series in 2006.

9. Bruce Fleming, *Bridging the Military-Civilian Divide: What Each Side Must Know about the Other, and about Itself* (Washington, DC: Potomac, 2010). For a historical overview of these issues in the United States, see Arthur A. Ekirch, Jr., *The Civilian and the Military: A History of the American Antimilitarist Tradition* (Oakland, CA: Independent Institute, [1956] 2010).

10. We must be careful to not exaggerate the dearth of public support for the SDF or to confuse lack of support with resistance to its possible use of force abroad. But to suggest that the SDF's lack of popularity is a nothing more than myth is to deny that the organization and its personnel have continually been engaged in a "search for legitimacy," or perhaps more aptly, greater legitimacy, both before and after they won the support of most citizens in the second half of the 1960s. Paul Midford, "The GSDF's Quest for Public Acceptance and the 'Allergy' Myth," in *The Japanese Ground Self-Defense Force: Search for Legitimacy*, ed. Robert D. Eldridge and Paul Midford (New York: Palgrave Macmillan, 2017), 334.

11. Constitution of Japan.

12. According to the Stockholm International Peace Research Institute, Japan ranked as the world's sixth-largest military spender in 2010, expending $41 billion, about 1 percent of the country's GDP, for defense. Sheila Smith, *Japan Rearmed: The Politics of Military Power* (Cambridge, MA: Harvard University Press, 2019), 11.

13. I have decided to use the term Police Reserve Force, which is the most accurate translation of the Japanese name for the force, Keisatsu Yobitai. Most scholars have used the name National Police Reserve because Douglas MacArthur used it in his July 1950 letter to Prime Minister Yoshida "authoriz[ing]" the Japanese government to create what he called the "national police reserve" (as well as the expansion of the existing Maritime Safety Board) and because it is the English term that occupation officials called the organization. Frank Kowalski, *An Inoffensive Rearmament: The Making of the Postwar Japanese Army*, ed. Robert D. Eldridge (Annapolis, MD: Naval Institute Press, 2013), 23. I prefer Police Reserve Force, which a few scholars have used, because this appellation reflects the powerful influence that the US military had on the force while signaling how Japanese officials, civilian and uniformed, transformed the force to make it a hybrid of the US military and Japanese models, lending it both a postwar democratic and an imperial military character. In addition, the inclusion of the word "Force" (the *tai* at the end of Keisatsu Yobitai) highlights the continuities between the Police Reserve Force (1950–52) and its two successors, the National Safety Force (Hoantai, 1952–54) and the Ground Self-Defense Force (Rikujō Jieitai, 1954–present), as well as connections between these postwar forces and the pre-1945 Imperial Army (Teikoku guntai). Although almost all primary and secondary sources refer to the Jieitai as the Self-Defense Force in English, people at the time and scholars since have almost always used the term "National Safety Force" for Hoantai, except for a few scholars, including John Welfield, who calls it the National Security Force. In this instance, I think National Safety Force is more accurate because it better reflects the attempt by officials to soften the image of the Hoantai by using "safety" rather than "security" in English. See John Welfield, *An Empire in Eclipse: Japan in the Postwar American Alliance System* (London: Atlantic Highlands, 1988). As a result of MacArthur's memo, the Maritime Safety Board became the Maritime Reserve Force (Kaijō Yobitai), then the Maritime Safety Force (Kaijō Hoantai) in 1952, and finally the Maritime Self-Defense Force (Kaijō Jieitai) in 1954.

14. Paul Midford, *Rethinking Japanese Public Opinion and Security: From Pacifism to Realism?* (Stanford, CA: Stanford University Press, 2011), 1; Paul Midford, "The Logic of Reassurance and Japan's Grand Strategy," *Security Studies* 11, no. 3 (Spring 2002): 1.

15. Cynthia Enloe, *Maneuvers: The International Politics of Militarizing Women's Lives* (Berkeley: University of California Press, 2000), 3.

16. Michael Geyer, "The Militarization of Europe, 1914–1945," in *The Militarization of the Western World*, ed. John Gillis (New Brunswick, NJ: Rutgers University Press, 1989), 79; Michael S. Sherry, *In the Shadow of War: The United States since the 1930s* (New Haven, CT: Yale University Press, 1995), xi.

17. Phillip Babcock Gove, ed., *Webster's Third New International Dictionary of the English Language*, unabridged (New York: Merriam-Webster, 2002), 1174.

18. J. W. Dower, *Embracing Defeat: Japan in the Wake of World War II* (New York: W. W. Norton, 1999), 58–61.

19. Constitution of Japan.

20. Kenneth J. Ruoff, *Japan's Imperial House in the Postwar Era, 1945-2019* (Cambridge, MA: Harvard University Press, 2020), 314.

21. For more on the representations of Japan as feminized and emasculated, which had domestic and international inflections, see Dower, *Embracing Defeat*, 135–37; Yoshikuni Igarashi, *Bodies of Memory: Narratives of War in Postwar Japanese Culture, 1945–1970* (Princeton, NJ: Princeton University Press, 2000); Naoko Shibusawa, *America's Geisha Ally: Reimagining the Japanese Enemy* (Cambridge, MA: Harvard University Press, 2010); Yoshikuni Igarashi, *Homecomings: The Belated Return of Japan's Lost Soldiers* (New York: Columbia University Press, 2016).

22. Etō Jun, "'Haha' no hōkai ga kodomo o dame ni shita," *Gendai*, August 1979, 230. Etō's essay was translated and appeared slightly abridged in English as "The Breakdown of Motherhood Is Wrecking Our Children," *Japan Echo* 11, no. 4 (1979): 102–9.

23. Nakamura Eri, "Nihon rikugun ni okeru dansei sei no kōchiku: Dansei no 'kyōfushin' o meguru kaishaku o jiku ni," in *Jendā to shakai: Dansei shi, rikugun, sekushuariti*, ed. Kimoto Kimiko and Kido Yoshiyuki (Tokyo: Junpōsha, 2010), 179.

24. Airgram A-38, from American Consulate Sapporo to Department of State, "The Japanese Military Establishment in Northern Japan," December 29, 1970, 11, Department of State Files, US National Archives, Washington, DC. Nakasone made the comment in an interview with the *Mainichi* newspaper.

25. Ralph Ellison, *Invisible Man* (New York: Random House, 1952), 3.

26. See, for example, Sabine Frühstück, *Uneasy Warriors: Gender, Memory, and Popular Culture in the Japanese Army* (Berkeley: University of California Press, 2007), 3, 5.

27. Alex Martin, "Military Flexes Relief Might, Gains Newfound Esteem," *Japan Times*, April 15, 2011.

28. Mishima Takashi, *Nippon no "heishi"tachi* (Tokyo: Jiji Kahō sha, 2007), 1.

29. James S. Corum, "Adenauer, Amt Blank, and the Founding of the Bundeswehr 1950–1956," in *Rearming Germany*, ed. James S. Corum (Leiden, The Netherlands: Brill, 2011), 35. See also James S. Corum, "American Assistance to the New German Army and Luftwaffe," in Corum, *Rearming Germany*, 93–116.

30. Thomas U. Berger, *Cultures of Antimilitarism: National Security in Germany and Japan* (Baltimore: Johns Hopkins University Press, 1998), 36–37. See also Alexandra

Sakaki et al., *Reluctant Warriors: Germany, Japan, and Their U.S. Alliance Dilemma* (Washington, DC: Brookings Institution Press, 2020).

31. David Clay Large, *Germans to the Front: West German Rearmament in the Adenauer Era* (Chapel Hill: University of North Carolina Press, 1996), 7.

32. In addition to Large, *Germans to the Front*, see Donald Abenheim, *Reforging the Iron Cross: The Search for Tradition in the West German Forces* (Princeton, NJ: Princeton University Press, 1988); Jay Lockenour, *Soldiers as Citizens: Former Wehrmacht Officers in the Federal Republic of Germany, 1945–1955* (Lincoln: University of Nebraska Press, 2001); Robert G. Moeller, *War Stories: The Search for a Usable Past in the Federal Republic of Germany* (Berkeley: University of California Press, 2001); Alaric Searle, *Wehrmacht Generals, West German Society, and the Debate on Rearmament, 1949–1959* (Westport, CT: Praeger, 2003).

33. See, for example, Uta G. Poiger, "A New, 'Western' Hero? Reconstructing German Masculinity in the 1950s," *Signs: Journal of Women in Culture and Society* 24, no. 1 (1998): 147–62.

34. See William L. Hauser, *America's Army in Crisis: A Study in Civil-Military Relations* (Baltimore: Johns Hopkins University Press, 1973), 22–35; and Michel L. Martin, *Warriors to Managers: The French Military Establishment since 1945* (Chapel Hill: University of North Carolina Press, 1981).

35. Catherine Lutz, *Homefront: A Military City and the American Twentieth Century* (Boston: Beacon, 2001), 168.

36. Susan Jeffords, *The Remasculinization of America: Gender and the Vietnam War* (Bloomington: Indiana University Press, 1989).

37. Paula Reed Ward, "DoD Paid $53 Million of Taxpayers' Money to Pro Sports for Military Tributes, Report Says," *Pittsburgh Post-Gazette*, November 5, 2015, https://www.post-gazette.com/news/nation/2015/11/06/Department-of-Defense-paid-53-million-to-pro-sports-for-military-tributes-report-says/stories/2015 11060140.

38. Scholars have generally paid little attention to this sort of public service by militaries. Usually it does not get mentioned at all, and when it does, it is often just a passing reference. See, for example, Suchit Bunbongkarn, "The Thai Military and Its Role in Society in the 1990s," in *The Military, the State, and Development in Asia and the Pacific*, ed. Viberto Selochan (Boulder, CO: Westview, 1991), 72; Thak Chaloemtiarana, *Thailand: The Politics of Despotic Paternalism* (Ithaca, NY: Cornell University Southeast Asia Program Publications, 2007), 171. Thanks to Shane Strate for guiding me to these examples. The SDF's active role conducting civil engineering, agricultural assistance, and disaster relief throughout its history, including when Japan was still recovering from the war, is certainly more unusual in developed countries than in developing countries like Thailand.

39. Mark R. Grandstaff, "Making the Military American: Advertising, Reform, and the Demise of an Antistanding Military Tradition, 1945–1955," *Journal of Military History* 60 (April 1996): 299.

40. Benjamin L. Alpers, "This is the Army: Imagining a Democratic Military in World War II," in *The World War Two Reader*, ed. Gordon Martel (London: Routledge, 2004), 147.

41. Grandstaff, "Making the Military American," 303, 305, 323.

42. Charles C. Moskos, "Toward a Postmodern Military: The United States as a Paradigm," *The Postmodern Military: Armed Forces after the Cold War*, ed. Charles C. Moskos, John Allen Williams, and David R. Segal (New York: Oxford University Press, 2000), 15.

43. Robert D. Eldridge and Paul Midford, introduction to *The Japanese Ground Self-Defense Force*, ed. Robert D. Eldridge and Paul Midford (New York: Palgrave Macmillan, 2017), 3.

44. US Military Assistance Advisory Group—Japan, *A Decade of Defense in Japan* (Washington, DC: Headquarters, Military Assistance Advisory Group, 1964), 5, 8.

45. The GSDF has used the terms "corps" and "army" in English to refer to these regional organizations, which contain two to four divisions each (e.g., the Northern Army in Hokkaido). In Japanese, officials have used the vaguer and softer term *hōmentai*, which can be translated as "area force," (the *tai* is the same character as in Jieitai, Self-Defense Force), "area corps," or "area army," rather than a term like *hōmengun*, which means "area military" or "area army." As early as the 1960s, GSDF publications in English began to exclusively use the term "army" to refer to these area organizations, but did not change the nomenclature in Japanese. Thus, "corps" rather than "army" most accurately captures the regional organizations' meaning in Japan.

46. Alessio Patalano, *Post-War Japan as a Sea Power: Imperial Legacy, Wartime Experience and the Making of a Navy* (London: Bloomsbury, 2015), 37.

47. Beatrice Trefalt, *Japanese Army Stragglers and Memories of the War in Japan, 1950–1975* (London: RoutledgeCurzon, 2003); Igarashi, *Homecomings*.

48. These articles were published in English in James Auer, ed., *From Marco Polo Bridge to Pearl Harbor: Who Was Responsible?* (Tokyo: Yomiuri shinbun, 2006).

49. Patalano, *Post-War Japan as a Sea Power*, 9.

50. Patalano, *Post-War Japan as a Sea Power*, 85.

51. In 1954, just before the National Safety Force became the Self-Defense Force, an estimated 80 percent of officers in the Maritime Safety Force had been officers in the Imperial Navy. In contrast, only 24.4 percent of officers in the ground forces had been officers in the Imperial Army. Morris, *Nationalism and the Right Wing in Japan*, 236–37.

52. Patalano, *Post-War Japan as a Sea Power*, 37–59.

53. Eldridge and Midford, introduction, 4.

54. Smith, *Japan Rearmed*, 173–74.

55. Smith, *Japan Rearmed*, 173–74.

56. Eldridge and Midford, introduction, 5.

57. Leonard A. Humphreys, *The Way of the Heavenly Sword: The Japanese Army in the 1920's* (Stanford, CA: Stanford University Press, 1995), vii; D. Colin Jaundrill, *Samurai to Soldier: Remaking Military Service in Nineteenth-Century Japan* (Ithaca, NY: Cornell University Press, 2016), 157.

58. Martin, *Warriors to Managers*.

59. Ayako Kusunoki, "The Early Years of the Ground Self-Defense Forces, 1945–1960," in Eldridge and Midford, *The Japanese Ground Self-Defense Force*, 59–131.

60. Lewis Austin, *Japan: The Paradox of Progress* (New Haven, CT: Yale University Press, 1976), 255.

61. Jennifer M. Miller, *Cold War Democracy: The United States and Japan* (Cambridge, MA: Harvard University Press, 2019), 98–107.

62. Donald T. Roden, "Thoughts on the Early Meiji Gentleman," in *Gendering Modern Japanese History*, ed. Barbara Molony and Kathleen Uno (Cambridge, MA: Harvard University Asia Center, 2005), 64.

63. Fumika Sato, "A Camouflaged Military: Japan's Self-Defense Forces and Globalized Gender Mainstreaming," *Asia-Pacific Journal* 10, no. 3 (2012): 4–5.

64. Sato, "A Camouflaged Military," 5.

65. Frühstück, *Uneasy Warriors*, 89.

66. Sato, "A Camouflaged Military," 7.

67. Sato, "A Camouflaged Military," 11.

## 1. The Police Reserve Force and the US Army

1. Irikura Shōzō, interview by author, February 9, 2006, Sapporo, Japan.

2. Irikura interview, February 9, 2006; Irikura Shōzō, "'Keisatsu Yobitai uramen shi,'" *Asagumo shinbun*, June 15, 2000, 3.

3. Irikura interview, February 9, 2006.

4. Douglas MacArthur letter to Yoshida Shigeru, July 8, 1950, RG-10: VIP Correspondence, Yoshida Collection, June–December 1950, US National Archives, College Park, Maryland.

5. Richard B. Finn, *Winners in Peace: MacArthur, Yoshida and Postwar Japan* (Berkeley: University of California Press, 1992), 266.

6. Natsuyo Ishibashi, "Different Forces in One: The Origin and Development of Organizational Cultures in the Japanese Ground and Maritime Self-Defense Forces, 1950–Present," *Japan Forum* 28, no. 2 (2016): 162; Thomas French, *National Police Reserve: The Origin of Japan's Self Defense Forces* (Leiden, The Netherlands: Brill, 2014), 242.

7. Sado Akihiro, *The Self-Defense Forces and Postwar Politics in Japan* (Tokyo: Japan Publishing Industry Foundation for Culture, 2017), 131–47.

8. Katō Yōzō, *Shiroku, Jieitai shi: Keisatsu Yobitai kara konnichi made* (Tokyo: "Gekkan seigaku" seiji geppō sha, 1979); Yomiuri shinbun sengo shi hanhen, ed., *"Saigunbi" no kiseki* (Tokyo: Yomiuri shinbun sha, 1981); J. W. Dower, *Empire and Aftermath: Yoshida Shigeru and the Japanese Experience, 1878–1954* (Cambridge, MA: Harvard University Press, 1988); Nagano Setsuo, *Jieitai ha dono yō ni shite umareta ka* (Tokyo: Gakuen kenkyūsha, 2003); Masuda Hiroshi, *Jieitai no tanjō: Nihon no saigunbi to Amerika* (Tokyo: Chūō Kōron, 2004); French, *National Police Reserve*; Kusunoki, "The Early Years"; Miller, *Cold War Democracy*.

9. Kusunoki, "The Early Years," 63.

10. Memo from MacArthur to Yoshida, vol. 8, 1950, R6-10: VIP Correspondence, "Yoshida," June–December 1950, MacArthur Memorial Archives and Library, Norfolk, Virginia.

11. Welfield, *An Empire in Eclipse*, 74.

12. Kusunoki, "The Early Years," 64. Kusunoki dates the meeting to July 8, the same day that MacArthur delivered his letter to Yoshida, but this is a typo. The meeting took place on July 13. Finn, *Winners in Peace*, 264.

13. Takamae Eiji, *The Allied Occupation of Japan*, trans. Robert Ricketts and Sebastian Swann (London: Continuum, 2002), 487.

14. Finn, *Winners in Peace*, 264.

15. Miller, *Cold War Democracy*, 87.

16. For more on Willoughby and Hattori, see John L. Weste, "Staging a Come-back: Rearmament Planning and *kyūgunjin* in Occupied Japan, 1945–52," *Japan Forum* 11, no. 2 (1999): 165–78.

17. Kenneth B. Pyle, *Japan Rising: The Resurgence of Japanese Power and Purpose* (New York: PublicAffairs, 2007), 227.

18. Yoshida quoted in Finn, *Winners in Peace*, 263.

19. Sigal Ben-Rafael Galanti, "Japan's Remilitarization Debate and the Projection of Democracy," in *Japan's Multilayered Democracy*, ed. Sigal Ben-Rafael Galanti, Nissim Otmazgin, and Alon Levkowitz (Landham, MD: Lexington, 2015), 95.

20. Yoshida as quoted by Dower, Dower, *Empire and Aftermath*, 416. For the shifting interpretations of "war potential" thereafter, see Richard J. Samuels, *Securing Japan: Tokyo's Grand Strategy and the Future of East Asia* (Ithaca, NY: Cornell University Press, 2007) 146–47.

21. Miller, *Cold War Democracy*, 74.

22. Kusunoki, "The Early Years," 78.

23. Bōei shō bōei kenkyūjo senshibu, ed., *Utsumi Hitoshi ōraru hisutorī, Keisatsu Yobitai, Hoantai jidai* (Tokyo: Bōei shō bōei kenkyūjo, 2008), 46, 101; Kusunoki, "The Early Years," 65–66.

24. Ishibashi, "Different Forces in One," 162–63.

25. Pyle, *Japan Rising*, 229–30.

26. Hajimu Masuda, "Fear of World War III: Social Politics of Japan's Rearmament and Peace Movements, 1950–3," *Journal of Contemporary History* 47, no. 3 (2012): 551–71.

27. Miller, *Cold War Democracy*, 85.

28. Bōei shō bōei kenkyūjo senshibu, ed., *Ōraru hisutorī: Reisenki no bōeiryoku seibi to dōmei seisaku, 1* (Tokyo: Bōei shō bōei kenkyūjo, 2012), 252.

29. "Keisatsu Yobitai sōsetsu ni tomonau bōshū gyōmu," *Bōshū jūnen-shi 1*, in *Sengo Nihon bōei mondai shiryōshū*, ed. Ōtake Hideo, 3 vols. (Tokyo: Sanichi shobō, 1991), 1:482.

30. "Public Safety Highlights," 10–11, file PRF, RG 331.2271.3, US National Archives, College Park, Maryland; Office of Military History, Officer Headquarters, United States Army Forces East Asia and Eighth United States Army, ed., *History of the National Police Reserve of Japan (July 1950–April 1952)*, 2 vols. (Washington, DC: Office of Military History, 1955), 1:126

31. "'Keisatsu Yobitai' to koshō," *Mainichi shinbun*, July 27, 1950, in *Shinbun shūsei Shōwa-shi no shōgen*, ed. Takada Kiyoshi, 26 vols. (Tokyo: SBB shuppankai, 1991), 25:338.

32. "Guntai-teki tsuyoi sōshiki: Keisatsu Yobitai no seikaku," *Yomiuri shinbun*, August 2, 1950, in Takada, *Shinbun shūsei Shōwa-shi no shōgen*, 25:349.

33. Office of Military History, *History of the National Police Reserve*, 127–28. The same artist or a different one produced another design. It is not clear if it was used for the recruitment drive or not. It features uniformed figures, one in the foreground saluting and four to the rear—two holding the Japanese flag and a flag with the golden dove on it between two shouldering rifles. Its text reads, "Securing peace and public safety is in our hands" (*heiwa to chian ha warera no te de!!*) and "Police Reserve

Force recruitment." Another poster that was later used to recruit PRF officers features a photograph of a force member in front of the Diet Building; it emphasizes democracy and public harmony with the words "Minshū Nihon no chitsujo o mamoru" (protecting order in democratic Japan). A mock-up of the first design and the actual poster of the second one are preserved in the Papers of Frank Kowalski, oversized materials box, Manuscript Division, Library of Congress, Washington, DC.

34. Sasaki Tomoyuki, *Japan's Postwar Military and Civil Society: Contesting a Better Life* (New York: Bloomsbury, 2017), 20.

35. "Guntai-teki tsuyoi sōshiki."

36. "Kaikyū o jūni ni: Keisatsu Yobitai fukusei mo kimaru," *Asahi shinbun*, August 14, 1950, 2.

37. "Kaikyū o jūni ni," 2. Hirazawa's death sentence was never carried out and he died in prison.

38. Office of Military History, *History of the National Police Reserve*, 133–36.

39. "Shonichi de san man-me kōyo," *Mainichi shinbun*, August 14, 1950, in Ōtake, *Sengo Nihon bōei mondai shiryōshū*, 1:477.

40. "Keisatsu Yobitai sōsetsu ni tomonau bōshū gyōmu," 1:480–84.

41. "Keisatsu Yobitai sōsetsu ni tomonau bōshū gyōmu," 1:480–84.

42. Satō Morio, interview, September 17, 2003; Satō Morio, *Keisatsu Yobitai to saigunbi he no michi* (Tokyo: Fuyō shobo, 2015), 39–41.

43. Welfield, *An Empire in Eclipse*, 371–75.

44. Steven Pinker, *The Better Angels of Our Nature: Why Violence Has Declined* (New York: Viking, 2011), 100.

45. Sasaki, *Japan's Postwar Military*, 33. In the early 1980s, the seven prefectures of Kyushu, which accounted for only 11 percent of the entire population at the time, continued to provide nearly one-third of SDF senior officers, petty officers, and rank-and-file personnel. Welfield, *An Empire in Eclipse*, 371.

46. Bōei shō bōei kenkyūjo senshibu, ed., *Ōraru hisutorī: Reisenki no bōeiryoku seibi to dōmei seisaku*, 2 (Tokyo: Bōei shō bōei kenkyūjo, 2013), 33.

47. Kuzuhara Kazumi, "The Korean War and the National Police Reserve of Japan: Impact of the US Army's Far East Command on Japan's Defense Capability," *NIDS Security Reports*, no. 7 (December 2006): 99. By September 1951, there were forty PRF installations. They were divided into four regions, northeast to southwest. In region one were Engaru, Bihoro, Obihiro, Sapporo, Eniwa, Hakodate, Aomori, and Akita. In region two were Funaoka, Takada, Kanazawa, Matsumoto, Utsunomiya, Shinmachi, Katsuta, Nerima, Narashino, the McKnight National Headquarters in Tokyo, Tachikawa, Kurihama, and Toyokawa. In region three were Maizuru, Fukuchiyama, Itami, Himeji, Mizushima, Yonago, Zentsuji, Fukuyama, Kaidaichi, and Mitsuhama. In region four were Ozuki, Nakatsu, Sone, Fukuoka, Miyakonojo, Kumamoto, Hario, and Kanoya. General Headquarters, Supreme Commander for the Allied Powers, Civil Affairs Section, Control and Advisory Group, "A Report on the Japanese National Police Reserve, October 1951," RG 333, GS-1 (4), US National Archives, College Park, Maryland.

48. Office of Military History, *History of the National Police Reserve*, 180.

49. Tetsuo Maeda, *The Hidden Army: The Untold Story of Japan's Military Forces*, ed. David J. Kenney, trans. Steven Karpa (Chicago: Edition Q, 1995), 17.

50. Miller, *Cold War Democracy*, 72.

51. Raymond Y. Aka, interview by author, July 19, 2002, Walnut Creek, California. "A Short History of the Military Assistance Effort in Japan," 2. Document, composed around 1980, shared with author by Raymond Y. Aka, longtime Military Assistance Advisory Group—Japan official. The author is unknown.

52. Kowalski, *An Inoffensive Rearmament*, 23.

53. Bōei chō "Jieitai no jūnen shi" henshū iinkai, ed., *Jieitai no jūnen shi* (Tokyo: Ōkura-shō, 1961), 375.

54. Dower, *Embracing Defeat*, 547.

55. Kowalski, *An Inoffensive Rearmament*, 127–28. The historian Thomas French casts doubt on the accuracy of Kowalski's memoir. Although Kowalski may have exaggerated aspects of his work with the PRF, given other evidence and his detailed descriptions there is little reason to doubt his characterization of the force as both gendarme-like and an embryonic army, or the nature of his interactions with senior PRF officers like Hayashi. French, *National Police Reserve*, 13–14.

56. Kowalski, *An Inoffensive Rearmament*, 79.

57. Kowalski, *An Inoffensive Rearmament*, 99.

58. Dower, *Embracing Defeat*, 550.

59. Kitamura Morimitsu letter to Frank Kowalski, July 2, 1954, Papers of Frank Kowalski, box 1, folder 3, Manuscript Division, Library of Congress, Washington, DC. Despite the gendered characterization of US military advisers as male parents to the PRF, it appears that at least three women numbered among the hundreds of advisers assigned to oversee the camps. A Civil Affairs document makes note of "two officers female" and "one enlisted female" assigned to Camp Kurihama. It is unknown what roles they filled. "Information Concerning Quarters for Advisory Groups to the NPR," undated, 4, US National Archives, College Park, Maryland.

60. See, for example, Satō interview, February 16, 2004; Irikura interview, February 9, 2006.

61. William Sebald, *With MacArthur in Japan: A Personal History of the Occupation* (New York: W. W. Norton, 1965), 198.

62. Papers of Frank Kowalski, box 4, folder 3, 4, and 5, Manuscript Division, Library of Congress, Washington, DC.

63. Satō Morio, interview, September 17, 2005.

64. Office of Military History, *History of the National Police Reserve*, 194.

65. Foster Hailey, "US Army Manual Poor Fit in Japan," *New York Times*, December 9, 1956, 29.

66. Kusunoki, "The Early Years," 67.

67. Miller, *Cold War Democracy*, 106.

68. Lockenour, *Soldiers as Citizens*, 183.

69. Kowalski, *An Inoffensive Rearmament*, 106.

70. Kowalski, *An Inoffensive Rearmament*, 109.

71. Kyushu Civil Affairs Section Annex, "Operational Policy for Direction of PRF by Chief, 4th Region with KCASA Assistance," January 8, 1951, 2, record information unknown, US National Archives, College Park, Maryland.

72. Memo, to: Camp Commanders, Chiefs, All Divisions and Sections, R. Hq, Subject: "Concerning Operational Procedures and Supervision," translation, 4th Region Headquarters, National Police Reserve, June 6, 1951, 1–2, US National Archives, College Park, Maryland.

73. Memo, Subject: "Advisory Policy," General Headquarters, Supreme Commander for the Allied Powers, Civil Affair Section, October 11, 1951, 1, US National Archives, College Park, Maryland.

74. Furukawa Kumio, interview by author, May 15, 2006, Sapporo, Japan.

75. General Headquarters (GHQ), SCAP, Government Section, "National Police Reserve," January 15, 1952, 1, RG 331.2271.5, US National Archives, College Park, Maryland.

76. Maeda, *Hidden Army*, 8.

77. "Jieitai no jūnen shi" henshū iinkai, *Jieitai no jūnen shi*, 25.

78. Kuboi Masayuki, interview by author, November 30, 2005, Kita Hiroshima, Japan; Satō interview, September 17, 2005.

79. Satō Yukio, "Takada Camp," undated, Papers of Frank Kowalski, box 7, folder 11, Manuscript Division, Library of Congress, Washington, DC.

80. Fujii Shigeru, interview by author, March 4, 2008, Sapporo, Japan.

81. Takashi Yoneyama, "The Establishment of the ROK Armed Forces and the Japan Self-Defense Forces and the Activities of the US Military Advisory Groups to the ROK and Japan," *NIDS Security Studies*, no. 15 (December 2014): 82.

82. Satō interview, September 17, 2005; Satō, *Keisatsu Yobitai*, 52.

83. Sayuri Guthrie-Shimizu, *Transpacific Field of Dreams: How Baseball Linked the United States and Japan in Peace and War* (Chapel Hill: University of North Carolina Press, 2012), 199.

84. Irikura Shōzō, letter to author, February 10, 2020.

85. Irikura interview, February 9, 2006; Fujii interview, March 4, 2008; Nagano, *Jieitai*, 28–29; Satō, *Keisatsu Yobitai*, 52.

86. Fujii interview, March 4, 2008.

87. See, for example, a letter from Kunitomi Shigeru to his brother Kunitomi Masao; both were members of the PRF. Kunitomi Shigeru letter to Kunitomi Masao, Papers of Frank Kowalski, box 3, folder 23, Manuscript Division, Library of Congress, Washington, DC; Nagano, *Jieitai*, 28.

88. Yoshida Yutaka, *Nihon no guntai* (Tokyo: Iwanami shinsho, 2002), 34–35.

89. Irikura Shōzō, interview by author, February 8, 2006, Sapporo, Japan.

90. "Yūmoto Yūzo intabyū kiroku," September 18, 1980, in Ōtake, *Sengo Nihon bōei mondai shiryōshū*, 1:494; Nagano, *Jieitai*, 21. Kowalski notes that the PRF "cut down the boots to the feet of their new owners." Kowalski, *An Inoffensive Rearmament*, 81.

91. GHQ records show that a request for "75,000 [pairs of] small shoes or boots in sizes 5 to 7" was fulfilled by "Marine sources." A year and half later, a quartermaster memo noted the return of 72,915 pairs of Marine shoes and it was more valuable to scrap them than to salvage them. Message to Department of Army, Washington DC, from CINCFE Tokyo Japan, "CG Eighth Army Yokohama Japan," July 14, 1950, RG9 "War CXDA," US National Archives, College Park, Maryland; "Dropping Accountability of Shoes, Marine, Loaned to PRFJ," March 17, 1952, RG 331 B.397 F.20, US National Archives, College Park, Maryland.

92. Satō, "Takada Camp," 6.

93. Hailey, "US Army Manual Poor Fit in Japan," 29.

94. "Yūmoto Yūzo intabyū kiroku," 492.

95. Takamae, *The Allied Occupation of Japan*, 488

96. Kusunoki, "The Early Years," 115.

97. Fujii interview, March 4, 2008.

98. Satō interview, September 17, 2005.

99. Irikura interview, February 9, 2006.

100. Irikura interview, February 9, 2006.

101. Tanida Isamu, "Sājanto K: Kita Fuji de no Nichibei guhatsu funsō," *Asagumo gekkan* 22, no. 10 (October 1985): 35–36.

102. Eiichiro Azuma, "Brokering Race, Culture, and Citizenship: Japanese Americans in Occupied Japan and Postwar National Inclusion," *Journal of American–East Asian Relations* 16, no. 3 (Fall 2009): 185, 199, 201–4, 209.

103. Tanida, "Sājanto K," 36.

104. Sakamoto Chikara, "Jieitai zero sai kokkei dan," *Bungei shunjū*, June 1968, in Ōtake, *Sengo Nihon bōei mondai shiryōshū*, 1:495.

105. Dower, *Embracing Defeat*, 436–38.

106. Public Safety Division, Police Branch, "Newsreel Coverage of N.P.R.," October 13, 1950, 1–2, US National Archives, College Park, Maryland.

107. Masuda, "Fear of World War III," 554.

108. Office of Military History, *History of the National Police Reserve*, 143–46.

109. See, for example, Kagawa Yoshiaki, "Keisatsu Yobitai koto hajime," in *Keisatsu Yobitai no kaiko: Jieitai no yoake*, ed. Shichōkai and Nishida Hiroshi (Tokyo: Shinpūsha, 2003), 47; Kuboi Masayuki, *Higashi Hiroshima kara Kita Hiroshima made: 80 nen no kaisō* (Kita Hiroshima, Japan: Kuboi Masayuki, 2004), 79.

110. Tessa Morris-Suzuki, "A Fire on the Other Shore? Japan and the Korean War Order," in *The Korean War in Asia: A Hidden History*, ed. Tessa Morris-Suzuki (Lanham, MD: Rowman & Littlefield, 2018), 11, 15–18.

111. Irikura interview, February 9, 2006.

112. "Yūmoto Yūzo intabyū kiroku," 492.

113. "Yūmoto Yūzo intabyū kiroku," 493.

114. Welfield, *An Empire in Eclipse*, 76. Welfield stated that in "June 1950 some 300 former imperial second lieutenants were taken into the Police Reserve," but this is a typo. They entered the force in June 1951 rather than June 1950, when the force had not yet been formed.

115. Morris, *Nationalism and the Right Wing in Japan*, 214; Hanji Kinoshita, "Echoes of Militarism in Japan," *Pacific Affairs* 26, no. 3 (September 1953): 246.

116. Kuboi interview, November 30, 2005.

117. Pulliam G-2, GHQ Inter-Office Memorandum to Willoughby, "Appointment of Mr. Hayashi, Keizo CofS of NPR," September 26, 1950, record information unknown, US National Archives, College Park, Maryland.

118. Kusunoki, "The Early Years," 67; David Hunter-Chester, *Creating Japan's Ground Self-Defense Force: A Sword Well Made* (Lanham, MD: Lexington, 2016), 91–92.

119. Rikujō bakuryō kanbu sōmuka, ed., *Keisatsu Yobitai sōtai shi* (Tokyo: Bōei chō rikujō bakuryō kanbu, 1958), 13.

120. "Kanbu kōshū kai ni okeru Hayashi sōtai sōkan no kunji," *Keisatsu Yobitai shūhō*, December 25, 1950, 2, Papers of Frank Kowalski, box 3, folder 12, Manuscript Division, Library of Congress, Washington, DC.

121. "Kanbu kōshū kai ni okeru Hayashi sōtai sōkan no kunji," *Keisatsu Yobitai shūhō*, 1–8.

122. Rikujō bakuryō kanbu sōmuka, *Keisatsu Yobitai sōtai shi*, 13.

123. "Kanbu kōshū kai ni okeru Hayashi sōtai sōkan no kunji," *Keisatsu Yobitai shūhō*, 1–8.

124. Sasaki, *Japan's Postwar Military and Civil Society*, 55.

125. Irikura Shōzō, interview by author, July 11, 2019, Sapporo, Japan.

126. Hatano Sumio and Satō Susumu, "'Ajia moderu toshite no 'Yoshida dokutorin,'" *Gunji shigaku* 40, no. 156 (March 2004): 13.

127. Hatano and Satō, "'Ajia moderu toshite no 'Yoshida dokutorin,'" 13.

128. Memo from MacArthur to Yoshida.

129. Welfeld, *An Empire in Eclipse*, 73.

130. Welfeld, *An Empire in Eclipse*, 73.

131. French, *National Police Reserve*, 128.

132. Welfield, *An Empire in Eclipse*, 77.

133. Rikujō bakuryō kanbu sōmuka, *Keisatsu Yobitai sōtai shi*, ii.

134. "Fighters for the Public Peace and Security," a police march, RG 331. 2570.13.24, US National Archives, College Park, Maryland.

135. Welfield, *An Empire in Eclipse*, 77.

136. Kusunoki, "The Early Years," 77.

137. Humphreys, *The Way of the Heavenly Sword*, 43; Edward J. Drea, *Japan's Imperial Army: Its Rise and Fall, 1853–1945* (Lawrence: University of Press of Kansas, 2009), 143.

138. Dower, *Embracing Defeat*, 554–55.

139. Kusunoki, "The Early Years," 75.

140. Kusunoki, "The Early Years," 75–76; Yomiuri shinbun sengo shi hanhen, ed., *"Saigunbi" no kiseki*, 8–16.

141. Yoshida Shigeru, *The Yoshida Memoirs: The Story of Japan in Crisis*, trans. Kenichi Yoshida (Boston: Houghton Mifflin, 1962), 190.

142. Yoshida Ritsuto, "Guntai no 'saigai shutsudō' seido no kakuritsu: Daikibo saigai e no taiō to eiju no henka kara," *Shigaku zasshi* 117, no. 10 (October 2008): 73, 93–94. See also Arakawa Shōji, *Guntai to chiiki* (Tokyo: Aoki Shoten, 2001), 195–96.

143. Charles Davison, *The Japanese Earthquake of 1923* (London: Thomas Merby, 1931), 16–23; J. Charles Schencking, "1923 Tokyo as a Devastated War and Occupation Zone: The Catastrophe One Confronted in Post Earthquake Japan," *Japanese Studies* 29, no. 1 (2009): 111–29.

144. Humphreys, *The Way of the Heavenly Sword*, 52.

145. Richard Smethurst, *A Social Basis for Prewar Japanese Militarism: The Army and the Rural Community* (Berkeley: University of California Press, 1974), 150–52.

146. Tomoaki Murakami, "The GSDF and Disaster Relief Dispatches," in Eldridge and Midford, *The Japanese Ground Self-Defense Force*, 268–70; Kusunoki, "The Early Years," 95.

147. "Address by Major Dilworth at Camp near Maebashi," August 9, 1952, National Defense Academy Archives, Yokosuka, Japan.

148. Masuda, *Jieitai no tanjō*, 33; Miller, *Cold War Democracy*, 102.

149. "A Short History of the Military Assistance Effort in Japan," 5, 9; US Military Assistance Advisory Group—Japan, *A Decade of Defense in Japan*, 2; Pyle, *Japan Rising*, 234–35.

150. "A Short History of the Military Assistance Effort in Japan," 6. William S. Biddle, the chief of MAAG from June 1955 to July 1957, attended an array of official social events that year during which he rubbed shoulders with GSDF officers, Japanese government officials, and businessmen from both countries. These events included a duck-netting party at the Imperial Palace, a bird-hunting outing near Tachikawa, the SDF Commemoration Day, the Fifth All-Japan GSDF Softball Tournament, US Armed Forces Day, a judo tournament, the Green Grass Golf Tournament, and the Far East Command Inter-Service Football Championships, which featured three games: the Sukiyaki Bowl between the Marines and the Air Force, the Torii Bowl between the Army and the Navy, and the Rice Bowl between Japan and Korea at the Korakuen Football Stadium. William S. Biddle Collection, boxes 25 and 39, Military History Institute, US Army War College Archives, Carlisle, Pennsylvania.

151. "Jieitai no jūnen shi" henshū iinkai, *Jieitai no jūnen shi*, 374.

152. "A Short History of the Military Assistance Effort in Japan," 6. See also Congressional Quarterly Service, *Global Defense: U. S. Military Commitments Abroad* (Washington, DC: Congressional Quarterly Service, 1969), 44; "Status of MAAG Japan," briefing paper, 1966, no. 1326, Kaihara Osamu Papers, National Diet Library, Tokyo.

153. Staff of the *Asahi Shimbun*, *The Pacific Rivals: A Japanese View of Japanese-American Relations* (New York: Weatherhill, 1972), 328.

154. Sado, *The Self-Defense Forces*, 57. In contrast, because the MSDF "assumed collaborations with the U.S. Navy as its basic stance from the beginning, it conducted joint drills with the U.S. Navy . . . from the early days of its founding." Sado, *The Self-Defense Forces*, 57.

155. Smith, *Japan Rearmed*, 44.

## 2. Establishing the National Defense Academy and Overcoming the Past

1. Shima Atsushi, interview by author, October 18, 2016, Tokyo.

2. Tanaka Hiromi, "Kaisetsu," afterword to Maki Tomoo, *Bōei no tsutome: Jieitai no seishinteki kyoten.* (Tokyo: Chūō kōron sha, 2004), 316–22.

3. In 2014, the academy began to require graduates who did not join the SDF to reimburse part of their academic expenses. Garren Mulloy, *Defenders of Japan: The Post-Imperial Armed Forces 1964–2016* (London: Hurts, 2021), 240.

4. Shima interview, October 18, 2016.

5. Gojū nenshi henshū jigyō iinkai, ed., *Bōei Daigakkō gojū nenshi* (Yokosuka, Japan: Bōei Daigakkō, 2004), 4.

6. Nishihara Masashi, "U.S. Military Advisors and the Establishment of the Japanese National Defense Academy," translated and annotated by Robert D. Eldridge, unpublished manuscript. The original Japanese article was published as Nishihara Masashi, "Bōdai sōsetsu ki no Beigunjin komontachi: Sōritsu gojū shūnen o mukaeta Bōdai o furikaeru," *Obaradai*, no. 83 (2003): 84–95.

7. Takahashi Kazuhiro, interview by author, July 1, 2019, Tokyo, Japan.

8. Nishihara, "U.S. Military Advisors."

9. Takahashi Kazuhiro, "Bōei Daigakko ni okeru Beigun kōmondan no yakuwari ni kansuru jisshō kenkyū," *Bōei Daigakkō kiyō* 118 (2019): 33.

10. Nishihara, "U.S. Military Advisors," 4.

11. Dower, *Empire and Aftermath*, 398–99.

12. Dower, *Empire and Aftermath*, 267–69.

13. Yoshida, *The Yoshida Memoirs*, 190.

14. "A Plan for the Training of the Cadre of the Defence Corps of Japan," 4, Okinawa Prefectural Archives, Okinawa, Japan; "Memorandum of Conversation: Proposed Establishment of a Japanese Military Academy," US Foreign Service, February 14, 1952, 2, Okinawa Prefectural Archives, Okinawa, Japan.

15. Gojū nenshi henshū jigyō iinkai, *Bōei Daigakkō gojū nenshi*, 3; Takahashi, "Bōei Daigakkō ni okeru Beigun kōmondan," 32.

16. Bōei shō bōei kenkyūjo senshibu, ed., *Utsumi Hitoshi ōraru hisutorī, Keisatsu Yobitai, Hoantai jidai* (Tokyo: Bōei shō bōei kenkyūjo, 2008), 61.

17. For an analysis of the curriculum of the Imperial Army Academy, see Hirota Teruyuki, *Rikugun shōkō no kyōiku shakai shi: Risshin shusse to tennōsei* (Yokohama, Japan: Seori shobō, 1997), 173–201.

18. Hirota, *Rikugun shōkō no kyōiku shakai-shi*, 62.

19. "A Plan for the Training of the Cadre of the Defence Corps of Japan."

20. Nishihara, "U.S. Military Advisors," 5.

21. Nishihara, "U.S. Military Advisors," 5.

22. George B. Pickett, Jr., "My Years in Japan," May 20, 2002, 1, National Defense Academy Archives, Yokosuka, Japan.

23. "Memorandum of Conversation," February 14, 1952, 2.

24. Nishihara, "U.S. Military Advisors," 6; Bōei shō bōei kenkyūjo senshibu, *Utsumi Hitoshi ōraru hisutorī*, 62.

25. John W. Masland and Laurence I. Radway, *Soldiers and Scholars: Military Education and National Policy* (Princeton, NJ: Princeton University Press, 1957), 106.

26. Nishihara, "U.S. Military Advisors," 6–7.

27. See, for example, Kobayashi Sunao, "Beikoku rikugun shikan gakkō," *Keisatsu Yobitai shiryō shū* 3 (March 1952): 1–7; Joel J. Dilworth, "A Tribute to the Japanese National Defense Academy," June 16, 2002, National Defense Academy Archives, Yokosuka, Japan.

28. US Military Assistance Advisory Group—Japan, *A Decade of Defense in Japan*, 11.

29. Masland and Radway, *Soldiers and Scholars*, 107.

30. For more on Koizumi's political thought, see Taeju Kim, "The Moral Realism of the Postwar Intellectuals" (PhD dissertation, University of Chicago, 2018), 137–38. For a description of Koizumi's activities in the Imperial Household Agency and how he, like Maki, was inspired by Fukuzawa Yukichi, see Ruoff, *Japan's Imperial House in the Postwar Era*, 76–78. Koizumi is not related to the Koizumi family of politicians, including Jun'ya, who served as director of the Defense Agency from 1964 to 1965, and his son, Jun'ichirō, who served as prime minister from 2001 to 2006 and is mentioned at the end of this chapter and in the epilogue.

31. Nakamori Shizuo, *Bōei daigakkō no shinjitsu* (Tokyo: Keizai kai, 2004), 27.

32. Pickett, "My Years in Japan," 2.

33. Yoshida, *The Yoshida Memoirs*, 191.

34. Carter Eckert, *Park Chung Hee and Modern Korea: The Roots of Militarism, 1866–1945* (Cambridge, MA: Belknap Press of Harvard University Press, 2016), 109.

35. Maekawa Kiyoshi, interview by author, October 20, 2016, Tokyo.

36. Pickett, "My Years in Japan," 3.

37. Yoshida, *The Yoshida Memoirs*, 191.

38. Maki was joined at Keiō by his younger brother, Aritsune (Yūkō), who went on to become a famous mountaineer. Maki's studies in Britain and those of his brother at Columbia University were made possible by the financial support of an uncle who became wealthy in the sugar industry in colonial Taiwan. For more on Maki Aritsune, see David Fedman, "Mounting Modernization: Itakura Katsunobu, the Hokkaido University Alpine Club and Mountaineering in Pre-War Hokkaido," *Asia-Pacific Journal*, October 19, 2009, 1–18. After completing his studies at Oxford, the older Maki spent time climbing in the Alps before returning to Japan.

39. Justin Aukema, "Cultures of (Dis)remembrance and the Effects of Discourse at the Hiyoshidai Tunnels," *Japan Review* 32 (2019): 130.

40. Roden, "Thoughts on the Early Meiji Gentleman," 80.

41. J. M. Winter, "Oxford and the First World War," in *The History of the University of Oxford*, vol. 8: *The Twentieth Century*, ed. Brian Harrison (Oxford: Clarendon, 1994), 8–10, 18–24.

42. Julia Stapleton, *Englishness and the Study of Politics: The Social and Political Thought of Ernest Barker* (Cambridge: Cambridge University Press, 1994), 172, 180.

43. For assessments of Barker, see Stapleton, *Englishness and the Study of Politics*; Andrzej Olechnowicz, "Liberal Anti-Fascism in the 1930s: The Case of Sir Ernest Barker," *Albion* 36, no. 4 (2005): 636–60. For more about the academic and cultural milieu of universities like Oxford and the relationship of dons and students, see Reba N. Soffer, *Discipline and Power: The University, History, and the Making of an English Elite, 1870–1930* (Stanford, CA: Stanford University Press, 1994), 24–25. Like other intellectuals, Barker contributed to the war effort. He helped lead a group of historians of "different political sensitivities" at Oxford who published *Why We Are at War: Great Britain's Case*, which "reconstructed a century of Germanic aggression." Anne Rasmussen, "Mobilizing Minds," in *The Cambridge History of the First World War: Civil Society*, ed. Jay Winter, vol. 3 (Cambridge: Cambridge University Press, 2014), 403.

44. Keiō Gijuku shi jiten henshū iinkai, ed., *Keiō Gijiku shi jiten* (Tokyo: Keiō Gijuku, 2008), 586.

45. Keiō Gijuku shi jiten henshū iinkai, *Keiō Gijiku shi jiten*, 749.

46. See Aukema, "Cultures of (Dis)remembrance," 131–33.

47. Maki only published seven articles in *Mita shinbun* during his time as a professor and administrator at Keiō. Only one, which like nearly all his earlier articles was about student participation in sports, was published after the Manchurian Incident. "Rīgu jōka niha futatsu no hōhō ga aru," *Mita shinbun*, October 21, 1932, 3. This was long before Japanese society was mobilized for war after the Marco Polo Incident in 1937 led to a full-scale assault on China. Koizumi made his statements in the *Mita shinbun* and major national daily newspapers that encouraged students to serve in the military from 1937 to 1944. Aukema, "Cultures of (Dis)remembrance," 131–32.

48. Gojū nenshi henshū jigyō iinkai, *Bōei Daigakkō gojū nenshi*, 15.

49. Tanaka, "Kaisetsu," 318–19.

50. Iokibe Makoto, "Jō," introduction to Maki, *Bōei no tsutome*, 2.

51. Dower, *Empire and Aftermath*, 442.

52. "'Hakushi' o tsukuru Hoan Daigakkō," *Mainichi shinbun*, February 25, 1953, 7.

53. Todoroki Takao, "Maki Tomoo shodai Bōei Daigakkō gakuchō no kyōiku ri'nen to sono engen: Ānesuto Bākā to no kankei o chūshin ni," *Bōei Daigakkō kiyō* 97 (2008): 6–8.

54. Maki, *Bōei no tsutome*, 20–21.

55. For an analysis of postwar conservative academics, see Kim, "The Moral Realism of the Postwar Japanese Intellectuals."

56. Eckert, *Park Chung Hee and Modern Korea*, 282; Danny Orbach, *Curse on this Country: The Rebellious Army of Imperial Japan* (Ithaca, NY: Cornell University Press, 2017), 226.

57. Maeda, *The Hidden Army*, 58–59.

58. Maki, *Bōei no tsutome*, 268. Maki provided both the Japanese terms and their English equivalents in parentheses in his text.

59. Yumiko Mikanagi, *Masculinity and Japan's Foreign Relations* (Boulder, CO: First Forum, 2011), 60.

60. Roden, "Thoughts on the Early Meiji Gentleman," 74.

61. Maekawa Kiyoshi, "Maki sensei to Inoue Shigeyoshi kaigun taishō," *Bōdai dōsō kai shi* (1969): 185.

62. Orbach, *Curse on this Country*, 161–256.

63. Jason G. Karlin, "The Gender of Nationalism: Competing Masculinities in Meiji Japan," *Journal of Japanese Studies* 28, no. 1 (Winter 2002): 68–70; Mikanagi, *Masculinity and Japan's Foreign Relations*, 26–29. For a deeper exploration of competing notions of masculinity during the Meiji period, see Jason G. Karlin, *Gender and Nation in Meiji Japan* (Honolulu: University of Hawai'i Press, 2014), chap. 1.

64. Donald T. Roden, *Schooldays in Imperial Japan: A Study in the Culture of a Student Elite* (Berkeley: University of California Press, 1980), 113–24.

65. Paul R. Deslandes, *Oxbridge Men: British Masculinity and the Undergraduate Experience, 1850–1920* (Bloomington: Indiana University Press, 2005), 156.

66. "Visit of Doctor Tomo-O Maki, Superintendent, Japan Defense Academy to the U. S. Naval Academy on Thursday, 16 February and Friday, February 17, 1956," RG 405 Entry 56 A, Records of the Superintendent, Directives, Notices 1956–1963, box 2, folder 1, Records of the United States Naval Academy, Annapolis, MD.

67. Maki, *Bōei no tsutome*, 190. Originally published in *Shūshin*, January 1963. Todoroki, "Maki Tomoo," 3.

68. In the early 1920s, the Army Academy briefly introduced sports that were popular in regular middle schools at the time, such as baseball, tennis, and soccer, but these were soon abandoned as "anti-foreign" attitudes emerged. Theodore F. Cook, "The Japanese Officer Corps: The Making of a Military Elite, 1872–1945," PhD dissertation, Princeton University, 1987, 101; Stewart Lone, *Provincial Life and the Military in Imperial Japan: The Phantom Samurai* (London: Routledge, 2009), 153n6.

69. Takahashi interview, July 1, 2019.

70. Eckert, *Park Chung Hee and Modern Korea*, 109–10.

71. Tanaka Hiromi, "Bōei Daigakkō," in *Shin Yokosuka shi shi: Betsuhen gunji*, ed. Yokoshuka-shi (Yokosuka, Japan: Yokosuka shi, 2012), 795.

72. Maki, *Bōei no tsutome*, 144.

NOTES TO PAGES 79-84

73. Ueda Naruhiko, interview by author, October 18, 2016, Tokyo.

74. Maeda, *The Hidden Army*, 59–60.

75. Bōei shō bōei kenkyūjo senshibu, ed., *Sakuma Makoto ōraru hisutorī, moto sōgō bakuryō kaigi gichō, jōkan* (Tokyo: Bōei shō bōei kenkyūjo, 2007), 26.

76. Matsutani Sei, "Hoan Daigakkō sōritsu no omoide," in Ōtake, *Sengo Nihon bōei mondai shiryōshū*, 2:481–86.

77. For example, Yamazaki Makoto, a cadet in the ninth graduating class, recalled that one of his instructors who had a strong influence on him was a member of the first graduating class. Yamazaki, interview by author, October 17, 2016, Tokyo.

78. For an analysis of socioeconomic backgrounds of Imperial Army Academy cadets, see Hirota, *Rikugun shōkō no kyōiku shakai-shi*, 137–68.

79. "Kamera Hoan Daigakkō ni hairu," *Asahi kurabu*, June 3, 1953, 4.

80. Ueda interview, October 18, 2016.

81. Bōei shō bōei kenkyūjo senshibu, ed., *Suzuki Akio ōraru hisutorī, moto kōkū bakuryō chō* (Tokyo: Bōei shō bōei kenkyūjo, 2011), 30; Bōei shō bōei kenkyūjo senshibu, ed., *Ishizu Sadamasu ōraru hisutorī* (Tokyo: Bōei shō bōei kenkyūjo, 2014), 23.

82. Satō Morio, the overworked Mitsubishi machinist who joined the PRF in 1950, applied to the NDA but was not accepted. Satō, *Keisatsu Yobitai*, 111.

83. Shima interview, October 18, 2016.

84. Thomas M. Brendle, "Recruitment and Training in the SDF," in *The Modern Japanese Military System*, ed. James H. Buck (Beverly Hills, CA: Sage, 1975), 85. The proportion of successful applicants to the academy from Kyushu remained high for decades. From 1959 until 1978, the average percentage of academy students from the island was just over 31 percent. Welfield, *An Empire in Eclipse*, 376.

85. Sasaki, *Japan's Postwar Military*, 29; Welfield, *An Empire in Eclipse*, 375. For NDA admissions data, see Brendle, "Recruitment and Training in the SDF," 85.

86. Sōrifu tōkeikyoku, *Nihon no jinkō: Shōwa 30 nen kokusei chōsa no kaisetsu* (Tokyo: Nihon tōkei kyōkai, 1960), 216–19.

87. Sasaki, *Japan's Postwar Military*, 33.

88. Bōei shō bōei kenkyūjo senshibu, ed., *Nishimoto Tetsuya ōraru hisutorī, moto sōgō bakuryō kaigi chō, jōkan* (Tokyo: Bōei shō bōei kenkyūjo, 2010), 45.

89. Shikata Toshiyuki, interview by author, October 20, 2016, Tokyo. See also Bōei shō bōei kenkyūjo senshibu, *Ishizu Sadamasu ōraru hisutorī*, 21.

90. Ueda interview, October 18, 2016.

91. Shima interview, October 18, 2016.

92. Robert W. Aspinall, *Teachers' Unions and the Politics of Education in Japan* (Albany: State University of New York Press, 2001), 37.

93. Bōei shō bōei kenkyūjo senshibu, *Suzuki Akio ōraru hisutorī*, 27.

94. Bōei shō bōei kenkyūjo senshibu, *Nishimoto Tetsuya ōraru hisutorī*, 47.

95. Ueda Naruhiko, interview in Bōei Daigakkō sōgō toshokan, ed., *Bōei Daigakkō ōraru hisutorī, ikkisei* (Yokosuka, Japan: Bōei shō Bōei Daigakkō, 2019), 27. Ueda was interviewed by NDA faculty members on November 10, 2016, a month after I interviewed him.

96. Tomizawa Hikaru, "Rikujō Jieitai kanbu no sodachikata (sono ichi)," *Kaikō*, August 2002, 1–5; Tomizawa Hikaru, "Rikujō Jieitai kanbu no sodachikata (sono ni)," *Kaikō*, September 2002, 1–5.

97. Tomizawa, "Rikujō Jieitai kanbu no sodachikata (sono ni)," 1–5.

98. Shima interview, October 18, 2016.

99. Bōei shō bōei kenkyūjo senshibu, ed., *Yoshikawa Keisuke ōraru hisutorī, moto Ōminato chihō sōkan* (Tokyo: Bōei shō bōei kenkyūjo, 2014), 138.

100. Bōei shō bōei kenkyūjo senshibu, *Sakuma Makoto ōraru hisutorī*, 27.

101. One cadet recalled that it seemed like Yoshida came to the academy almost every month, though this was obviously not the case. Another remembered that, thanks to Yoshida's frequent visits to the academy, cadets felt an affinity with him that went beyond him being prime minister. Shima interview, October 18, 2016; Bōei shō bōei kenkyūjo senshibu, *Sakuma Makoto ōraru hisutorī*, 30.

102. Bōei shō bōei kenkyūjo senshibu, *Ishizu Sadamasu ōraru hisutorī*, 22.

103. Shima interview, October 18, 2016.

104. Copy of "Bōei Daigakkō gakuseitai uta," provided by Maekawa Kiyoshi, in the author's possession. The translation is a slightly modified version of a translation found in the papers of William S. Biddle, box 25, Military History Institute, US Army War College, Carlisle, Pennsylvania. The music for the song was composed by the prolific musician Hirai Kenzaburō.

105. Shikata interview, October 20, 2016.

106. Bōei shō bōei kenkyūjo senshibu, *Yoshikawa Keisuke ōraru hisutorī*, 139.

107. Shikata interview, October 20, 2016.

108. See, for example, Bōei shō bōei kenkyūjo senshibu, *Yoshikawa Keisuke ōraru hisutorī*, 138; Shima interview, October 18, 2016.

109. Ikeda Kiyoshi, *Jiyū to kiritsu: Igirisu no gakkō seikatsu* (Tokyo: Iwanami shoten, 1949), 154.

110. Bōei shō bōei kenkyūjo senshibu, *Nishimoto Tetsuya ōraru hisutorī*, 50; Bōei shō bōei kenkyūjo senshibu, *Yoshikawa Keisuke ōraru hisutorī*, 25; Francis E. Kramer, "Memories of the National Defense Academy," June 27, 2002, 2–3. National Defense Academy Archives, Yokosuka, Japan.

111. Guthrie-Shimizu, *Transpacific Field of Dreams*, 201.

112. Bōei shō bōei kenkyūjo senshibu, *Nishimoto Tetsuya ōraru hisutorī*, 51; Ken Belson, "The Organized Chaos of Botaoshi, Japan's Wildest Game," *New York Times*, August 22, 2018.

113. Nishihara, "U.S. Military Advisors"; Joel J. Dilworth, letter to Nishihara Masashi, May 16, 2002, National Defense Academy Archives, Yokosuka, Japan.

114. Nishihara, "U.S. Military Advisors," 3.

115. "National Safety Academy: Camp Kurihama," "Controversial Issues" addendum, National Defense Academy Archives, Yokosuka, Japan.

116. Dilworth, "A Tribute," 1.

117. Maki Tomoo, *Bei-Ei-Futsu shikan gakkō rekihō no tabi* (Tokyo: Kōyō shobō, 1969), 18. One indication of the closeness of Maki's relationship with Fisken is that that latter's father and mother drove from Seattle to meet Maki in San Francisco at the beginning of his trip.

118. Maki, *Bei-Ei-Futsu*, 70.

119. See, for example, Maki, *Bōei no tsutome*, 182–85.

120. Kramer, "Memories," 1–2.

121. Kramer, "Memories," 3.

122. Fumio Ota, "Japanese Warfare Ethics," *Routledge Handbook of Military Ethics*, ed. George Lucas (New York: Routledge, 2015), 167.

123. Kramer, "Memories," 1, 3.

124. William J. Brake, "Historic Milestones" letter to Nishihara Masashi, July 2002, National Defense Academy Archives, Yokosuka, Japan.

125. Shikata interview, October 20, 2016.

126. David C. Evans and Mark R. Peattie, *Kaigun: Strategy, Tactics, and Technology in the Imperial Japanese Navy, 1887–1941* (Annapolis, MD: Naval Institute Press, 1997), 9.

127. Yokosuka shi shi henshū iinkai, ed., *Yokosuka shi shi* (Yokosuka, Japan: Yokosuka shichō, 1957), 577.

128. Yokosuka shi shi henshū iinkai, *Yokosuka shi shi*, 577.

129. Bōei shō bōei kenkyūjo senshibu, *Ishizu Sadamasu ōraru hisutorī*, 140; Mishima Yukio, "Gendai shōnen no mujun o han'ei," *Shūkan Asahi*, July 26, 1953, 6.

130. Tomizawa Hikaru, interview by author, October 19, 2016, Tokyo.

131. "Tokushū: Shimin ha Bōdai-sei o dō miru ka," *Obaradai*, July 10, 1957, 2. The temptations faced by students was aptly captured in an *Obaradai* cartoon showing a cadet, in uniform of course, entering a dark, narrow street lined with signs of drinking establishments advertising "o-saké" and, in English, "BAR" and "BEER," along with signs proclaiming, "Underage individuals are not welcome." *Obaradai*, May 8, 1958, 1.

132. Maekawa interview, October 20, 2016.

133. Mishima, "Gendai shōnen no mujun o han'ei," 5–7.

134. Ōya Sōichi and Miyagi Otoya, "Hoan daigaku ni nyūgaku shita dōki," *Shūkan Sankei*, January 17, 1954, 4–7.

135. Ōya Sōichi, "Hotondo tennōsei ni ha bōkanteki," *Shūkan Sankei*, January 17, 1954, 7–8.

136. Miyagi Otoya, "Saigunbi o chōetsu," *Shūkan Sankei*, January 17, 1954, 8–9.

137. Miyagi, "Saigunbi o chōetsu," 8–9.

138. John Toland, *The Rising Sun: The Decline and Fall of the Japanese Empire, 1936–1945* (New York: Random House, 1970); John Costello, *The Pacific War, 1941–1945* (New York: Quill, 1981), 97–98; Michael Norman and Elizabeth M. Norman, *Tears in the Darkness: The Story of the Bataan Death March and its Aftermath* (New York: Farrar, Straus and Giroux, 2009), 371–72. Also see Ian Ward, *The Killer They Called God* (Singapore: Media Masters, 1992). The historian Hayashi Hirofumi believed that although Tsuji was a key figure in the planning and execution of the massacres, researchers have overestimated his role. Hayashi, "Massacre of Chinese in Singapore and Its Coverage in Postwar Japan," in *New Perspectives on the Japanese Occupation in Malaya and Singapore, 1941–1945*, ed. Akashi Yoji and Yoshimura Mako (Singapore: NUS Press, 2008), 237–38.

139. For a personal account of his travels through Southeast Asia and China, see Tsuji Masanobu, "Underground Escape," in *Ukiyo: Stories of "the Floating World" of Postwar Japan*, third edition, ed. Jay Gluck (New York: Vanguard, 1963), 48–66.

140. Robert Guillain, "The Resurgence of Military Elements in Japan," *Pacific Affairs* 25, no. 3 (September 1952): 219.

141. Morris, *Nationalism and the Right Wing in Japan*, 223.

142. Morris, *Nationalism and the Right Wing in Japan*, 223.

143. The historian Robert Bickers wrote of early twentieth-century China: "The foxtrot and the waltz had once been acts of social and cultural revolution

for educated urbanites, the types who flocked to Guangzhou in the mid-1920s and played at revolution: the country might indeed be 'saved by dancing,' and by being in all ways modern and Western. That was part of their thinking back then. Now these steps were seen by some as acts of treachery." Robert Bickers, *Out of China: How the Chinese Ended the Era of Western Domination* (Cambridge, MA: Harvard University Press, 2017), 175. Sayyid Qutb, the intellectual forefather of later radical Islamic thought, is said to have been scandalized by a church dance in Greeley, Colorado, in 1948. Daniel Brogan, "Al Qaeda's Greeley Roots," 5280.com, August 28, 2010, https://www.5280.com/2010/08/al-qaedas-greeley-roots/, accessed May 4, 2019.

144. John Hunter Boyle, *Modern Japan: The American Nexus* (Orlando, FL: Harcourt Brace Jovanovich, 1993), 117. See also Karlin, "The Gender of Nationalism," 44–47.

145. Tanizaki Junichiro, *Naomi*, trans. Anthony H. Chambers (New York: Vintage International, 2001).

146. James L. McClain, *Japan: A Modern History* (New York: W. W. Norton, 2002), 464–65.

147. Nagato Toru, "Maki kōchō to Akashiya-kai," in *Maki no mi: Maki Tomoo sensei tsuisō shū*, ed. Bōei Daigakko dōsō kai (Tokyo: Bōei Daigakko dōsō kai Maki ki'nen shuppan iinkai, 1972), 357–58.

148. Roden, "Thoughts on the Early Meiji Gentleman," 78–79.

149. Deslandes, *Oxbridge Men*, 174.

150. "Dansu kōyūkai no genjō," *Obaradai*, March 26, 1957, 3. The recollections of Nagato, a graduate of the eighth class writing many years later, about how the Akashiya was founded differed from those in the *Obaradai* article. He wrote that the club was formed while the academy was located at Kurihama. Nagato, "Maki kōchō to Akashiya-kai," in Bōei Daigakko dōsō kai, *Maki no mi*. The Obaradai article seems like a more reliable source.

151. Haraguchi Toshirō, "Omoitsuku mama ni," in Bōei Daigakko dōsō kai, *Maki no mi*, 307–8. It is unknown if Tsuji's daughter attended the dance or not. It is rumored that the cadet who invited her decided to go with another young woman instead, but perhaps that was because Tsuji would not allow his daughter to go.

152. Uchida Shūhei, "Shinnen no hito," in Bōei Daigakko dōsō kai, *Maki no mi*, 473.

153. Patalano, *Post-War Japan as a Sea Power*, 182n28.

154. Bōei shō bōei kenkyūjo senshibu, *Ishizu Sadamasu ōraru hisutorī*, 22. Although Ishizu mistakenly remembered Maki rather than Takeshita interacting with Tsuji, there is no reason to doubt the accuracy and essence of the rest of his memories of the incident, which are essentially corroborated by other cadets.

155. *Naikaku iinkai kiroku, dai 11 go*, March 7, 1958, 10.

156. *Naikaku iinkai kiroku, dai 11 go*, March 7, 1958, 10–11.

157. Maki, *Bōei no tsutome*, 183–84.

158. *Naikaku iinkai kiroku, dai 11 go*, March 7, 1958, 11.

159. *Naikaku iinkai kiroku, dai 11 go*, March 7, 1958, 12.

160. "Bōdai-sei no dansu shikaru," *Yomiuri shinbun*, March 8, 1958, 2. See also "'Dansu dake ichininmae no Bōei daisei,'" *Mainichi shinbun*, March 8, 1958, 1; "'Shin kokugun kanbu' no dansu rongi," *Asahi shinbun*, March 8, 1958, 2.

161. Nagato, "Maki kōchō to Akashiya-kai," 358. In the wake of the Diet hearing, cartoonist Katō Yoshirō poked fun at the uproar in the pages of the *Mainichi shinbun*, depicting cadets changing the theme of the dance to a costume party in response to Tsuji's criticism and dancing with women clad in costumes of missiles and rocket launchers. The cartoon was number 1497 in a series of 13,615 that Katō published in the paper from 1954 to 2001. Katō Yoshirō, "Mappira-kun," *Mainichi shinbun* (evening edition), March 10, 1958, 3.

162. Morris, *Nationalism and the Right Wing in Japan*, 215.

163. "Kaikō irai no daikangei: Arima Ineko, Bōei Daigakkō o hōmon," *Mainichi shinbun*, June 15, 1958, 6.

164. Ōe Kenzaburō, "Joyū to Bōei daisei," *Mainichi shinbun*, June 25, 1958 (evening), 5.

165. Yamaguchi Susumu, "Genjitsu o mushi no pen no ogori," *Mainichi shinbun*, July 7, 1958, 3.

166. "'Hokori' to 'chijoku': Wakai sedai to Bōeidai sei," *Mainichi shinbun*, July 18, 1958, 6.

167. A few years later, in January 1961, Ōe published a novella, *Seventeen*, in which the protagonist calls the SDF "parasites" who are dependent on the US army to keep Japan secure. Over the course of the story, the protagonist, who is seventeen, veers from the left to the right and joins an ultranationalist gang. In a sequel to *Seventeen* published the following month, Ōe depicted the protagonist's "final deliverance through assassination and suicide." Ōe modeled the stories on the life of seventeen-year-old Yamaguchi Otoya, the son of a GSDF officer, who with a sword assassinated Asanuma Inejirō, the leader of the Socialist Party, while he was speaking in a televised political debate. Yamaguchi then hung himself in his cell after writing on the wall, "Seven lives for my country. Long live [*banzai*] His Imperial Majesty, the Emperor." As he had done more implicitly regarding NDA cadets in his *Mainichi* op-ed, Ōe ridiculed the manliness of the protagonist and, by extension, Yamaguchi, by portraying him as a compulsive masturbator, which along with his insults of the emperor in the stories infuriated right-wing gangsters. Masao Miyoshi, introduction to *Two Novels: Seventeen, J*, by Kenzaburō Ōe, trans. Luk Van Haute (New York: Blue Moon, 1996), vi–vii, 10. Thanks to Jonathan Zwicker for introducing me to these stories.

168. National Defense Academy of Japan, "Bōdai shōyō uta no tanjō to genjō," https://www.bodaidsk.com/activity/000637.html, accessed on October 2, 2019. Another student, Shiose Susumu, composed the music.

169. National Defense Academy of Japan, "Bōdai shōyō uta no tanjō to genjō."

170. Shima interview, October 18, 2016.

171. Tomizawa interview, October 19, 2016.

172. It appears that the only mention within the academy at the time was a collage of newspaper clippings in the yearbook of the third graduating class. Bōei Daigakkō dai san ki sotsugyō ki'nen shasshinchō iinkai, ed., *Bōei Daigakkō dai san ki sotsugyō ki'nen shasshinchō* (Yokosuka, Japan: Bōei Daigakkō, 1959), unpaginated.

173. Shikata interview, October 20, 2016.

174. See, for example, "Jieitai no 'seishin kyōiku' yōkō," *Yomiuri shinbun*, November 15, 1960. For a translation of the Imperial Precepts to Soldiers and Sailors, see Arthur E. Tiedemann, *Modern Japan: A Brief History* (Princeton, NJ: D. Van Nostrand, 1955), 107–12. For an English translation of the Imperial Rescript of Education, see

Wm. Theodore de Bary, Carol Gluck, and Arthur E. Tiedemann, *Sources of Japanese Tradition*, vol. 2: *1600 to 2000*, second edition (New York: Columbia University Press, 2005), 780–81.

175. Japan Defense Agency, "Ethical Principles for Personnel of the Self Defense Force," undated. Manuscript in author's possession.

176. Katō, *Shiroku, Jieitai shi*, 170–80.

177. Morris, *Nationalism and the Right Wing in Japan*, 248–50.

178. Welfield, *An Empire in Eclipse*, 371.

179. James H. Buck, "The Japanese Self-Defense Forces," *Asian Survey* 7 (1967): 610. The ratios for the SDF as a whole are about the same. For those percentages, see Emmerson, *Arms, Yen and Power*, 126.

180. Shikata interview, October 20, 2016.

181. Buck, "The Japanese Self-Defense Forces," 610. In the 1970s, of the 500 new GSDF officers who rose through the ranks, around 50 entered the GSDF after graduation from other universities, and approximately 250 others were NDA graduates. All officer aspirants, including NDA graduates, must complete an officers' candidate course, the length of which depends on their experience. Edward J. Drea, "Officer Education in Japan," *Military Review*, September 1980, 32.

182. Maeda, *The Hidden Army*, 59.

183. Robert D. Eldridge, "Organization and Structure of the Contemporary Ground Self-Defense Force," in *The Japanese Ground Self-Defense Force: Search for Legitimacy*, ed. Robert D. Eldridge and Paul Midford (New York: Palgrave Macmillan, 2017), 21.

184. Yamazaki interview, October 17, 2016.

185. For more about the creation of majors in the social sciences, see Hitoshi Kawano, "The Expanding Role of Sociology at Japan National Defense Academy," *Armed Forces & Society* 35, no. 1 (October 2008): 122–44.

186. Inoki first issued the text to cadets as an academy superintendent directive on December 16, 1970, and then it was disseminated within the SDF.

187. Nishihara Masashi, interview by author, October 12, 2015, Tokyo, Japan.

188. Iokibe Makoto, *Nihon ha suitai suru no ka* (Tokyo: Chikura shobō, 2014), 73–76. The article was originally published in the *Mainichi shinbun* on September 7, 2008.

189. "'Ajia gaikō mahi': Bōei Daigakkō Iokibe Makoto shi, Koizumi meru maga de shushō hihan," *Asahi shinbun*, September 7, 2006, 4.

190. Hiroko Willcock, "The Political Dissent of a Senior General: Tamogami Toshio's Nationalist Thought and a History Controversy," *Asian Politics & Policy* 3, no 1 (2011): 38–39; Oleg Benesh, *Inventing the Way of the Samurai: Nationalism, Internationalism, and Bushidō in Modern Japan* (Oxford: Oxford University Press, 2014), 237.

191. Iokibe Makoto, interview by author, June 27, 2015, Tokyo; Wakamiya Yoshibumi, "Bōei Daigakkō: Kōchō o nayamasu 'Tamogami' ōendan," *Asahi shinbun*, March 16, 2009, 11.

192. "Bōei Daigakkō Iokibe Makoto: Shita 'Tamogami mondai' de basshingu mo," *Asahi shinbun*, March 24, 2012, B09.

193. Shikata interview, October 20, 2016. Inoki became president of the NDA at the beginning of Tamogami's final year at the academy. The president during his first three years was Ōmori Hiroshi, the former chief of staff of the GSDF.

194. Iokibe, *Nihon ha suitai suru no ka*, 178. This article was originally published in the *Mainichi shinbun* on November 9, 2008.

195. Nishihara Masashi, interview by author, June 24, 2015, Tokyo.

196. Iokibe Makoto, "Maki ki'nen shitsu kaisetsu ni atatte," in *Maki ki'nen shitsu zuroku: Kengaku no seishin—Jishu jiritsu, shodai gakkōchō Maki Tomoo no jidai*, ed. Maki ki'nen shitsu secchi nado kento iinkai (Yokosuka, Japan: Bōei Daigakkō, 2008), i.

197. Nishihara interview, October 12, 2015.

## 3. Becoming a "Beloved Self-Defense Force" in Hokkaido and Beyond

1. Thanks to Oleg Benesch for his help understanding the probable inspiration for this snow castle.

2. Dai 50 Sapporo yuki matsuri jikkō iinkai, *Dai 50 Sapporo yuki matsuri ki'nen shashinshū bekkan—kiroku/shiryōhen* (Sapporo, Japan: Sapporo yuki matsuri jikkō iinkai, 1999), 17; Kanechika Kentarō, "Yuki matsuri," *Junkan Yomiuri*, March 21, 1952, 34–35.

3. "'Sapporo yuki matsuri' kyōryoku no suii," undated internal Northern Corps public relations document, author's collection. See also Dai 50 Sapporo yuki matsuri jikkō iinkai, *Dai 50 Sapporo yuki matsuri*.

4. Airgram A-38, from US Consulate Sapporo to Department of State, "The Japanese Military Establishment in Northern Japan," December 29, 1970, 10, Department of State Files, US National Archives, Washington, DC.

5. Toyoshima Yasuhiro, interview by author, June 5, 2006, Sapporo, Japan.

6. Frühstück, *Uneasy Warriors*; Sabine Frühstück and Eyal Ben-Ari, "'Now We Show It All!' Normalization and the Management of Violence in Japan's Armed Forces," *Journal of Japanese Studies* 28, no. 1 (Winter 2002): 1–39; Satō Fumika, *Gunji soshiki to jendā: Jieitai no joseitachi* (Tokyo: Keiō Gijuku Daigaku shuppankai, 2004); Sudō Noriko, *Jieitai kyōryoku eiga: "Kyō mo ware daizora ni ari" kara "Meitantei Konan" made* (Tokyo: Ōtsuki shoten, 2013).

7. Asahi shinbun, ed., *Jieitai* (Tokyo: Asahi shinbun sha, 1968), 233.

8. Robert Trumbull, "Japan Bolsters Hokkaido Islands," *New York Times*, September 11, 1956, 6. Because of this concentration of SDF bases, Hokkaido can be compared to Okinawa, which is home to 75 percent of all US bases in Japan. There is of course a huge gap in geographic size that makes the burden associated with bases much heavier for the latter island. In 2010, Hokkaido hosted fifty-one bases and camps and some forty thousand personnel. Ministry of Defense, *Defense of Japan 2010* (Tokyo: Erklaren, 2010), 421.

9. "Fuyu o mukaeta Hokkaidō Jieitai," *Asahi shinbun*, November 22, 1954, 3.

10. Chitose shi shi hensan iinkai, ed., *Chitose shi shi* (Chitose, Japan: Chitose, 1983), 1216–38.

11. Foreign Service Dispatch 790, US Embassy Tokyo to Department of State, "Public Image of Japan Self Defense Forces," "Submission by Consul at Sapporo," January 10, 1961, unpaginated, State Department Files, US National Archives, Washington, DC.

12. Tadaki Tatsuo, "Warera yuki no geijutsu butai: 'Sapporo yuki matsuri' no kushin dan," *Nihon keizai shinbun*, January 18, 1964, 10.

13. Kishimoto Shigekazu, "Dō kaihatsu no senkusha tare," *Akashiya*, November 25, 1960, 3.

14. Brett L. Walker, *The Conquest of Ainu Lands: Ecology and Culture in Japanese Expansion, 1590–1800* (Berkeley: University of California Press, 2001), 5.

15. Ann Irish, *Hokkaido: A History of Ethnic Transition and Development on Japan's Northern Island* (Jefferson, NC: McFarland, 2009), 119.

16. Irish, *Hokkaido*, 291; Juha Saunavaara, "Postwar Development in Hokkaido: The U.S. Occupation Authorities' Local Government Reform in Japan," *Journal of American-East Asian Relations* 21 (2014): 134–55.

17. Matsushita Takaaki, *Guntai o yūchi seyo: Rikukaigun to toshi keisei* (Tokyo: Yoshikawa kōbunkan, 2013), 259.

18. Ikeda Kōtarō, *Watashi no kaisōroku* (Nayoro, Japan: Ikeda Mitsui, 1990), 110–11.

19. Sakuraba Yasuki, interview by author, December 19, 2005, Nayoro, Japan; Nayoro shi shi hensan iinkai, ed., *Shin Nayoro shi shi*, 3 vols. (Nayoro, Japan: Nayoro shi, 2000), 2:688–89.

20. Ōkoda Yahiro, *Kita no daichi o mamorite gojū nen: Sengo Nihon no hoppō jūshi senryaku* (Tokyo: Kaya shobō, 2005), 143. For a history of the Seventh Division in Asahikawa and its relationship with society, see Hirano Tomohiko, "Dai nana shidan to Asahikawa," in *Kita no guntai to gunto: Hokkaidō, Tōhoku*, ed. Yamamoto Kazushige (Tokyo: Yoshikawa kōbunkan, 2015), 44–78.

21. Nayoro shi shi hensan iinkai, *Shin Nayoro shi shi*, 2:817.

22. Asagumo shinbun sha henshū-kyoku, ed., *Hanran no hanseiki: Rikujō Jieitai no 50 nen* (Tokyo: Asagumo shinbun sha, 2000), 33.

23. Sakuraba interview, December 19, 2005.

24. Sakuraba interview, December 19, 2005.

25. Bibai shi hyaku nen shi hensan iinkai, ed., *Bibai shi hyaku nen shi: Tsūshi hen* (Bibai, Japan: Bibai shichō Taki Tadashi, 1991), 1426–28.

26. Lone, *Provincial Life and the Military in Imperial Japan*, 116–17.

27. Lee K. Pennington, "Wives for the Wounded: Marriage Mediation for Japanese Disabled Veterans during World War II," *Journal of Social History* 53, no. 3 (2020): 667–97.

28. Irikura Shōzō, interview by author, February 9, 2006.

29. Irikura interview, February 8, 2006.

30. Sasaki, *Japan's Postwar Military and Civil Society*, 75.

31. Sasaki, *Japan's Postwar Military and Civil Society*, 75–78.

32. "Tondenhei mondai," *Hokkaidō nenkan*, 1957, 131.

33. Airgram, A-38, 6. See also Sasaki, *Japan's Postwar Military and Civil Society*, 81–82.

34. Irikura interview, February 8, 2006.

35. Asahi shinbun, *Jieitai*, 59; Brendle, "Recruitment and Training in the SDF," 79.

36. "Hajime no Kyōryoku kai shōnen bu hassoku," *Akashiya*, November 25, 1964, 2.

37. Foreign Service Dispatch 790, enclosure no. 4, estimate by the army attaché, 3.

38. Sasaki Masanobu postcard to Irikura Shōzō, January 10, 1985.

39. Irikura Shōzō, interview by author, July 11, 2019.

40. Foreign Service Dispatch 790, enclosure no. 4, estimate by the army attaché, 3.

41. Miyazawa Sakutarō and Katsuki Toshichika, interview by author, October 30, 2002, Tokyo. Soon thereafter, as the number of imperial military officer veterans dwindled as they passed away, the Kaiko-sha and Suiko-sha began to allow SDF officers to join their associations.

42. Morris, *Nationalism and the Right Wing in Japan*, 241.

43. Hitoshi Kawano, "A Comparative Study of Combat Organizations: Japan and the United States during World War II" (PhD dissertation, Northwestern University, 1996), 61; Smethurst, *A Social Basis for Prewar Japanese Militarism*, i.

44. Peter J. Katzenstein, *Cultural Norms and National Security: Police and Military in Postwar Japan* (Ithaca, NY: Cornell University Press, 1996), 108-9.

45. Sasaki, *Japan's Postwar Military and Civil Society*, chap. 4.

46. Peter J. Katzenstein and Nobuo Okawara, *Japan's National Security: Structures, Norms and Policy Reponses in a Changing World* (Ithaca, NY: Cornell East Asia Program, 1993), 58.

47. Asahi shinbun, *Jieitai*, 232.

48. Foreign Service Dispatch 790, 1. In 1964, US military advisers observed, "To 'accept' the [SDF] does not denote a real enthusiasm for them. The majority of the people surveyed indicated they preferred the status quo to any real increase in strength. Interviewees stated that excellent impressions gained of the JSDF were due mostly to their participation in disaster relief operations and in national civil works projects. A key point revealed again and again in the surveys is that improved social welfare of the people should take precedence over augmentations of defense potential." US Military Assistance Advisory Group—Japan, *A Decade of Defense in Japan*, 16.

49. Morris Janowitz, *The Professional Soldier: A Social and Political Portrait* (New York: Free Press, 1960), 395, 399–401. For more on the US military's public relations and advertising campaigns during the first decade after World War II, see Grandstaff, "Making the Military American."

50. Tanaka Takamasa, "Bōei cho no kōhō seisaku ni kansuru ichi kōsatsu," *Seiji, seisaku daiarōgu*, January 2004, 81.

51. Leonard A. Humphreys, "The Japanese Military Tradition," in *The Modern Japanese Military System*, ed. James H. Buck, (Beverly Hills, CA: Sage, 1975), 37.

52. "Self-Defense Forces Law," in author's collection, 27.

53. See also Murakami, "The GSDF and Disaster Relief Dispatches," 270.

54. Murakami, "The GSDF and Disaster Relief Dispatches," 269–72.

55. "Jieitai no jūnen shi" henshū iinkai, *Jieitai no jūnen shi*, 357.

56. Nayoro shi shi hensan iinkai, *Shin Nayoro shi shi*, 2:684; "Saigai hakken," *Hokkaidō nenkan*, 1961, 162.

57. "Hondō no bōei," *Hokkaidō nenkan*, 1967, 161.

58. James H. Buck, Notes on the Contributors to *The Modern Japanese Military System*, ed. James H. Buck (Beverly Hills, CA: Sage, 1975), 251; Buck, "The Japanese Self-Defense Forces," 605.

59. Murakami, "The GSDF and Disaster Relief Operations," 273. After retiring from the force in 1965, Ōmori succeeded Maki as the president of the National Defense Academy.

60. Robert Trumbull, "U.S. Forces Assist Typhoon Victims," *New York Times*, October 7, 1959, 18.

61. "Taiin no kenketsu o kotowari," *Asahi shinbun*, February 18, 1964, 14.

62. Yoshida, "Guntai no 'saigai shutsudō.'"

63. "Jieitai no jūnen shi" henshū iinkai, *Jieitai no jūnen shi*, 361.

64. Foreign Service Dispatch 790, 4.

65. "Jimoto he no kyōryoku," *Hokkaidō nenkan*, 1960, 155.

66. "Jimoto he no kyōryoku," *Hokkaidō nenkan*, 1959, 146.

67. Sasaki, *Japan's Postwar Military and Civil Society*, 61.

68. Sasaki, *Japan's Postwar Military and Civil Society*, 65.

69. "Burudozā unkō no kihō," *Nayoro shinbun*, February 2, 1953.

70. Kuboi Masayuki, interview by author, November 7, 2005.

71. Sakuraba interview, December 19, 2005.

72. Kuboi interview, November 7, 2005.

73. "SDF Members to Be Dispatched to Farm Villages," *Nihon keizai shinbun*, August 18, 1962, US Embassy Tokyo Summaries of Japanese Press, RG84, P422, 350.78.30.3, Department of State Files, US National Archives, Washington, DC.

74. Irikura interview, February 8, 2006.

75. Akikuni Tamehachi, "Ore ha hohei. No. 3," *Kashiwadai*, June 1, 1969, in "Tōkō sukurappu (44.4.1–50.4)," scrapbook of Akikuni's published work that he kindly allowed me to copy; Akikuni Tamehachi, interview by author, June 29, 2007, Obihiro, Japan.

76. Toyohira, "Bangai-kun," *Akashiya*, June 1, 1969, 7. The cartoonist's first name is unknown. Bangai, the name of the strip's protagonist, means an extra in a theatrical or cinematic production. "Kun," like "san," as in Tanaka-san, is a common informal honorific title.

77. Zaidan hōjin Sapporo orinpikku toki taikai sōshiki iinkai, ed., *Dai 11 orinpikku toki taikai koshiki hōkokusho* (Sapporo, Japan: Zaidan hōjin Sapporo orinpikku toki taikai sōshiki iinkai, 1972), 366.

78. Sakuraba interview, December 19, 2005.

79. "Migoto na moriagari," *Nayoro shinbun*, March 3, 1970; Sakuraba interview, December 19, 2005.

80. Sakuraba interview, December 19, 2005.

81. "Kokudo kensetsu tai to keisatsu ni: Shakai-to ga Jieitai no keihen an," *Asahi shinbun*, November 23, 1959, 1.

82. Yoshida Shigeru, *Sekai to Nihon* (Tokyo: Ōshima Hideichi, 1963), 205.

83. Irikura Shōzō, interview by author, June 30, 2007, Sapporo, Japan.

84. Sasaki, *Japan's Postwar Military and Civil Society*, 60.

85. Foreign Service Dispatch 790, 6.

86. "Jieitai no jūnen shi" henshū iinkai, *Jieitai no jūnen shi*, 366.

87. "Bugai kyōryoku gyōmu," *Hokkaidō nenkan*, 1961, 162.

88. Yoshida, *The Yoshida Memoirs*, 190.

89. Asagumo shinbun sha henshū kyoku, *Hanran no hanseiki*, 23.

90. "Jieitai ki'nenbi gyōji kankei shiryō (43 nen) 2/2," 1968, 4A.34.155, 5-2303, National Archives of Japan, Tokyo.

91. Irikura interview, February 8, 2006.

92. "Tonai akirame Asakusa de," in *Asahi Shinbun*, August 10 1973 (evening edition), 2.

93. "Shōwa 34 nen, Chōkan nado kunji shū," October 29 and November 1, 1959, 4A.34.144, 8-476, National Archives of Japan, Tokyo.

94. "Ichimi seifū: Hyaku bun ha ikken shikazu," *Akashiya*, July 25, 1958, 1.

95. "'Makomanai kaijō' shasshin tokushū," *Akashiya*, July 25, 1958, 2.

96. "Dōraku no kora to mutsumi no natsu suzushi," *Akashiya*, July 25, 1959, 1.

97. Sapporo shi keizai bu, ed., *Hokkaidō dai hakurankai shi: Hokkaido Grand Fair* (Sapporo, Japan: Sapporo shi, 1959), 96.

98. Rikujō Jieitai Hakodate chūtonchi, "Rikujō Jieitai Hakodate chūtonchi kaisetsu 12 shūnen ki'nen gyōji," 1963, Hakodate City Central Library, Hakodate, Japan.

99. Yamafuji insatsu kabushiki kaisha, ed., *Hokubu hōmentai 50 nen no ayumi, shashin shū* (Sapporo, Japan: Yamafuji insatsu kabushiki kaisha, 2004), 60.

100. "Jieitai no jūnen shi" henshū iinkai, *Jieitai no jūnen shi*, 366.

101. Hokkai 45 shūnen ki'nenshi henshū iinkai, ed., *Hokkai, warera ga jidai: Hanseiki no kiseki* (Sapporo, Japan: Mainichi shinbun sha Hokkaidō shisha, 2004), 101–06.

102. "'Sapporo yuki matsuri' kyōryoku no suii."

103. Dai 50 Sapporo yuki matsuri jikkō iinkai, *Dai 50 Sapporo yuki matsuri*, 6–7.

104. Dai 50 Sapporo yuki matsuri jikkō iinkai, *Dai 50 Sapporo yuki matsuri*, 45–46.

105. See, for example, "Chūgakusei ga 'ichi nichi nyūtai,'" *Mainichi shinbun*, October 19, 1956, 7.

106. Mori Michio, interview by author, May 23, 2006. Mori is a former Hokkaido Broadcasting Company producer who made several films for the Northern Corps and the GSDF as a whole. Unfortunately, it appears that probably none of these and other similar films have survived.

107. "Dōmin to tomo ni 16 nen," *Hokkai taimusu*, October 28, 1966. The *Hokkai taimusu* closed in 1998.

108. Smethurst, *A Social Basis for Prewar Japanese Militarism*, xiv.

109. Nogawa Yasuharu, "'Gunto' Kanazawa ni okeru rikugun ki'nenbi shukuga gyōji in tsuite no obegaki," *Chihōshi kenkyū* 63, no. 4 (August 2013): 49–52.

110. Tokizane Makoto, "Gunkisai," *Rekishi gunzō* 24, no. 1 (2015): 18–21.

111. Lone, *Provincial Life and the Military in Imperial Japan*, 18–20. See also Nakano Ryō, "Taishō ki Nihon gun no gunji enshū: Chiiki shakai to no kankei o chūshin ni," *Shigaku zasshi* 114, no. 4 (April 2005): 53–74. For firsthand observations of grand maneuvers and a military flag festival by a British army attaché based in Japan from 1917 to 1920, see M. D. Kennedy, *The Military Side of Japanese Life* (Boston: Houghton Mifflin, 1923), 43, 76–77.

112. Edward J. Drea, "Trained in the Hardest School," in *In the Service of the Emperor: Essays on the Imperial Japanese Army* (Lincoln: University of Nebraska Press, 1998), 87.

113. Daigaku kyōdō riyō kikan hōjin ningen bunka kenkyū kikō, *Sakura rentai ni miru sensō no jidai* (Sakura, Japan: Kokuritsu rekishi minzoku hakubutsukan, 2006), 45.

114. Drea, "Trained in the Hardest School," 88.

115. Irikura interview, June 30, 2007.

116. Other GSDF regional newspapers are, moving east to west, the Northeastern Corps's *Michinoku*, the Eastern Corps's *Azuma*, the Middle Corps's *Asuka*, and the *Chinzei* published by the Western Corps in Kyushu (and Okinawa after reversion in 1972). Unfortunately, some regional headquarters have not preserved old editions. Early editions of the *Azuma*, for example, do not appear to be extant.

117. Irikura interview, February 8, 2006.

118. In 1962, a poll conducted as the paper neared its hundredth issue found that 39 percent of personnel read the *Akashiya* every month and 45 percent read it occasionally. A 1966 poll found that 60 percent of personnel read it every month and 40 percent did so sometimes. "Honshi no ankēto kekka," *Akashiya*, November 25, 1962, 6; "Butai no nyūsu chūshin ni," *Akashiya*, March 10, 1966, 4. According to Irikura, officers generally read the *Asagumo*, which had more general content and was concerned with national security issues, whereas enlisted personnel tended to read the regional newspapers like the *Akashiya*. Irikura interview, June 30, 2007.

119. Irikura interview, June 30, 2007.

120. In the early twenty-first century, the GSDF Second Division, which is headquartered in Asahikawa, has been less reticent about linking the GSDF to the Imperial Army. In 1964, the Northern Corps reopened the Hokuchin Museum, which had originally been established in 1934 on the grounds of the Hokkaido Gokoku Shrine, on the nearby base that had become the headquarters of the division two years before. It is unclear what the content of the exhibits were like when the museum opened, but 2013 exhibits in the museum, which reopened in a new building in 2007, connected the Second Division to both the tondenhei and the Imperial Army's Seventh Division. For an analysis of the current Hokuchin Museum, see André Hertrich, "War Memory, Local History, Gender: Self-Representation in Exhibitions of the Ground Self-Defense Force," in *Local History and War Memories in Hokkaido*, ed. Philip A. Seaton (London: Routledge, 2016), 179–97.

121. Michelle E. Mason, *Dominant Narratives of Colonial Hokkaido and Imperial Japan: Envisioning the Periphery and the Modern Nation-State* (New York: Palgrave Macmillan, 2012), 31–54.

122. "Tondenhei monogatari, sono 2," *Akashiya*, November 25, 1962, 6.

123. Shiryōkan: Tondenhei kara Jieitai made (Sapporo, Japan: Hokkai taimusu, 1968), Hokkaido Prefectural Library Collection, Sapporo, Japan.

124. David Fedman, *Seeds of Control: Japan's Empire of Forestry in Colonial Korea* (Seattle: University of Washington Press, 2020), 3–4, 103. In colonial Korea, the acacia became a preferred tree of Japanese forestry officials for erosion control, and it is associated with colonial oppression by some Koreans today.

125. The words of "Kono michi" were written by the poet Kitahara Hakushū and the music was arranged by the composer Yamada Kōsaku. Corps officials chose "Akashiya" over words associated with the island and the defense of peripheral regions such as *sakimori* (soldiers garrisoned at strategic posts in Kyushu in ancient times), *saihate* (the furthest ends), *kitaguni* (north country), and *suzuran* (lilies). Irikura Shōzō, "Honshi sōkan 100 go o kaerimite," *Akashiya*, February 20, 1963, 2.

126. Hokubu hōmen sōkanbu dai ichi bu kōhō han and Irikura Shōzō, eds., *Hokkaidō to Jieitai* (Sapporo, Japan: Kan Hideo, 1963), unpaginated.

127. Irikura Shōzō, interview by author, February 9, 2006.

128. Hokubu hōmen sōkanbu dai ichi bu kōhō han and Irikura, *Hokkaidō to Jieitai*, unpaginated.

129. *Akashiya*, May 25, 1964, 1.

130. Satō, *Gunji soshiki to jendā*, 183–203.

131. Frühstück, *Uneasy Warriors*; Eyal Ben-Ari, "Normalization, Democracy, and the Armed Forces: The Transformation of the Japanese Military," in *Japan's Multilayered Democracy*, ed. Sigal Ben-Rafael Galanti et al. (Lanham, MD: Lexington, 2014), 113.

132. "Gikai hi'nin seitō," *Akashiya*, February 1, 1966, 2; Irikura interview, June 30, 2007.

133. "Shimin no koe: Seinen yo dokushin no hokori o," *Akashiya*, March 15, 1961, 4.

134. "Watakushi no mita parēdo: Shimin ha hatten o kitai," *Akashiya*, November 25, 1966, 3.

135. Ezra F. Vogel, *Japan's New Middle Class* (Berkeley: University of California Press, 1963), 9.

136. Vogel, *Japan's New Middle Class*, 9–10.

137. Miyata Yoshifumi, "Taiin no taidō ni manabu," *Akashiya*, December 10, 1964, 1.

138. "Dōmin no hiroba: Kono hito ni kiku," *Akashiya*, February 25, 1964, 2.

139. Frühstück, *Uneasy Warriors*, 53. See also Sabine Frühstück, "After Heroism: Must Real Soldiers Die?," in *Recreating Japanese Men*, ed. Sabine Frühstück and Anne Walthall (Berkeley: University of California Press, 2011).

140. "Beigun no kieru Hokkaidō," *Yomiuri shinbun*, July 10, 1954, 7.

141. Foreign Service Dispatch 790, enclosure no. 4, estimate by the army attaché, 1.

142. "SDF's New Course," *Tokyo shinbun*, September 20, 1962, State Department press summary, Tokyo Embassy, US National Archives, Washington, DC.

143. Kuboi interview, November 7, 2005. Kuboi, who graduated from the Imperial Army's officer-training school months before Japan's surrender and was a proud member of the GSDF, said that he only gave up wearing a uniform for the latter reason while commuting by train in Tokyo during the early 1960s.

144. Foreign Service Dispatch 790, 9. This issue too was not without precedent in the prewar period, though the dynamics were different and much briefer. During the early 1920s, some soldiers began wearing civilian clothes while commuting as a form of self-protection, because civilian anger at the army's role in restoring order during the Rice Riots, disappointment in the Siberian intervention, disapproval of the military's ballooning share of the national budget, and resentment of the military's arrogance led to confrontations. Humphreys, *The Way of the Heavenly Sword*, 43–49.

145. "Dōmin no hiroba, kono hito ni kiku: Jieitai o shiritai," *Akashiya*, February 1, 1965, 2.

146. "Watashi no hitokoto: Gaishutsu ha seifuku o kite," *Akashiya*, April 28, 1967, 5.

147. Satō Morio, interview by author, February 16, 2004.

148. "Taiin ha taiinrashiku—BG no zaidankai kara," *Akashiya*, November 25, 1966, 2. The Beatles had performed in a series of five concerts at the Budokan Hall in Tokyo that summer. Right-wing ultranationalists protested the concerts being held at the hall because it was the venue for the annual National Memorial Service for War Dead and because John Lennon spoke out against the Vietnam War in a press conference the day the Beatles arrived. For a summary of their visit to Tokyo, see Steve Turner, *Beatles '66: The Revolutionary Year* (New York: Ecco, 2016), 223–34.

149. Irikura interview, February 8, 2006.

150. "Butai no hana," *Akashiya*, July 1, 1969, 1.

151. Irikura interview, February 8, 2006.

152. Sato, "A Camouflaged Military," 5.

153. Frühstück, *Uneasy Warriors*, 90.

154. Irikura Shōzō, "WAC (Minazawa nii) ni kiku," *Akashiya*, September 25, 1968, 4.

155. "Shōrai ha Makomanai, Shimamatsu ni mo," *Akashiya*, September 25, 1968, 4; "WAC no zaidankai," *Akashiya*, February 1, 1970, 2.

156. "Zūmu appu," *Akashiya*, August 1, 1974, 1.

157. "Fōto nyūsu," *Akashiya*, August 1, 1974, 4.

158. Foreign Service Dispatch 790, estimate by MAAG, 5.

159. Takashi Oka, "Hokkaido, Facing Soviet, Vital in Japan's Defense," *New York Times*, February 25, 1970, 5.

160. Airgram A-38.

161. Kuboi, *Higashi Hiroshima kara Kita Hiroshima made*, 118.

162. Irikura interview, February 8, 2006.

163. Humphreys, "The Japanese Military Tradition," 39.

164. Airgram A-04, US Consulate Sapporo to Department of State, "Northern Army Commander Publicly Supports Security Treaty; Defines Roles of Self-Defense Forces," January 29, 1969, 2.

165. Toyoshima interview, June 5, 2006.

166. For several years, a park called Satoland served as the venue until it was moved to the current location at Tsūdome.

167. Tsujimoto Naohiro, chief of Sapporo City Tourism Section, interview by author, July 12, 2019.

## 4. Public Service/Public Relations during Anpo, the Olympics, and the Mishima Incident

1. Although the SDF's support for the 1964 games is celebrated by the force, it is generally little remembered by society as a whole. A special exhibit at the Edo-Tokyo Museum in the fall of 2014 marking the fiftieth anniversary of the Olympics, for example, did not mention the SDF's substantial contributions, despite highlighting others, such as IBM's supercomputer group, whose work behind the scenes was also essential to the success of the games. Yukiyoshi Shōichi and Yoneyama Jun'ichi, eds., *Tōkyō Orinpikku to shinkansen* (Tokyo: Seigensha, 2014), 155.

2. One of those allies, Watanabe Yōko, who has written for SDF publications such as *Securitarian* and *MAMORI*, published a book on the SDF's support for all of the Olympic games held in Japan. Watanabe Yōko, *Orinpikku to Jieitai* (Tokyo: Namiki shobō, 2016).

3. Bōei-shō, Jieitai, "Bōei-shō Jieitai Tōkyō 2020 Orinpikku, Paraorinpikku kyōgi taikai tokusetsu pēji, Orinpikku, Paraorinpikku o sasae Jieitai," accessed on October 20, 2021, https://www.mod.go.jp/j/publication/olympic/support.html.

4. Ono took great though puzzling liberties in adapting a photograph of this scene. In the painting, the Olympic Stadium, where the race began and ended, looms in the background, but it does not appear in the photograph. And in the painting, the Japanese runner, whose number does not match that of any of the three Japanese

competitors, runs a few meters ahead of a black African athlete, whereas in the photograph, Tsuburaya, Japan's top marathoner, runs evenly with him.

5. Irikura Shōzō, interview by author, June 30, 2007.

6. Leonard Humphreys, interview by author, July 17, 2001, Lodi, California.

7. Hanson W. Baldwin, "Armies without Friends: Apathy of Public in Germany and Japan Viewed as Handicap to Military Forces," *New York Times*, May 4, 1964, 10. Baldwin quoted the commentator Horie Yoshitaka, an Imperial Army veteran and one of only four officers to survive the Battle of Iwo Jima, as calling the SDF "puppet troops."

8. Perhaps one indication of this desire to improve the international view of Japan and specifically the SDF was the Defense Agency's publication of an English-language color map of Tokyo showing on one side the locations of the many events where the force would be providing logistical support and on the other side photographs and a detailed description of that support. I suspect that the audience for this map was also domestic and internal—that it was meant to boost the morale of personnel. Irikura Shōzō kindly gave me his personal copy of this map. Japan Defense Force, "Tokyo Olympic Games and Self Defense Force," September 1, 1964, map in possession of the author.

9. Funabashi Yōichi, "Seikaijū aozora o atsumeta," *Foresight* 11, no. 1 (January 2000): 62.

10. Funabashi, "Seikajiū aozora o atsumeta," 62.

11. Andrew Gordon, *A Modern History of Japan: From Tokugawa Times to the Present*, third edition (Oxford: Oxford University Press, 2014), 274.

12. Gordon, *A Modern History of Japan*, 274; Masumi Junnosuke, *Contemporary Politics in Japan*, trans. Lonny E. Carlile (Berkeley: University of California Press, 1995), 37–38.

13. Gordon, *A Modern History of Japan*, 274–75; Masumi, *Contemporary Politics in Japan*, 38–43.

14. Sado, *The Self-Defense Forces*, 53–54.

15. Fujiwara Akira, *Nihon kindaishi no kyozō to jitsuzō* (Tokyo: Ōtsuki shoten, 1989), 208–9.

16. Sado, *The Self-Defense Forces*, 54.

17. Akagi Muneyoshi, "60 nen to watakushi," *THIS IS*, May 1990, 177.

18. Sado, *The Self-Defense Forces*, 54

19. Akagi, "60 nen to watakushi," 177. See also Akagi Muneyoshi, *Ima dakara iu* (Tokyo: Bunka sōgō shuppan, 1973), 102–6. One of the best overviews of the security treaty crisis is found in Masumi, *Contemporary Politics in Japan*, chap. 1. Also see George R. Packard, III, *Protest in Tokyo: The Security Treaty Crisis of 1960* (Princeton, NJ: Princeton University Press, 1966); Igarashi, *Bodies of Memory*, 132–43.

20. Berger, *Cultures of Antimilitarism*, 45

21. Nick Kapur, *Japan at the Crossroads: Conflict and Compromise after Anpo* (Cambridge, MA: Harvard University Press, 2018), 75–107.

22. Martin E. Weinstein, *Japan's Postwar Defense Policy, 1947–1968* (New York: Columbia University Press, 1971), 120–21.

23. Akagi, *Ima dakara iu*, 103–6. See also Sugita Ichirō, *Wasurerarete iru anzen hoshō* (Tokyo: Jiji tsūshin sha, 1967), 96–104.

24. Organizing Committee of the Games of the XVIII Olympiad, ed., *Games of the XVIII Olympiad Tokyo 1964*, 2 vols. (Tokyo: Organizing Committee of the Games of the XVIII Olympiad, 1964), 1:495.

25. "Seika rirē shukushi, shukuho narabi ni," *Chinzei*, September 30, 1964, 3.

26. David Clay Large, *Nazi Games: The Olympics of 1936* (New York: W. W. Norton, 2007).

27. Organizing Committee of the Games of the XVII Olympiad, *The Games of the XVII Olympiad: Rome 1960* (Rome: Organizing Committee of the Games of the XVII Olympiad, 1960).

28. Ernst-Heinrich von Zimmer, "Die Bundeswehr bei den XX. Olympischen Sommerspielen 1972," *Wehrkunde* 20, no. 8 (1972): 402–6.

29. Congressional Quarterly Service, *Global Defense: U.S. Military Commitments Abroad* (Washington, DC: Congressional Quarterly Service, 1969), 44.

30. Satō Noboru, interview by author, March 3, 2008; "Supaingo o Eigo de narau," *Hokkaidō shinbun*, June 30, 1964. For a sample of internal newspaper coverage of the Northern Corps's participation, see *Akashiya*, October 25, 1964, 1–3.

31. Organizing Committee of the Games of the XVIII Olympiad, *Games of the XVIII Olympiad Tokyo*, 1:496.

32. Organizing Committee of the Games of the XVIII Olympiad, *Games of the XVIII Olympiad Tokyo*, 1:496, 499.

33. For a more in-depth treatment of the television coverage, see Hashimoto Kazuo, *Nihon supōtsu hōsō shi* (Tokyo: Taishūkan shoten, 1992), 261–87.

34. Paul Droubie, "Playing the Nation: 1964 Tokyo Olympics and Japanese Identity" (PhD dissertation, University of Illinois at Urbana-Champaign, 2009), 56.

35. Roy Tomizawa, *1964—The Greatest Year in the History of Japan: How the Tokyo Olympics Symbolized Japan's Miraculous Rise from the Ashes* (Austin, TX: Lioncrest, 2019), 178.

36. Takashima Kō, *Guntai to supōtsu no kindai* (Tokyo: Seikyūsha, 2015), 58, 68–69. After the Amsterdam Olympics, Tsurata left the navy to study law at Meiji University, and by 1932 he had joined the South Manchurian Railway corporation, which sponsored his training and competition trips.

37. Takashima, *Guntai to supōtsu no kindai*, 157.

38. Satō, *Keisatsu yobitai to saigunbi he no michi*, 80–83; Satō Noboru, interview by author, February 16, 2004.

39. Bōei-shō, Jieitai, "Bōei-shō Jietai Tōkyō 2020 Orinpikku, Paraorinpikku kyōgi taikai tokusetsu pēji, Jieikan senshu no katsuyaku," accessed on October 20, 2021, https://www.mod.go.jp/j/publication/olympic/index.html.

40. Tony Mason and Eliza Riedi, *Sport and the Military: The British Armed Forces, 1880–1960* (Cambridge: Cambridge University Press, 2010); Wanda Ellen Wakefield, *Playing to Win: Sports and the American Military, 1896–1945* (Albany: State University of New York Press, 1997).

41. Armed Forces Sports Committee, ed., *Achieving Excellence: The Story of America's Military Athletes in the Olympic Games* (Alexandria, VA: Armed Forces Sports Committee, 1992), 41.

42. "Orinpikku o gyūjiru Jieitai," *Shūkan Yomiuri supōtsu*, January 6, 1961, 95.

43. "Katsu koto dake," *Yomiuri shinbun*, March 5, 1963 (evening edition), 1. The SDF began to focus on fewer sports, especially shooting, wresting, and weightlifting,

after the 1964 games. The organization also supplies the national Olympic team with most of biathlon competitors for the winter games. Since the 1990s, the SDF has trained female athletes as well.

44. Watanabe, *Orinpikku to Jieitai*, 240.

45. Watanabe, *Orinpikku to Jieitai*, 250–52.

46. Uchimi Katsuo, *Sengo supōtsu taisei no kakuritsu* (Tokyo: Fumaido Shuppan, 1993), 267.

47. Uchimi, *Sengo supōtsu taisei*, 267. For one example of concern about state amateurism or, as the article's author terms it, "military amateurism," see "Guntai ama: Kateneba imi nai," *Asahi shinbun*, August 13, 1964, 1.

48. Miyake's niece, Miyake Hiromi won a bronze medal in the 48 kg weight class at the 2012 London games. Her father, Yoshiyuki, won a bronze medal in the featherweight class at the Mexico City games. He, and of course her uncle, were members of the SDF, but she was not.

49. See for example, "Tsuburaya Kōkichi," *Asahi shinbun*, April 13, 1964, 14.

50. Hashimoto Katsuhiko, *Orinpikku ni ubawareta inochi: Tsuburaya Kōkichi, sanjūnen me no shishōgen* (Tokyo: Shōgakkan, 1999).

51. Rie Otomo, "Narratives, the Body and the 1964 Tokyo Olympics," *Asian Studies Review* 31, no. 2 (June 2007): 126.

52. That said, because of technical challenges and influenced by internal guidelines that its coverage not be nationalistic, NHK broadcast less video of Tsurubaya than many television audience members hoped and expected, even though they heard from the announcer that he had moved from fourth to third and then into second place as the race led to the finish in the National Stadium. Hashimoto, *Nihon supōtsu hōsō shi*, 281–83.

53. Ichikawa Kon, dir., *Tokyo Olympiad* (Toho, 1965; Janus Films, 1965), VHS.

54. Ichikawa, *Tokyo Olympiad*.

55. "Hada de kanjita sekai no Nippon," *Yomiuri shinbun*, October 25, 1964, 8–9.

56. See, for example, "Chiho butai mo dōin," *Asahi shinbun*, March 22, 1964, 5; "Katsu koto dake," 1.

57. Tabata Ryōichi, "Rikujō Jieitai no Orinpikku shien kōsō," *Shūshin* 6, no. 9 (September 1963): 43.

58. "Toki no hito," *Yomiuri shinbun*, September 15, 1964, 2.

59. Asagumo shinbun sha, ed., *Tōkyō Orinpikku sakusen* (Tokyo: Asagumo shinbun sha, 1965), 8.

60. Murakami Hyōe, "Kin medaru kyū no karei naru shūdan, Jieitai," *Sandē Mainichi*, November 1964, 100–1.

61. Hara Hideki, "Orinpikku to Jieitai," *Bunka hyōron* 27 (January 1964): 149.

62. See, for example, "Rikukaiku no ichiman dōin," *Asahi shinbun*, September 13, 1964, 5.

63. "Shien butai hajime no gisei," *Yomiuri shinbun*, October 19, 1964, 11.

64. "Orinpikku butai saiten," *Asahi shinbun*, October 10, 1964 (evening edition), 10.

65. See, for example, "Konjō, fuyō no jidai?" *Yomiuri shinbun*, August 10, 1964, 3.

66. These conclusions are based on keyword searches of the *Yomiuri* and *Asahi* newspapers' full-text databases.

67. Igarashi, *Bodies of Memory*, 156.

68. Daimatsu Hirobumi, *Ore ni tsuite koi* (Tokyo: Kōdansha, 1963), 154.

69. See, for example, Tajima Naoto, *Konjō no kiroku* (Tokyo: Kōdansha, 1964); Kamiyama Makoto, *Nihon no konjō: Matsushita Konnosuke no ningen no kangaekata* (Tokyo: Nanboku sha, 1964); Oogya Shōzō, *Sararīman no dokonjō* (Tokyo: Kurabu sha, 1964).

70. Orinpikku Tōkyō taikai junbi sokushin tokubetsu iinkai, National Diet, February 8, 1963.

71. Motoaki Hiroshi, *Konjō—Nihonjin no bitaritī* (Tokyo: Diamond sha, 1964).

72. Harumi Befu, *Cultural Nationalism in East Asia: Representation and Identity* (Berkeley: Institute of East Asian Studies, University of California, 1993), 113. In Nihonjinron literature in the prewar and postwar periods, konjō has sometimes been used in *shimaguni konjō* (island-country spirit) to indicate a supposedly different mentality unique to people of island nations, but in the 1960s konjō was rarely paired with *shimaguni* and was usually used alone.

73. "Konjō, fuyō no jidai?," 3.

74. Murakami, "Kin medaru kyū," 101.

75. "Jietaiin wa naze tsuyoi," *Asahi shinbun*, September 6, 1964, 14.

76. "1964 nen, Tōkyō gorin no toshi o mukaeru," *Asagumo shinbun*, January 2, 1964, 1.

77. "Tōkyō gorin ni hi no maru o," *Asagumo shinbun*, January 2, 1964, 4.

78. "1964 nen," 1.

79. See, for example, "'Konjō' ga dai ichi da," *Asagumo shinbun*, January 2, 1964, 4; "Sakurama, konjō no yon'i," *Asagumo shinbun*, October 22, 1964, 1.

80. "Shikaku shita Kawano senshū o gōrin mura kara 'tsuihō,'" *Yomiuri shinbun*, October 14, 1964, 15.

81. Murakami, "Kin medaru kyū," 101.

82. "Yomiuri sunhyō," *Yomiuri shinbun*, October 29, 1964 (evening edition), 1.

83. Naikaku sōridaijin kanbō kōhōshitsu, *Jieitai ni kansuru seiron chōsa* (Tokyo: Naikaku sōridaijin kanbō kōhōshitsu, 1963); Naikaku sōridaijin kanbō kōhōshitsu, *Jieitai no kōhō oyobi bōei mondai ni kansuru seiron chōsa* (Tokyo: Naikaku sōridaijin kanbō kōhōshitsu, 1966). The latter survey was conducted in 1965 but not published until the next year.

84. Shōwa 34 nen chōkan nado kunji shū, 4A.34.144, National Archives of Japan, Tokyo.

85. Letter from Leonard Humphreys to author, September 27, 2014.

86. Murakami, "The GSDF and Disaster Relief Dispatches," 275.

87. "Yuki to tatakau Jieitaiin," *Asahi shinbun*, February 1, 1963, 13.

88. Humphreys interview, July 17, 2001.

89. Airgram 13, from US Embassy Tokyo to Department of State, "Public Attitudes towards the Self Defense Forces and Japan's Defense Problems," July 31, 1964, State Department Files, US National Archives, Washington, DC.

90. Asagumo shinbun sha, *Tōkyō Orinpikku sakusen*, 205.

91. Asagumo shinbun sha, *Tōkyō Orinpikku sakusen*, 195–96. See also "Sekai ichi no guntai to shōsan," *Chinzei*, November 30, 1964, 4.

92. Franziska Seraphim, *War Memory and Social Politics in Japan, 1945–2005* (Cambridge, MA: Harvard University Asia Center, 2006), 209.

93. Sado, *The Self-Defense Forces*, 75; Robert D. Eldridge, "The GSDF during the Cold War Years, 1960–1989," in *The Japanese Ground Self-Defense Force: Search for*

*Legitimacy*, ed. by Robert D. Eldridge and Paul Midford (New York: Palgrave Macmillan, 2017), 141–44.

94. A TV variety show, for example, aired a program about Kasai's engagement and the advertisement for the show focused on two words: "Olympics" and "SDF." USO hōsō, *Yomiuri shinbun*, April 25, 1965, 15.

95. "Izumi," *Yomiuri shinbun*, April 23, 1965, 15.

96. Arata Masafumi, *"Tōyō no majo" ron* (Tokyo: Īsuto shinsho, 2013), 204.

97. "Kasai-san hare no kyoshiki," *Yomiuri shinbun*, May 31, 1965 (evening edition), 9.

98. Brendle, "Recruitment and Training in the SDF," 77–78.

99. Brendle, "Recruitment and Training in the SDF," 78.

100. Brendle, "Recruitment and Training in the SDF," 77–79.

101. Welfield, *An Empire in Eclipse*, 370.

102. "Boshū hōhō no kaizen he," *Asahi shinbun*, February 8, 1964 (evening edition), 6.

103. US Military Assistance Advisory Group—Japan, *A Decade of Defense in Japan*, 15.

104. US Military Assistance Advisory Group—Japan, *A Decade of Defense in Japan*, 15.

105. Tsukasa Matsueda and George Moore, "Japan's Shifting Attitudes toward the Military," *Asian Survey* 7, no. 9 (1967): 620.

106. Brendle, "Recruitment and Training in the SDF," 81.

107. Brendle, "Recruitment and Training in the SDF," 83.

108. Brendle, "Recruitment and Training in the SDF," 82, 84, 88.

109. Frühstück, *Uneasy Warriors*, 36–79.

110. Asada Jirō, "Nyūei," in *Hohei no honryō* (Tokyo: Kodansha, [1999] 2004), 147–82.

111. Sato, "A Camouflaged Military," 5.

112. Sato, "A Camouflaged Military," 7.

113. "Jieitai ichinichi nyūtai kanyū o tsuikyū," *Yomiuri shinbun*, July 6, 1962 (evening edition), 2.

114. "Botsugen kobanashi: Josei o nerau Jieitai," *Yomiuri shinbun*, July 26, 1965, 10.

115. Thomas Rohlen, "'Spiritual Education' in a Japanese Bank," *American Anthropologist* 75, no. 5 (October 1973): 1543.

116. Robert Trumbull, "Army Helps Train Workers in Japan," *New York Times*, March 13, 1966, 6.

117. "Hanashi no minato," *Yomiuri shinbun*, July 12, 1962 (evening edition), 9.

118. "Shain kyōiku hikiukemasu: Shageki kunren kara keieigaku made," *Shūkan Asahi*, April 26, 1963, 21.

119. "Mochikomi zokuzoku," *Asahi shinbun*, April 4, 1963 (evening edition), 6.

120. Kichiji Shun'ei and Hatano Motoji, "Taiken nyūtai to hitozukuri," *Keieisha* 20, no. 6 (June 1966): 48.

121. "Shinnyū shain kyōiku kunren seido no chūmoku subeki jisshi rei: Jieitai be no nyūtai kunren de seika wo agete iru Mitsutoyo seisakujo seisakusho," *Rōsei jihō* 2, no. 11 (February 1967): 2–11; Rohlen, "'Spiritual Education,'" 1542–62.

122. Rohlen, "'Spiritual Education,'" 1547–48.

123. "Shain kyōiku ha Jieitai de," *Nihon*, September 1961, 208–9.

124. "Shain kyōiku hikiukemasu," 21–23.

125. Cook, "The Japanese Officer Corps," 400.

126. Trumbull, "Army Helps Train Workers;" Jieitai he no taiken nyūtai," *Yomiuri shinbun*, September 11, 1967, 16; "Taiken nyūtai," *Yomiuri shinbun*, April 8, 1969, 14.

127. "Jitsuryoku jidai no sararīman zō," *Yomiuri shinbun*, May 30, 1968, 20.

128. Mizukami Tōru, "Mōretsu shain no imi to haikei," *Gekkan rōdō mondai* 136 (1969): 13.

129. "Tenmei jingo," *Asahi shinbun*, April 25, 1963, 1.

130. Ogawauchi Kazuo, "'Shujū no jōgi,' no bōrei: Shain kyōiku to 'ichinichi nyūtai,'" *Asahi shinbun*, April 29, 1963, 3. An article in *Asahi gurafu*, which was referenced by several successive articles, seems to have unleashed a flurry of coverage on experiential enlistment. "Etajima de shain kyōiku," *Asahi gurafu*, April 19, 1963, 19–23.

131. Rohlen, "'Spiritual Education,'" 1543.

132. "Shain kyōiku hikiukemasu," 23.

133. Brendle, "Recruitment and Training in the SDF," 72.

134. "Uyoku dantai, Jieitai he taiken nyūtai," *Yomiuri shinbun*, July 20, 1966, 14.

135. "Yoku aru shitsumon: Taiken nyūtai," Ministry of Defense, accessed May 13, 2019, http://www.mod.go.jp/j/faq.html#Q1. In 1985, an estimated 41,000 employees from 1,200 organizations participated in experiential enlistment. Fukumoto Hirofumi, "Kawatta zo! Kigyō kenshū," *Asahi jānaru*, July 4, 1986, 109.

136. Some authors report that Mishima approached the SDF for permission to engage in training, presumably alone, in 1966, but that his request was rejected. The unnamed group reported by the *Yomiuri* is most likely unrelated to him. Robert Jay Lifton, Shūichi Katō, and Michael R. Reich, *Six Lives, Six Deaths: Portraits from Modern Japan* (New Haven, CT: Yale University Press, 1979), 263; John Nathan, *Mishima: A Biography* (New York: Little, Brown, 1974), 220.

137. Mishima Yukio, *Patriotism*, trans. Geoffrey W. Sargent (New York: New Directions, 1966). John Nathan speculated that, perhaps like Ōe, who "without question . . . had in mind" Yamaguchi Otoya's assassination of Socialist Party chairman Asanuma Inejirō in 1960, "it is not unlikely that Mishima was 'inspired' by the same incident." Nathan, *Mishima*, 183–84.

138. Nathan, *Mishima*, 227.

139. Nathan, *Mishima*, 220; Mishima, "Jieitai o taiken suru," *Sandē Mainichi*, June 5, 1967, in Mishima Yukio, *Mishima Yukio zenshū*, 35 vols. (Tokyo: Shinchōsha, 1973–76), 33:16–25.

140. Mishima, "Jieitai o taiken suru," 17. Mishima also reflected on his six-week enlistment in this fashion in Mishima Yukio, *Sun and Steel*, trans. John Bester (London: Martin Secker & Warburg, 1971), 57–59.

141. Mishima, "Jietai o taiken suru," 17.

142. Mishima, "Jieitai o taiken suru," 17; "Jietaiin, Mishima Yukio: Otokorashisa hada de," *Mainichi shinbun*, May 30, 1967, 15.

143. Naoki Inose and Hiroaki Sato, *Persona: A Biography of Yukio Mishima* (Berkeley, CA: Stone, 2012), 261.

144. Yamanouchi Hisaaki, "Mishima and His Suicide," *Modern Asian Studies* 6, no. 1 (1972): 10.

145. Damian Flanagan, *Yukio Mishima* (London: Reaktion, 2014), 8.

146. Nathan, *Mishima*, 222–23.

147. Nathan, *Mishima*, 223.

148. Yamamoto Tsunetomo, *Hagakure: The Book of the Samurai*, trans. William Scott Wilson (Tokyo: Kodansha International, 1979), 17.

149. Mishima Yukio, *The Way of the Samurai: Yukio Mishima on "Hagakure" in Modern Life*, trans. Kathryn Sparling (New York: Basic Books, [1967] 1977).

150. Nathan, *Mishima*, 223.

151. Nathan, *Mishima*, 225.

152. Flanagan, *Yukio Mishima*, 214.

153. Mishima Yukio, "Tsuburaya nii no jijin—kokō ni shite ōshii jishonshin," *Sankei shinbun*, January 3, 1968, in Mishima, *Mishima Yukio zenshū*, 33:166–68.

154. Nathan, *Mishima*, 226.

155. Welfield, *An Empire in Eclipse*, 355; Sado, *The Self-Defense Forces*, 55–56.

156. Thomas Havens, *Fire across the Sea: The Vietnam War and Japan 1965–1975* (Princeton, NJ: Princeton University Press, 1987), 169–70.

157. Inose and Sato, *Persona*, 589.

158. Havens, *Fire across the Sea*, 189–90.

159. Kapur, *Japan at the Crossroads*, 222–25.

160. As quoted in Nathan, *Mishima*, 260.

161. Sado, *The Self-Defense Forces*, 55.

162. Nathan, *Mishima*, 261.

163. Inose and Sato, *Persona*, 669.

164. Joyce Lebra, "Eyewitness: Mishima," *New York Times*, November 28, 1970, 26.

165. Mishima, "Mishima's Manifesto." In these longer passages, I have slightly adapted Christopher Smith's online translation of Mishima's manifesto, https://www.japaneseempire.info/post/mishima-yukio-s-manifesto, accessed October 15, 2021.

166. Mishima, "Mishima's Manifesto."

167. Mishima, "Mishima's Manifesto."

168. Inose and Sato, *Persona*, 728–29.

169. Nakasone Yasuhiro, *The Making of the New Japan: Reclaiming the Political Mainstream*, translated and annotated by Lesley Connors (Richmond, UK: Curzon, 1999), 165.

170. Takashi Oka, "Japan's Self-Defense Force Wins a Skirmish with the Past," *New York Times*, February 28, 1971, 12–13.

171. Nakasone, *The Making of the New Japan*, 165. The full statement can be found in Inoki Masamichi, *Watakushi no niju seiki: Inoki Masamichi kaikoroku* (Tokyo: Sekai shisō sha, 2000), 338–40.

172. The incident did lead the SDF to make some policy changes in experiential enlistment. The Defense Agency dictated that no groups that aimed to overthrow the government would be accepted into experiential-enlistment programs. It also cut back on the programs, warning bases to not spend much money on them, to limit them to a single week in March, and to not offer any weapons training.

173. Eldridge, "The GSDF during the Cold War Years, 1960–1989," 150.

174. NHK hōsō seiron chōsa sho, ed., *Zusetsu: Sengo seiron shi* (Tokyo: NHK Bukkusu, 1975), 172–75.

175. Shiba Ryōtarō, one of the country's most popular writers of historical fiction, was typical in his response to the incident. The response appeared on the front page of the *Mainichi* newspaper the following day. Shiba Ryōtarō, "Bungaku-ronteki na sono shi: Taishū ni ha muryoku datta," *Mainichi shinbun*, November 26, 1970, 1.

176. Oka, "Japan's Self-Defense Force Wins a Skirmish with the Past," 12.

177. Katrin Bennhold, "As Neo-Nazis Seed Military Ranks, Germany Confronts 'an Enemy Within,'" *New York Times*, July 3, 2020. Zolen Kanno-Youngs and David E. Sanger, "Extremist Emboldened by Capitol Attack Pose Rising Threat, Homeland Security Says," *New York Times*, January 27, 2021, https://www.nytimes.com/2021/01/27/us/politics/homeland-security-threat.html.

## 5. The Return of the "Japanese Army" to Okinawa

1. Agnew quoted in "Reversion Ceremonies Held," *Japan Times*, May 16, 1972, 1.

2. Tillman Durdin, "Okinawa Islands Returned by U.S. to Japanese Rule," *New York Times*, May 15, 1972, 1, 3.

3. "Era Ends: Okinawa Given Back," *Pacific Stars and Stripes*, May 16, 1972, 1, 24.

4. "Thousands Protest Retention of U.S. Bases," *Pacific Stars and Stripes*, May 17, 1972, 7.

5. Eiji Oguma, *The Boundaries of "the Japanese,"* vol. 1: *Okinawa 1818–1972— Inclusion and Exclusion*, trans. Leonie R. Stickland (Melbourne, Australia: Trans Pacific, 2014), 272–81.

6. Havens, *Fire across the Sea.*

7. Arasaki Moriteru, *Okinawa gendai shi* (Tokyo: Iwanami shoten, 2005), 85.

8. Ryūkyū shinpō sha henshū kyoku, ed., *Gendai Okinawa jiten: Fukkigo zen kiroku* (Naha, Japan: Ryūkyū shinpō sha, 1992), 647.

9. See, for example, "Miyakojima Residents' Association Members Call on Defense Agency Bureau to Stop SDF Missile Base Deployment," *Ryūkyū shinpō*, August 27, 2019.

10. George H. Kerr, *Okinawa: The History of an Island People* (Tokyo: Tuttle, [1958] 2000), 10. For more detailed overview of Ryukyu *shobun*, see Koji Taira, "Troubled National Identity: The Ryukyuans/Okinawans," in *Japan's Minorities: The Illusion of Homogeneity*, ed. Michael Weiner (London: Routledge, 1997), 140–77.

11. Kensei Yoshida, *Democracy Betrayed: Okinawa under U.S. Occupation* (Bellingham: Western Washington University Center for East Asian Studies, 2002), 157–65.

12. Robert K. Sakai, "The Ryukyu (Liu-ch'iu) Islands as a Fief of Satsuma," in *The Chinese World Order: Traditional China's Foreign Policy*, ed. John King Fairbank (Cambridge, MA: Harvard University Press, 1968), 112–34.

13. Gavan McCormack, *Client State: Japan in the American Embrace* (New York: Verso, 2007), 155.

14. Alan S. Christy, "The Making of Imperial Subjects in Okinawa," *Positions: East Asia Cultures Critique* 1, no. 3 (Winter 1993): 607–39.

15. Sakaya Chatani, *Nation-Empire: Ideology and Rural Youth Mobilization in Japan and Its Colonies* (Ithaca, NY: Cornell University Press, 2018), 102.

16. Haruko Taya Cook and Theodore F. Cook, *Japan at War: An Oral History* (New York: New Press, 1992), 367.

17. Ōta Masahide, *This Was the Battle of Okinawa* (Haebaru, Japan: Naha, 1981).

18. As quoted in Ōta Masahide, "War Memories Die Hard in Okinawa," *Japan Quarterly*, January 1988, 11–13; Yoshida, *Democracy Betrayed*, 25–27; Takamae, *The Allied Occupation of Japan*, 443–44.

19. Yoshida, *Democracy Betrayed*, 40.

20. David Tobaru [John] Obermiller, "Dreaming Ryūkyū: Shifting and Contesting Identities in Okinawa," in *Japan since 1945: From Postwar to Post-Bubble*, ed. Christopher Gerties and Timothy S. George (London: Bloomsbury, 2013), 69–88.

21. Laura Hein and Mark Selden, "Culture, Power, and Identity in Contemporary Okinawa," in *Islands of Discontent: Okinawan Responses to Japanese and American Power*, ed. Laura Hein and Mark Selden (Lanham, MD: Rowman & Littlefield, 2003), 21.

22. Satō quote in Masumi, *Contemporary Politics in Japan*, 101.

23. Satō as quoted in Gavan McCormack and Satoko Oka Norimatsu, *Resistant Islands: Okinawa Confronts Japan and the United States* (Lanham, MD: Rowman & Littlefield, 2012), 86.

24. Fukuchi Hiroaki, "Okinawa no 'Nihon fukki,'" *Shūkan kin'yōbi*, May 12, 2006, 30–33, as quoted in McCormack and Norimatsu, *Resistant Islands*, 86.

25. Telegram, from: High Command Ryukyu, to: Department of the Army, Subj: Okinawa Negotiations, Okinawa Defense JSDF Deployment, June 1970, 2, RG 319, History of USCAR, box 17, F6, Okinawa Prefectural Archives, Haebaru, Japan.

26. Quoted in Yoshida, *Democracy Betrayed*, 158.

27. Quoted in Ōshiro Masayasu, *Okinawa sen no shinjitsu to waikyoku* (Tokyo: Kōbunken, 2007), 113.

28. Narita Chihiro, "Okinawa henkan to Jieitai haibi," *Dōjidai shi kenkyū* 10 (2017): 44. See also Sado, *The Self-Defense Forces*, 79–90.

29. "Yara Objects to Plan for SDF in Okinawa," *Japan Times*, October 9, 1970, 3.

30. "Naha kūkō kinpaku," *Ryūkyū shinpō*, October 7, 1970, 3; "'Kenmin mushi, sugu kaere,'" *Okinawa taimusu*, October 8, 1970, 11.

31. "Okinawa Negotiations—Okinawa Defense JSDF Deployments," Department of the Army, 3, translation of an excerpt from a May 11, 1970, *Ryūkyū shinpō* editorial, Okinawa Prefectural Archives, Haebaru, Japan.

32. The headquarters of all three branches in Okinawa was on Naha Base. In 1974, the GSDF maintained sub-bases at Minami Yoza, Chinen, Katsuren (Uruma), Koza, and Yoza. The ASDF had sub-bases at Yoza, Miyako, Kumejima, and Onna. Almost all MSDF operations were at Naha.

33. Yamagata Masaaki, interview by author, May 20, 2010, Naha, Japan.

34. "Okinawa Negotiations," *Ryūkyū shinpō*, 5.

35. Okinawa taimusu sha, ed., *Tetsu no bōfū: Genchijin ni yoru Okinawa senki* (Tokyo: Asahi shinbun sha, 1950).

36. Arasaki, *Okinawa gendai shi*, 47.

37. Mikio Higa, *Politics and Parties in Postwar Okinawa* (Vancouver: University of British Columbia Press, 1963), 40–56.

38. Ōta Masahide, *Minikui Nihonjin: Nihon no Okinawa ishiki* (Tokyo: Simul, 1969). Ōta's title alludes to *The Ugly American* (1958), a bestselling novel that depicted the failures of the US diplomatic corps in Southeast Asia.

39. David Tobaru [John] Obermiller, "The United States Military Occupation of Okinawa: Politicizing and Contesting Okinawan Identity, 1945–1955" (PhD dissertation, University of Iowa, 2006), 9.

40. Mikio Higa, "The Okinawan Reversion Movement (I)," *Ryūdai hōgaku* 17 (November 1975): 160.

41. Okinawa ken kyōshokuin kumiai, ed., *Kore ga Nihon gun da: Okinawa sen ni okeru zangyaku kōi*, sixth edition (Naha, Japan: Okinawa ken kyōshokuin kumiai, [1972] 1975), i. Thanks to Akamine Yukinori for helping to secure permission to use this image.

42. Ōshiro, *Okinawa sen no shinjitsu to waikyoku*, 112–13.

43. "Nana hyaku hachi jū nin o gyakusatsu: Kyū Nihon-gun," *Ryūkyū shinpō* April 15, 1972, 11; Ōshiro, *Okinawa sen no shinjitsu to waikyoku*, 125–26; John K. Emmerson, "Troubles Ahead for Okinawa," *New York Times*, March 9, 1972, 41.

44. Ōta Masahide, Miyagi Etsujiro, and Hosaka Hiroshi, *Fukkigo ni okeru Okinawa jūmin no ishiki to hen'yō* (Naha, Japan: Ōta Masahide, 1984), 124.

45. "Nakamura Ryūhei ōraru hisutorī," in *Nakamura Ryūhei ōraru hisutorī*, ed. Bōei shō bōei kenkyūjo senshibu (Tokyo: Bōei shō bōei kenkyūjo, 2008), 285.

46. "Relocation Units to Leave for Okinawa on 1st of Next Month; to Make Soft Landing, with Military Color Weakened: JDA," *Tōkyō shinbun* (evening), February 16, 1972, full USCAR translation of article, Okinawa Prefectural Archives, Haebaru, Japan.

47. Quoted in "1,000 GSDF Men Train for Duty on Okinawa," *Japan Times*, May 4, 1972.

48. Ishimine Kunio, interview by author, July 9, 2019, Naha, Japan. The SDF also sent a female official to help with recruitment after reversion. Sato, "A Camouflaged Military," 8. Like other Okinawans before reversion, Tameyoshi joined the SDF on the mainland. It was not until a decade later that the first Okinawan woman applying from Okinawa entered the WAC. "Nankan o toppa shita 19 nin," *Okinawa gurafu*, May 1978.

49. Kuniyoshi Nagahiro, "Shōkai: Okinawa gunji jiten," unpublished manuscript in author's possession, 376.

50. Kuniyoshi Nagahiro, interview by author, May 25, 2010, Naha, Japan. See also "Kuwae Ryōhō ōraru hisutorī," in Bōei shō bōei kenkyūjo senshibu, *Nakamura Ryūhei ōraru hisutorī*, 454; Yamada Takaji, *Ichirō hei kaisō* (Tokyo: Yamada Takaji, 2005), 165–66.

51. "'Jieitai hantai ha seiron de nai,'" *Ryūkyū shinpō*, October 9, 1970, 1; Ishimine interview, July 9, 2019.

52. Kuniyoshi Nagahiro, interview by author, May 21, 2010, Naha, Japan.

53. The ASDF appointed one officer from Okinawa, Tomon Hiroshi, to serve there immediately after reversion. The MSDF's officer corps did not include any Okinawans. Ishimine interview, July 9, 2019.

54. "Shikikan ni Kuwae issa," *Okinawa taimusu*, January 11, 1972, 8.

55. "Kuwae Ryōhō ōraru hisutorī," 425, 456–57.

56. Yamagata Masaaki, email message to author, July 13, 2020.

57. Narita, "Okinawa henkan to Jieitai haibi," 39.

58. "Okinawa Negotiations," *Ryūkyū shinpō*, 5.

59. Ishimine Kunio, interview by author, July 5, 2019, Naha, Japan.

60. Shin Kumamoto shi shi henshū iinkai, ed., *Shin Kumamoto shi shi, tsūshi hen, gendai II* (Kumamoto, Japan: Kumamoto shi, 2000), 9:78; Okinawa bōei kyōkai, ed., *Sōritsu 30 shūnen ki'nen shi* (Naha, Japan: Okinawa bōei kyōkai, 2002), 9.

61. Konishi Makoto, *Hansen jieikan: Kenryōku o yurugasu seinen kūsō no zōhan* (Tokyo: Shakai hihyō sha, 2018), 208–12.

62. "'Okinawa hahei chūshi seyo,'" *Okinawa taimusu*, April 28, 1972, 11.

63. Ōshiro, *Okinawa sen no shinjitsu to waikyoku*, 122; "5 SDF Men Fired for Okinawa Appeal," *Japan Times*, April 30, 1972. The Konishi incident prompted Defense Agency and SDF officials to worry about more trouble emerging from within the organization as well as discussions about how to improve training and living conditions to prevent such problems. "Jieitai, hatachi no nayami," *Yomiuri shinbun*, August 15, 1970, 5.

64. "Kuwae Ryōhō ōraru hisutorī," 456.

65. Katsu Hidenari, interview by author, May 13, 2010, Kokubun, Japan.

66. "Sato Orders Tighter Controls on Agency," *Japan Times*, March 13, 1972.

67. "Sato Orders Tighter Controls on Agency."

68. "Okinawa shōkai," *Chinzei*, March 25, 1972, 7.

69. "Sōkan kunji: Seikyō muhi no Seibu hōmentai no rensei ni zenryoku o tsukusu," *Chinzei*, April 25, 1972, 3.

70. Shin Kumamoto shi shi henshū iinkai, *Shin Kumamoto shi shi*, 77.

71. "Okinawa no rekishi fūzoku ni tsuite no ensetsu," *Shurei*, June 1, 1972, 1.

72. Kinjō Kazuhiko and Ohara Masao, *Minna mi no iwao no hate ni* (Tokyo: Kōbunsha, 1959); Kinjō Kazuhiko, *Ai to senketsu no kiroku* (Tokyo: Zenbō sha, 1966); Kinjō Kazuhiko, *Himeyuri butai no saigo* (Tokyo: Kaisei sha, 1966).

73. Kinjō Kazuhiko, *Okinawa sen no gakutotai* (Tokyo: Tōkyō shokan sentā, [1966] 1992).

74. Kyle Ikeda, *Okinawan War Memory: Transgenerational Trauma and the War Fiction of Medoruma Shun* (London: Routledge, 2014), 18.

75. "Okinawa bijutsuten taiin no sakuhin ni kyōtan," *Chinzei*, April 25, 1972, 1. For more on Orion during the occupation period, see Jeffrey W. Alexander, *Brewed in Japan: The Evolution of the Japanese Beer Industry* (Honolulu: University of Hawai'i Press, 2013), chap. 5.

76. Ōmine Shinichi, "Taiin no bijutsuhin o mite," *Chinzei*, April 25, 1972, 1.

77. Ishimine interview, July 9, 2019.

78. Ōshiro, *Okinawa sen no shinjitsu to waikyoku*, 116.

79. Ōshiro, *Okinawa sen no shinjitsu to waikyoku*, 116.

80. Gordon, *A Modern History of Japan*, 281–84.

81. Masumi, *Contemporary Politics in Japan*, 390–93.

82. Yoshida, *Democracy Betrayed*, 156–57.

83. "Bombs Hurled into Japan Gov't Office," *Japan Times*, February 18, 1972, 3; "Kaenbin nagekomu," *Okinawa taimusu*, February 17, 1972, 9.

84. "Sanpai-chū ni kaen-bin," *Okinawa taimusu*, July 17, 1975, 3.

85. Katsu interview, May 13, 2010.

86. Okinawa ken kyōiku shokuin gumiai, ed., *Okinawa no heiwa kyōiku: Tokusetsu jugyō o chūshin to shita jissenrei* (Naha, Japan: Okinawa ken kyōiku shokuin gumiai, 1978); Gibo Yukio, ed., *Okinawa to heiwa kyōiku: Tokusetsu jugyō no kiroku* (Naha, Japan: Okinawa ken kyōiku bunka shiryō sentā, 1979); Okinawa ken kyōiku bunka shiryō sentā heiwa kyōiku kenkyū iinkai, ed., *Heiwa kyōiku no jissen shū I: Okinawa ken to kichi no gakushū o fukameru tame ni* (Naha, Japan: Okinawa ken kyōiku bunka shiryō, 1983).

87. Yamagata Masaaki, "Okinawa ni okeru Jieitai jōchū o meguru kenmin ishiki no haikei to Okinawa Jieitai no hatasu yakuwari" (master's thesis, Meiō Daigakuin, 2007), 29.

88. Kuniyoshi interview, May 25, 2010.

89. "Okinawa Negotiations," *Ryūkyū shinpō*.

90. Ryūkyū shinpō, ed., *Yo kawari uramen shi: Shōgen ni miru Okinawa fukki no kiroku* (Naha, Japan: Ryūkyū shinpō-sha, 1983), 289; Yamagata, "Okinawa ni okeru Jieitai jōchū," 29.

91. Kuwae Ryōhō, *Ikusanga* (Tokyo: Hara shobō, 1982), 263–66. Kuwae published this book recounting his experiences on the tenth anniversary of reversion, May 15, 1982.

92. Takayoshi Egami, "Politics in Okinawa since the Reversion of Sovereignty," *Asian Survey* 34, no. 9 (September 1994): 834.

93. Kuniyoshi, "Shōkai," 374; Taira Ryōshō, *Taira Ryōshō kaiganryoku* (Naha, Japan: Okinawa taimusu sha, 1987), 242–45.

94. "Jieitai no gomi ha o-kotowari," *Ryūkyū shinpō*, August 17, 1972, 1; "Naha Mayor Suspends SDF Personnel Status," *Japan Times*, December 7, 1972; "Defense Agency, Naha Argue SDF Resident Registration," *Japan Times*, December 9, 1972.

95. Koyama Takashi, "Okinawa no jiseiken henkan ni tomonau Okinawa he no Jieitai haibi o meguru ugoki," *Bōei kenkyū sho kiyō* 20, no. 1 (December 2017): 154.

96. "Naha Mayor to End Curbs on SDF Resident Status," *Japan Times*, February 4, 1973.

97. Tanaka Kisaburō, interview by author, May 13, 2010, Kokubun, Japan.

98. Yamagata Masaaki, interview by author, July 5, 2019, Naha, Japan. Yamagata served as a senior GSDF commander in Okinawa near the end of his career in the early 2000s and retired as a major general in Tokyo in 2012. He wrote the master's thesis referenced in this chapter.

99. "Jieitaiin ni shōtaijō," *Okinawa taimusu*, January 11, 1979, 8; "Jieikan sanka mata momeru," *Yomiuri shinbun*, January 16, 1979, 23.

100. "Kidōtai mo shutsudō, keibi," *Okinawa taimusu*, January 16, 1983, 15.

101. Arasaki, *Okinawa gendai shi*, 86.

102. "Kirawareta Jieitai," *Yomiuri shinbun*, October 19, 1954, 7.

103. Emmerson, *Arms, Yen and Power*, 117.

104. "'Sabetsu' ha yokunai; Jieikan no nyūgaku de kenkai," *Asahi shinbun*, September 19, 1967, 2.

105. "3 Students Begin Hunger Strike," *Japan Times*, May 21, 1975.

106. "Jieikan no nyūgaku kyoka o tekkai seyo," *Okinawa taimusu*, April 16, 1975, Okinawa Prefectural Archives, Haebaru, Japan. See also Yamagata, "Okinawa ni okeru Jieitai jōchū," 28–29.

107. Arasaki Moriteru, *Yo kawari no uzu no naka de: 1973–1977* (Tokyo: Gaifū sha, 1992), 22.

108. "'Jieitai kōgi' tsuzuku," *Okinawa taimusu*, May 5, 1973, 3.

109. Katsu interview, May 13, 2010.

110. Ishimine Kunio, interview by author, May 26, 2010, Naha, Japan; Ishimine Kunio, *Kakebashi* (Naha, Japan: Ishimine Kunio, 1987), 61–62.

111. Sato, "A Camouflaged Military," 8.

112. Jieitai Okinawa chihō renrakubu sōritsu 20 nen ki'nen gyōji jikkō iinkai, ed., *Okinawa chiren 20 nen shi* (Nishihara chō, Japan: Jieitai Okinawa chihō renrakubu, 1992). Also see "SDF Trying to Win Okinawans," *Japan Times*, April 21, 1975, 2, which has slightly lower figures (10, 54, and 121) for these years. But these likely only represent enlistments in the GSDF.

113. Yamagata, "Okinawa ni okeru Jieitai jōchū," 62.

114. "Jieikan boshū gyōmu no kaishi o kokuji," *Okinawa taimusu*, August 1, 1979, 1.

115. Yamagata Masaaki, interview by author, July 9, 2019. In the mid-1990s, the number of applicants in Okinawa increased threefold compared to 1991, though the economic recession may have been a significant contributing factor to this rise. Frühstück, *Uneasy Warriors*, 38. Very few Okinawans applied and even fewer were accepted to the National Defense Academy in the last several years before 2019. Yamagata interview, July 9, 2019.

116. Even more ironically, *Shurei no hikari*, one of the magazines of USCAR, appropriated the name of the gate.

117. Although no one seems to have made this observation at the time, the SDF's figurative appropriation of Shuri Castle reenacted the Japanese Army's literal appropriation of the castle when it established its command headquarters there and in caverns deep beneath it before the Battle of Okinawa. This led US naval ships to fire thousands of rounds of artillery at the castle and to its decimation. As Michael Molasky observed, the Japanese Army's appropriation, in turn, reenacted the early historical domination of the Ryukyu Kingdom by the Satsuma domain. Michael S. Molasky, *The American Occupation of Japan and Okinawa: Literature and Memory* (London: Routledge, 1990), 16. For more on the history and memory of Shuri Castle, see Tze May Loo, *Heritage Politics: Shuri Castle and Okinawa's Incorporation into Modern Japan, 1879–2000* (Lanham, MD: Lexington, 2014).

118. Gerald Figal, *Beachheads: War, Peace, and Tourism in Postwar Okinawa* (Lanham, MD: Rowman & Littlefield, 2012), 58, 89–127.

119. "Kun," like "san," as in Tanaka-san, is a common honorific title. "Kun" is informal and mostly used for males, such as boys or junior employees at work. It is used by superiors to inferiors, by males of the same age and status to each other, and to address male children.

120. See, for example, Hasegawa Katsuki, "Shurei-kun," *Shurei*, November 29, 1975; Hasegawa Katsuki, "Shurei-kun," *Shurei*, July 18, 1976, 2.

121. Kuwae Ryōhō, "Seihō sōkan chokusetsu taiin o gekirei," *Shurei*, June 1, 1972, 1.

122. Kuwae Ryōhō, "Shinsei Okinawa ken no tanjō ni atari," *Shurei*, June 1, 1972, 1.

123. Kuwae Ryōhō, "Hakkan no kotoba," *Shurei*, June 1, 1972, 1.

124. Arasaki, *Yo kawari no uzu no naka de*, 39–40.

125. "SDF Girds for Okinawa Reversion," *Japan Times*, January 17, 1972.

126. Yamagata interview, July 9, 2019.

127. Ishimine interview, July 5, 2019.

128. "Dud Shells Pose Issue in Okinawa," *Japan Times*, December 8, 1972.

129. Shiratani Kozue, interview by author, July 5, 2019, Naha, Japan; Eldridge, "The GSDF during the Cold War Years," 153. See also Yamagata, "Okinawa ni okeru Jieitai jōchū," 36.

130. "Oroku bakuhatsu jiko," *Ryūkyū shinpō*, March 3, 1974, 1; "Oroku de fuhatsudan bakuhatsu," *Okinawa taimusu*, March 3, 1974, 1.

131. "Yomigaeru senso no akuyume," *Okinawa taimusu*, March 3, 1974, 12.

132. Yamagata interview, July 9, 2019.

133. Bōei cho, "Saigai hakken, bugai kyōryoku nado, Shōwa 50 nen 2/2" (1), 4A, 35 1469, National Archives of Japan, Tokyo.

134. "Naha chūtonchi Okinawa chihō renraku bu kaisetsu ki'nen gyōji," *Shurei*, March 20, 1973, 2. The printed date of the issue of this newspaper is incorrect. It should be the 48th year of Shōwa (1973) rather than 47th year of Shōwa (1972).

135. Ōta Masahide, interview by author, May 19, 2010, Naha, Japan.

136. Tanaka Kisaburō and Yanagita Mitsuhara, interview by author, May 13, 2010, Kokubun, Japan. The first commander of the ASDF in Okinawa, Yamada Takaji, also recalled that many force members wanted to return as quickly as possible to the mainland and recounted the continuing hostility experienced by personnel. Ryūkyū shinpō, *Yo kawari uramen shi*, 290; "Yamada Takaji ōraru hisutorī," in *Nakamura Ryūhei ōraru hisutorī*, ed. Bōei shō bōei kenkyūjo senshibu (Tokyo: Bōei shō bōei kenkyūjo, 2008), 406–7.

137. "Josei maneki pātī: taiin, hitokazu sukunai to fuman," *Ryūkyū shinpō*, March 11, 1973; "Ano te kono te no shintō sakusen," *Okinawa taimusu*, January 26, 1974, Okinawa Prefectural Archives, Haebaru, Japan.

138. See, for example, "Okinawa no hana *'diego*,'" *Shurei*, May 18, 1973, 3; "Okinawa no hana *būgenbirea*," *Shurei*, July 6, 1973, 5.

139. "Nadeshiko," *Chinzei*, June 1, 1979, 4.

140. The other genre in which women appeared frequently in the *Shuri* were articles about family life in Okinawa. These told of or were written by wives (and sometimes daughters) of male personnel who, despite the challenges of living in Okinawa, spoke almost invariably of how much they enjoyed living on the islands.

141. "Jieitai ni kekkon sōdansho," *Yomiuri shinbun*, June 10, 1973, 22.

142. Although many international marriages had occurred between US soldiers and Okinawan women from 1945 to 1972 (and have occurred since), the US military has generally discouraged such marriages, and it briefly prohibited them in 1948. It did not seek to leverage them to gain greater acceptance for the US military presence during the occupation, and has not done since. Though it does not deal explicitly with this question, Etsuko Takushi Crissley's book sheds light on these marriages. Etsuko Takushi Crissey, *Okinawa's GI Brides: Their Lives in America*, trans. Steve Rabson (Honolulu: University of Hawai'i Press, 2017).

143. Katsu interview, May 13, 2010.

144. "Sude ni 40 gumi ga kekkon," *Okinawa taimusu*, June 21, 1974, Okinawa Prefectural Archives, Haebaru, Japan.

145. Katsu interview, May 13, 2010; Ishimine interview, July 5, 2019.

146. "Sude ni 40 gumi ga kekkon." The *Japan Times* reported that forty-seven GSDF members had married "local girls" as of April 1975. "SDF Trying to Win Okinawans."

147. "Wadai ♥♥♥ kekkon," *Shurei*, July 20, 1974, 2.

148. "Fukki go 410 nin ga totsugu," *Ryūkyū shinpō*, May 14, 1982, 20.

149. Ishimine, *Kakebashi*, i.

150. Kokuba gumi shi henshū iinkai, ed., *Kokuba gunmi shashi: Sōritsu 50 shūnen ki'nen* (Naha, Japan: Kokuba gumi, 1984).

151. Ishimine interview, July 9, 2019.

152. Ishimine interview, July 9, 2019.

153. Ishimine interview, July 9, 2019; Okinawa bōei kyōkai, *Sōritsu 30 shūnen ki'nen shi.*

154. Egami, "Politics in Okinawa," 835.

155. Tanaka and Yanagita interview, May 13, 2010.

156. *Okinawa taimusu*, ed., *Okinawa nenkan* (Naha, Japan: Okinawa taimusu sha, 1980), 204–5.

157. Egami, "Politics in Okinawa," 835–36.

158. Yoshida, *Democracy Betrayed*, 167.

159. Ōta, Miyagi, Hosaka, *Fukkigō ni okeru Okinawa jūmin no ishiki to hen'yō*, 125.

160. Kuniyoshi interview, May 25, 2010.

161. "Tadashikatta senso mokuteki," *Okinawa taimusu*, December 8, 1972, 1.

162. Kuwae, *Ikusanga*, 145.

163. Kuwae, *Ikusanga*, 147–50.

164. "Irei no hi," *Okinawa taimusu*, June 24, 1976, 9.

165. "Irei no hi," 9.

166. "Shimin, kao o shikameru," *Ryūkyū shinpō*, June 25, 1976, 11.

167. Kuwae, *Ikusanga*, 150.

168. Hiromichi Yahara, *The Battle of Okinawa*, trans. Roger Pineau and Matatoshi Uehara (New York: John Wiley & Sons, 1995), 6; Toland, *The Rising Sun*, 683, 721.

169. "Kuwae Ryōhō ōraru hisutorī," 434.

170. Kuwae Ryōhō, "Retsusei no ju," *Shurei*, July 18, 1976, 3; Kuwae, *Ikusanga*, 38–39.

171. "Irei no hi."

172. "Kuwae kōsei danchō," *Okinawa taimusu*, August 3, 1976, 2.

173. The brigade band did parade through the streets of the northern town of Motobu and held a concert afterward during the Ocean Exposition in 1975, apparently without incident.

174. For one example, see "Jieitai bando ga Kokusai-dori kōshin," *Okinawa taimusu*, October 7, 1979, 11.

175. Arasaki Moriteru, *Ryūkyū ko shiten kara: 1978–1982, Okinawa dōji jidai shi*, vol. 2 (Tokyo: Gaifū sha, 1992), 199. The *Okinawa taimusu* used similar language in its evaluation of the parade. "Jieitai no 'gosan' shōmei," *Okinawa taimusu*, December 12, 1982, 1. See also Arasaki Moriteru, "The Struggle against Military Bases in Okinawa—Its History and Current Situation," *Inter-Asia Cultural Studies* 2, no. 1 (2001): 104.

176. "Sanpi uzumaku chū parēdo," *Okinawa taimusu*, December 12, 1982. 1.

177. Chibana Shōichi, *Burning the Rising Sun: From Yomitan Village, Okinawa; Islands of U.S. Bases* (Kyoto: South Wind, 1992). For a secondary treatment of Chibana, see Norma Field, *In the Realm of a Dying Emperor: Japan at Century's End* (New York: Vintage, 1993) 33–104.

178. Ruoff, *Japan's Imperial House in the Postwar Era*, 296–97.

179. Sheryl WuDunn "Rage Grows in Okinawa over U.S. Military Bases," *New York Times*, November 4, 1995, 3.

180. "Okinawa Negotiations," *Ryūkyū shinpō*, 1–2, 5, 6.

181. Steve Rabson, introduction to *Okinawa: Two Postwar Novellas*, by Ōshiro Tatsuhiro and Higashi Mineo (Berkeley: Institute of East Asian Studies, University of California, 1989), 29.

182. *Ryūkyū shinpō*, April 21, 1975.

## Epilogue

1. Pyle, *Japan Rising*, 270.

2. Smith, *Japan Rearmed*, 44–45.

3. Smith, *Japan Rearmed*, 57.

4. Smith, *Japan Rearmed*, 69–70; Samuels, *Securing Japan*, 97–98.

5. Smith, *Japan Rearmed*, 209–14.

6. Richard J. Samuels, *3.11* (Ithaca, NY: Cornell University Press, 2013), 63.

7. Japanese media and publishers have devoted a lot of attention to the role of the SDF in responding to 3.11. For a narrative account in English of the triple disaster that describes the GSDF operations, see Lucy Birmingham and David McNeill, *Strong in the Rain: Surviving Japan's Earthquake, Tsunami, and Fukushima Nuclear Disaster* (New York: Palgrave Macmillan, 2012).

8. Smith, *Japan Rearmed*, 165.

9. Midford, "The GSDF's Quest for Public Acceptance and the 'Allergy' Myth," 332–33.

10. Akane Okutsu, "Japan's Self-Defense Forces Start Mass-Vaccination Mission," *Nikkei Asia*, May 24, 2021, accessed on October 22, 2021, https://asia.nikkei.com/Spotlight/Coronavirus/Japan-Self-Defense-Forces-start-mass-vaccination-mission.

11. Eldridge, "Organization and Structure of the Contemporary Ground Self-Defense Force," 47.

12. Smith, *Japan Rearmed*, 168.

13. Frühstück, *Uneasy Warriors*, 70.

14. See, for example, Sankei shinbun Iraku shūzai han, ed., *Bushidō no kuni kara kita Jieitai: Iraku jindō fukkō shien no shinjitsu* (Tokyo: Sankei shinbun nyūsu sābisu, 2004).

# BIBLIOGRAPHY

Abenheim, Donald. *Reforging the Iron Cross: The Search for Tradition in the West German Forces*. Princeton, NJ: Princeton University Press, 1988.

Akagi Muneyoshi. "60 nen to watakushi," *THIS IS*, May 1990, 176–78.

Akagi Muneyoshi. *Ima dakara iu*. Tokyo: Bunka sōgō shuppan, 1973.

Alexander, Jeffrey W. *Brewed in Japan: The Evolution of the Japanese Beer Industry*. Honolulu: University of Hawai'i Press, 2013.

Alpers, Benjamin L. "This Is the Army: Imagining a Democratic Military in World War II." In *The World War Two Reader*, edited by Gordon Martel, 145–79. London: Routledge, 2004.

Arakawa Shōji. *Guntai to chiiki*. Tokyo: Aoki shoten, 2001.

Arasaki Moriteru. *Okinawa gendai shi*. Tokyo: Iwanami shoten, 2005.

Arasaki Moriteru. *Ryūkyū ko shiten kara: 1978–1982, Okinawa dōji jidai shi*, vol. 2. Tokyo: Gaifū sha, 1992.

Arasaki Moriteru. "The Struggle against Military Bases in Okinawa—Its History and Current Situation." *Inter-Asia Cultural Studies* 2, no. 1 (2001): 101–8.

Arasaki Moriteru. *Yo kawari no uzu no naka de: 1973–1977*. Tokyo: Gaifū sha, 1992.

Arata Masafumi. *"Tōyō no majo" ron*. Tokyo: Īsuto shinsho, 2013.

Armed Forces Sports Committee, ed. *Achieving Excellence: The Story of America's Military Athletes in the Olympic Games*. Alexandria, VA: Armed Forces Sports Committee, 1992.

Asada Jirō. "Nyūei." In *Hohei no honryō*, 147–82. Tokyo: Kōdansha, [1999] 2004.

Asagumo shinbun sha, ed. *Tōkyō Orinpikku sakusen*. Tokyo: Asagumo shinbun sha, 1965.

Asagumo shinbun sha henshū kyoku, ed. *Hanran no hanseiki: Rikujō Jieitai no 50 nen*. Tokyo: Asagumo shinbun sha, 2000.

Asahi shinbun, ed. *Jieitai*. Tokyo: Asahi shinbun sha, 1968.

Aspinall, Robert W. *Teachers' Unions and the Politics of Education in Japan*. Albany: State University of New York Press, 2001.

Auer, James, ed. *From Marco Polo Bridge to Pearl Harbor: Who Was Responsible?* Tokyo: Yomiuri shinbun, 2006.

Auer, James. *The Post-War Rearmament of Japanese Maritime Forces, 1945–71*. New York: Praeger, 1973.

Aukema, Justin. "Cultures of (Dis)remembrance and the Effects of Discourse at the Hiyoshidai Tunnels." *Japan Review* 32 (2019): 127–50.

Austin, Lewis. *Japan: The Paradox of Progress*. New Haven, CT: Yale University Press, 1976.

Azuma, Eiichiro. "Brokering Race, Culture, and Citizenship: Japanese Americans in Occupied Japan and Postwar National Inclusion." *Journal of American–East Asian Relations* 16, no. 3 (Fall 2009): 183–211.

Befu, Harumi. *Cultural Nationalism in East Asia: Representation and Identity.* Berkeley: Institute of East Asian Studies, University of California, 1993.

Ben-Ari, Eyal. "Normalization, Democracy, and the Armed Forces: The Transformation of the Japanese Military." In *Japan's Multilayered Democracy*, edited by Sigal Ben-Rafael Galanti, Nissim Otmazgin, and Alon Levkowitz, 105–21. Lanham, MD: Lexington, 2014.

Benesh, Oleg. *Inventing the Way of the Samurai: Nationalism, Internationalism, and Bushidō in Modern Japan.* Oxford: Oxford University Press, 2014.

Berger, Thomas U. *Cultures of Antimilitarism: National Security in Germany and Japan.* Baltimore: Johns Hopkins University Press.

Bibai shi hyaku nen shi hensan iinkai, ed. *Bibai shi hyaku nen shi: Tsūshi hen.* Bibai, Japan: Bibai shichō Taki Tadashi, 1991.

Bickers, Robert. *Out of China: How the Chinese Ended the Era of Western Domination.* Cambridge, MA: Harvard University Press, 2017.

Birmingham, Lucy, and David McNeill. *Strong in the Rain: Surviving Japan's Earthquake, Tsunami, and Fukushima Nuclear Disaster.* New York: Palgrave Macmillan, 2012.

Bōei Daigakkō dai san ki sotsugyō ki'nen shasshinchō iinkai, ed. *Bōei Daigakkō dai san ki sotsugyō ki'nen shasshinchō.* Yokosuka, Japan: Bōei Daigakkō, 1959.

Bōei Daigakkō dōsō kai, ed. *Maki no mi: Maki Tomoo sensei tsuisō shū.* Tokyo: Bōei Daigakkō dōsō kai Maki ki'nen shuppan iinkai, 1972.

Bōei chō "Jieitai no jūnen shi" henshū iinkai, ed. *Jieitai no jūnen shi.* Tokyo: Ōkurashō, 1961.

Bōei shō bōei kenkyūjo senshibu, ed. *Ishizu Sadamasu ōraru hisutorī.* Tokyo: Bōei shō bōei kenkyūjo, 2014.

Bōei shō bōei kenkyūjo senshibu, ed. *Nakamura Ryūhei ōraru hisutorī.* Tokyo: Bōei shō bōei kenkyūjo, 2008.

Bōei shō bōei kenkyūjo senshibu, ed. *Nishimoto Tetsuya ōraru hisutorī, moto sōgō bakuryō kaigi chō, jōkan.* Tokyo: Bōei shō bōei kenkyūjo, 2010.

Bōei shō bōei kenkyūjo senshibu, ed. *Ōraru historī: Reisenki no bōeiryoku seibi to dōmei seisaku, 1.* Tokyo: Bōei shō bōei kenkyūjo, 2012.

Bōei shō bōei kenkyūjo senshibu, ed. *Ōraru historī: Reisenki no bōeiryoku seibi to dōmei seisaku, 2.* Tokyo: Bōei shō bōei kenkyūjo, 2013.

Bōei shō bōei kenkyūjo senshibu, ed. *Sakuma Makoto ōraru hisutorī, moto sōgō bakuryō kaigi gichō, jōkan.* Tokyo: Bōei shō bōei kenkyūjo, 2007.

Bōei shō bōei kenkyūjo senshibu, ed. *Suzuki Akio ōraru hisutorī, moto kōkū bakuryō chō.* Tokyo: Bōei shō bōei kenkyūjo, 2011.

Bōei shō bōei kenkyūjo senshibu, ed. *Utsumi Hitoshi ōraru hisutorī, Keisatsu Yobitai, Hoantai jidai.* Tokyo: Bōei shō bōei kenkyūjo, 2008.

Bōei shō bōei kenkyūjo senshibu, ed. *Yoshikawa Keisuke ōraru hisutorī, moto Ōminato chihō sōkan.* Tokyo: Bōei shō bōei kenkyūjo, 2014.

Boyle, John Hunter. *Modern Japan: The American Nexus.* Orlando, FL: Harcourt Brace Jovanovich, 1993.

Brendle, Thomas M. "Recruitment and Training in the SDF." In *The Modern Japanese Military System*, edited by James H. Buck, 67–98. Beverly Hills, CA: Sage, 1975.

Buck, James H. "The Japanese Self-Defense Forces." *Asian Survey* 7 (1967): 597–613.

Buck, James H. Notes on the Contributors to *The Modern Japanese Military System*, edited by James H. Buck, 251–53. Beverly Hills, CA: Sage, 1975.

Bunbongkarn, Suchit. "The Thai Military and Its Role in Society in the 1990s." In *The Military, the State, and Development in Asia and the Pacific*, edited by Viberto Selochan, 67–81. Boulder, CO: Westview, 1991.

Chaloemtiarana, Thak. *Thailand: The Politics of Despotic Paternalism*. Ithaca, NY: Cornell University Press, 2007.

Chatani, Sakaya. *Nation-Empire: Ideology and Rural Youth Mobilization in Japan and Its Colonies*. Ithaca, NY: Cornell University Press, 2018.

Chibana Shōichi. *Burning the Rising Sun: From Yomitan Village, Okinawa; Islands of U.S. Bases*. Kyoto: South Wind, 1992.

Chitose shi shi hensan iinkai, ed. *Chitose shi shi*. Chitose, Japan: Chitose, 1983.

Christy, Alan S. "The Making of Imperial Subjects in Okinawa." *Positions: East Asia Cultures Critique* 1, no. 3 (Winter 1993): 607–39.

Congressional Quarterly Service. *Global Defense: U.S. Military Commitments Abroad*. Washington, DC: Congressional Quarterly Service, 1969.

Cook, Haruko Taya, and Theodore F. Cook. *Japan at War: An Oral History*. New York: New Press, 1992.

Cook, Theodore F. "The Japanese Officer Corps: The Making of a Military Elite, 1872–1945." PhD dissertation, Princeton University, 1987.

Cortazzi, Hugh, ed. *The Growing Power of Japan, 1967–1972: Analysis and Assessments from John Pilcher and the British Embassy, Tokyo*. Folkestone, UK: Renaissance, 2015.

Corum, James S. "Adenauer, Amt Blank, and the Founding of the Bundeswehr 1950–1956." In *Rearming Germany*, edited by James S. Corum, 29–52. Leiden, The Netherlands: Brill, 2011.

Corum, James S. "American Assistance to the New German Army and Luftwaffe." In *Rearming Germany*, edited by James S. Corum, 93–116. Leiden, The Netherlands: Brill, 2011.

Costello, John. *The Pacific War, 1941–1945*. New York: Quill, 1981.

Crissey, Etsuko Takushi. *Okinawa's GI Brides: Their Lives in America*. Translated by Steve Rabson. Honolulu: University of Hawai'i Press, 2017.

Dai 50 Sapporo yuki matsuri jikkō iinkai. *Dai 50 Sapporo yuki matsuri ki'nen shashinshū bekkan—kiroku/shiryōhen*. Sapporo, Japan: Sapporo yuki matsuri jikkō iinkai, 1999.

Daigaku kyōdō riyō kikan hōjin ningen bunka kenkyū kikō. *Sakura rentai ni miru sensō no jidai*. Sakura, Japan: Kokuritsu rekishi minzoku hakubutsukan, 2006.

Daimatsu Hirobumi. *Ore ni tsuite koi*. Tokyo: Kōdansha, 1963.

Davison, Charles. *The Japanese Earthquake of 1923*. London: Thomas Merby, 1931.

de Bary, Wm. Theodore, Carol Gluck, and Arthur E. Tiedemann. *Sources of Japanese Tradition*, vol. 2: *1600 to 2000*. Second edition. New York: Columbia University Press, 2005.

Deslandes, Paul R. *Oxbridge Men: British Masculinity and the Undergraduate Experience, 1850–1920*. Bloomington: Indiana University Press, 2005.

Dower, J. W. *Embracing Defeat: Japan in the Wake of World War II*. New York: W. W. Norton, 1999.

Dower, J. W. *Empire and Aftermath: Yoshida Shigeru and the Japanese Experience, 1878–1954*. Cambridge, MA: Harvard University Press, 1988.

Drea, Edward J. *In the Service of the Emperor: Essays on the Imperial Japanese Army*. Lincoln: University of Nebraska Press, 1998.

Drea, Edward J. *Japan's Imperial Army: Its Rise and Fall, 1853–1945*. Lawrence: University Press of Kansas, 2009.

Drea, Edward J. "Officer Education in Japan." *Military Review*, September 1980, 31–39.

Droubie, Paul. "Playing the Nation: 1964 Tokyo Olympics and Japanese Identity." PhD dissertation, University of Illinois Urbana-Champaign, 2009.

Eckert, Carter. *Park Chung Hee and Modern Korea: The Roots of Militarism, 1866–1945*. Cambridge, MA: Belknap Press of Harvard University Press, 2016.

Egami, Takayoshi. "Politics in Okinawa since the Reversion of Sovereignty." *Asian Survey* 34, no. 9 (September 1994): 828–40.

Ekirch, Arthur A., Jr. *The Civilian and the Military: A History of the American Antimilitarist Tradition*. Oakland, CA: Independent Institute, 2010.

Eldridge, Robert D. "The GSDF during the Cold War Years, 1960–1989." In *The Japanese Ground Self-Defense Force: Search for Legitimacy*, edited by Robert D. Eldridge and Paul Midford, 133–81. New York: Palgrave Macmillan, 2017.

Eldridge, Robert D. "Organization and Structure of the Contemporary Ground Self-Defense Force." In *The Japanese Ground Self-Defense Force: Search for Legitimacy*, edited by Robert D. Eldridge and Paul Midford, 19–55. New York: Palgrave Macmillan, 2017.

Eldridge, Robert D., and Paul Midford. Introduction to *The Japanese Ground Self-Defense Force*, edited by Robert D. Eldridge and Paul Midford, 3–17. New York: Palgrave Macmillan, 2017.

Ellison, Ralph. *Invisible Man*. New York: Random House, 1952.

Emmerson, John K. *Arms, Yen and Power: The Japanese Dilemma*. New York: Dunellen, 1971.

Enloe, Cynthia. *Maneuvers: The International Politics of Militarizing Women's Lives*. Berkeley: University of California Press, 2000.

"Etajima de shain kyōiku." *Asahi gurafu*, April 19, 1963, 19–23.

Etō Jun. "The Breakdown of Motherhood Is Wrecking Our Children." *Japan Echo* 11, no. 4 (1979): 102–9.

Etō Jun. "'Haha' no hōkai ga kodomo o dame ni shita." *Gendai*, August 1979, 222–31.

Evans, David C., and Mark R. Peattie. *Kaigun: Strategy, Tactics, and Technology in the Imperial Japanese Navy, 1887–1941*. Annapolis, MD: Naval Institute Press, 1997.

Fedman, David. "Mounting Modernization: Itakura Katsunobu, the Hokkaido University Alpine Club and Mountaineering in Pre-War Hokkaido." *Asia-Pacific Journal*, October 19, 2009, 1–18.

Fedman, David. *Seeds of Control: Japan's Empire of Forestry in Colonial Korea*. Seattle: University of Washington Press, 2020.

Field, Norma. *In the Realm of a Dying Emperor: Japan at Century's End*. New York: Vintage, 1993.

Figal, Gerald. *Beachheads: War, Peace, and Tourism in Postwar Okinawa*. Lanham, MD: Rowman & Littlefield, 2012.

Finn, Richard B. *Winners in Peace: MacArthur, Yoshida and Postwar Japan.* Berkeley: University of California Press, 1992.

Flanagan, Damian. *Yukio Mishima.* London: Reaktion, 2014.

Fleming, Bruce. *Bridging the Military-Civilian Divide: What Each Side Must Know about the Other, and about Itself.* Washington DC: Potomac, 2010.

French, Thomas. *National Police Reserve: The Origin of Japan's Self Defense Forces.* Leiden, The Netherlands: Brill, 2014.

Frühstück, Sabine. "After Heroism: Must Real Soldiers Die?" In *Recreating Japanese Men,* edited by Sabine Frühstück and Anne Walthall, 91–111. Berkeley: University of California Press, 2011.

Frühstück, Sabine. *Uneasy Warriors: Gender, Memory, and Popular Culture in the Japanese Army.* Berkeley: University of California Press, 2007.

Frühstück, Sabine, and Eyal Ben-Ari. "'Now We Show It All!' Normalization and the Management of Violence in Japan's Armed Forces." *Journal of Japanese Studies* 28, no. 1 (Winter 2002): 1–39

Fujiwara Akira. *Nihon kindaishi no kyozō to jitsuzō.* Tokyo: Ōtsuki shoten, 1989.

Fukuchi Hiroaki. "Okinawa no 'Nihon fukki.'" *Shūkan kin'yōbi,* May 12, 2006, 30–33.

Fukumoto Hirofumi. "Kawatta zo! Kigyō kenshū." *Asahi jānaru,* July 4, 1986, 106–11.

Funabashi Yōichi. "Seikaijū aozora o atsumeta." *Foresight* 11, no. 1 (January 2000): 62–64.

Galanti, Sigal Ben-Rafael. "Japan's Remilitarization Debate and the Projection of Democracy." In *Japan's Multilayered Democracy,* edited by Sigal Ben-Rafael Galanti, Nissim Otmazgin, and Alon Levkowitz, 89–103. Lanham, MD: Lexington, 2015.

Geyer, Michael. "The Militarization of Europe, 1914–1945." In *The Militarization of the Western World,* edited by John Gillis, 65–102. New Brunswick, NJ: Rutgers University Press, 1989.

Gibney, Frank. "The View from Japan." *Foreign Affairs* 50, no. 10 (October 1971): 97–111.

Gibo Yukio, ed. *Okinawa to heiwa kyōiku: Tokusetsu jugyō no kiroku.* Naha, Japan: Okinawa ken kyōiku bunka shiryō sentā, 1979.

Gojū nenshi henshū jigyō iinkai, ed. *Bōei Daigakkō gojū nenshi.* Yokosuka, Japan: Bōei Daigakkō, 2004.

Gordon, Andrew. *A Modern History of Japan: From Tokugawa Times to the Present.* Third edition. Oxford: Oxford University Press, 2014.

Gove, Phillip Babcock, ed. *Webster's Third New International Dictionary of the English Language,* unabridged. New York: Merriam-Webster, 2002.

Grandstaff, Mark R. "Making the Military American: Advertising, Reform, and the Demise of an Antistanding Military Tradition, 1945–1955." *Journal of Military History* 60, no. 2 (April 1996): 299–324.

Guillain, Robert. "The Resurgence of Military Elements in Japan." *Pacific Affairs* 25, no. 3 (September 1952): 211–25.

Guthrie-Shimizu, Sayuri. *Transpacific Field of Dreams: How Baseball Linked the United States and Japan in Peace and War.* Chapel Hill: University of North Carolina Press, 2012.

Hanmura Ryō. *Sengoku Jieitai.* Tokyo: Kakugawa shunju, 2000.

Hara Hideki. "Orinpikku to Jieitai." *Bunka hyōron* 27 (January 1964): 148–51.

Hashimoto Katsuhiko. *Orinpikku ni ubawareta inochi: Tsuburaya Kōkichi, sanjūnen me no shishōgen*. Tokyo: Shōgakkan, 1999.

Hashimoto Kazuo. *Nihon supōtsu hōsō shi*. Tokyo: Taishūkan shoten, 1992.

Hatano Sumio and Susumu Satō. "Ajia moderu toshite no 'Yoshida dokutorin.'" *Gunji shigaku*, no. 156 (March 2004): 4–20.

Hauser, William L. *America's Army in Crisis: A Study in Civil-Military Relations*. Baltimore: Johns Hopkins University Press, 1973.

Havens, Thomas. *Fire across the Sea: The Vietnam War and Japan 1965–1975*. Princeton, NJ: Princeton University Press, 1987.

Havens, Thomas. *Marathon Japan: Distance Racing and Civic Culture*. Honolulu: University of Hawai'i Press, 2015.

Hayashi, Hirofumi. "Massacre of Chinese in Singapore and Its Coverage in Postwar Japan." In *New Perspectives on the Japanese Occupation in Malaya and Singapore, 1941–1945*, edited by Akashi Yoji and Yoshimura Mako, 234–49. Singapore: NUS Press, 2008.

Hein, Laura, and Mark Selden. "Culture, Power, and Identity in Contemporary Okinawa." In *Islands of Discontent: Okinawan Responses to Japanese and American Power*, edited by Laura Hein and Mark Selden, 1–38. Lanham, MD: Rowman & Littlefield, 2003.

Hertrich, André. "War Memory, Local History, Gender: Self-Representation in Exhibitions of the Ground Self-Defense Force." In *Local History and War Memories in Hokkaido*, edited by Philip A. Seaton, 179–97. London: Routledge, 2016.

Hirano Tomohiko "Dai nana shidan to Asahikawa." In *Kita no guntai to gunto: Hokkaido, Tōhoku*, edited by Yamamoto Kazushige, 44–78. Tokyo: Yoshikawa kōbunkan, 2015.

Hirota Teruyuki. *Rikugun shōkō no kyōiku shakai shi: Risshin shusse to tennōsei*. Yokohama, Japan: Seori shobō, 1997.

Hokkai 45 shūnen ki'nenshi henshū iinkai, ed. *Hokkai, warera ga jidai: Hanseiki no kiseki*. Sapporo, Japan: Mainichi shinbun sha Hokkaidō shisha, 2004.

Hokubu hōmen sōkanbu dai ichi bu kōhō han and Irikura Shōzō, eds. *Hokkaidō to Jieitai*. Sapporo, Japan: Kan Hideo, 1963.

Humphreys, Leonard A. "The Japanese Military Tradition." In *The Modern Japanese Military System*, edited by James H. Buck, 21–40. Beverly Hills, CA: Sage, 1975.

Humphreys, Leonard A. *The Way of the Heavenly Sword: The Japanese Army in the 1920's*. Stanford, CA: Stanford University Press, 1995.

Hunter-Chester, David. *Creating Japan's Ground Self-Defense Force: A Sword Well Made*. Lanham, MD: Lexington, 2016.

Igarashi, Yoshikuni. *Bodies of Memory: Narratives of War in Postwar Japanese Culture, 1945–1970*. Princeton, NJ: Princeton University Press, 2000.

Igarashi, Yoshikuni. *Homecomings: The Belated Return of Japan's Lost Soldiers*. New York: Columbia University Press, 2016.

Ikeda Kiyoshi. *Jiyū to kiritsu: Igirisu no gakkō seikatsu*. Tokyo: Iwanami shoten, 1949.

Ikeda Kōtarō. *Watashi no kaisōroku*. Nayoro, Japan: Ikeda Mitsui, 1990.

Ikeda, Kyle. *Okinawan War Memory: Transgenerational Trauma and the War Fiction of Medoruma Shun*. London: Routledge, 2014.

Inoki Masamichi. *Watakushi no niju seiki: Inoki Masamichi kaikoroku*. Tokyo: Sekai shisō sha, 2000.

Inose, Naoki, and Hiroaki Sato. *Persona: A Biography of Yukio Mishima*. Berkeley, CA: Stone, 2012.

Iokibe Makoto. *Nihon ha suitai suru no ka*. Tokyo: Chikura shobō, 2014.

Irish, Ann. *Hokkaido: A History of Ethnic Transition and Development on Japan's Northern Island*. Jefferson, NC: McFarland, 2009.

Ishibashi, Natsuyo. "Different Forces in One: The Origin and Development of Organizational Cultures in the Japanese Ground and Maritime Self-Defense Forces, 1950–Present." *Japan Forum* 28, no. 2 (2016): 155–75.

Ishimine Kunio. *Kakebashi*. Naha, Japan: Ishimine Kunio, 1987.

Janowitz, Morris. *The Professional Soldier: A Social and Political Portrait*. New York: Free Press, 1960.

Japan Defense Agency. "Ethical Principles for Personnel of the Self Defense Force." Undated. Manuscript in author's possession.

Jaundrill, D. Colin. *Samurai to Soldier: Remaking Military Service in Nineteenth-Century Japan*. Ithaca, NY: Cornell University Press, 2016.

Jeffords, Susan. *The Remasculinization of America: Gender and the Vietnam War*. Bloomington: Indiana University Press, 1989.

Jieitai Okinawa chihō renrakubu sōritsu 20 nen ki'nen gyōji jikkō iinkai, ed. *Okinawa chiren 20 nen shi*. Nishihara chō, Japan: Jieitai Okinawa chihō renrakubu, 1992.

Kagawa Yoshiaki. "Keisatsu Yobitai koto hajime." In *Keisatsu Yobitai no kaiko: Jieitai no yoake*, edited by Shichōkai and Nishida Hiroshi. Tokyo: Shinpūsha, 2003.

"Kamera Hoan Daigakkō ni hairu." *Asahi kurabu*, June 3, 1953, 4–5.

Kamiyama Makoto. *Nihon no konjō: Matsushita Konnosuke no ningen no kangaekata*. Tokyo: Nanboku sha, 1964.

Kanechika Kentarō. "Yuki matsuri." *Junkan Yomiuri*, March 21, 1952, 34–35.

Kapur, Nick. *Japan at the Crossroads: Conflict and Compromise after Anpo*. Cambridge, MA: Harvard University Press, 2018.

Karlin, Jason G. *Gender and Nation in Meiji Japan*. Honolulu: University of Hawai'i Press, 2014.

Karlin, Jason G. "The Gender of Nationalism: Competing Masculinities in Meiji Japan." *Journal of Japanese Studies* 28, no. 1 (Winter 2002): 41–77.

Katō Yōzō. *Shiroku, Jieitai shi: Keisatsu Yobitai kara konnichi made*. Tokyo: "Gekkan seigaku" seiji geppō sha, 1979.

Katzenstein, Peter J. *Cultural Norms and National Security: Police and Military in Postwar Japan*. Ithaca, NY: Cornell University Press, 1996.

Katzenstein, Peter J., and Nobuo Okawara. *Japan's National Security: Structures, Norms and Policy Reponses in a Changing World*. Ithaca, NY: Cornell East Asia Program, 1993.

Kawano, Hitoshi. "A Comparative Study of Combat Organizations: Japan and the United States during World War II." PhD dissertation, Northwestern University, 1996.

Kawano, Hitoshi. "The Expanding Role of Sociology at Japan National Defense Academy." *Armed Forces & Society* 35, no. 1 (October 2008): 122–44.

Keiō Gijuku shi jiten henshū iinkai, ed. *Keiō gijiku shi jiten*. Tokyo: Keiō gijuku, 2008.

Kennedy, M. D. *The Military Side of Japanese Life*. Boston: Houghton Mifflin, 1923.

Kerr, George H. *Okinawa: The History of an Island People*. Tokyo: Tuttle, [1958] 2000.

Kichiji Shun'ei and Hatano Motoji. "Taiken nyūtai to hitozukuri." *Keieisha* 20, no. 6 (June 1966): 48–53.

Kim, Taeju. "The Moral Realism of the Postwar Intellectuals." PhD dissertation, University of Chicago, 2018.

Kinjō Kazuhiko. *Ai to senketsu no kiroku*. Tokyo: Zenbō sha, 1966.

Kinjō Kazuhiko. *Himeyuri butai no saigo*. Tokyo: Kaisei sha, 1966.

Kinjō Kazuhiko. *Okinawa sen no gakutotai*. Tokyo: Tōkyō shokan sentā, [1966] 1992.

Kinjō Kazuhiko and Ohara Masao. *Minna mi no iwao no hate ni*. Tokyo: Kōbunsha, 1959.

Kinoshita, Hanji. "Echoes of Militarism in Japan." *Pacific Affairs* 26, no. 3 (September 1953): 244–51.

Kobayashi Sunao. "Beikoku rikugun shikan gakkō." *Keisatsu Yobitai shiryō shū* 3 (March 1952): 1–7.

Koji Taira. "Troubled National Identity: The Ryukyuans/Okinawans." In *Japan's Minorities: The Illusion of Homogeneity*, edited by Michael Weiner, 140–77. London: Routledge, 1997.

Kokuba gumi shi henshū iinkai, ed. *Kokuba gumi shashi: Sōritsu 50 shūnen ki'nen*. Naha, Japan: Kokuba gumi, 1984.

Konishi Makoto. *Hansen jieikan: Kenryōku o yurugasu seinen kūsō no zōhan*. Tokyo: Shakai hihyō sha, 2018.

Kowalski, Frank. *An Inoffensive Rearmament: The Making of the Postwar Japanese Army*. Edited by Robert D. Eldridge. Annapolis, MD: Naval Institute Press, 2013.

Koyama Takashi. "Okinawa no jiseiken henkan ni tomonau Okinawa he no Jieitai haibi o meguru ugoki." *Bōei kenkyū sho kiyō* 20, no. 1 (December 2017): 115–57.

Kuboi Masayuki. *Higashi Hiroshima kara Kita Hiroshima made: 80 nen no kaisō*. Kita Hiroshima, Japan: Kuboi Masayuki, 2004.

Kusunoki, Ayako. "The Early Years of the Ground Self-Defense Forces, 1945–1960." In *The Japanese Ground Self-Defense Force: Search for Legitimacy*, edited by Robert D. Eldridge and Paul Midford, 59–131. New York: Palgrave Macmillan, 2017.

Kuwae Ryōhō. *Ikusanga*. Tokyo: Hara shobō, 1982.

Kuzuhara Kazumi. "The Korean War and the National Police Reserve of Japan: Impact of the US Army's Far East Command on Japan's Defense Capability." *NIDS Security Reports*, no. 7 (December 2006): 95–116.

Large, David Clay. *Germans to the Front: West German Rearmament in the Adenauer Era*. Chapel Hill: University of North Carolina Press, 1996.

Large, David Clay. *Nazi Games: The Olympics of 1936*. New York: W. W. Norton, 2007.

Lifton, Robert Jay, Shūichi Katō, and Michael R. Reich. *Six Lives, Six Deaths: Portraits from Modern Japan*. New Haven, CT: Yale University Press, 1979.

Lockenour, Jay. *Soldiers as Citizens: Former Wehrmacht Officers in the Federal Republic of Germany, 1945–1955*. Lincoln: University of Nebraska Press, 2001.

Lone, Stewart. *Provincial Life and the Military in Imperial Japan: The Phantom Samurai*. London: Routledge, 2009.

Loo, Tze May. *Heritage Politics: Shuri Castle and Okinawa's Incorporation into Modern Japan, 1879–2000*. Lanham, MD: Lexington, 2014.

Lutz, Catherine. *Homefront: A Military City and the American Twentieth Century.* Boston: Beacon, 2001.

Maeda, Tetsuo. *The Hidden Army: The Untold Story of Japan's Military Forces.* Edited by David J. Kenney. Translated by Steven Karpa. Chicago: Edition Q, 1995.

Maekawa Kiyoshi. "Maki sensei to Inoue Shigeyoshi kaigun taishō." *Bōdai dōsō kai shi* (1969): 183–91.

Maki ki'nen shitsu secchi nado kento iinkai. *Maki ki'nen shitsu zuroku: Kengaku no seishin—Jishu jiritsu, shodai gakkōchō Maki Tomoo no jidai.* Yokosuka, Japan: Bōei Daigakkō, 2008.

Maki Tomoo. *Bei-Ei-Futsu shikan gakkō rekihō no tabi.* Tokyo: Kōyō shobō, 1969.

Maki Tomoo. *Bōei no tsutome: Jieitai no seishinteki kyoten.* Tokyo: Chūō kōron sha, 2004.

Martin, Michel L. *Warriors to Managers: The French Military Establishment since 1945.* Chapel Hill: University of North Carolina Press, 1981.

Masao Miyoshi. Introduction to *Two Novels: Seventeen, J,* by Kenzaburō Ōe, translated by Luk Van Haute, v–xvii. New York: Blue Moon, 1996.

Masland, John W., and Laurence I. Radway. *Soldiers and Scholars: Military Education and National Policy.* Princeton, NJ: Princeton University Press, 1957.

Mason, Michelle E. *Dominant Narratives of Colonial Hokkaido and Imperial Japan: Envisioning the Periphery and the Modern Nation-State.* New York: Palgrave Macmillan, 2012.

Mason, Tony, and Eliza Riedi. *Sport and the Military: The British Armed Forces, 1880–1960.* Cambridge: Cambridge University Press, 2010.

Masuda, Hajimu. "Fear of World War III: Social Politics of Japan's Rearmament and Peace Movements, 1950–3." *Journal of Contemporary History* 47, no. 3 (2012): 551–71.

Masuda Hiroshi. *Jieitai no tanjō: Nihon no saigunbi to Amerika.* Tokyo: Chūō kōron, 2004.

Masumi Junnosuke. *Contemporary Politics in Japan.* Translated by Lonny E. Carlile. Berkeley: University of California Press, 1995.

Matsueda, Tsukasa, and George Moore. "Japan's Shifting Attitudes toward the Military." *Asian Survey* 7, no. 9 (1967): 614–25.

Matsushita Takaaki. *Guntai o yūchi seyo: Rikukaigun to toshi keisei.* Tokyo: Yoshikawa kōbunkan, 2013.

McClain, James L. *Japan: A Modern History.* New York: W. W. Norton, 2002.

McCormack, Gavan. *Client State: Japan in the American Embrace.* New York: Verso, 2007.

McCormack, Gavan, and Satoko Oka Norimatsu. *Resistant Islands: Okinawa Confronts Japan and the United States.* Lanham, MD: Rowman & Littlefield, 2012.

Midford, Paul. "The GSDF's Quest for Public Acceptance and the 'Allergy' Myth." In *The Japanese Ground Self-Defense Force: Search for Legitimacy,* edited by Robert D. Eldridge and Paul Midford, 297–345. New York: Palgrave Macmillan, 2017.

Midford, Paul. "The Logic of Reassurance and Japan's Grand Strategy." *Security Studies* 11, no. 3 (Spring 2002): 1–43.

Midford, Paul. *Rethinking Japanese Public Opinion and Security: From Pacifism to Realism?* Stanford, CA: Stanford University Press, 2011.

Mikanagi, Yumiko. *Masculinity and Japan's Foreign Relations*. Boulder, CO: First Forum, 2011.

Mikio Higa. "The Okinawan Reversion Movement (I)." *Ryūdai hōgaku* 17 (November 1975): 147–74.

Mikio Higa. *Politics and Parties in Postwar Okinawa*. Vancouver: University of British Columbia Press, 1963.

Miller, Jennifer M. *Cold War Democracy: The United States and Japan*. Cambridge, MA: Harvard University Press, 2019.

Ministry of Defense. *Defense of Japan 2010*. Tokyo: Erklaren, 2010.

Mishima Takashi. *Nippon no "heishi"tachi*. Tokyo: Jiji Kahō sha, 2007.

Mishima Yukio. "Gendai shōnen no mujun o han'ei." *Shūkan Asahi*, July 26, 1953, 5–7.

Mishima Yukio. *Mishima Yukio zenshū*. 35 vols. Tokyo: Shinchōsha, 1973–76.

Mishima Yukio. *Patriotism*. Translated by Geoffrey W. Sargent. New York: New Directions, 1966.

Mishima Yukio. *Sun and Steel*. Translated by John Bester. London: Martin Secker & Warburg, 1971.

Mishima Yukio. *The Way of the Samurai: Yukio Mishima on "Hagakure" in Modern Life*. Translated by Kathryn Sparling. New York: Basic Books, [1967] 1977.

Miyagi Otoya. "Saigunbi o chōetsu." *Shūkan Sankei*, January 17, 1954, 8–9.

Mizukami Tōru. "Mōretsu shain no imi to haikei." *Gekkan rōdō mondai* 136 (1969): 12–17.

Moeller, Robert G. *War Stories: The Search for a Usable Past in the Federal Republic of Germany*. Berkeley: University of California Press, 2001.

Molasky, Michael S. *The American Occupation of Japan and Okinawa: Literature and Memory*. London: Routledge, 1990.

Morris, Ivan. *Nationalism and the Right Wing in Japan: A Study of Post-War Trends*. Oxford: Oxford University Press, 1960.

Morris-Suzuki, Tessa. "A Fire on the Other Shore? Japan and the Korean War Order." In *The Korean War in Asia: A Hidden History*, edited by Tessa Morris-Suzuki, 7–38. Lanham, MD: Rowman & Littlefield, 2018.

Moskos, Charles C. "Toward a Postmodern Military: The United States as a Paradigm." In *The Postmodern Military: Armed Forces after the Cold War*, edited by Charles C. Moskos, John Allen Williams, and David R. Segal, 14–31. New York: Oxford University Press, 2000.

Motoaki Hiroshi. *Konjō—Nihonjin no bitaritī*. Tokyo: Diamond sha, 1964.

Mulloy, Garren. *Defenders of Japan: The Post-Imperial Armed Forces 1964–2016*. London: Hurts, 2021.

Murakami Hyōe. "Kin medaru kyū no karei naru shūdan, Jieitai." *Sandē Mainichi*, November 1964, 100–3.

Murakami, Tomoaki. "The GSDF and Disaster Relief Dispatches." In *The Japanese Ground Self-Defense Force: Search for Legitimacy*, edited by Robert D. Eldridge and Paul Midford, 265–96. New York: Palgrave Macmillan, 2017.

Nagano Setsuo. *Jieitai ha dono yō ni shite umareta ka*. Tokyo: Gakuen kenkyūsha, 2003.

Naikaku sōridaijin kanbō kōhōshitsu. *Jieitai ni kansuru seiron chōsa*. Tokyo: Naikaku sōridaijin kanbō kōhōshitsu, 1963.

Naikaku sōridaijin kanbō kōhōshitsu. *Jieitai no kōhō oyobi bōei mondai ni kansuru seiron chōsa*. Tokyo: Naikaku sōridaijin kanbō kōhōshitsu, 1966.

Nakamori Shizuo. *Bōei Daigakkō no shinjitsu*. Tokyo: Keizai kai, 2004.

Nakamura Eri. "Nihon rikugun ni okeru dansei sei no kōchiku: Dansei no 'kyōfushin' o meguru kaishaku o jiku ni." In *Jendā to shakai: Dansei shi, rikugun, sekushuariti*, edited by Kimoto Kimiko and Kido Yoshiyuki, 170–90. Tokyo: Junpōsha, 2010

Nakano Ryō. "Taishō ki Nihon gun no gunji enshū: Chiiki shakai to no kankei o chūshin ni." *Shigaku zasshi* 114, no. 4 (April 2005): 53–74.

Nakasone Yasuhiro. *The Making of the New Japan: Reclaiming the Political Mainstream*. Translated and annotated by Lesley Connors. Richmond, UK: Curzon, 1999.

Narita Chihiro. "Okinawa henkan to Jieitai haibi." *Dōjidai shi kenkyū* 10 (2017): 37–53.

Nathan, John. *Mishima: A Biography*. New York: Little, Brown, 1974.

Nayoro shi shi hensan iinkai, ed. *Shin Nayoro shi shi*. 3 vols. Nayoro, Japan: Nayoro shi, 2000.

NHK hōsō seiron chōsa sho, ed. *Zusetsu: Sengo seron shi*. Tokyo: NHK Bukkusu, 1975.

Nishihara Masashi. "Bōdai sōsetsu ki no Beigunjin komontachi: Sōritsu gojū shūnen o mukaeta Bōdai o furikaeru." *Obaradai*, no. 83 (2003): 84–95.

Nogawa Yasuharu. "'Guntō' Kanazawa ni okeru rikugun ki'nenbi shukuga gyōji in tsuite no obegaki." *Chihōshi kenkyū* 63, no. 4 (August 2013): 49–52.

Norman, Michael, and Elizabeth M. Norman. *Tears in the Darkness: The Story of the Bataan Death March and Its Aftermath*. New York: Farrar, Straus and Giroux, 2009.

Obermiller, David Tobaru [John]. "The United States Military Occupation of Okinawa: Politicizing and Contesting Okinawan Identity, 1945–1955." PhD dissertation, University of Iowa, 2006.

Obermiller, David Tobaru [John]. "Dreaming Ryūkyū: Shifting and Contesting Identities in Okinawa." In *Japan since 1945: From Postwar to Post-Bubble*, edited by Christopher Gerties and Timothy S. George, 69–88. London: Bloomsbury, 2013.

Office of Military History, Officer Headquarters, United States Army Forces East Asia and Eighth United States Army, ed., *History of the National Police Reserve of Japan (July 1950–April 1952)*. 2 vols. Washington, DC: Office of Military History, 1955.

Oguma, Eiji. *The Boundaries of "the Japanese,"* vol. 1: *Okinawa 1818–1972—Inclusion and Exclusion*. Translated by Leonie R. Stickland. Melbourne, Australia: Trans Pacific, 2014.

Okinawa bōei kyōkai, ed. *Sōritsu 30 shūnen ki'nen shi*. Naha, Japan: Okinawa bōei kyōkai, 2002.

Okinawa ken kyōiku bunka shiryō sentā heiwa kyōiku kenkyū iinkai, ed. *Heiwa kyōiku no jissen shū I: Okinawa ken to kichi no gakushū o fukameru tame ni*. Naha, Japan: Okinawa ken kyōiku bunka shiryō, 1983.

Okinawa ken kyōiku shokuin gumiai, ed. *Okinawa no heiwa kyōiku: Tokusetsu jugyō o chūshin to shita jissenrei*. Naha, Japan: Okinawa ken kyōiku shokuin gumiai, 1978.

Okinawa ken kyōshokuin kumiai, ed. *Kore ga Nihon gun da: Okinawa sen ni okeru zangyaku kōi*. Sixth edition. Naha, Japan: Okinawa ken kyōshokuin kumiai, 1972.

*Okinawa taimusu*, ed., *Okinawa nenkan*. Naha, Japan: Okinawa taimusu sha, 1980.

Okinawa taimusu sha, ed. *Tetsu no bōfū: Genchijin ni yoru Okinawa senki*. Tokyo: Asahi shinbun sha, 1950.

Ōkoda Yahiro. *Kita no daichi o mamorite gojū nen: Sengo Nihon no hoppō jūshi senryaku*. Tokyo: Kaya shobō, 2005.

Olechnowicz, Andrzej. "Liberal Anti-Fascism in the 1930s: The Case of Sir Ernest Barker." *Albion* 36, no. 4 (2005): 636–60.

Oogya Shōzō. *Sararīman no dokonjō*. Tokyo: Kurabu sha, 1964.

Orbach, Danny. *Curse on this Country: The Rebellious Army of Imperial Japan*. Ithaca, NY: Cornell University Press, 2017.

Organizing Committee of the Games of the XVII Olympiad. *The Games of the XVII Olympiad: Rome 1960*. Rome: Organizing Committee of the Games of the XVII Olympiad, 1960.

Organizing Committee of the Games of the XVIII Olympiad. *Games of the XVIII Olympiad Tokyo 1964*. 2 vols. Tokyo: Organizing Committee of the Games of the XVIII Olympiad, 1964.

Ōshiro Masayasu. *Okinawa sen no shinjitsu to waikyoku*. Tokyo: Kōbunken, 2007.

Ota, Fumio. "Japanese Warfare Ethics." In *Routledge Handbook of Military Ethics*, edited by George Lucas, 163–69. New York: Routledge, 2015.

Ōta Masahide. *Minikui Nihonjin: Nihon no Okinawa ishiki*. Tokyo: Simul, 1969.

Ōta Masahide. *This Was the Battle of Okinawa*. Haebaru, Japan: Naha, 1981.

Ōta Masahide. "War Memories Die Hard in Okinawa." *Japan Quarterly*, January 1988, 11–13.

Ōta Masahide, Miyagi Etsujiro, and Hosaka Hiroshi. *Fukkigō ni okeru Okinawa jūmin no ishiki to hen'yō*. Naha, Japan: Ōta Masahide, 1984.

Ōtake Hideo, ed. *Sengo Nihon bōei mondai shiryōshū*. 3 vols. Tokyo: Sanichi shobō, 1991.

Otomo, Rie. "Narratives, the Body and the 1964 Tokyo Olympics." *Asian Studies Review* 31, no. 1 (June 2007): 117–32.

Ōya, Sōichi. "Hotondo tennōsei ni ha bōkanteki." *Shūkan Sankei*, January 17, 1954, 7–8.

Ōya, Sōichi and Miyagi Otoya. "Hoan Daigaku ni nyūgaku shita dōki." *Shūkan Sankei*, January 17, 1954, 4–7.

Packard, George R., III. *Protest in Tokyo: The Security Treaty Crisis of 1960*. Princeton, NJ: Princeton University Press, 1966.

Patalano, Alessio. *Post-War Japan as a Sea Power: Imperial Legacy, Wartime Experience and the Making of a Navy*. London: Bloomsbury, 2015.

Pennington, Lee K. "Wives for the Wounded: Marriage Mediation for Japanese Disabled Veterans during World War II." *Journal of Social History* 53, no. 3 (2020): 667–97.

Pinker, Steven. *The Better Angels of Our Nature: Why Violence Has Declined*. New York: Viking, 2011.

Poiger, Uta G. "A New, 'Western' Hero? Reconstructing German Masculinity in the 1950s." *Signs: Journal of Women in Culture and Society* 24, no. 1 (1998): 147–62.

Pyle, Kenneth B. *Japan Rising: The Resurgence of Japanese Power and Purpose*. New York: PublicAffairs, 2007.

Rabson, Steve. Introduction to *Okinawa: Two Postwar Novellas*, by Ōshiro Tatsuhiro and Higashi Mineo. Berkeley: Institute of East Asian Studies, University of California, 1989.

Rasmussen, Anne. "Mobilizing Minds." In *The Cambridge History of the First World War: Civil Society*, edited by Jay Winter, vol. 3. Cambridge: Cambridge University Press, 2014.

Rikujō bakuryō kanbu sōmuka, ed. *Keisatsu Yobitai sōtai shi*. Tokyo: Bōei chō rikujō bakuryō kanbu, 1958.

Roden, Donald T. *Schooldays in Imperial Japan: A Study in the Culture of a Student Elite*. Berkeley: University of California Press, 1980.

Roden, Donald T. "Thoughts on the Early Meiji Gentleman." In *Gendering Modern Japanese History*, edited by Barbara Molony and Kathleen Uno, 61–98. Cambridge, MA: Harvard University Asia Center, 2005.

Rohlen, Thomas. "'Spiritual Education' in a Japanese Bank." *American Anthropologist* 75, no. 5 (October 1973): 1542–62.

Ruoff, Kenneth J. *Japan's Imperial House in the Postwar Era, 1945–2019*. Cambridge, MA: Harvard University Press, 2020.

Ruoff, Kenneth J. *The People's Emperor: Democracy and the Japanese Monarchy, 1945–1995*. Cambridge, MA: Harvard University Asia Center, 2001.

Ryūkyū shinpō, ed. *Yo kawari uramen shi: Shōgen ni miru Okinawa fukki no kiroku*. Naha, Japan: Ryūkyū shinpō sha, 1983.

Ryūkyū shinpō sha henshū kyoku, ed. *Gendai Okinawa jiten: Fukkigo zen kiroku*. Naha, Japan: Ryūkyū shinpō sha, 1992.

Sado Akihiro. *The Self-Defense Forces and Postwar Politics in Japan*. Tokyo: Japan Publishing Industry Foundation for Culture, 2017.

Sakai, Robert K. "The Ryukyu (Liu-ch'iu) Islands as a Fief of Satsuma." In *The Chinese World Order: Traditional China's Foreign Policy*, edited by John King Fairbank, 112–34. Cambridge, MA: Harvard University Press, 1968.

Sakaki, Alexandra, Hann W. Maull, Kerstin Lukner, Ellis S. Krauss, and Thomas U. Berger. *Reluctant Warriors: Germany, Japan, and Their U.S. Alliance Dilemma*. Washington, DC: Brookings Institution Press, 2020.

Samuels, Richard J. *3.11*. Ithaca, NY: Cornell University Press, 2013.

Samuels, Richard J. *Securing Japan: Tokyo's Grand Strategy and the Future of East Asia*. Ithaca, NY: Cornell University Press, 2007.

Sankei shinbun Iraku shūzai han, ed. *Bushidō no kuni kara kita Jieitai: Iraku jindō fukkō shien no shinjitsu*. Tokyo: Sankei shinbun nyūsu sābisu, 2004.

Sapporo shi keizai bu, ed. *Hokkaidō dai hakurankai shi: Hokkaido Grand Fair*. Sapporo, Japan: Sapporo shi, 1959.

Sasaki Tomoyuki. *Japan's Postwar Military and Civil Society: Contesting a Better Life*. New York: Bloomsbury, 2017.

Sato, Fumika. "A Camouflaged Military: Japan's Self-Defense Forces and Globalized Gender Mainstreaming." *Asia-Pacific Journal*, August 28, 2021, 1–28.

Satō Fumika. *Gunji soshiki to jendā: Jieitai no joseitachi*. Tokyo: Keiō Gijuku Daigakku shuppankai, 2004.

Satō Morio. *Keisatsu Yobitai to saigunbi he no michi*. Tokyo: Fuyō shobō, 2015.

Schencking, J. Charles. "1923 Tokyo as a Devastated War and Occupation Zone: The Catastrophe One Confronted in Post Earthquake Japan." *Japanese Studies* 29, no. 1 (2009): 111–29.

Searle, Alaric. *Wehrmacht Generals, West German Society, and the Debate on Rearmament, 1949–1959.* Westport, CT: Praeger, 2003.

Sebald, William. *With MacArthur in Japan: A Personal History of the Occupation.* New York: W. W. Norton, 1965.

Seraphim, Franziska. *War Memory and Social Politics in Japan, 1945–2005.* Cambridge, MA: Harvard University Asia Center, 2006.

"Shain kyōiku ha Jieitai de." *Nihon,* September 1961, 208–9.

"Shain kyōiku hikiukemasu: Shageki kunren kara keieigaku made." *Shūkan Asahi,* April 26, 1963, 20–23.

Sherry, Michael S. *In the Shadow of War: The United States since the 1930s.* New Haven, CT: Yale University Press, 1995.

Shibusawa, Naoko. *America's Geisha Ally: Reimagining the Japanese Enemy.* Cambridge, MA: Harvard University Press, 2010.

Shin Kumamoto shi shi henshū iinkai, ed. *Shin Kumamoto shi shi, tsūshi hen, gendai II.* 9 vols. Kumamoto, Japan: Kumamoto shi, 2000.

"Shinnyū shain kyōiku kunren seido no chūmoku subeki jisshi rei: Jieitai be no nyūtai kunren de seika wo agete iru Mitsutoyo seisakujo seisakusho." *Rōsei jihō* 2, no. 11 (February 1967): 2–11.

Smethurst, Richard. *A Social Basis for Prewar Japanese Militarism: The Army and the Rural Community.* Berkeley: University of California Press, 1974.

Smith, Sheila. *Japan Rearmed: The Politics of Military Power.* Cambridge, MA: Harvard University Press, 2019.

Soffer, Reba N. *Discipline and Power: The University, History, and the Making of an English Elite, 1870–1930.* Stanford, CA: Stanford University Press, 1994.

Sōrifu tōkeikyoku. *Nihon no jinkō: Shōwa 30 nen kokusei chōsa no kaisetsu.* Tokyo: Nihon tōkei kyōkai, 1960.

Staff of the *Asahi Shimbun. The Pacific Rivals: A Japanese View of Japanese-American Relations.* New York: Weatherhill, 1972.

Stapleton, Julia. *Englishness and the Study of Politics: The Social and Political Thought of Ernest Barker.* Cambridge: Cambridge University Press, 1994.

Sudō Noriko. *Jieitai kyōryoku eiga: "Kyō mo ware daizora ni ari" kara "Meitantei Konan" made.* Tokyo: Ōtsuki shoten, 2013.

Sugita Ichirō. *Wasurerarete iru anzen hoshō.* Tokyo: Jiji tsūshin sha, 1967.

Saunavaara, Juha. "Postwar Development in Hokkaido: The U.S. Occupation Authorities' Local Government Reform in Japan." *Journal of American-East Asian Relations* 21 (2014): 134–55.

Tabata Ryōichi. "Rikujō Jieitai no Orinpikku shien kōsō." *Shūshin* 6, no. 9 (September 1963): 42–46.

Taira Ryōshō. *Taira Ryōshō kaiganryoku.* Naha, Japan: Okinawa taimusu sha, 1987.

Tajima Naoto. *Konjō no kiroku.* Tokyo: Kōdansha, 1964.

Takada Kiyoshi, ed. *Shinbun shūsei Shōwa-shi no shōgen.* 26 vols. Tokyo: SBB shuppankai, 1991.

Takahashi Kazuhiro. "Bōei Daigakkō ni okeru Beigun kōmondan no yakuwari ni kansuru jisshō kenkyū." *Bōei Daigakkō kiyō* 118 (2019): 19–34.

Takamae Eiji. *The Allied Occupation of Japan*. Translated by Robert Ricketts and Sebastian Swann. London: Continuum, 2002.

Takashima Kō. *Guntai to supōtsu no kindai*. Tokyo: Seikyūsha, 2015.

Tanaka Hiromi. "Bōei Daigakkō." In *Shin Yokosuka shi shi: Betsuhen gunji*, edited by Yokoshuka shi, 794–96. Yokosuka, Japan: Yokosuka shi, 2012.

Tanaka Takamasa. "Bōei cho no kōhō seisaku ni kansuru ichi kōsatsu." *Seiji, seisaku daiarōgu*, January 2004, 79–86.

Tanizaki Junichiro. *Naomi*. Translated by Anthony H. Chambers. New York: Vintage International, 2001.

Tanida Isamu. "Sājanto K: Kita Fuji de no Nichibei guhatsu funsō." *Asagumo gekkan* 22, no. 10 (October 1985): 35–36.

Tiedemann, Arthur E. *Modern Japan: A Brief History*. Princeton, NJ: D. Van Nostrand, 1955.

Todoroki Takao. "Maki Tomoo shodai Bōei Daigakkō gakuchō no kyōiku ri'nen to sono engen: Ānesuto Bākā to no kankei o chūshin ni." *Bōei Daigakkō kiyō* 97 (2008): 1–23.

Tokizane Makoto. "Gunkisai." *Rekishi gunzō* 24, no. 1 (2015): 18–21.

Toland, John. *The Rising Sun: The Decline and Fall of the Japanese Empire, 1936–1945*. New York: Random House, 1970.

Tomizawa Hikaru. "Rikujō Jieitai kanbu no sodachikata (sono ichi)." *Kaikō*, August 2002, 1–5.

Tomizawa Hikaru. "Rikujō Jieitai kanbu no sodachikata (sono ni)." *Kaikō*, September 2002, 1–5.

Tomizawa, Roy. *1964—The Greatest Year in the History of Japan: How the Tokyo Olympics Symbolized Japan's Miraculous Rise from the Ashes*. Austin, TX: Lioncrest, 2019.

Trefalt, Beatrice. *Japanese Army Stragglers and Memories of the War in Japan, 1950–1975*. London: RoutledgeCurzon, 2003.

Tsuji Masanobu. "Underground Escape." In *Ukiyo: Stories of "the Floating World" of Postwar Japan*, edited by Jay Gluck, third edition, 48–66. New York: Vanguard, 1963.

Turner, Steve. *Beatles '66: The Revolutionary Year*. New York: Ecco, 2016.

Uchimi Katsuo. *Sengo supōtsu taisei no kakuritsu*. Tokyo: Fumaido shuppan, 1993.

Ueda Naruhiko. Interview in *Bōei Daigakkō ōraru hisutorī, ikkisei*, edited by Bōei Daigakkō sōgō toshokan. Yokosuka, Japan: Bōei shō Bōei Daigakkō, 2019.

US Military Assistance Advisory Group—Japan. *A Decade of Defense in Japan*. Washington DC: Headquarters, Military Assistance Advisory Group, 1964.

Vogel, Ezra F. *Japan's New Middle Class*. Berkeley: University of California Press, 1963.

von Zimmer, Ernst-Heinrich. "Die Bundeswehr bei den XX. Olympischen Sommerspielen 1972." *Wehrkunde* 20, no. 8 (1972): 402–6.

Wakefield, Wanda Ellen. *Playing to Win: Sports and the American Military, 1896–1945*. Albany: State University of New York Press, 1997.

Walker, Brett L. *The Conquest of Ainu Lands: Ecology and Culture in Japanese Expansion, 1590–1800*. Berkeley: University of California Press, 2001.

Ward, Ian. *The Killer They Called God*. Singapore: Media Masters, 1992.

Watanabe Yōko. *Orinpikku to Jieitai*. Tokyo: Namiki shobō, 2016.

Weinstein, Martin E. *Japan's Postwar Defense Policy, 1947–1968*. New York: Columbia University Press, 1971.

Welfield, John. *An Empire in Eclipse: Japan in the Postwar American Alliance System.* London: Atlantic Highlands, 1988.

Weste, John L. "Staging a Comeback: Rearmament Planning and *kyugūnjin* in Occupied Japan, 1945–52." *Japan Forum* 11, no. 2 (1999): 165–78.

Willcock, Hiroko. "The Political Dissent of a Senior General: Tamogami Toshio's Nationalist Thought and a History Controversy." *Asian Politics & Policy* 3, no 1 (2011): 29–47.

Winter, J. M. "Oxford and the First World War." In *The History of the University of Oxford*, vol. 8: *The Twentieth Century*, edited by Brian Harrison. Oxford: Clarendon, 1994.

Yahara, Hiromichi. *The Battle of Okinawa.* Translated by Roger Pineau and Matatoshi Uehara. New York: John Wiley & Sons, 1995.

Yamada Takaji. *Ichirō hei kaisō.* Tokyo: Yamada Takaji, 2005.

Yamafuji insatsu kabushiki kaisha, ed. *Hokubu hōmentai 50 nen no ayumi, shashin shū.* Sapporo, Japan: Yamafuji insatsu kabushiki kaisha, 2004.

Yamagata Masaaki. "Okinawa ni okeru Jieitai jōchū o meguru kenmin ishiki no haikei to Okinawa Jieitai no hatasu yakuwari." Master's thesis, Meiō Daigakuin, 2007.

Yamamoto Tsunetomo. *Hagakure: The Book of the Samurai.* Translated by William Scott Wilson. Tokyo: Kodansha International, 1979.

Yamanouchi Hisaaki. "Mishima and His Suicide." *Modern Asian Studies* 6, no. 1 (1972): 1–16.

Yokosuka shi shi henshū iinkai, ed. *Yokosuka shi shi.* Yokosuka, Japan: Yokosuka shichō, 1957.

Yomiuri shinbun sengo shi hanhen, ed. *"Saigunbi" no kiseki.* Tokyo: Yomiuri shinbun sha, 1981.

Yoneyama, Takashi. "The Establishment of the ROK Armed Forces and the Japan Self-Defense Forces and the Activities of the US Military Advisory Groups to the ROK and Japan." *NIDS Security Studies*, no. 15 (December 2014): 69–98.

Yoshida, Kensei. *Democracy Betrayed: Okinawa under U.S. Occupation.* Bellingham: Western Washington University Center for East Asian Studies, 2002.

Yoshida Ritsuto. "Guntai no 'saigai shutsudō' seido no kakuritsu: Daikibo saigai e no taiō to eiju no henka kara." *Shigaku zasshi* 117, no. 10 (October 2008): 73–97.

Yoshida Shigeru. *Sekai to Nihon.* Tokyo: Ōshima Hideichi, 1963.

Yoshida Shigeru. *The Yoshida Memoirs: The Story of Japan in Crisis.* Translated by Kenichi Yoshida. Boston: Houghton Mifflin, 1962.

Yoshida Yutaka. *Nihon no guntai.* Tokyo: Iwanami shinsho, 2002.

Yukiyoshi Shōichi and Yoneyama Jun'ichi, eds. *Tōkyō Orinpikku to shinkansen.* Tokyo: Seigensha, 2014.

Zaidan hōjin Sapporo Orinpikku toki taikai sōshiki iinkai, ed. *Dai 11 orinpikku toki taikai koshiki hōkokusho.* Sapporo, Japan: Zaidan hōjin Sapporo orinnpikku toki taikai sōshiki iinkai, 1972.

# INDEX

Page numbers in *italics* refer to figures.

Abe Shinzō, 253, *255*
acacia tree, 98, 144–45; eponymous for *Akashiya*, 144–45; on National Defense Academy campus, 98; in Sapporo, 144–45;
Adenaur, Konrad, 11
Afghanistan, 12
Agnew, Spiro, 203, 205
agricultural assistance: by Imperial military, 58, 129; by GSDF, 4, 129–32, *130*, *131*, 143, 145, 234
Air Force Academy (US), 90
Air Self-Defense Force (ASDF), 3–4, 11, 14–15, 20, 81, 107, 109, 123, 138, 167, 175, 213, 218, 220–22, 228, 231, 235, 238, 243, 256, 297n32
Aka, Raymond, *166*
Akagi Munemori, 127, 137, 163–64, 195, 199
*Akashiya* (newspaper), 129–30, *130*, *131*, 137, 142–54, *146*, *152*, 181, 233–34, 239, 286n118
Akihito (emperor), 249; as crown prince 71, 227, 249. *See also* emperor
Akutagawa Prize, 102, 105
Algeria, 11
Amami Islands, 205, 221, 227, 231, 240
Annapolis. *See* US Naval Academy
anti-communism, 6, 8, 18, 38, 42
Arima Ineko, 102, 104
Army Anniversary Day, 140
Army Language School (US), 90
Army Nursing Corps (NSF/GSDF), 20
"army without war potential" (*senryoku naki guntai*), 31
Army-Navy football game, the, 71
Article 9, 2–3, 15, 22, 28–29, 32, 34, 66, 74, 109, 162, 194, 220, 251–53, 255, 257
Asada Jirō, 186
*Asagumo shinbun* (newspaper), 174, 181

*Asahi shinbun* (newspaper), 35, 161, 175, 181, 190, 227
Asahikawa, *26*, 118–19, 126, 147, 150, 156, 286n120
Asahikawa Base: as GSDF base, 118, 154, 156, 286n120; as Imperial Army base, 118, 282n20
Asaka Base (GSDF), *26*, 135, 158, *159*, 170
Asanuma Inejirō, 279n167, 294n137
Ash, D. R., 259n2
Australia, 169
"autonomous defense," 199, 212. *See also* Nakasone Yasuhiro

Barker, Ernest, 74, 273n43
Bataan Death March, 97, 106
Beatles, The, 152, 287n148
Beauvoir, Simone de, 96
Bekkai training grounds (GSDF), *26*, 123, 136
Bibai, 44, 119
Bibai Base, 119
Bikila, Abebe, 172
Black September, 165
*Bōei no tsutome* (Duty of defense) (Maki), 108, 110
bomb disposal, 235–37; by SDF, 235–37; by US military, 236
boots, 45–46, 47, 268n90, 268n91
*bōtaoshi* (topple the pole), 88–89, *88*
*bougainvillea* flower, 239
Boy Scouts, 140, 190, 242
Brake, William J., 92
Britain, 68–69, 71, 90, 169, 172, 273n38
Budōkan Hall, 203
Bundeswehr, 11, 13
Bush, George, 109
bushido, 176; and the Imperial military, 18, 106; and Mishima Yukio, 193; and the SDF, 9, 109, 143; and Tamogami Toshio, 109, 256

Cadet Code (NDA), 92, 110
California Institute of Technology, 90
Cambodia, 158, 253
Cambridge University, 87
Cannon, 189
"checkbook diplomacy," 253
Chiba Prefecture, 141
Chibana Hideo, 243
Chibana Shōichi, 248–49
Chijin no ai (Naomi) (Tanizaki), 97
Children's Day, 137, 146, 146
China, 14, 26, 97, 156, 177, 253, 273n47, 278n139, 278n143
Chinen, 204, 235
Chinen Base, 245, 298n32
Chinzei (newspaper), 143, 181, 222, 224, 234, 239–40, 286n116
Chitose, 26; site of US Air Force Base, 114, 166
Chitose Base (ASDF), 123
Chō Isamu, 245
Civil Affairs Section Annex (CASA), 38–39, 41–42, 61–62
civil engineering, 12; by GSDF, 107, 128–29, 133, 155, 161, 207, 216, 218, 232, 234; by Imperial Army, 128; by US Army Corps of Engineers, 128; by US Navy Seabees, 79, 91
Coast Guard, 235
Coca-Cola, 45
Cold War defense identity, 4–5, 6–10, 20–23, 38, 65, 124, 154, 161, 164, 199, 200, 208, 237, 251–52, 256
Coming-of-Age Day (Seijin no hi), 230–31
Communist Party. See Japan Communist Party
compulsory group suicide, 210, 213, 215, 223–24, 228. See also Okinawa, Battle of
Confessions of a Mask (Mishima), 95
"corporate warrior" (kigyō senshi), 8, 189. See also salaryman
Coubetin, Pierre de, 170

Daimatsu Hirobumi, 176–77, 183
Daisetsuzan National Park, 145
dancing, social, 95, 97–100, 104, 277n143, 279n161
Defense Agency, 4, 9–10, 62, 99–100, 106, 109, 118–24, 127–28, 134, 137, 139, 149, 150, 156, 163–65, 169, 173–74, 179–82, 185–87, 195, 199, 209, 212, 216, 220–22, 232, 243, 252, 253, 289n8, 295n172, 299n63

Defense for Peace Expo, 137
Defense, Ministry of, 253
"defensive defense" (senshu bōei), 5, 257
deigo flower, 239
depurging, 18, 51, 68
Diet, National, 30–31, 97, 99, 102, 104, 115, 139, 147, 162–63, 170, 177–78, 182, 194, 212, 266n33, 279n161
Dilworth, Joel J., 59–61, 71, 90
disaster relief, 12, 262n38; by imperial military, 58–59; by postwar military, 13–14, 21, 54, 57, 60, 125–27, 129, 133, 145, 155, 157, 161, 181, 207, 218, 232, 235, 251, 254, 256, 283n48
Dodge, Joseph, 36
dokuritsu jison (independence and self-respect), 73
Don Carlos (Schiller), 105
Dulles, John Foster, 32, 68
Dutch East Indies, 37

Ebine Shundō, 35
École Polytechnique, 90
Education, Ministry of, 231
Edo-Tokyo Museum, 288n1
Eihei Temple, 36
Eisenhower, Dwight D., 162–64
El Paso, 166
emperor, 7, 9, 50, 54, 59, 96, 106, 140–41, 149, 190, 191, 199, 209, 213, 215, 224, 279n167. See also Akihito; Hirohito
Empress Teimei (Kujo Sadako), 68
Ennis, William P., 69
Esaki Masumi, 150, 169, 170
Etajima Training School, 26, 44, 107
Ethical Principles for Personnel of the SDF (Jieikan no kokorogamae), 105–6, 109, 199
Etō Jun, 8
Ezo, 116
Ezo sakura, 147

Fathers and Brothers Association (Fukei kai), 122
Fayetteville, 12
femininity, 19–20, 153–54, 170, 186–87
Fisken, Archibald D., 90, 91, 276n117
Floyd, George, 12
Fuji, Camp (GSDF), 192
Fuji, Mt., 78, 86, 104, 196
Fujii Shigeru, 44, 45, 48
Fujitsu, 189
Fukuchiyama, 26, 59, 266
Fukuchiyama Base, 59

Fukui Prefecture, 36
Fukushima Prefecture, 171
Fukuzawa Yukichi, 73–74, 98
Furukawa Kumio, 43

gentlemanliness, 19, 39, 48, 65, 77, 87, 98, 104, 107. *See also* masculinity; noblesse oblige
Germany, 11, 76, 257
Ginza, 135
Godzilla, 3
Gotōda Masaharu, 31, 69, 252
Gōyū Renmei (Native Friend League), 122
Grand Hill Hotel, 183, 243
Great Hanshin Earthquake, 158, 237, 254
Great Kantō Earthquake, 56, 58, 94, 242
Ground Self-Defense Force (GSDF), 13–16. *See also* agricultural assistance; bomb disposal; civil engineering; disaster relief; indoctrination; newspapers, internal; recruitment; training, military; Tokyo Summer Olympics
GSDF Central Band, 134
GSDF field manual, 41
Guam Doctrine. *See* Nixon Doctrine

Hagerty, James, 162–63
Hakodate, 266n47
Hakodate Base, 44, 137
Hansen, Camp, 242
Harvard University, 90
Hashimoto Masakata, 156
Hattori Takushirō, 31, 33, 52, 97
Hayama, 79
Hayashi Keizō, 8, 19, 21, 23, 39–40, 42, 51–54, *52*, 57, 61, 63, 66, 73, 84, 105–6, 113
Hayashi Yasakichi, 52
Heatley, Basil, *172*, 173
Heflin, Martin, 112
Hibiscus flower, 233, 239
*Himeyuri* (Lily Corps), 223
*hinomaru* flag, 92, 161, 205
Hirohito (emperor), 205, 210, 227, 247. *See also* emperor
Hiroshima, 44, 72, 107, 219
"Hiroshima Death March," 106
Hirozawa Sadamichi, 35
Hitachi, 189
Hitler, Adolf, 165
Hiyoshi campus (Keiō University), 74
*Hokkai taimusu* (newspaper), 140
Hokkaido, 9, 14, 21, 37, 44, 48, 54, 83, 111–57, 165–66, 181, 194, 201, 207, 216–17,

219, 221, 233–34, 238, 240, 263n45, 273n38, 286n120. *See also* Asahikawa; Bekkai training grounds; Bibai; Chitose; Ezo; Hakodate; Hokkaido Industrial and Science Exposition; Nayoro; Northern Corps; Obihiro; Sapporo; Shibetsu; Yūbari
Hokkaido Colonization Agency (Kaitakushi), 116, *143*
Hokkaido Industrial and Science Exposition, 137
*Hokkaidō shinbun* (newspaper), 140
Hokkaido University, 145, 151
Hokuriku, 180–81, *180*
Home Ministry, 28, 30, 32, 52, 106
Honduras, 158
Honshu, 26, 37, 72, 117, 127, 129, 171, 180, 254
Horie Masao, 222–23, 234
Horie Yoshitaka, 289n7
Hōsei University, 170
House of Representatives (US), 162
Hull, John E., 90
Humphreys, Leonard A., 125, 155, 160, 180–81
Hungary, 169

Ichikawa Kon, 172
Ikeda Hayato, 163–64, 181
Ikeda Kiyoshi, 87–88
Ikeda Kōtarō, 118
Imperial Blood and Iron Youth Corps (*Tekketsu kinnokai*), 223
Imperial Household Agency, 52, 71, 272n30
imperial military, 2, 3, 9, 22, 27, 32; bases, 38, 44, 117; and domestic security, 56; former personnel, 26, 33, 42–43, 45, 50, 61, 66, 70, 72, 79–80, 85, 90, 105, 107, 189, 207, 216–19; legacies of, 23, 28–29, 40, 53, 65, 69, 105, 142, 149; officer academies, 68, 71, 78; relationship with society, 140–41. *See also* agricultural assistance; civil engineering; disaster relief; indoctrination; Okinawa, Battle of; spirit; sports; training, military; Tsuji Masanobu
Imperial Palace, 57, 83, 199, 271n150
(in)visibility, 10, 29, 115, 141, 161, 168, 249
Incheon, 50
indoctrination: in imperial military, 18, 106, 144; of postwar military personnel, 18, 55, 105–6
Inoki Masamichi, 109–10, 200, 280n186, 280n193
Inoue Shigeyoshi, 76–77

International Anti-War Day, 194
International Association of Athletics Federation, *172*
International Ocean Exposition, 237
International Olympic Committee (IOC), 158, 165, 172
*Invisible Man* (Ellison), 10
Iokibe Makoto, 109–10
Iran-Iraq War, 252
Iraq, 4, 112, 156, 158, 253, 256
Iraq War, 12, 109
Irikura Shōzō, 25–27, *27*, 32, 43, 45–46, 48, 50, 54, 72, 122, 130, 142, 145–47, 151–53, 155, 160, 233, 286n118, 289n8
Ise Bay Typhoon, 127, 180
Ishimine Kunio, 224, 232, 242, 243
Ishizu Sadamasa, 85, 99, 104, 278m154
Israel, 165
Italy, 11, 76
Itō Hirobumi, 97
Iwo Jima, Battle of, 289n7

Japan Communist Party, 55–56, 114, 147
Japan Socialist Party, 100, 109, 114, 118, 133, 147, 187, 230, 254, 279n167, 294n137
Japan Teacher's Union (*Nikkyōso*), 83
*Jieikan no kokorogamae. See* Ethical Principles for Personnel of the SDF
*Jiyū to kiritsu: Igirisu no gakkō seikatsu* (Freedom and discipline: English school life) (Ikeda), 87
Johnson, Earl D., 69–70
juvenile delinquents (*ochikobore*), 1, 186

Kabeno Yōko, 150
Kadena Base (USAF), 226
Kagoshima, *26*, 82–83,
Kagoshima Prefecture, 220–21
Kaitakushi. *See* Hokkaido Colonization Agency
Kamakura, 92
Kami Kazuhiko, 181–82
Kanagawa Prefecture, 25, 72
Kanazawa, *26*, 117
Kanazawa University, 117
Kanba Michiko, 163
Kasai Masae, 182–83
Katō Yoshirō, 279n161
Katsu Hidenari, 221, 227, 231, 240
Kawamoto Nobumasa, 173
Kawano Shun'ichi, 179
*Kawashidai* (newspaper),130
Keimatsu Rumiko, 150

Keiō University, 65, 71, 73–77, 84, 87, 98, 110, 273n38
Kenpeitai, 68
Kim Il-sung, 29
*Kimi ga yo* (national anthem), 161
Kimura Yoshihiro, *85*
Kinjō Kazuhiko, 223–24, 247
Kishi Nobusuke, 97, 100, 162–64, 252
Kishida Fumio, 255
Kishimoto Shigekazu, 116
Kita Kumamoto Base, 222
Kitahara Hakushu, 286n125
Kobe (Hanshin/Owaji) Earthquake. *See* Great Hanshin Earthquake
Kobe University, 109
"Koinobori" (song), 146
Koizumi Jun'ichirō, 109, 253, 272n30
Koizumi Junya, 182, 272n30
Koizumi Shinzō, 71, 73, 74, 84, 87, 272n30, 273n47
Kokuba Kōshō, 243
Kokuba Kōtarō, 242–43
Kokubun Ryōsei, 110
Komatsu Makiko, 154
Konishi Makoto, 220
*konjō* (willpower), 148, 176, 183, 190; in imperial military, 178; and Japanese Olympic athletes, 176–79; and salaryman, 148, 189; and SDF personnel, 177–79, 187, 189. *See also* indoctrination; spirit
Korea (colonial), 286n124
Korea, North, 26, 156, 253
Korea (peninsula), 8, 15, 25, 28, 69, 182
Korea, South, 26, 29, 61, 182
Korean War, 8, 11, 28, 30, 32, 35, 38–40, 44, 48–50, 55, 62, 67, 113–14, 117, 207, 214
Kowalski, Frank, 39–42, 61, 267n55
Koza Riot, 226
Kramer, Francis E., 90–92
Kuboi Masayuki, 51, 129, 155, 287n143
Kumamoto, 14, *26*, 218, 222, 223–24, 226, 247
Kuniyoshi Nagahiro, 218
Kure, 72
Kurihama, Camp, 25–26, *27*, 28, 38, 44, 72, 266n47, 267n59
Kurihama (NSA/NDA campus), 72, 78–79, 83, 89, 93, 95, 278n150
Kurile Islands, *26*, 217
Kurume, *26*, 85, 107
Kuwae Ryōhō, 218–23, 227–29, 232, 234, 244–48, *246*, 250,
Kyoto, 37

Kyoto Prefecture, 59
Kyoto University, 200
Kyūshū danji (Kyushu man), 82
Kyūshū, 14, 26, 37, 42, 58, 81–82, 85,
    117, 120, 129, 143–44, 165, 181, 209,
    213, 218, 220–22, 224, 238, 239–40,
    247, 266n45, 275n84, 286n125. See also
    Western Corps

legitimization, 5, 257
Leys Public School, 87
Liberal Democratic Party (Jiminto), 120,
    123, 125, 139, 242–43, 252–53, 254
London Metropolitan Police, 31

Mabuni, 204, 245–46, 246, 248
MacArthur, Douglas, 28, 29–31, 33, 38, 40,
    61, 67, 97, 113–14, 205, 210
Machimura Kingo, 120–21
Maekawa Kiyoshi, 86, 95
Mainichi shinbun (newspaper), 36, 102–3,
    105, 139, 191, 227,
Maki Tomoo, 8, 21, 23, 65–67, 71–80, 84–96,
    85, 91, 98–107, 200, 273n38; and dancing,
    98–100; and democracy 74–76; and
    gentlemanliness, 19, 76–77, 87; and Keiō
    University, 73–74; memory of, 109–10,
    256; and Obaradai, 78–79; and Oxford
    University, 73–74; and sports 77–78;
    upbringing, 73. See also Bōei no tsutome;
    noblesse oblige
Makomanai Base, 138, 143; and history
    museum, 144; as Meiji-era ranch, 144;
    as one site of Hokkaido Industrial and
    Science Exhibition, 137; as Sapporo Snow
    Festival site, 111–12, 119, 139–49, 156; as
    US Army base, 144
Manchuria, 14, 247
Manchurian Incident, 247n47
Maritime Safety Agency, 3, 15
Maritime Safety Board, 28, 260n13
Maritime Safety Force, 50, 93, 260n13,
    263n51
Maritime Self-Defense Force (MSDF), 3–4,
    14–15, 20, 50, 107, 181, 213, 218, 231,
    260n13, 271n154, 297n32
marriages, 115, 120, 122, 142, 151, 154,
    183, 207, 238, 239–42, 255. See also
    matchmaking
Maruyama Tadayuki, 178
masculinity, 7–9, 11–12, 19, 37, 53, 76–77,
    85, 87, 96, 104–5, 120, 148–51, 186–87,
    192, 198, 237, 256, 279n167. See also

bushido; gentlemanliness; Kyūshū danji;
    noblesse oblige
Mashita Kanetoshi, 196, 199–200
Masuhara Keikichi, 52, 68
Matayoshi Kōsuke, 216–19, 221, 224, 232,
    243, 247
matchmaking, 120, 122, 145, 154, 240–41
Matsuno Raizō, 139
Matsutani Sei, 72, 79–80
May Day, 56, 83, 105
McGill, Camp, 78
medical flights, 235, 237
Meiji Shrine, 56, 135, 188
Melendez, Mrs., 166
Micronesia, 247
militarization, 5–6, 140, 141
Military Assistance Advisory Group
    (MAAG), 62, 89, 91, 92, 160, 166, 271n150
military base communities, 12, 116, 117–24
military bases. See imperial military: bases;
    SDF bases; US military bases
military flag festivals, 140
military-society integration, 5–6, 10, 112,
    119–20, 124, 132, 161, 237, 249, 250, 252
Ming Dynasty, 209
Mishima Incident, 2, 22, 196–201, 197, 253.
    See also Mishima Yukio
Mishima Yukio, 2, 8, 16, 22, 109, 191–201;
    association with senior SDF officers,
    193–94; and bushido, 193; commentary
    on Tsuburaya's suicide, 194; coup
    attempt and suicide of; establishment
    of paramilitary force (Shield Society),
    194; experiential enlistment of, 191–92;
    fetishization of military training, 191–92;
    hopes for coup, 194–95; and Nakasone
    Yasuhiro, 195, 199–200; right-wing
    radicalization of, 191; twenty-first century
    SDF sympathies for, 256; visit to National
    Safety Academy 95–96. See also Mashita
    Kanetoshi; Mishima Incident; Morita
    Masakatsu; patriotism; Sunday Mainichi;
    Tanaka Yoshio; Yamamoto Kiyokatsu
Mita shinbun (newspaper), 74, 273n47
Mitsubishi, 37, 44, 48
Mitsuya Kenkyū scandal, 182
Miura Peninsula, 79, 93
Miyagi Otoya, 96
Miyake Hiromi, 291n48
Miyake Yoshinobu, 168, 170–71, 173,
    177–79, 291n48
Miyake Yoshiyuki, 291n48
Miyano Masatoshi, 70

Miyata Yoshifumi, 148
Moiwa, Mt., *138*
Mori Shigehiro, 37
Morita Masakatsu, 199
Moscow, 55, 176
Motoaki Hiroshi, 177
Mukden, 140
Murayama Tomiichi, 254
museums, base, 110, 144, 286n120
Mutual Security Assistance (MSA), 61–62

Naganuma case, 226
Nagoya, 37
Naha, 203, *204*, 205, *206*, 216, 218, 221, 224, 229–30, 235–36, 242, 247
Naha Base, 213, *214*, 235, 238, *239*, 242, 245
Nakamura Kazuo, 182–83
Nakamura Ryūhei, 216
Nakasone Yasuhiro: and "autonomous defense," 252; as Defense Agency director, 10, 109, 195, 199–200, 212, 218, 243; and Mishima Yukio, 195, 199–200; as prime minister, 252
Nara, *26*, 107
Nara Prefecture, 137
National Athletic Festival, 231
National Defense Academy, 8, 64–110, *78*, *85*, *88*, *91*, 219, 252, 256; athletics, 78–79, 88–89; background of students, 80–83; daily life at, 83–84; establishment of, 64–72; and masculinity, 87–88, 104; philosophical underpinnings, 72–78; and US military advisors, 89–95; and Yokosuka, 78–79, 93–95. *See also* Maki Tomoo; Ōe Kenzaburō; Tsuji Masanobu
National Safety Academy, 64, 191
National Safety Force (*Hoantai*), 3–4, 17, 20–21, 51, *52*, 53, 57, 59, 61, 75, 81–83, 90, 118, 122, 126, 128–29, 134–35, *135*, 169, 260n13
Nayoro, *26*, 117–19, 123, 126, 129, 132, 156, 282
Nerima Base, *26*, *135*, 135, 266n47
newspapers, internal (SDF), 23, 130, 167, 174, 233, 286n116. *See also* Akashiya; Kawashidai; Shurei
Niigata, 177, 217
Niigata Prefecture, 44
Nisei military linguists, 48
Nishi Takeichi, 168–69
Nishibō, 170
Nishihara Masashi, 110
Nishime Jinji, 243–44

Nishimoto Tetsuya, 82, 83
Nissan, 189
Nixon Doctrine, 211
Nixon, Richard, 208, 211
noblesse oblige, 19, 21, 76, 110
Northern Corps (GSDF), 9, 14, 21, 54, 111–14, *113*, 116, 120, 122, 128, 129–32, *130*, 134, *136*, 137–56, *146*, *152*, 165–66, 194, 219, 256

*Obaradai* (newspaper), 80, 90, 94, 98, 105, 277n131, 278n150
Obaradai campus (NDA), 78, *78*–79, 83, 86, 89, 93,
Obihiro, *26*, 128, 130, 154
Ochanomizu University, 105
Ōdori Park, 111–12, *113*, 136, *136*, 151, *152*, 156. *See also* parades; Sapporo Snow Festival
Ōe Kenzaburō, 102–5, 226, 279n167
Officer Candidate School (GSDF), 70, 77, 107
Ogawauchi Kazuo, 190
Okada Haruo, 182
Okazaki Katsuo, 30, 31
Okinawa, 14, 22, *26*, 156, 165, 194, *204*; disposal (*shobun*) of, 208–10; post-reversion opposition to SDF, 225–32; post-reversion SDF strategies, 232–47; SDF deployment to, 211–13; US occupation of, 210–11. *See also* Okinawa, Battle of
Okinawa, Battle of, 22, 202, 209–10, 215–16, 219, 222–23, 227–28, 233, 235, 245–48, 301n117
*Okinawa keizai shinbun* (newspaper), 228
Okinawa Memorial Day, 245, *246*
Okinawa Teachers Association, 205, 215, 227, 231. *See also* peace education
*Okinawa taimusu* (newspaper), 218–19, 224, 227–28, 233, 235–36, 238, 241, 245, 247
Ōkouchi, Colonel, *166*
Olympic games: Amsterdam, 290; Berlin, 165, 175; Los Angeles (1932), 169, 177; Mexico City, 171, 291n48; Munich, 165; Rome, 165, 169–70, 172, 178; Sapporo, 201; Tokyo (2020), 158, 255. *See also* Tokyo Summer Olympics (1964)
Ōmine Shinichi, 224
Ōmori Hiroshi, 280n193
Ōmori Kan, 127
Ono Hisako, 158–59, *159*

open-base events: by imperial military, 138–39; by SDF, 132, 137–38, 237–38
Operation Tomodachi, 254, 256
Orion Beer, 224, 243
Oroku Airfield, 242
Osaka, 14, 26, 221
Osaka Castle, 113
Ōshima Kenkichi, 177–78
Ōta Fumio, 92, 110
Ōta Masahide, 215, 224, 238, 244
"outcasts" (hikagemono), 1, 10, 174, 259
Oxford University, 65, 71, 73–77, 83, 90
Ōya Sōichi, 96, 103
Ōzato, 234
Ōzu Yasujirō, 104

Palia, Colonel, 166
parades, 134–36, 135–36, 147, 155, 180, 201, 226, 243, 247–48, 303n173
paramilitary: Mishima's Shield Society, 2, 194; PRF as, 17, 34;
patriotism, 8, 12, 42, 91, 106, 142; Hayashi's redefinition of, 53–54; Maki's definition of, 75–76; and SDF youth group, 122
Patriotism (Yūkoku) (Mishima), 191
peace education (heiwa kyōiku), 227
"Peace National Construction Force" (Kokudō kensetsu tai), 133
Peace Plaza (Heiwa no hiroba), 245, 246
Peacekeeping Operations (PKO), 4, 253–55
Pearl Harbor, 15
Pentagon, 12, 90
Perry, Matthew C., 25, 90, 144
Perseus, 104
Persian Gulf, 252
Pickett, George B., Jr., 69–72
Police Reserve Force (PRF), 1, 3, 15, 17, 25–63; camp conditions, 43–51; and disaster relief, 54, 57–59; enlistees view of, 25–26, 44–48; establishment of, 29–33; and former imperial soldiers, 26, 45, 51; formulation of identity, 51–54; and internal security, 54–57; list of installations, 266n47; recruitment, 33–38; society's view of, 49; training, 41–42; and US military, 38–43. See also PRF anthem; PRF pledge
"postmodern military," 13
Potsdam Declaration, 7, 50
PRF anthem, 55
PRF pledge, 55

protests, 21, 160; anti-security treaty (Anpo), 21, 161–64, 191, 194–95, 199; International Anti-War Day, 194–95; May Day, 56, 83, 105; for Okinawan reversion, 214; against SDF parade, 248; against SDF participation in Coming-of-Age Day, 230–31; against terms of Okinawa's reversion, 203–5, 206, 212, 216, 226; against US bases, 225, 249. See also Rice Riots
Provincial Liaison Office (Chihō renraku bu), 216, 224, 233
public relations: US military, 12–13, 125–26; SDF, 124, 130, 161, 173, 191, 216, 232, 252
punishment, corporal, 66
Purdue University, 90

Qing Dynasty, 209

Rambo, 12
rearmament, 6, 11, 28, 30–32, 57, 59, 66–68, 70, 75, 95–97, 102–3, 117–18, 133, 162, 164, 207, 231
Red Purge, 32
recruitment: PRF, 25, 33–34, 36–37, 42, 51, 59; SDF, 19–20, 121, 129, 146, 154, 183–87, 190, 218–19, 228, 230, 232–33, 254, 259n2, 265n33, 298n48, 301n115; US military, 12
recruitment posters, 34, 146, 233, 265n33
"residual sovereignty," 210
Rice Riots, 56, 58, 287n144
Ridgeway, Matthew, 51
Rokumeikan, 97
Rōnin, 81–82
Roppongi, 195
Royal Airforce College, 90
Royal Military College, 90
Royal Naval College, 90
Rumoi, 154
Russo-Japanese War, 58, 77
Ryūkyū shinpō (newspaper), 224, 227–28, 233, 235–36, 238, 241, 244–45, 247

Safety Advisor Group, 62, 70, 80
Sakarajima, 58
Sakuma Makoto, 79, 84
Sakura, 141
Sakura Castle, 141
Sakuraba Yasuki, 118–19, 132
salaryman (sararīman), 148, 187, 189; and SDF personnel, 8, 9, 148–49, 186, 237
Samawah, 158
samurai, 2, 8–9, 17, 19, 54, 73, 76–77, 81–83, 86, 92, 116, 142–43, 192–94, 215, 221, 256

San Francisco Treaty, 210
Sankei shinbun (newspaper), 194
Sanyo, 189
Sapporo, 14, 111–12, 114, 117, 119, 122, 129, 132, 136–38, 145, 148, 150–51, 152, 154–55, 201, 226. See also Makomanai Base; Sapporo Snow Festival˙
Sapporo Clock Tower, 145
Sapporo Snow Festival, 14, 83; criticism of SDF involvement, 139; establishment of, 111; sponsors of, 139–40; SDF support for, 111–12, 113, 115, 128, 134, 138–39, 143, 156, 194, 256
Sartre, Jean-Paul, 96
Sasaki Masanobu, 122
Sasaki Tetsuo, 118
Sasebo, 26, 181
Satō Eisaku, 163–64, 183, 203, 208, 211–12
Satō Morio, 1, 9, 15, 36–37, 48, 50, 169
Satō Noboru, 166
Satō Yukio, 44, 46
Satsu Kazuo, 139
Satsuma domain, 209, 215–16, 220–21, 301n117. See also Kagoshima
Sebald, William, 41
Seiyō seiji seido shi (History of Western political systems) (Maki), 74
Sekai (magazine), 96
SDF bases, 14, 21, 113–14, 116–19, 123, 134, 136, 139, 209, 213–14, 225, 235, 237–38, 281n8. See also Asahikawa Base; Chinen Base; Chitose Base; Fuji Camp; Fukuchiyama Base; Hakodate Base; Makomanai Base; Naha Base; Nerima Base
SDF Law (1954), 59, 121, 126, 163, 183
Self-Defense League (Jiei dōmei), 97
Sendai, 14, 73, 137, 217
Sengoku Jieitai (Warring-States SDF), 3
Senkaku Islands (Daioyutai), 208
September 11 (9/11) attacks, 12, 112, 253
"Sergeant K," 48
Shepard, Whitfield P., 38–39
Seventeen (Ōe), 280n167
Shibetsu, 119
Shield Society (Tate no kai), 194–96, 198
Shiga Kenjirō, 149–50
Shikata Toshiyuki, xiii, 82–83, 87, 93, 105, 107, 110
Shikoku, 14, 26, 82, 117
Shima Atsushi, 64–65, 83–85, 105, 107
Shizuoka Prefecture, 190
Shōheikō Neo-Confucian academy, 73

"Shōwa Restoration," 191
Shurei (newspaper), 233–36, 238–41, 240, 246
Sino-Japanese War, 77
Socialist Party. See Japan Socialist Party
Sony, 190
Sook Ching Massacre, 97
South Manchuria Railway, 290n36
Soviet Union, 5, 9, 26, 83, 113, 117, 119, 127, 143, 147, 169
"special vehicles" (tokusha)
spirit (seishin), 18, 177, 189–90; imperial military, 77, 102, 178; NDA, 69; PRF, 42, 53; SDF, 7, 106, 150, 176. See also konjō
sports: imperial military participation in, 168–69; at the NDA, 77–78, 88–89; in PRF, 44–45; SDF participation in, 169, 231; SDF support for, 4, 134. See also Tokyo Summer Olympics (1964)
Squaw Valley, 165
"Student K," 147
subordinate independence, 5, 61
Suga Yoshihide, 255
Sugihara, Willy N., 89
Sunday Mainichi (magazine), 191
Supreme Commander for the Allied Powers (SCAP), 28, 30–32, 36, 38–41, 43, 46, 49, 52, 55, 56, 66–67, 69, 75, 97
Suzuki Akio, 83

Tabata Ryōichi, 166
Tachikawa, 229
Taira Koichi, 234, 245
Taira Ryōshō, 229
Taiyū-kai (Force Friends Association), 122, 224
Takada, 26, 44
Takada, Camp, 44, 46
Takayama Shinobu, 72
Takeshita Masahiko, 99, 278n154
Tameyoshi Yaeyako, 218, 232, 298n48
Tamogami Toshio, 109–10
Tanaka Kisaburō, 230, 238, 243
Tanaka Yoshio, 182
Tanizaki Junichirō, 97
Tatsumi Eiichi, 68–69
"tax thieves" (zeikin dorobo), 1, 16, 179, 255
Teigin Incident, 35
Tohoku, 14, 37, 82, 171
Tōjō Hideki, 31, 79
Tokugawa period, 17, 77, 93, 193
Tokugawa shogunate, 25, 93, 116, 209

Tokyo, 14, 21, *25*, 36, *52*, 56, 59, 72, 82–83, 100, 105, 117–19, 134–35, *135*, 150–51, 153–54, 158, 164–66, 168–69, 188, 194–95, *197*, 202, 220, 223, 226, 231, 242, 243, 289n8

Tokyo Bay, 78, *93*

Tokyo Institute of Technology, 71

*Tōkyō shinbun* (newspaper), 150

*Tokyo Olympiad*, 172

Tokyo Station, 99–100

Tokyo Summer Olympics (1964), 22, 148, 161, 255; as public relations, 173–76; SDF athletic involvement in, 168–73; SDF logistical support for, 164–68

Tokyo University, 96, 102, 122, 163, 190

Tokyo University of Education, 223

Tokyo war crimes trial, 14, 109

Tokunoshima Island, 221. *See also* Amami Islands

Tomizawa Hikaru, xiv, 84, 105

Tomizawa Uio, 105

*tondenhei* (farmer-soldiers), 9, 21, 116, 121, 142–44, *143*, 145, 149, 286n120

Toyohira River, 138, *138*

training, military: Imperial Army, SDF, PRF, 33, 38, 40; joint US-Japan, 23, 29

Tripartite Pact, 76

Trump, Donald, 12, *253*

Tsuburaya Kōkichi, *159*, 168, 170–73, *172*, 177–79, 194, 289n4; Mishima's commentary on, 194

Tsuji Masanobu, 96–97, 99–100, 102, 104–5

uniforms, 20, 83, 94–95, 134, 150–51, 167, 207, 230, 232, 250; and PRF, 35–36, 43, 45–46

United Nations, 158, 252–53, 255

US Air Force, 62, 114, 166, 226, 229, 271n150

US Army Far East Command, 90

US Army field manual, 41

US military, 9, 11–13, 16–17, 19–20, 22, 50–51, 61–63, 67, 124, 162, 166, 178, 210, 234–36, 249, 252–54; NDA and, 64–66, 70–71, 76, 89–93, *91*, 95, 102, 108; PRF and, 15, 28–29, 32, 37–44, 46, 48; SDF and, 1–2, 114, 148–49, 180, 185, 188, 207, 232, 250, 256–57. *See also* Military Assistance Advisory Group, US military bases

US military academy, 39, 66, 69, 70–71, 76, 89–92, 98, 100, 107–8

US military bases, 2, 9, 16, 22, 28, 38, 203, *204*, 207–14, 222, 225, 249, 250. *See also* Hansen, Camp; Kadena Base; McGill, Camp; Zama, Camp

US Naval Academy, 70, 76, 89, 108

University of Ryukyus, 215, 231

Urasoe, 229–30, 238

Ushijima Mitsuru, 245, 247

Utsumi Hitoshi, 31–32, 69, 70

Vietnam War, 5, 194, 212, 220, 225–26

Waseda University, 148

Washington Heights, 166

Watson, LeRoy, 70

Wehrmacht, 11, 165

West Point. *See* US military academy

Western Corps, 14, 143, 165, 181, 216, 218, 220–22, 239, 286n116

Whalen, Horace K., 149

Whitney, Courtney, 30–31

Willoughby, Charles A., 31, *52*, 97

Women's Army Corps (GSDF), 20, 153, 186

World War I, 73

World War II, 2, 23, 94, 124, 161, 176, 222, 257. *See also* Okinawa, Battle of; Iwo Jima, Battle of

Worthington, General, *166*

Yamada Kōsaku, 286n125

Yamada Takaji, 302n136

Yamagata Prefecture, 74

Yamaguchi Otoya, 279n167

Yamaguchi Prefecture, 37, *60*

Yamaguchi Susumu, 103, 105

Yamamoto Isoroku, 15

Yamamoto Kiyokatsu, 193

Yamamoto Tsunetomo, 193–94

Yamanaka cottage (Keiō University), 74

Yamaoka Tesshu, 92

Yamato spirit, 176–77, 193. *See also* bushido; *konjō*; spirit

Yamazaki Makoto, 108, 275n77

Yanagita Mitsuhara, 238, 243

Yara Chōbyō, 205, 210–12, 217–18, 229, 235, 243

Yasukuni Shrine, 109

Yokohama, 56, 74, 94, 98, 242

Yokosuka, *26*, 66, 70, *78*, 78–79, 93–95, 98, 105

Yokosuka Naval Station (US Navy), 66, 79, 94

Yomitan, 216

*Yomiuri shinbun* (newspaper), 15, 173, 177, 179, 189–90, 191, 229

Yonemine Hitoshi, 220

Yoshida Doctrine, 5, 31, 252

Yoshida Shigeru, 5, 8, 15, 23, 60, 158, 162, 163–64, 210, 212, 252; NDA, 10, 21, 65–75, 80, 84, 108, 277n101; NSF, *52*; PRF and, 21, 28, 29–32, 38, 39, 51–52, 54, 57–59, 125, 134, 149; SDF, 133. *See also* Yoshida Doctrine

Yoshii Takeshige, 178

Yoshiide, Colonel, *166*

Yoshikawa Keisuke, 84

Yoyogi, 166

Yūbari, 126

Yūmoto Yūzo, 45–46, 50

Zama, 72

Zama, Camp, 89

Zengakuren (All-Japan Student Federation), 163

Zushi, 98

# Studies of the Weatherhead East Asian Institute
# Columbia University

## Selected Titles

(Complete list at: weai.columbia.edu/content/publications)

*Outsourcing Repression: Everyday State Power in Contemporary China*, by Lynette H. Ong. Oxford University Press, 2022.

*Diasporic Cold Warriors: Nationalist China, Anticommunism, and the Philippine Chinese, 1930s–1970s,* by Chien-Wen Kung. Cornell University Press, 2022.

*Dream Super-Express: A Cultural History of the World's First Bullet Train*, by Jessamyn Abel. Stanford University Press, 2022.

*The Sound of Salvation: Voice, Gender, and the Sufi Mediascape in China*, by Guangtian Ha. Columbia University Press, 2022.

*Carbon Technocracy: Energy Regimes in Modern East Asia*, by Victor Seow. The University of Chicago Press, 2022.

*Disunion: Anticommunist Nationalism and the Making of the Republic of Vietnam*, by Nu-Anh Tran. University of Hawai'i Press, 2022.

*Learning to Rule: Court Education and the Remaking of the Qing State, 1861–1912*, by Daniel Barish. Columbia University Press, 2022.

*Policing China: Street-Level Cops in the Shadow of Protest*, by Suzanne Scoggins. Cornell University Press, 2021.

*Mobilizing Japanese Youth: The Cold War and the Making of the Sixties Generation*, by Christopher Gerteis. Cornell University Press, 2021.

*Middlemen of Modernity: Local Elites and Agricultural Development in Modern Japan*, by Christopher Craig. University of Hawai'i Press, 2021.

*Isolating the Enemy: Diplomatic Strategy in China and the United States, 1953–1956*, by Tao Wang. Columbia University Press, 2021.

*A Medicated Empire: The Pharmaceutical Industry and Modern Japan*, by Timothy M. Yang. Cornell University Press, 2021.

*Dwelling in the World: Family, House, and Home in Tianjin, China, 1860–1960*, by Elizabeth LaCouture. Columbia University Press, 2021.

*Made in Hong Kong: Transpacific Networks and a New History of Globalization*, by Peter Hamilton. Columbia University Press, 2021.

*China's influence and the Center-periphery Tug of War in Hong Kong, Taiwan and Indo-Pacific*, by Brian C.H. Fong, Wu Jieh-min, and Andrew J. Nathan. Routledge, 2020.

*The Power of the Brush: Epistolary Practices in Chosŏn Korea*, by Hwisang Cho. University of Washington Press, 2020.

*On Our Own Strength: The Self-Reliant Literary Group and Cosmopolitan Nationalism in Late Colonial Vietnam*, by Martina Thucnhi Nguyen. University of Hawai'i Press, 2020.

*A Third Way: The Origins of China's Current Economic Development Strategy*, by Lawrence Chris Reardon. Harvard University Asia Center, 2020.

*Disruptions of Daily Life: Japanese Literary Modernism in the World*, by Arthur M. Mitchell. Cornell University Press, 2020.

*Recovering Histories: Life and Labor after Heroin in Reform-Era China,* by Nicholas Bartlett. University of California Press, 2020.

*Figures of the World: The Naturalist Novel and Transnational Form,* by Christopher Laing Hill. Northwestern University Press, 2020.

*Arbiters of Patriotism: Right Wing Scholars in Imperial Japan,* by John Person. University of Hawai'i Press, 2020.

Printed in the USA
CPSIA information can be obtained
at www.ICGtesting.com
LVHW092321141023
760911LV00027B/321/J